# THE ESSENTIAL GUIDE TO
# INTERNAL AUDITING

# THE ESSENTIAL GUIDE TO INTERNAL AUDITING

## Second Edition

### K H Spencer Pickett

A John Wiley & Sons, Ltd., Publication

**British Library Cataloguing in Publication Data**

A catalogue record for this book is available from the British Library.

ISBN 978-0-470-74693-6 (paperback)
ISBN 978-1-119-97382-9 (ebk)
ISBN 978-1-119-97383-6 (ebk)
ISBN 978-1-119-97705-6 (ebk)

Typeset in 9.5/12 Gill Sans Light by Laserwords Private Limited, Chennai, India.

This book is dedicated with love to my wife, Jennifer, and my two children, Dexter and Laurel-Jade

A very special thanks goes out to Stuart, Carol, Suzanne and Charlotte

# CONTENTS

# LIST OF ABBREVIATIONS

| | |
|---|---|
| AC | Audit Committee |
| ACCA | Chartered Association of Certified Accountants |
| AICPA | American Institute of Certified Public Accountants |
| CAE | Chief Audit Executive |
| CBOK | Common Body of Knowledge |
| CEO | Chief Executive Officer |
| CFO | Chief Finance Officer |
| CG | Corporate Governance |
| CICA | Canadian Institute of Chartered Accountants |
| CIMA | Chartered Institute of Management Accountants |
| CIO | Chief Information Officer |
| COSO | Committee of Sponsoring Organizations of the Treadway Commission |
| CPA | Certified Public Accountant |
| CPD | Continuing Professional Development |
| CPE | Continuing Professional Education |
| CRO | Chief Risk Officer |
| CRSA | Control Risk Self-Assessment |
| CRSA | Control and Risk Self-Assessment |
| CSA | Control Self-Assessment |
| DF | Director of Finance |
| DP | Data Protection |
| EA | External Audit |
| ERM | Enterprise Risk Management |
| FCO | Foreign and Commonwealth Office |
| FSA | Financial Services Authority |
| GAAP | Generally Accepted Accounting Policies |
| GAIN | Global Audit Information Network |
| GAO | Government Accountability Office |
| GRC | Governance, Risk and Control |
| HM | Her Majesty's |
| HR | Human Resource |
| HRM | Human Resource Management |
| IA | Internal Audit |
| IC | Input Control |
| ICAEW | Institute of Chartered Accountants in England and Wales |
| ICE | Internal Control Evaluation |
| ICQ | Internal Control Questionnaire |
| IIA | Institute of Internal Auditors |
| IPPF | International Professional Practices Framework |

| | |
|---|---|
| IRC | INFOSEC Research Council |
| IS | Information Systems |
| ISO | International Standards Organization |
| IT | Information Technology |
| KPIs | Key Performance Indicators |
| KRCM | Key Risk and Control Matrix |
| MIS | Management Information System |
| MUS | Monetary Unit Sampling |
| NAO | National Audit Office |
| NED | Non-Executive Director |
| NYSE | New York Stock Exchange |
| OECD | Organization for Economic Cooperation and Development |
| PAC | Public Accounts Committee |
| PC | Personal Computer |
| PESTL | Political, Economical, Social, Technical and Legal |
| PPF | Professional Practices Framework |
| PSR | Preliminary Survey Report |
| PwC | PricewaterhouseCoopers |
| QA | Quality Assurance |
| RaCE | Risk-Assessed Control Evaluation |
| RBSA | Risk-Based Systems Auditing |
| SD | Systems Development |
| SD | Standard Deviation |
| SEC | Securities and Exchange Commission |
| SEC | Stock Exchange Commission |
| SIC | Statement on Internal Control |
| SWOT | Strengths, Weaknesses, Opportunities and Threats |
| US | United States of America |
| USA | United States of America |
| VFM | Value for Money |

Chapter 1

# INTRODUCTION

## Introduction

The 1000 page *Internal Auditing Handbook 3rd Edition* contains a comprehensive account of the role, responsibilities and work of the internal audit profession and this new book is a streamlined text from the same author that draws heavily from the main *Handbook*. The second edition of *The Essential Guide to Internal Auditing* reflects the significant changes in the field of internal auditing over the last few years. Since the last edition there have been many developments that impact the very heart of the audit role. There really are 'new look' internal auditors who carry the weight of a heightened expectation from society on their shoulders. Auditors no longer spend their time looking down at detailed working schedules in cramped offices before preparing a comprehensive report on low-level problems that they have found for junior operational managers. They now spend much more time presenting 'big picture' assurances to executive boards after having considered the really high-level risks that need to be managed properly. Moreover, the internal auditor also works with and alongside busy managers to help them understand the task of identifying and managing risks to their operations. At the same time the internal auditor has to retain a degree of independence so as to ensure the all-important professional scepticism that is essential to the audit role. The auditor's report to the board via the Audit Committee must have a resilience and dependability that is unquestionable and the audit product must add value to the employing organization. These new themes have put the internal auditor at the forefront of business, commerce and public sector entities as one of the cornerstones of corporate governance – and the new *The Essential Guide to Internal Auditing* has been updated to take this on board. The second edition of *The Essential Guide* contains much of the material that formed the basis of the first edition and has been expanded in the following manner:

1. The new edition has been updated to reflect the Institute of Internal Auditors' International Standards for the Professional Practice of Internal Auditing that were released during 2009.
2. Each chapter has a new section on new developments to reflect changes that have occurred since the first edition was published.
3. There is a new worked example of auditing the risk management process contained in the appendices.

Change is now a constant and we have tried not to focus too much on specific events such as the 2007/08 banking failures/Credit Crunch, the resulting recession and isolated incidents such as the Madoff fraud or the BP oil leaks in the Gulf Coast, since it is the principles of internal auditing that remain constant, regardless of the latest scandal to impact the economy. Please take a look at the Institute of Internal Auditors' web site at www.theiia.org to keep up to date with new developments and the latest corporate scandals.

The first edition of *The Essential Guide* described internal auditing as a growing quasi-profession. The quantum leap that occurred between the old and new millennium is that internal auditing has now achieved the important status of being a full-blown profession, led by a chief audit executive.

Note that the term 'chief audit executive' (CAE) is used throughout the book and this person is described by the Institute of Internal Auditors (IIA):

> The chief audit executive is a senior position within the organization responsible for internal audit activities. Normally, this would be the internal audit director. In the case where internal audit activities are obtained from external service providers, the chief audit executive is the person responsible for overseeing the service contract and the overall quality assurance of these activities, reporting to senior management and the board regarding internal audit activities, and follow-up of engagement results. The term also includes titles such as general auditor, head of internal audit, chief internal auditor, and inspector general.

With the growing influence of internal auditing comes the need to ensure expectations of a professional service are fully understood and fully met. Regulators around the world have now recognized the real impact a fully professional internal audit function can make in promoting good governance. However, with greater recognition comes a greater responsibility to deliver the goods, which is why *The Essential Guide* has been prepared with the need for auditors to live up to this enhanced role kept fully in mind.

The areas that are included in this chapter are:

1.1   Reasoning behind the Book
1.2   The IIA Standards and Links to the Book
1.3   How to Navigate around the Book
1.4   *The Essential Guide* as a Development Tool
1.5   The Development of Internal Auditing
       Summary and Conclusions

# 1.1   Reasoning behind the Book

The original *Essential Guide* focused on the practical aspects of performing the audit task. It contained basic material on managing, planning, performing and reporting the audit, recognizing the underlying need to get the job done well. The new edition has a different focus. Now we need first and foremost to understand the audit context and how we fit into the wider corporate governance agenda. It is only after having done this that we can go on to address the response to changing expectations. In fact, we could argue that we need to provide an appropriate response to the call for better and more effective governance of both private and public sector organizations, rather than think of the audit position as being more or less static. It is no longer possible to simply write about an audit plan, preparing the audit programme and how best to perform the audit task. To do justice to the wealth of material on internal auditing, we must acknowledge the impact of internal audit standards and the work of writers, thought leaders, academics and journalists.

The new context for internal auditing is set firmly within the corporate governance and risk management arena. The Institute of Internal Auditors' (IIA) definition of internal auditing was not changed when the standards were revised in January 2009 and remains as follows:

> Internal auditing is an independent, objective assurance and consulting activity designed to add value and improve an organization's operations. It helps an organization accomplish its objectives by bringing a systematic, disciplined approach to evaluate and improve the effectiveness of risk management, control and governance processes.

As a result, *The Essential Guide* has early chapters on Corporate Governance Perspectives, Managing Risk and Internal Controls. It is only after having addressed these three interrelated topics that we can really appreciate the internal audit role. There are also chapters covering professional standards, audit approaches, managing internal audit, planning, performance and reporting audit work and specialist areas such as fraud and information system (IS) auditing. The final chapter attempts to peer into the future at some of the changes that may well be on the way. *The Essential Guide* rests firmly on the platform provided by the IIA's International Standards for the Professional Practice of Internal Auditing as part of the International Professional Practices Framework (IPPF). Internal auditing is a specialist career and it is important that we note the efforts of a professional body that is dedicated to this chosen field. Note that despite the recent changes in the field of internal auditing there is much of the first book that is retained in the new edition. Change means we build on what we, as internal auditors, have developed over the years rather than throw away anything that is more than a few years old. This is why much of the original material from the first edition has not been discarded – as the saying goes, it is important not to throw away the baby with the bath water. Note that all references to IIA definitions, code of ethics, IIA attribute and performance standards, practice advisories and practice guides relate to the International Professional Practices Framework (IPPF) prepared by the Institute of Internal Auditors in 2009.

## 1.2   The IIA Standards and Links to the Book

*The Essential Guide* addresses many aspects of internal auditing that are documented in the Institute of Internal Auditors (IIA) International Standards for the Professional Practice of Internal Auditing. Some years ago, the Institute of Internal Auditors (IIA) Executive Committee commissioned an international Steering Committee and Task Force to review the Professional Practices Framework (PPF), the IIA's guidance, structure and related processes. The Task Force's efforts were focused on reviewing the scope of the framework and increasing the transparency and flexibility of the guidance development, review and issuance processes. The results culminated in a new International Professional Practices Framework (IPPF) and a reengineered Professional Practices Council, the body that supports the IPPF. The Attribute Standards outline what a good internal audit set-up should look like, while the Performance Standards set a benchmark for the audit task. Together with the Practice Advisories, Position Statements and Practice Guides and other reference material, they constitute a worldwide professional framework for internal auditing. The IIA's main Attribute and Performance Standards are listed below.

### Attribute Standards

**1000: Purpose, Authority, and Responsibility**   The purpose, authority, and responsibility of the internal audit activity must be formally defined in an internal audit charter, consistent with the Definition of Internal Auditing, the Code of Ethics, and the *Standards*. The chief audit executive must periodically review the internal audit charter and present it to senior management and the board for approval.

**1100: Independence and Objectivity**   The internal audit activity must be independent and internal auditors must be objective in performing their work.

**1200: Proficiency and Due Professional Care**   Engagements must be performed with proficiency and due professional care.

**1300: Quality Assurance and Improvement Program**   The chief audit executive must develop and maintain a quality assurance and improvement program that covers all aspects of the internal audit activity.

## Performance Standards

**2000: Managing the Internal Audit Activity**   The chief audit executive must effectively manage the internal audit activity to ensure it adds value to the organization.

**2100: Nature of Work**   The internal audit activity must evaluate and contribute to the improvement of governance, risk management, and control processes using a systematic and disciplined approach.

**2200: Engagement Planning**   Internal auditors must develop and document a plan for each engagement, including the engagement's objectives, scope, timing, and resource allocations.

**2300: Performing the Engagement**   Internal auditors must identify, analyze, evaluate, and document sufficient information to achieve the engagement's objectives.

**2400: Communicating Results**   Internal auditors must communicate the engagement results.

**2500: Monitoring Progress**   The chief audit executive must establish and maintain a system to monitor the disposition of results communicated to management.

**2600: Resolution of Senior Management's Acceptance of Risks**   When the chief audit executive believes that senior management has accepted a level of residual risk that may be unacceptable to the organization, the chief audit executive must discuss the matter with senior management. If the decision regarding residual risk is not resolved, the chief audit executive must report the matter to the board for resolution.

## 1.3   How to Navigate around the Book

A brief synopsis of *The Essential Guide* will help the reader work through the material. Although most chapters contain 10 main sections, they are each of variable length:

## Chapter 1 – Introduction

This, the first chapter, deals with the content of *The Essential Guide* and lists the International Standards for the Professional Practice of Internal Auditing. It also covers the way *The Essential Guide* can be used as a development tool for internal audit staff. The way internal auditing has developed over the years is an important aspect of the chapter, whereby the progress of the profession is tracked in summary form from its roots to date. It is important to establish the role of internal audit at the start of the book in order to retain this focus throughout the next few chapters, which cover corporate perspectives. Note that the internal audit process appears in some detail from Chapter 5 onwards. Likewise our first encounter with the IPPF appears in this chapter, which will underpin the entire *Essential Guide*.

## Chapter 2 – Corporate Governance Perspectives

Chapter 2 covers corporate governance in general in that it summarizes the topic from a business standpoint rather than focusing just on the internal audit provisions. A main driver for 'getting things right' is the constant series of scandals that have appeared in developed (as well as developing) economies. The governance equation is quickly established and then profiles of some of the well-known scandals are used to demonstrate how fragile accountability frameworks can be. New-look models of corporate governance are detailed using extracts from various codes and guidance to form a challenge to business, government and not-for-profit sectors. Note that the chapter may be used by anyone interested in corporate governance as an introduction to the subject. The section on internal auditing is very brief and simply sets out the formal role and responsibilities, without going into too much detail. One topic that stands out in the chapter relates to audit committees, as many view this forum as the key to ensuring corporate responsibility and transparency. The corporate governance debate is ongoing and each new code refers to the need to start work on updates almost as soon as they are published. As such, it is never really possible to be up to date at publication and the reader is advised to keep an eye on new developments as and when they arise.

## Chapter 3 – Managing Risk

Many writers argue that we have entered a new dimension of business, accounting and audit whereby risk-based strategies are essential to the continuing success of all organizations. Reference is made to various risk standards and policies and we comment on the need to formulate a risk management process as part of the response to threats and opportunities. The corporate aspiration to embed risk management into the way organizations work is discussed. The growing importance of control self-assessment has ensured this appears in *The Essential Guide*, although this topic is also featured in the chapter on audit approaches (Chapter 7). The chapter closes with an attempt to work through the audit role in risk management and turns to the published professional guidance to help clarify respective positions. There is a link from this chapter to risk-based planning in the later chapter on setting an audit strategy (Chapter 8). Throughout *The Essential Guide* we try to maintain a link between corporate governance, risk management and internal control as integrated concepts that impact the internal audit role.

## Chapter 4 – Internal Controls

Some argue that internal control is the most important concept for internal auditors to get to grips with. Others simply suggest that we need to understand where controls fit into the risk management equation. Whatever the case, it is important to address this topic before we can get into the detailed material on internal auditing. An auditor armed with a good control model is more convincing that one who sees controls only as isolated mechanisms. Chapter 4 takes the reader through the entire spectrum of control concepts from control models, procedures and the link to risk management. One key section concerns the fallacy of perfection, where gaps in control and the reality of imperfection are discussed. For most business ventures it is uncertainty that creates business opportunities and new thinking. With the advent of risk management this does not mean controls take a back seat; it just means controls need to add value to the business equation to be of any real use.

## Chapter 5 – The Internal Audit Role

This chapter moves into the front line of internal audit material. Having gone through the reasoning behind the audit role (governance, risk management and the need for sound controls), we can turn to the actual role. The basic building blocks of the audit charter, independence, ethics and so on are important aspects of *The Essential Guide*. Much of the material builds on the original first edition of *The Essential Guide* and is updated to reflect new dimensions of auditing. One key component is the section on audit competencies, which forms the balancing factor in the equation – 'the challenges' and 'meeting the challenges'.

## Chapter 6 – Professionalism

The auditors' work will be determined by the needs of the organization and the experiences of senior auditors, and most audit shops arrive at a workable compromise. One feature of the upwards direction of the internal audit function is the growing importance of professional standards, while the main footing for *The Essential Guide* revolves around the IIA's IPPF. Moreover, quality is a theme that has run across business for many years. If there are quality systems in place for internal auditing, we are better able to manage the risk of poor performance. It would be ironic for internal audit reports to recommend better controls over operations that are reviewed when the audit team has no robust system in place that ensures it can live up to its own professional standards. Processes that seek to improve the internal audit product are covered in this chapter, including the important internal and external reviews that are suggested by auditing standards.

## Chapter 7 – The Audit Approach

The range and variety of audit services that fall under the guise of internal auditing have already been mentioned. A lot depends on the adopted approach and, rather than simply fall into one approach, it is much better to assess the possible positions armed with a knowledge of what is out there. Once we know what services we will be providing, we can think about a suitable structure for the audit shop. There is a note on control risk self-assessment (CRSA) and consideration of how it is possible to integrate the CRSA technique with the audit process. Other specialist aspects of audit work involving fraud investigations and information systems auditing are also mentioned. The IPPF acknowledges the linked trend towards more consulting work by internal audit outfits and therefore the consulting approach has its own section in this chapter.

## Chapter 8 – Setting an Audit Strategy

One view is that formulating an internal audit strategy is one of the most important tasks for the chief audit executive. In itself, this task depends on an intimate understanding of the corporate governance context, the audit role and competencies and challenge to add value to the business. The CAE needs to define a strategy, set standards, motivate staff and then measure what is done to have a half chance at delivering a successful audit service.

## Chapter 9 – Audit Fieldwork

Audit fieldwork covers the entire audit process from planning the assignment to reporting the results, while interviewing is seen as the primary means of obtaining information for the audit.

Various models are used throughout the chapter to explain the way risk-based auditing can be applied and there is coverage of planning, ascertaining, evaluating and reporting the audit assignment. The bridge between good working papers and audit findings and preparing the draft report is established using a key audit schedule as the pivotal document. Chapter 9 is quite involved and goes through the entire audit process in some detail.

## Chapter 10 – Meeting the Challenge

This final short chapter attempts to track key developments that impact on internal auditing and includes comments from various authoritative sources on future directions.

## Appendix – Auditing the Risk Management Process: A Case Study

The Appendix provides a case study on auditing the risk management process, which is provided in presentation format.

## 1.4 *The Essential Guide* as a Development Tool

All internal auditors need to be professionally competent and all internal audit shops need likewise to demonstrate that they add value to the task of enhancing risk management, control and governance processes. While a great deal of high-level work may be undertaken by the chief audit executive in terms of strategy, budgets and audit plans, the bottom line comes down to the performance of each and every individual auditor. It is this person who must carry the burden of heightened expectations where internal audit seeks a seat at the governance table. *The Essential Guide* is a resource that can be used to help support the internal auditor's constant drive to greater professionalism. It contains a basic minimum of knowledge that should be assimilated by competent internal auditors. *The Essential Guide* can also be used as an induction tool for new auditors who could work through each chapter and have a look at the case study in the Appendix.

## 1.5 The Development of Internal Auditing

Internal audit is now a fully developed profession. An individual employed in internal audit 10 years ago would find an unrecognizable situation in terms of the audit role, services provided and approach. For a full appreciation of internal auditing, it is necessary to trace these developments and extend trends into the future. It is a good idea to start with the late Lawrence Sawyer, the Godfather of internal audit, to open the debate on the audit role. Sawyer has said that audit has a long and noble history: 'Ancient Rome "hearing of accounts" one official compares records with another – oral verification gave rise to the term "audit" from the Latin "auditus" – a hearing'.[1]

## The Evolution of the Audit Function

It is important to understand the roots of internal auditing and the way it has developed over the years. One American text has detailed the history of internal audit:

> Prior to 1941, internal auditing was essentially a clerical function.... Because much of the record keeping at that time was performed manually, auditors were needed to check the accounting records after it was completed in order to locate errors... railroad companies are usually

credited with being the first modern employers of internal auditors . . . and their duty was to visit the railroads' ticket agents and determine that all monies were properly accounted for. The old concept of internal auditing can be compared to a form of insurance; the major objective was to discover fraud . . . .[2]

It is clear that the internal audit function has moved through a number of stages in its development which can be tracked as follows:

*Extension of external audit*   Internal audit developed as an extension of the external audit role in testing the reliability of accounting records that contribute to published financial statements. Internal audit was based on a detailed programme of testing accounting data. Where this model predominates, there can be little real development in the professionalism of the internal audit function. It would be possible to disband internal audit by simply increasing the level of testing in the external auditor's work plan. Unfortunately there are still organizations whose main justification for resourcing an internal audit service is to reduce the external audit fee. The IIA UK&Ireland have suggested this link between external and internal audit:

> The nineteenth century saw the proliferation of owners who delegated the day-to-day management of their businesses to others. These owners needed an independent assessment of the performance of their organizations. They were at greater risk of error, omissions or fraud in the business activities and in the reporting of the performance of these businesses than owner-managers. This first gave rise to the profession of external auditing. External auditors examine the accounting data and give owners an opinion on the accuracy and reliability of this data. More slowly the need for internal auditing of business activities was recognized. Initially this activity focused on the accounting records. Gradually it has evolved as an assurance and consulting activity focused on risk management, control and governance processes. Both external audit and internal audit exist because owners cannot directly satisfy themselves on the performance and reporting of their business and their managers cannot give an independent view of these.[3]

*Internal check*   The testing role progressed to cover nonfinancial areas, and this equated the internal audit function to a form of internal check. Vast numbers of transactions were double-checked to provide assurances that they were correct and properly authorized by laid-down procedures. The infamous 'audit stamp' reigned supreme, indicating that a document was checked by the auditor and deemed correct and above board. Internal control was seen as internal check and management was presented with audit reports listing the sometimes huge number of errors found by internal audit. The audit function typically consisted of a small team of auditors working under an assistant chief accountant. This actually encouraged management to neglect control systems on the grounds that errors would be picked up by the in-house auditors on the next visit. It locked the audit role tightly into the system of control, making it difficult to secure real independence. Moreover, most internal auditors assumed a 'Got-Ya' mentality, where their greatest achievements resided in the task of finding errors, abuse and/or neglect by managers and their staff. One writer has said:

> The old concept of internal auditing can be compared to a form of insurance; the major objective was to discover fraud more quickly than it could be discovered by the public accountant during an annual audit.[4]

**Probity work**  Probity work arrived next as an adaptation of checking accounting records, where the auditors would arrive unannounced at various locations and local offices, and perform a detailed series of tests according to a preconceived audit programme. Management was again presented with a list of errors and queries that were uncovered by the auditors. The auditors either worked in small teams based in accountancy or had dual posts where they had special audit duties in addition to their general accounting role. Audit consisted mainly of checking, with the probity visits tending to centre on cash income, stocks, purchases, petty cash, stamps, revenue contracts and other minor accounting functions. The main purpose behind these visits was linked to the view that the chief accountant needed to check on all remote sites to ensure that accounting procedures were complied with and that local books and records were correct. The audit was seen as an inspection routine on behalf of management. This militates against good controls, as the auditor is expected to be the main avenue for securing information on whether local office records were correct. Insecure head office management may then feel that their responsibility stops at issuing a batch of detailed procedures to local offices and nothing more. The auditors would then follow up these procedures without questioning why they were not working. The fundamental components of the control systems above local office level fell outside the scope of audit work, which was centred on low-level, detailed checking.

**Nonfinancial systems**  The shift in low-level checking arose when audit acquired a degree of separation from the accounting function with internal audit sections being purposely established. This allowed a level of audit management to develop, which in turn raised the status of the audit function away from a complement of junior staff completing standardized audit programmes. The ability to define an audit's terms of reference stimulated the move towards greater professionalism, giving rise to the model of audit as a separate entity. Likewise, the ability to stand outside basic financial procedures allowed freedom to tackle more significant business problems. It was now possible to widen the scope of audit work and bring to bear a whole variety of disciplines and not just accounting experience.

**Chief auditors**  Another thrust towards a high-profile, professional audit department was provided through employing chief internal auditors (or chief audit executives, CAEs) with high organizational status. They could meet with all levels of senior management and represent the audit function. This tended to coincide with the removal of audit from the finance function. The audit department as a separate high-profile entity encourages career auditors, able to develop within the function. This is as well as employing people who are able to use this audit experience as part of their managerial career development. The current position in many large organizations establishes a firm framework from which the audit function may continue to develop the professional status that is the mark of an accepted discipline. When assessing risk for the audit plan one asks what is crucial to the organization before embarking on a series of planned audits that in the past may have had little relevance to top management. Professionalism is embodied in the ability to deal with important issues that have a major impact on success.

**Audit committees**  Audit committees bring about the concept of the audit function reporting to the highest levels and this had a positive impact on perceived status. Securing the attention of the board, chief executive, managing director, nonexecutive directors and senior management also provides an avenue for high-level audit work able to tackle the most sensitive corporate issues. This is far removed from the early role of checking the stock and petty cash. Internal audit was now poised to enter all key parts of an organization. An important development in the US occurred when the Treadway Commission argued that listed companies should have an audit committee composed of nonexecutive directors. Since then, most stock exchange rules around the world require listed companies to have an audit committee and most also require an internal audit presence.

**Professionalism**   The Institute of Internal Auditors has some history going back over 50 years. *Brink's Modern Internal Auditing* has outlined the development of the IIA:

> In 1942, IIA was launched. Its first membership was started in New York City, with Chicago soon to follow. The IIA was formed by people who were given the title internal auditor by their organizations and wanted to both share experiences and gain knowledge with others in this new professional field. A profession was born that has undergone many changes over subsequent years.[5]

The importance of sound organizational systems came to the fore in the US where the Foreign Corrupt Practices Act, passed in 1997, stated that an organization's management was culpable for any illegal payments made by the organization even where they claimed they had no knowledge of the payments. The only way to ensure legality and propriety of all payments was to install reliable systems and controls. The systems-based approach offers great potential with the flexibility in applying this approach to a multitude of activities and developing a clear audit methodology at corporate, managerial and operational levels. Many internal audit shops have now moved into risk-based auditing, where the audit service is driven by the way the organization perceives and manages risk. Rather than start with set controls and whether they are being applied throughout the organization properly, the audit process starts with understanding the risks that need to be addressed by these systems of internal control. Much of the control solution hinges on the control environment in place and whether a suitable control framework has been developed and adopted by the organization. Internal audit can provide formal assurances regarding these controls. Moreover, many internal audit shops have also adopted a consulting role, where advice and support are provided to management.

There is no linear progression in audit services, with many forces working to take the profession back to more traditional models of the audit role where compliance and fraud work (including financial propriety) are the key services in demand. Many of the trends behind the development of internal audit point to the ultimate position where the audit function becomes a high-profile autonomous department reporting at the highest level. This may depend on moving out audit functions currently based in accountancy. The true audit professional is called upon to review complicated and varied systems even if the more complicated and sensitive ones may sometimes be financially based. A multidisciplined approach provides the flexibility required to deal with operational areas. Again, this move is strengthened by the growing involvement in enterprise-wide risk management. The latest position is that there is normally no longer a clear logic to the chief audit executive to continue to hold a reporting line to the DF. The debate now revolves around whether the CAE should report directly into the main board and not just to the audit committee.

## The Expectation Gap

Audit services will have to be properly marketed, which is essentially based on defining and meeting client needs. This feature poses no problem as long as clients know what to expect from their internal auditors. It does, however, become a concern when this is not the case, and there is a clear gap in what is expected and what is provided. Management may want internal auditors to:

- Check on junior staff on a regular basis.
- Investigate fraud and irregularity and present cases to the police and/or internal disciplinaries.
- Draft procedures where these are lacking.
- Draft information papers on items of new legislation or practice.
- Investigate allegations concerning internal disputes and advise on best resolution.
- Advise on data privacy and security, and check that the rules are complied with.
- Identify key risks for senior management.

One cannot give up professional integrity but, at the same time, the above expectations cannot simply be ignored. If new resources are brought in to cover these services, they may end up competing for the internal audit role. It is important not to sacrifice assurance work by diverting audit resources to carrying out pure consulting services. We must also keep an eye on the wider societal expectations. If internal audit is seen as professionally independent, then there will come a time when audit reports will be of increasing interest to stakeholders who sit outside the corporate entity.

The emergence of a Governance, Risk and Compliance process in many larger organizations derives from an attempt to integrate these three concepts into a meaningful whole. New legislation and regulations should be considered and the effects anticipated. The audit strategy and business plan should take on board these additional factors in a way that promotes the continuing success of the audit function. This means that the CAE must resource the continual search for new legislation that affects the organization's control systems or impacts on the future of internal audit. As suggested by the current definition of internal auditing, these three concepts now form the framework for the design and provision of the internal audit service. One major issue is the growth of risk committees that are being established by main boards along with the appointment of high-level chief risk officers, and the impact this has on the internal audit role. This is why the next three chapters deal with these topics.

## Summary and Conclusions

This first chapter of *The Essential Guide* takes the reader through the structure of the book and highlights the pivotal role of the IIA standards. We have also provided a brief snapshot of the development of the internal audit role as an introduction to the subject. Many of the points mentioned above are dealt with in some detail in the main part of the book, although it is as well to keep in mind the basics of internal audit while reading more widely. The concept of internal audit is really quite simple – it is the task of putting the ideals into practice that proves more trying. Internal auditors have a noble history as guardians of good governance and as the need for better accountabilty becomes more profound, the auditor will need to step further and further into the corporate spotlight. We have mentioned Sawyer's views in this chapter, which is why we close with another quote on the wide range of benefits from a good internal audit team:

IA can assist top management in:

- monitoring activities top management cannot itself monitor
- identifying and minimizing risks

- validating reports to senior management
- protecting senior management in technical analysis beyond its ken
- providing information for the decision-making process
- reviewing for the future as well as for the past
- helping line managers manage by pointing to violation of procedures and management principles.[6]

Whatever the new risk-centric jargon used to describe the audit role, much of the above benefits described by Sawyer remain constant. For those embarking on a career in internal auditing, these are exciting new times, where the contribution of the competent auditor will be immense in helping locate integrity and transparency right at the forefront of the way large organizations are governed.

## Endnotes

1. Sawyer, Lawrence B. and Dittenhofer, Mortimer A., Assisted by Scheiner, James H. (1996) *Sawyer's Internal Auditing*, 4th edition, Florida: The Institute of Internal Auditors, p. 8.
2. Flesher, Dale (1996) *Internal Auditing: A One-Semester Course*, Florida: The Institute of Internal Auditors, pp. 5–6.
3. Internal Auditing (2002) *Distance Learning Module*, Institute of Internal Auditors UK&Ireland.
4. Flesher, Dale (1996) *Internal Auditing: A One-Semester Course*, Florida: The Institute of Internal Auditors, p. 7.
5. Moeller, Robert and Witt, Herbert (1999) *Brink's Modern Internal Auditing*, 5th edition, New York: John Wiley & Sons, Inc.
6. Sawyer, Lawrence B. and Dittenhofer, Mortimer A., Assisted by Scheiner, James H. (1996) *Sawyer's Internal Auditing*, 4th edition, Florida: The Institute of Internal Auditors, p. 13.

Chapter 2

# CORPORATE GOVERNANCE PERSPECTIVES

## Introduction

Corporate governance is a term that, over the years, has now found its way into popular literature. It has been described by Sir Adrian Cadbury as the way organizations are directed and controlled. This simple statement contains many profound elements including the performance/conformance argument of whether good governance is about complying with codes of practice or whether it also underpins better business performance. There is also some debate as to whether companies should follow a fixed set of rules or be guided by less rigid principles. An organization's main task is to achieve the level of performance that it was established for. However, at the same time, it must adhere to all relevant standards, rules, laws, regulations, policies and expectations that form a framework within which this performance will be assessed. This, in turn, may cause many difficulties in the real world. Our first reference to corporate governance comes from Ireland:

> Improved standards of corporate governance, like 'motherhood', cannot be argued against. It is critical to a small economy like Ireland, which is seeking to develop business in the more sophisticated sectors, that we are seen to operate to high standards.[1]

A widely reported case, involving a large law firm, recounts the pressures placed on the legal teams who were told to charge a set number of fee paying hours each month, which resulted in the routine falsification of timesheets to achieve this target. While the firm's performance was excellent, as measured in terms of income achieved, it broke many rules in its charging practices and even committed the criminal offence of false accounting; i.e. there was little conformance with rules, procedures and ethical values. The firm's tone at the top was weak in that it created a culture of abuse and control was lacking in that routine working practices broke many rules. Short-term gains in income were secured, while in the long run a great deal of damage was done to the firm's reputation when the scandal was eventually uncovered. The firm's partners, investors, employees and everyone else connected with the entity expected a high return, so the pressures this expectation created built up to force otherwise perfectly respectable people to falsify their charge sheets.

This simple illustration can be multiplied many times in all major developing and developed economies to give an insight into the type of problem that undermines the foundations of both business and public services. Moreover, there are many well-known corporate scandals involving large companies and public sector bodies that have occurred with frequent regularity over the years, each serving to undermine public trust in large organizations. Corporate governance codes and policies have come to be relied on to reestablish the performance/conformance balance to help ensure integrity, openness and accountability. The codes call for boardroom arrangements that support these three ideals and the internal audit function is a key component of governance structures in promoting good governance as part of the audit review process. The internal auditor who has a sound grasp of corporate governance is best placed to play a major role in the drive to ensuring sustainability as well as success in all business and service sectors. Note that all references to IIA definitions, code of ethics, IIA attribute and performance standards, practice advisories and practice guides relate to the International Professional Practices Framework (IPPF) prepared by the Institute of Internal Auditors in 2009. The sections covered in this chapter are:

2.1  The Agency Model
2.2  Corporate Ethics and Accountability
2.3  International Scandals and Their Impact
2.4  Models of Corporate Governance
2.5  The Institute of Internal Auditors
2.6  The External Audit
2.7  The Audit Committee
2.8  Internal Audit
2.9  The Link to Risk Management and Internal Control
2.10 Reporting on Governance, Risk and Internal Controls
2.11 New Developments
      Summary and Conclusions

## 2.1   The Agency Model

The main driver for corporate governance is based on the agency concept. Here corporate bodies are overseen by directors who are appointed by the owners, i.e. the shareholders. The directors formulate a corporate strategy to achieve set objectives and meet market expectations, and, in turn, employ managers and staff to implement this strategy. Throughout the course of this chapter we will develop a simple model that will set out the main elements of one version of the corporate governance framework, starting with Figure 2.1.

**FIGURE 2.1**   Corporate governance (1).

If everyone was totally competent and totally honest then the model in Figure 2.1 would work quite well. The shareholders appoint the board of directors who oversee their managers, while managers run the business through their operational and support staff, led by a combination of team leaders, supervisors and unit heads. To achieve their published objectives the directors set targets for their management team, authorize a budget and then establish a mechanism for measuring performance. All business activity feeds into the accounting system and the directors report the results back to their shareholders in the annual report on performance and accompanying final accounts. Shareholders check the overall performance and financial results each year and ensure that their investment is intact. They have a right to any dividends and may well see a growth in the value of their investment through strong share prices. Meanwhile, the directors have a duty to take all reasonable steps to protect the business and account for their activities. The Stewardship concept means directors owe this responsibility to the parties who have a vested interest in the organization. They work for and on behalf of the owners and need to demonstrate adequate competence. A hint at what could go wrong with this simple model is illustrated by the following article:

Many directors have virtually no idea of their powers, or of the legal obligations that they face . . . . Examples of rules directors commonly break – either deliberately or unintentionally – include: borrowing money from companies over which they exercise control; failing to hold and minute board meetings as and when required by law; failing to declare an interest in contracts that involve the company; blindly battling to save a company in difficulties or technically insolvent when this presents a risk to the creditors; failing to understand the 'five year' directors' employment contract rule.[2]

There are further mechanisms that need to be included in our model to reflect both the performance and accountability dimensions that are important in agency theory, i.e. strategic performance measures and published accounts, shown in Figure 2.2.

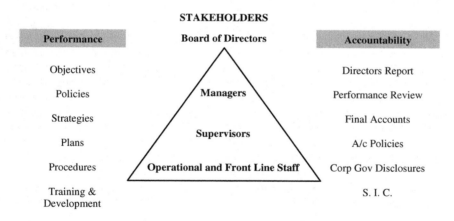

**FIGURE 2.2**   Corporate governance (2).

The board will set out the corporate objectives and strategy to achieve these objectives, formed within the defined policies that constrain the way the workforce behaves. Plans, procedures and well-trained staff will work to deliver their team and personal targets. Again, this simple model means that the shareholders get the performance returns they signed up to. The right side of the model closes the loop whereby the board reports formally back to the shareholders through the annual report and accounts. Most regulations require the disclosure of adopted governance arrangements and the statement of internal control (SIC), which says that controls are sound and work. In the past this model of basic corporate governance was used to establish the corporate entity, whereby owners used managers to run their investment and report back on results. Notice that the term 'shareholders' has been replaced with the term 'stakeholders' in our model, and this change is now explained.

## Defining Stakeholders

The agency model is based on changing the one-dimensional concept of *shareholders* to the wider concept of *stakeholders*. Most commentators argue that corporations need to acknowledge a wide range of people and groups affected by their operations and presence. Andrew Chambers has devised a 'Court of public opinion' as consisting of key figures including:

| | |
|---|---|
| Customers | Regulators |
| Financiers | Business partners |
| Politicians | Shareholders |
| The media | Competitors |
| Employees | Government |
| Business leaders | Local communities[3] |

This does not mean the shareholders can be sidelined in preference to all groups that come into contact with an organization. Shareholders have a right to have their investment managed with care and should expect some return (dividends) from the enterprise. They can vote on important matters such as who should be in charge of the company and how much they should receive for this task. Companies are paying much more attention to the needs of the shareholders and, as one commentator states:

> Twenty years ago management had scant if any regard for shareholders, unless they were part of the family! In the 1980s two things happened. One, management thought they had better start talking to investors because they could sack the board. Then we had firms being bid for and normally they weren't the ones which had achieved much. As they tried to defend what they had done, you heard the great cry of short-termism which really meant – we failed to perform for the last three years but don't worry, we will do for the next three. Suddenly the bulb went on in our brains that we had power and could influence management. Boards also recognised they had to talk to their shareholders. Today we do have sensible dialogues.[4]

Providing lots of information to the shareholders may represent good intentions but at times information alone may not be enough:

> Royal Bank of Scotland's annual report, published this week, devoted seven pages to executive pay. Barclay's report has eight if you count the page on directors' pay. Every year, it gets harder for the reader to have a clue what is really going on. It is now virtually impossible to grasp how generous these schemes could be. Even remuneration consultants who devise them admit to being frequently baffled, at least when trying to unpick them on the basis of the information published in the annual report.[5]

In general there are two types of stakeholders: those that have a direct *influence* on the organization's future activities, such as investors, customers, regulators and shareholders, and those that simply have an *interest* in the organization, such as local community groups and journalists. It is the stakeholders who are affected by the way corporations behave. In a sense this means almost everyone in society is affected by private corporations, listed companies and public sector bodies. Some argue that in the long run the interests of shareholders and general stakeholders tend to coincide so that all sides can be catered for via a single corporate strategy.

## 2.2   Corporate Ethics and Accountability

We have argued that if everyone were honest and competent there would always be good governance in most organizations. In terms of ethics, the first question to ask is whether we need to establish corporate ethics within organizations? A survey by Management Today and KPMG Forensic Accounting of more than 800 directors, managers and partners illustrates why business ethics needs to be carefully considered:

- More than 2 out of 3 say that everyone lies to their boss on occasion.
- Less than half consider the people at the top to be strong ethical role models.
- Over 20% felt it was okay to surf the net for pleasure during work time.
- Around 25% would not say that favouring friends or family in awarding contracts was totally unacceptable.
- Some 7% agreed it was okay to artificially inflate profits so long as no money was stolen.
- Only 1 in 5 were prepared to say that charging personal entertainment to expenses was totally unacceptable (less than 15% for board directors).
- People over 40, those in financial positions and those in the public sector take a more judgemental approach to ethical behaviour.
- A dishonest member of staff may receive a clean reference from 3 in 10 managers.
- Reasons for not reporting a fraud include – alienate myself, none of my business, jeopardise my job, everybody's doing it, it is fair game.
- Nearly 10% of board directors say it is acceptable to massage their profit figures as long as no money is stolen.[6]

The agency model required still more refinement to cope with the demands of the competitive economy that impact the ethical compass for the proper running of business, as shown in Figure 2.3.

The new model includes legislation and regulations, the external publication of the final accounts that are prepared by the board and a strong set of ethical standards. Meanwhile, external auditors are appointed to serve shareholders in making sure that the final accounts can be relied on. All countries have a raft of laws covering issues such as maximum working hours, minimum wage, antidiscrimination, consumer protection, environmental impacts, anticompetition, insider trading and health and safety, along with stock exchange and industry specific regulations set by various regulators to guide the way business is conducted and the way people are treated. Final accounts are checked by an external firm of accountants to ensure they show a true and fair view of the company's financial performance and position. Most organizations have a set of ethical standards that are made clear to employees and others, which help define unacceptable conduct. In this way the growth, stability and even demise of businesses is essentially dependent on the free flow of funds along with fair and open competition. The fittest companies survive while the less able must change, collapse or be consumed by stronger and more enterprising companies. The above model is straightforward and well understood as the proper basis for a capitalist system. The

**FIGURE 2.3**    Corporate governance (3).

public sector approach has some similarities, which are catered for by replacing the board with the accounting officer (for central government bodies) or chief executive for local authorities and other public service organizations. Not-for-profit organizations would have a similar responsible person at the helm. For public bodies, the owners are the taxpayers and the external auditors have an additional role in assessing performance and value for money (VFM) as well as verifying the financial statements. In this way public sector service strategies and performance measures are validated in the absence of the private sector profit motive, which is a fairly simple model of corporate accountability.

There is much that can be gained where a strong ethical foundation is in place:

> The pharmaceutical company mentioned in the COSO report was Johnson and Johnson. In the 1980s it faced a massive crisis when a malefactor inserted a deadly poison in bottles of one of its widely distributed products. The company had to decide whether to treat this as an isolated incident or take more drastic corrective action. Using its statement of ethical values as justification to recall and pull the entire product line, it averted a more serious crisis and received favourable publicity for its action.[7]

It is now a criminal offence for UK companies to bribe overseas public officials under the Bribery Act 2010, similar to the position for US companies. Most people agree that corruption has two sides – the offer and acceptance – and that companies that offer bribes simply encourage a continuation of corrupt practices. There is a subsidiary argument that, at times, company officials have to offer inducements (described, for example, as local licensing fees) to have any chance of securing business abroad. The OECD Convention on Combating Bribery of Foreign Officials led to the adoption of 17 Articles by OECD countries and five nonmember countries on 21 November 1997. In addition, the OECD have developed Recommendation on Improving Ethical Conduct in the Public Service (April 1998), which can be used to form the basis for an ethics management system:

- Ethical standards for the public service should be clear.
- Ethical standards should be reflected in the legal framework.

- Ethical standards should be made available to public servants.
- Public servants should know their rights and obligations when exposing wrongdoings.
- Political commitment to ethics should reinforce the ethical conduct of public servants.
- The decision making process should be transparent and open to scrutiny.
- There should be clear guidelines for interaction between the public and private sectors.
- Managers should demonstrate and promote ethical standards.
- Management policies, procedures and practices should promote ethical conduct.
- Public sector conditions and management of human resources should promote ethical conduct.
- Adequate accountability mechanisms should be in place with the public sector.
- Appropriate procedures and sanctions should exist to deal with misconduct.[8]

Some companies have taken a lead in ethical reporting. As an example there follows a quote from the late Anita Roddick, founder of the Body Shop, and further material posted on the Body Shop website:

> I would love it if every shareholder of every company wrote a letter every time they received a company's annual report and accounts. I would like them to say something like 'Okay that's fine, very good. But where are the details of your environmental audit? Where are your details of accounting to the community? Where is your social audit?'[9]

Unfortunately, there are certain flaws in this standard model, many of which hinder the degree of reliance that can be placed on the reports and representations published by large organizations and which serve to undermine the agency concept. These potential problems include:

- Boards dominated by a powerful chief executive officer (CEO) who manipulates the companies to their own personal agenda or who encourages excessive risk taking.
- Boards that are ineffectual and consist simply of a network of friends who fail to represent the shareholders to any real extent.
- Boards that are incompetent and/or who are overcommitted and meet on an irregular basis and simply rubber stamp the position set by the CEO or a small group of dominating board members.
- CEOs and chief finance officers (CFOs) who conspire with other board members to distort the published results of the company for reasons of personal gain or because of a fear that a fall in the share price will strip the value of shares and options they hold in the company, particularly where the market expects instant and large returns in rapid growth business sectors.
- Compensation schemes that encourage high rewards for excessive short-term risk taking based on huge bonuses.
- Employees who are regularly able to abuse company systems and exploit loopholes, again for personal gain, where managers either do not care or are implicated to some extent.
- Significant business ventures, takeovers and development projects that involve huge shifts of resources and large returns for entrepreneurs, but which involve major risks that have not been fully addressed.
- Short-term measures such as dumping waste, skipping important safety checks or exploiting third world labour and resources that reap significant returns but involve illicit hardship to third parties. Many of these acts are then concealed through misreporting or cover-ups.
- Organizations with great emphasis on success where bad news is not tolerated and losses, problems, errors or breach of procedure are either ignored or concealed.
- One-dimensional performance targets where operations are inappropriately skewed towards quick wins or figures are massaged to produce predetermined results.

- Organizations where accountabilities have not been properly established and where a blame culture means certain employees are unfairly targeted and whistleblowing is frowned on.
- External audit routines that are designed to protect top management where the in-charge audit partner has a basic allegiance to the company directors, particularly the CFO, who in reality determines the auditor's employment prospects, fees and extra consulting work.
- Published accounts that are so full of complicated material that the real picture is unclear, particularly where opaque accounting policies (relating to, say, off balance sheet financing) are applied in such as way as to present the picture that the board wants to publicise.
- Annual reports that fail to make clear the adopted strategy and how risks are identified and addressed. High impact risks may have been ignored because the board feel they are unlikely to arise, but which may spiral on to the radar in volatile market conditions.
- Tone at the top that fails to impress the need for high ethical standards, even when this may mean turning away from attractive business opportunities.

The list could go on and on and in general the basic agency model fails to ensure that the risks of all the above have been assessed and addressed to ensure they are unlikely to materialize. The normal performance/conformance model assumes people are competent and honest and takes no account of the fundamental pressures in society to place self-interest and short-term bonuses above absolute legitimacy and long-term sustainable growth. It also does not acknowledge the view that all players may not be competent in understanding their set responsibilities to grow and protect the resources entrusted to them.

## Shareowners

The focus on long-term sustainability has led to pressures on shareholders to mobilise and wield the great potential power they hold to drive executives away from short-termism. In fact, the California Public Employees' Retirement System (CalPERS) revised their Global Principles of Accountable Corporate Governance in March 2009, which recognizes the need to achieve long-term sustainable risk-adjusted investment returns. As such, they have adopted the term 'shareowner' rather than 'shareholder' to reflect a view that equity ownership carries with it active responsibilities and is not merely passively 'holding' shares. However, the growth and pace of big business, government reforms, virtual marketplaces and global competition has led to a cut-and-thrust climate where individuals are either required to achieve instant success or at least give the appearance of having done so. High ethical standards, which used to act as the glue that holds everything in place, are now more like the glue that slows everything down and can mean a second rather than first place medal. Competence, clarity of roles and the proper discharge of professional obligations is a good ideal. However, a two-year study by the Royal Society of Arts (Corporate Governance in the Public and Voluntary Sector) concluded:

> The report also found that there is confusion among many board members about roles, responsibilities, managerial hierarchy and levels of authority as well as the legislative framework that defines and sets limits for their activities.[10]

## 2.3  International Scandals and Their Impact

Corporate governance (CG) is the enhanced (and codified) process that is superimposed over the basic performance/accountability model to try to counter inappropriate behaviour. It is constructed in recognition of the need to encourage business performance, to demonstrate that this performance is really earned and to encourage more openness in reported results. Moreover, it is founded on good business sense as a way of promoting sustainable and realistic growth and enhanced corporate performances. We have touched on the types of problems that could undermine the agency model and before we delve into the many cases that set the context for the training, codes, guides and regulations on corporate governance, it is as well to recall the words of Sir Adrian Cadbury in the run-up to the first major attempt to tackle concerns over poor accountability:

> The country's economy depends on the drive and efficiency of its companies. Thus the effectiveness with which their boards discharge their responsibilities determines Britain's competitive position. They must be free to drive their companies forward, but exercise that freedom within a framework of effective accountability. This is the essence of any system of corporate governance (para. 1.1). By adhering to the code, listed companies will strengthen both their control over their business and their public accountability. In doing so, they will strike the right balance between meeting the standards of corporate governance now expected of them and retaining the essential spirit of enterprise (para. 1.5).[11]

Some of the more famous cases where these ideals have not been met are mentioned below:

## Guinness – 1986

Ernest Saunders, the Chief Executive of Guinness, paid himself £3 million plus interest, and paid large sums to those who helped him rig shares in order to try and take over another drinks company, Distillers. He rigged the shares to beat Argyll, the company in competition with him to try and take over Distillers. Ernest Saunders was not alone in the share-rigging; senior businessmen from outside Guinness were also involved.[12]

## Barlow Clowes – 1988

The Barlow Clowes business collapsed owing millions of pounds. The business was made up of a partnership and a company in the UK, with a total of 7000 investors; partnerships in Jersey and Geneva, with 11 000 investors; and Barlow Clowes International in Gibraltar. From November 1985 until April 1987, Spicer and Oppenheim provided a range of services, including audit, but did not audit the businesses in Jersey or Geneva. The Joint Disciplinary Scheme (JDS) states that there was in general inadequate planning of the Barlow Clowes audit work and that: 'in many respects the audit work was poorly controlled and inadequately focused to ensure that reliable audit opinions could be drawn'. Peter Clowes moved approximately £100 million from the accounts of investors and then spent it on planes, boats, jewellery and other things. In addition, £37 million pounds remained unaccounted for.[13]

## Polly Peck International – 1989

Asil Nadir was the head of Polly Peck International until its value dropped from £1 billion to less than half of that amount in 1989. The Stock Exchange had to suspend trading in Polly Peck International shares because of this fall in value. Asil Nadir was charged with false accounting and stealing a total of £31 million. There were also reports of insider trading. Asil Nadir fled to northern Cyprus in May 1993, shortly before his trial. Elizabeth Forsyth, Nadir's right-hand woman, however, was jailed for five years in March 1996 accused of laundering £400 000 Nadir allegedly stole from shareholders to pay off his debts. During 2010 Mr Nadir voluntarily returned to the UK to face the above charges.[14]

## BCCI (Bank of Credit and Commerce International) – 1991

BCCI, regarded as the world's biggest fraud, caused a bank operating in over 60 countries worldwide, and supposedly valued at $20 billion, to become worthless. The bank collapsed in 1991 owing $13 billion. PricewaterhouseCoopers (PwC) has been criticized for not spotting that BCCI, which was founded in 1975, was almost certainly insolvent before 1977. This was 10 years before PwC succeeded in becoming sole auditor of the bank over Ernst & Young. PwC, the external auditor, advised the Bank of England that the BCCI was riddled with fraud on 24 June 1991, and on 5 July 1991 the Bank of England shut BCCI.[15]

## Maxwell – 1991

Robert Maxwell, the founder and Chief Executive of the Maxwell publishing empire, manipulated funds to give the impression that the company was financially liquid, in order to disguise the fact that he had perpetrated a huge fraud, which came to light in 1991. The external auditors were Coopers and Lybrand.[16]

## Baring Futures (Singapore) – 1995

Baring Futures Singapore (BFS) was set up to enable the Baring Group to trade on the Singapore International Money Exchange (SIMEX). Nick Leeson, an inexperienced trader, was employed to manage both the dealing and settlement office (front and back office). Leeson was unable to trade in the UK due to a false statement made to the regulatory body for financial traders, the Securities and Futures Authority. On appointment by BFS, he opened an unauthorized account, which he used to cover up his large trading losses, which remained undiscovered until Barings collapsed in 1995.[17]

## Metropolitan Police – 1995

Anthony Williams, Deputy Director of Finance for the Metropolitan Police, was exposed as a fraudster. He stole £5 million over a period of eight years between 1986 and 1994 from a secret bank account, set up as part of a highly sensitive operation against terrorists. Anthony Williams was asked in the mid-1980s to set up the secret bank account. His signature was the only one required to authorize payments from the account, even though he had a co-signatory to the account. This enabled him to steal from the account to purchase homes in Spain, the South of England and Scotland, where he bought himself the title Laird of Tomintoul, and spent large amounts of money on property renovations. The internal controls in place were inadequate to manage the possible risks, and the external auditors failed to spot these risks early enough to prevent Williams perpetrating the fraud. The fraud was only discovered because a Scottish banker asked questions about the scale of Williams' spending on uneconomic renovations to his property in Scotland.[18]

## Sumitomo Corporation – 1996

Yasuo Hamanaka was a copper trader working for Sumitomo Corporation, the world's biggest copper merchant. 'The Hammer', as Hamanaka was known, was also known as Mr Five Per Cent, referring to the amount of the market he controlled on his own. He was the biggest 'player' in copper, selling about 10 000 tons a year and able to single-handedly sway prices. His early success, and the fact that he held such a large proportion of the market, allowed him to trade unchecked until it was too late. Yasuo Hamanaka was a rogue trader, who during 10 years of double-dealing in Tokyo ran up losses of £1.2 billion. One senior manager said: 'This is probably the biggest loss you will ever see.'[19]

## Daiwa Bank – 1996

Between 1984 and 1995 Toshihide Iguchi made bad trades in the bond market at the Manhattan branch of Daiwa Bank. He covered up his bad trades by selling bonds from Daiwa's own accounts and forging documentation for the bank's files to cover his tracks. He was in control of both the front and back offices of the bank, in a small understaffed branch, where his activities remained unmonitored for 11 years. In 1995, when he could no longer cope, he wrote to his employers admitting that he had lost the bank $1.1 billion. He claimed he kept the level of debt to himself for so long because he had not wanted to let anyone down. In 1996, Toshihide Iguchi was convicted of fraud and falsifying documents and jailed for four and half years in the US after losing the Daiwa Bank more than $1 billion in fraudulent trading over 11 years from 1984 onwards. Iguchi was ordered to pay $2.6 million in fines and restitution. Daiwa Bank paid $340 million in fines and had to close all its businesses in America, after being sued by the US authorities. Also in 2000, 11 senior executives were ordered to repay a total of $775 million in damages to the Daiwa Bank. Kenji Yasui, the former president of Daiwa Bank's New York branch, was ordered to repay the bulk of the damages – a massive $500 million. The executives may appeal against the ruling.[20]

## Morgan Grenfell – 1996

In 1996, it was revealed that Peter Young lost $600 million belonging to city bank Morgan Grenfell. Peter Young, as head of Morgan Grenfell's European Growth Unit Trust in 1995, a fund worth £788 million, became interested in buying shares in a company called Solv-Ex. Solv-Ex's US directors claimed to be able to extract oil from sand cheaply. Peter Young spent approximately £400 million of his company's money on Solv-Ex. He set up 'shell' companies in Luxembourg to buy Solv-Ex shares illegally. In 1996, Solv-Ex was under US federal investigation. By the time of his trial in 1998, Peter Young was declared mentally unfit. He attended court in women's clothing carrying a handbag. Morgan Grenfell was acquired by Deutsche Bank.[21]

## Inland Revenue – 1997

Michael Allcock was group leader of the Inland Revenue's Special Office 2, investigating foreign businessmen's tax affairs between 1987 and 1992, when he was suspended from duty charged with fraud, accepting cash bribes, a lavish overseas holiday with his family and the services of a prostitute, in exchange for information on cases. Allcock was jailed in 1997.[22]

## Liberty National Securities – 1999

Martin Frankel was banned from securities trading after being unable to account for $1 million from a fund he managed in 1992. In 1999, Frankel set up an unlicensed brokerage, Liberty National Securities, and defrauded insurance companies in five American states out of more than $200 million by gaining controlling stakes in them before absconding. He was extradited from Germany to the US in 2001 and pleaded guilty to 24 federal charges of fraud, racketeering and conspiracy in 2002.[23]

## Sellafield – 2000

Process workers were to blame for the scandal that hit Sellafield nuclear power plant and led to cancelled orders and the resignation of the chief executive. Process workers at the Sellafield nuclear plant falsified records measuring batches of fuel pellets processed from reprocessed plutonium and uranium. Safety inspectors gave managers at the plant two months to present an action plan to address their failures. The UK's nuclear watchdog, the Nuclear Installations Inspectorate (NII), focused on how the nature of the job, lack of supervision and poor training had contributed to the procedural failures. The data check was part of a quality assurance inspection, but the significance of the check had never been connected with safety and was not emphasized to staff, so falsifying the data became a way of avoiding what staff saw as a pointless task.[24]

## Equitable Life – 2001

Equitable Life is now an established financial scandal. Equitable Life gave contradictory information to savers, independent financial advisors and the media, and the regulator, the Financial Services Authority (FSA), has refused to comment on its role in the disaster. When Equitable announced its cuts of 16% to pensions and 14% to other with-profits savings, the insurer implied the money would only come from promised terminal bonuses, leaving guaranteed bonuses and capital safe. In fact, Equitable Life was prepared to dig into both guaranteed bonuses and capital that people had saved in order to claw back the full 16%. Therefore anyone who invested £100 000 with Equitable Life in autumn 2000 would be likely to walk away with just £77 000 a year on, instead of having the £104 000 that could have been expected. This has raised questions about the role of the regulator. An FSA spokesman said: 'It is up to investors to make their own investment decisions.' The FSA's hands-off approach appeared to be at odds with its responsibilities as outlined in the Financial Services and Markets Act. The Act says the FSA must take into account 'the needs that consumers may have for advice and accurate information'.[25]

## Alder Hey – 2001

Police are conducting an enquiry into Dutch pathologist Professor Dick Van Velzen, who worked at the Alder Hey Hospital in Liverpool between 1988 and 1995. The scandal came to light when a mother discovered that when her child, who died at three months, was buried in 1991, all of his organs were not intact. Eight years later organs belonging to him were discovered at Alder Hey Hospital in Liverpool, and she held a second funeral service. However, last year more body parts were discovered, and the bereaved mother held a third funeral service for her baby. The Government's Chief Medical Officer, Professor Liam Donaldson, revealed that 10 000 hearts, brains and other organs were still being held at other hospitals across England and that thousands of families remain unaware that the loved ones they buried have had organs illegally removed without their consent. These details were revealed by Professor Liam Donaldson in an official report into Alder Hey and into the scale of organ abuse in Britain.[26]

## Enron – 2001

Enron, a multinational energy trading company based in Houston, Texas, collapsed when credit rating firms prepared to lower their assessments of the company's debt. Enron would have been compelled to repay loans gained on the basis of its loan rating and faced weakened share price. Enron went from being worth $60 billion to bankruptcy. Enron collapsed because of its complicated trading activities and financial manipulation. The company's income came from buying and selling future prices of energy and other commodities. The amounts involved in the trades were shown incorrectly as income, rather than the marginal difference between each side of the transaction. Enron's actions were described as being akin to counting money it held temporarily on behalf of clients as all its own income. As well as responsibility for the external audit function, Andersen was also responsible for the internal audit at Enron.[27]

## WorldCom – 2002

Just as the US economy was recovering from the Enron saga another huge scandal appeared in the form of WorldCom. WorldCom was valued at $180 billion in 1999. The company was originally a small local telecommunications agency that grew very quickly into one of the largest providers in the industry. There was a change of senior management at WorldCom in 2002, who asked the internal auditor to examine particular accounting transactions. The internal auditor discovered that corporate expenses were being treated as capital investments; i.e. expenses were being set against long-term budgets, rather than being offset against profits immediately. This practice resulted in the inflation of WorldCom's profits and share value, creating the impression that the company was more valuable than it actually was.[28]

## Allied Irish Bank (AIB) Allfirst (US Subsidiary) – 2002

Allfirst, Allied Irish Bank's subsidiary, was based in Baltimore, Maryland, USA. In early 2002, AIB revealed that one of its traders, John Rusnak, had made transactions that resulted in a loss of almost $700 million (actual $691 million). Similarly to the Barings scandal, Rusnak had been allowed to trade unsupervised for almost five years before the scale of his losses was discovered.

Rusnak traded in what were regarded as low-risk transactions, yet was able to run up huge losses as AIB failed to oversee its Maryland activities as carefully as required. The Allfirst treasurer's conflicting responsibilities were in part responsible for this, as he was accountable for both trading profits and trading activities.[29]

## Xerox – 2002

The Securities and Exchange Commission, the US financial regulator, filed a suit against Xerox in April 2002 for misstating its profits to the tune of almost $3 billion. Xerox reached a settlement with the SEC and agreed to pay a fine of $10 million, but neither denied nor admitted any wrongdoing. The fine imposed by the Securities and Exchange Commission was the largest fine ever imposed on a publicly traded firm in relation to accounting misdeeds.[30]

## Merrill Lynch – 2002

The investment bank was fined by New York attorney general Eliot Spitzer to the tune of $10 million in 2002. The bank's analysts were suspected of advising investors to purchase worthless stocks, so the former could then secure investment banking business from the businesses concerned. The settlement imposed by Spitzer did not require Merrill Lynch to admit guilt for its actions.[31]

## Credit Suisse First Boston (CSFB) – 2002

The Financial Services Authority (FSA), the UK's financial watchdog, fined CSFB, the US-based investment banking arm of Switzerland's Credit Suisse, £4 million ($6.4 million) for trying to mislead the Japanese tax and regulatory authorities in 2002.[32]

Note that some of the more recent scandals are discussed towards the end of this chapter.

## 2.4   Models of Corporate Governance

We have established the classical model of corporate accountability and the ethical frameworks that are being used by organizations to promote sustainability. The last section provided a frightening insight into the fallout when things go wrong. The ripples caused by corporate scandals have recently become strong waves of discontent as the search has been made for workable and lasting solutions. Most solutions come in the guise of codes of practice that have been documented and appear as regulations or guidance for relevant organizations. Companies listed on various international stock markets are meant to subscribe to listing rules or make clear their reasons (and the implications) for failing to observe the rules. Health Trusts fall under the guidance provided for NHS organization and central government bodies have reference to guidance issued by the Treasury. Local authorities again have their own set of guidelines on promoting corporate governance, set within the local democracy and accountability framework for their environment. Not-for-profit organizations will also have their own set of standards for these types of voluntary, charitable and community-based organizations. Smaller family-run companies will have less stringent provisions and in countries where family-run enterprises are the norm, there is less concern with rules designed for the agency/stewardship relationship that was mentioned earlier on. Whatever the format and whatever the country, there is a growing trend towards corporate governance standards to be part of the way business and public services are conducted. We deal with some of the more well-known codes in this section of the chapter. Before we start, the IIA have provided a definition of governance:

> The combination of processes and structures implemented by the board to inform, direct, manage, and monitor the activities of the organization toward the achievement of its objectives.

The landmark 1992 Cadbury Report described corporate governance:

> The country's economy depends on the drive and efficiency of its companies. Thus the effectiveness with which their boards discharge their responsibilities determines Britain's competitive position. They must be free to drive their companies forward, but exercise that freedom within a framework of effective accountability. This is the essence of any system of corporate governance (para. 1.1).

Cadbury went on to document the simple but now famous phrase: 'Corporate governance is the system by which companies are directed and controlled' (para. 2.5).

Note that a synonym for governance is *controlling*. The globalization of governance processes is bringing the world closer in terms of commonality. Hand in hand with international accounting standards, we are approaching an era of closer comparability throughout the developed and developing world and it is as well to refer to the nonbinding Organization for Economic Cooperation and Development (OECD) Principles of Corporate Governance, because it has a global context. The principles are based on a philosophy that codes should be concise, understandable and accessible, the aim being to help improve the legal, institutional and regulatory framework as guidance to stock exchanges, corporations and investors. They see corporate governance as a set of relationships for company management, the board, shareholders and stakeholders, and setting objectives and monitoring performance in the context of the separation of ownership and control. They also make the point that corporate ethics and societal interests can affect the company's reputation and impact on the long-term success in attracting investors and 'patient' long-term capital through clear and understandable provisions. The OECD recognize that there is no single good model of corporate governance (CG) and that the principles are evolutionary and change with innovation in corporations. There are five key principles involved, summarized as follows:

1. **Rights of shareholders**   The CG framework should protect shareholders' rights.
2. **The equitable treatment of shareholders**   The CG framework should ensure the equitable treatment of all shareholders, including minority and foreign shareholders.
3. **The role of stakeholders in corporate governance**   The CG framework should ensure that timely and accurate disclosure is made of all material matters regarding the corporation, including the financial situation, performance, ownership and governance of the company.
4. **Disclosure and transparency**   The CG framework should ensure that timely and accurate disclosure is made on all material matters regarding the corporation, including the financial situation, performance, ownership and governance of the company – includes financial and operational results, company objectives, share ownership and voting, board membership and remuneration, material foreseeable risk factors, governance structures and policies and annual audit and access to information by users.

5. **Responsibility of the board**   The CG framework should ensure the strategic guidance of the company, the effective monitoring of management by the board, the board's accountability to the company and the shareholders. The board should be fully informed, fairly treat shareholders, ensure compliance with laws, etc., review performance and risk policy, etc., also ensuring that appropriate systems of internal control are in place, in particular, systems for monitoring risk, financial control and compliance with the law and disclosure and communications. The board should consider using Non-Executive Directors (NEDs) and have access to accurate, relevant and timely information (and access to key managers, such as the company secretary and the *internal auditor*, and recourse to independent external advice).

While these are fairly general in nature because of their global application, the principles do provide a good foundation for country-specific codes. One phrase that is often used by proponents of corporate government is that 'a one size fits all model will not work in practice'. Moreover, there is no point listing a set of rules that can be ticked off and filed under 'Job Done!' There needs to be a constant search for principles that set the right spirit of enterprise that has not run wild. European Union regulations mean member states' listed companies are now required to adopt International Accounting Standards with a view to bringing Europe closer to becoming a single equity market.

The saga continues and we expect to see further codes appear in the UK as time goes by. In fact, Nigel Turnbull's view on this likelihood has been formally reported:

> The Turnbull report on internal control is likely to be reviewed in five years time according to Rank Group Finance Director, Nigel Turnbull, the chairman of the English ICA-backed working party behind the review. Speaking at the launch of the paper, which has been endorsed by the Stock Exchange as part of its listing requirements, Turnbull said it did not mark the end of the debate. 'In a five year timetable something new might easily emerge but if there are problems with the current paper, they may well get resolved in practice,' he said.[33]

## Californian Public Employees' Retirement System (CalPERS)

The US experience is much the same as the UK's even though their corporate accountability structures and Securities and Exchange Commission (SEC) regulations differ in some respects. The CalPERS represents US investors and is a key stakeholder for corporate America. As such, it is concerned with the proper running of large corporations and the governance processes they adopt and report on. CalPERS has developed a set of US Corporate Governance Principles (Core Corporate Governance Principles), summarized as follows:

1. A substantial majority of the board consists of directors who are independent.
2. Independent directors meet periodically (at least once a year) without the CEO or other nonindependent directors.
3. When the chair of the board also serves as the company's CEO, the board designates formally or informally an independent director who acts in a lead capacity to coordinate the independent directors.
4. Certain board committees consist entirely of independent directors including:
   - audit;
   - director nomination;
   - board evaluation and governance;
   - CEO evaluation and management compensation;
   - compliance and ethics.

5. No director may also serve as a consultant or service provider to the company.
6. Director compensation is a combination of cash and stock in the company. The stock component is a significant portion of the compensation.

The theme for this code is the independence of directors and the use of committees to reinforce the oversight role. This is an important balancing mechanism where the huge power vested in the CEO is countered by the presence of independent persons who are able to ask tough questions where appropriate. Note that many of these types of codes are somewhat sidelined by developments in SEC rules that appeared towards the end of 2002. More recently, CalPERS has developed a set of Global Principles in 2009 that are broken down into four areas – Core, Domestic, International and Emerging Markets. CalPERS believes that the criteria contained in the Core Principles may be adopted by companies across all markets, which are summarized below:

There are many features that are important considerations in the continuing evolution of corporate governance best practices. However, the underlying tenet for CalPERS Core Principles of Accountable Corporate Governance is that fully accountable corporate governance structures produce, over the long term, the best returns to shareowners. CalPERS believes the following Core Principles should be adopted by companies in all markets – from developed to emerging – in order to establish the foundation for achieving long-term sustainable investment returns through accountable corporate governance structures.

1. Optimizing Shareowner Return: Corporate governance practices should focus the board's attention on optimizing the company's operating performance, profitability and returns to shareowners.
2. Accountability: Directors should be accountable to shareowners and management accountable to directors. To ensure this accountability, directors must be accessible to shareowner inquiry concerning their key decisions affecting the company's strategic direction.
3. Transparency: Operating, financial, and governance information about companies must be readily transparent to permit accurate market comparisons; this includes disclosure and transparency of objective globally accepted minimum accounting standards, such as the International Financial Reporting Standards ('IFRS').
4. One-share/One-vote: All investors must be treated equitably and upon the principle of one-share/one-vote.
5. Proxy Materials: Proxy materials should be written in a manner designed to provide shareowners with the information necessary to make informed voting decisions. Similarly, proxy materials should be distributed in a manner designed to encourage shareowner participation. All shareowner votes, whether cast in person or by proxy, should be formally counted with vote outcomes formally announced.
6. Code of Best Practices: Each capital market in which shares are issued and traded should adopt its own Code of Best Practices to promote transparency of information, prevention of harmful labor practices, investor protection, and corporate social responsibility. Where such a code is adopted, companies should disclose to their shareowners whether they are in compliance.
7. Long-term Vision: Corporate directors and management should have a long-term strategic vision that, at its core, emphasizes sustained shareowner value. In turn, despite differing investment strategies and tactics, shareowners should encourage corporate management to resist short-term behavior by supporting and rewarding long-term superior returns.
8. Access to Director Nominations: Shareowners should have effective access to the director nomination process.[34]

## Canada – The Dey Report

The Dey report was published in 1994 which set the framework for corporate governance in Canada. An updated view appeared in the November 2001 report, 'Beyond Compliance: Building a Governance Culture', by the Canadian Institute of Chartered Accountants, Canadian Venture Exchange, Toronto Stock Exchange. This report argued that there are several key issues that go beyond compliance and are fundamental to building a healthy governance culture:

1. Measures that can be taken to strengthen the capacity of the board to engage in a mature and constructive relationship with management – one that is grounded in a mutual understanding of respective roles and the ability of the board to act independently in fulfilling its responsibilities.
2. The critical role that the board must play in choosing the CEO . . . .
3. Particular issues that independent directors must face in corporations that have significant shareholders.

The Dey report, as with all governance material, is being continually updated to reflect current developments.

## The King Report

A major document from South Africa appeared in March 2002 and brought Africa into the corporate governance debate. The chairperson of the King Committee on Corporate Governance, Mervyne E. King, SC, prepared the report with support from the Institute of Directors (Centre for Directorship and Corporate Governance). Updating the 1994 King report, the Task Team also considered international best practice in recognition of what they termed 'our borderless world of the information'. The King report is now on version three and is remarkable because it has built on the wealth of knowledge and material that has been developed over the years since Cadbury was first reported.

## Australia

As with other developed economies, the Australians have derived material concerning the way companies and the public sector should be governed. The Australian Stock Exchange Rule 3C(3)(j) requires Australian companies to provide a statement of the main corporate governance practices that have been in place during the reporting period. The Australian *ASX Corporate Governance Council* has developed a set of Corporate Governance Principles and Recommendations that cover some important areas, and extracts from the foreword are reproduced below:

> This document cannot be the final word. It is offered as guidance and will be reviewed again. Nor is it the only word. Good corporate governance practice is not restricted to adopting the Council's Recommendations. The arrangements of many entities differ from the Recommendations but amount equally to good practice. What matters is disclosing those arrangements and explaining the governance practices considered appropriate to an individual company's circumstance. We are all – the Council, ASX and Australian market participants generally – in the business of preserving stakeholder confidence. That is the thread that runs through each of the Principles and Recommendations contained in this document. The wording may change, as necessary, from time to time, but that underlining theme will remain.[35]

## The OECD

The Organisation for Economic Co-operation and Development (OECD) has summed up many of the global principles of good corporate governance, and extracts are shown below:

I. Ensuring the Basis for an Effective Corporate Governance Framework
The corporate governance framework should promote transparent and efficient markets, be consistent with the rule of law and clearly articulate the division of responsibilities among different supervisory, regulatory and enforcement authorities.

II. The Rights of Shareholders and Key Ownership Functions
The corporate governance framework should protect and facilitate the exercise of shareholders' rights.

III. The Equitable Treatment of Shareholders
The corporate governance framework should ensure the equitable treatment of all shareholders, including minority and foreign shareholders. All shareholders should have the opportunity to obtain effective redress for violation of their rights.

IV. The Role of Stakeholders in Corporate Governance
The corporate governance framework should recognise the rights of stakeholders established by law or through mutual agreements and encourage active co-operation between corporations and stakeholders in creating wealth, jobs, and the sustainability of financially sound enterprises.

V. Disclosure and Transparency
The corporate governance framework should ensure that timely and accurate disclosure is made on all material matters regarding the corporation, including the financial situation, performance, ownership, and governance of the company.

VI. The Responsibilities of the Board
The corporate governance framework should ensure the strategic guidance of the company, the effective monitoring of management by the board, and the board's accountability to the company and the shareholders.[36]

## 2.5  The Institute of Internal Auditors

There are many other codes and guides from almost every country that has a developed market for shares and securities. The IIA has a leading role in considering issues relating to corporate governance and assessing how internal auditors can contribute to the growth in this evolution. Way back in 2002, the IIA Inc. prepared Professional Guidance that endorses the work of Kennesaw State University – Corporate Governance Center, involving over 20 professors from several universities who developed the following principles of corporate governance:

1. **Interaction** – Sound governance requires effective interaction among the board, management, the external auditor, and the internal auditor.
2. **Board Purpose** – The board of directors should understand that its purpose is to protect the interests of the corporation's stockholders, while considering the interests of other stakeholders (e.g., creditors, employees, etc.).
3. **Board Responsibilities** – The board's major areas of responsibility should be monitoring the CEO, overseeing the corporation's strategy, and monitoring risks and the corporation's control system. Directors should employ healthy skepticism in meeting these responsibilities.

4. **Independence** – The major stock exchanges should define an 'independent' director as one who has no professional or personal ties (either current or former) to the corporation or its management other than service as a director. The vast majority of the directors should be independent in both fact and appearance so as to promote arms-length oversight.

5. **Expertise** – The directors should possess relevant industry, company, functional area, and governance expertise. The directors should reflect a mix of backgrounds and perspectives. All directors should receive detailed orientation and continuing education to assure they achieve and maintain the necessary level of expertise.

6. **Meetings and Information** – The board should meet frequently for extended periods of time and should have access to the information and personnel it needs to perform its duties.

7. **Leadership** – The roles of Board Chair and CEO should be separate.

8. **Disclosure** – Proxy statements and other board communications should reflect board activities and transactions (e.g., insider trades) in a transparent and timely manner.

9. **Committees** – The nominating, compensation, and audit committees of the board should be composed only of independent directors.

10. **Internal Audit** – All public companies should maintain an effective, full-time internal audit function that reports directly to the audit committee.

11. **Reporting Model** – The current GAAP financial reporting model is becoming increasingly less appropriate for U.S. public companies. The industrial-age model currently used should be replaced or enhanced so that tangible and intangible resources, risks, and performance of information-age companies can be effectively and efficiently communicated to financial statement users. The new model should be developed and implemented as soon as possible.

12. **Philosophy and Culture** – Financial statements and supporting disclosures should reflect economic substance and should be prepared with the goal of maximum informativeness and transparency. A legalistic view of accounting and auditing (e.g., 'can we get away with recording it this way?') is not appropriate. Management integrity and a strong control environment are critical to reliable financial reporting.

13. **Audit Committees** – The audit committee of the board of directors should be composed of independent directors with financial, auditing, company, and industry expertise. These members must have the will, authority, and resources to provide diligent oversight of the financial reporting process. The board should consider the risks of audit committee member stock/stock option holdings and should set audit committee member compensation at an appropriate level given the expanded duties and risks faced by audit committee members. The audit committee should select the external auditor, evaluate external and internal auditor performance, and approve the audit fee.

14. **Fraud** – Corporate management should face strict criminal penalties in fraudulent financial reporting cases. The Securities and Exchange Commission should be given the resources it needs to effectively combat financial statement fraud. The board, management, and auditors all should perform fraud risk assessments.

15. **Audit Firms** – Audit firms should focus primarily on providing high-quality audit and assurance services and should perform no consulting for audit clients. Audit firm personnel should be selected, evaluated, compensated, and promoted primarily based on technical competence, not on their ability to generate new business. Audit fees should reflect engagements' scope of work and risk.

16. **External Auditing Profession** – Auditors should view public accounting as a noble profession focused on the public interest, not as a competitive business. The profession should carefully consider expanding audit reports beyond the current 'clean' versus modified dichotomy so as to enhance communication to financial report users.

17. **Analysts** – Analysts should not be compensated (directly or indirectly) based on the investment banking activities of their firms. Analysts should not hold stock in the companies they follow, and they should disclose any business relationships between the companies they follow and their firms.[37]

Note that, since 2002, the IIA have prepared a great deal of guidance that touches on governance for their members, and this will be referred to in later chapters.

## 2.6  The External Audit

External audit fits into the corporate governance jigsaw by providing a report on the final accounts prepared by the board. They check that these accounts show a fair view of the financial performance of the company and its assets and liabilities at the end of the accounting year and that governance reports are consistent with the financial accounts. The corporate governance model can be further developed to include an additional layer of accountability through the external audit process in Figure 2.4.

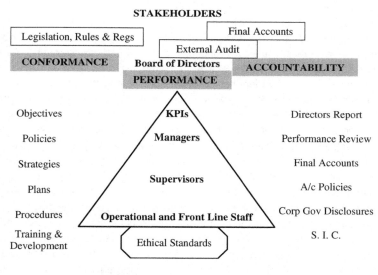

**FIGURE 2.4**   Corporate governance (4).

## The Different Objectives

The starting place is to clearly set out the different objectives of internal and external audit.

**The external auditor**  The external auditor seeks to test the underlying transactions that form the basis of the financial statements. In this way they may form an opinion on whether or not these statements show a true and fair view. Reliance may be placed on those systems that produce the accounts so that less testing will be necessary where the system is found to be sound. The systems are, however, perceived as a shortcut to examining all the financial transactions for the period in question.

*The internal auditor*  The internal auditor, on the other hand, seeks to advise management on whether its major operations have sound systems of risk management and internal controls. To this end the auditor will test the resultant transactions to confirm the evaluation and determine the implications of any system's weaknesses. These systems are primarily designed to ensure the future welfare of the organization rather than accounting for its activities. It should be clear from the above that the external auditor uses systems as a shortcut to verifying the figures in the accounts. In contrast the internal auditor is primarily concerned with all systems of control that enable organizational objectives to be met. Note that in the public sector, the National Audit Office, as well as their role in final accounts, also examines operational matters and value-for-money issues.

## The Main Similarities

The main similarities between internal and external audit are as follows:

- Both the external and internal auditors carry out testing routines and this may involve examining and analyzing many transactions. Where these revolve around financial systems they may appear to be very similar, particularly for the operational staff who have to supply the required information to assist the audit in hand. There are many auditors who have tried to explain the different roles of the two functions to a confused manager, who has seen both teams perform what appears to be exactly the same work. As testament to this, one will recall the many times where a client has handed a document to the internal auditor, who after much confusion is able to work out that the document actually belongs to the external audit team. This confusion is enhanced where the size of the audit means that the external audit team is located within the organization. Having said this, there are many ways that audit testing programmes applied to financial systems appear to be very similar and this does bring the two audit functions closer together in terms of working methodologies.
- Both the internal auditor and the external auditor will be worried if procedures were very poor and/or there was a basic ignorance of the importance of adhering to them. Obviously the external auditor will be involved in matters that impinge on the financial statements, although they may comment on the overall arrangements for setting standards and direction. Internal audit will tend to take this concept further in an attempt to promote suitable controls. The auditor's work is dependent on people doing things in the way that is laid down by the organization and they will not take this factor for granted without applying appropriate compliance tests.
- Both tend to be deeply involved in information systems since this is a major element of managerial control as well as being fundamental to the financial reporting process. New computerized developments that impact on the figures presented in the final accounts must incorporate basic controls to ensure the integrity of the database and ensuing reports. Information systems (IS) audit is a term applied to both external and internal audits as a follow-up to this principle. A good IS auditor may work in both types of audit roles throughout his/her career, as the skills applied to this type of work are wholly transferable. Take as an example computer interrogation routines that seek to identify correct functionality or, say, duplicate accounts; these may be applied to financial information systems by both external and internal audit although from different perspectives. The external auditor will seek to assess whether the information supplied by the computer that forms the basis of figures for the accounts is correct. The internal auditor will be concerned that the computer generates correct

reports that enable management to achieve their objectives efficiently. Obviously the internal auditor will consider all major systems that impact on organizational objectives as opposed to just the accounting-based ones. This makes for a concentration of resources on corporate managerial controls such as the systems development life cycle applied to new and developing computerized systems.

- Both are based in a professional discipline and operate to professional standards. The external auditor's work is in the main covered by external auditing standards, which cater for matters such as starting an engagement, planning work and carrying out the required tasks, while the internal auditor makes reference to either the IIA standards or equivalent internal auditing standards. There is one key difference in the form of an added impetus to subscribe properly to auditing standards that applies to the external auditor. This is the ever-present threat of legal action that may be taken by a client or a third party who has relied on the financial statements and suffered a loss as a result. The ability to prove that one has operated to professional standards is almost a prerequisite to a successful defence against any claims of professional negligence. The internal auditor has two main forces that encourage compliance with professional standards. These appear in the form of the CAE's stance on this issue and the quality assurance procedures that should call for a review of compliance done either in-house or through external resources. The key point, however, is the view that both internal and external audit should seek to adhere to formal auditing standards that should form the foundation of their work. This would be translated perhaps as an in-house audit manual supported by suitable training and development programmes.

- Both seek active cooperation between the two functions. IIA standards cover this point while the external auditor has a remit to place some reliance on the internal auditor's work wherever possible. This cooperation should operate on an equal footing and is partly designed to avoid embarrassing situations where both teams turn up at the same location at the same time.

- Both are intimately tied up with the organization's systems of internal control. Controls and the way they are interfaced with the organization's operational arrangements should be seen as an important concern, which is fundamental to the audit role. Considerations relating to authorization, segregation of duties, good documentation, audit trails, sound information systems and supervision all fall under the remit of control systems that are key to the success of the business in hand. There is one external audit view that proposes the use of extended interrogation software to perform 100% testing of financial systems and so moves away from the need to place any great reliance on controls. This, however, is based on the narrow definition of controls used by external audit based around the assumption that output from accounting systems is more or less correct. We can contrast this with the wider internal audit view on controls that considers them to be mechanisms that promote the achievement of organizational objectives. The importance of sound controls has been given greater recognition recently by the external audit world, with the general acceptance of this issue as part of the annual report issued by the directors. To this end we would expect the internal and external auditors to move closer together in relation to controls over financial systems. In practice we may speculate whether internal audit should have a key role in control evaluation by supporting relevant statements that appear in the annual report and accounts.

- Both are concerned with the occurrence and effect of errors and misstatement that affect the final accounts. This is a key concern of the external auditor, where it has an impact on the audit report that is issued after reviewing the items set out in the final accounts. In this situation the internal auditors would be interested in the system's weaknesses that have led to the resultant errors, in contrast to the external auditor's interest in the effect of incorrectly stated figures.

Where there is good cooperation between the two functions, we may expect a great deal of close working to identify and resolve such problems.

- Both produce formal audit reports on their activities. The external auditor has tended to report on an exception basis, where comments relate specifically to the type of audit opinion that is provided. More recently audit standards require more information in audit reports that provide a more rounded view of work done and responsibilities. The problem for the external auditor is that the more that is said in a report the more the writer can be held to account. The internal audit report can be differentiated by its resemblance to the more conventional type of report with a formal structure, i.e. a beginning, middle and end. This can become a detailed document for larger audits although one would expect an executive summary to provide a brief statement of opinion, making it closer to the model used by the external auditor. Notwithstanding the differences in the report formats, we can conclude that both sets of auditors have to assume the discipline of formally reporting their findings and carrying out their work with this obligation in mind.

## The Main Differences

There are, however, many key differences between internal and external audit and these are matters of basic principle that should be fully recognized:

- The external auditor is an external contractor and not an employee of the organization, as is the internal auditor. Note, however, that there is an increasing number of contracted-out internal audit functions where the internal audit service is provided by an external body. In fact this external body is likely to be the same type of organization (e.g. firm of accountants) as those that supply the external audit services. Having said this, there is a third model that is being increasingly applied that involves a small in-house internal audit team supplemented by an outsourced contract that covers more routine audits. In such a case we are still dealing with internal auditors who are normally employees of the company.
- The external auditor seeks to provide an opinion on whether the accounts show a true and fair view, whereas internal audit forms an opinion on the adequacy and effectiveness of systems of risk management and internal control, many of which fall outside the main accounting systems.
- The external audit role is really much removed from the considerations of the internal auditor both in terms of objectives and scope of work. The fact that there is some overlap in respect of controls over the accounting arrangements must be set within the context of these major differences.
- External audit is a legal requirement for limited companies and most public bodies, while internal audit is not essential for private companies and is only legally required in parts of the public sector. Much of the external auditor's work is prescribed in outline by law. To an extent, even working practices are affected by case law dealing with claims of professional negligence against the auditor. Rights, responsibilities and the role of external audit are found in legislation that contains clear definitions that are well understood by the business community. The world of the internal auditor, on the other hand, is determined mainly through professional standards.
- Internal audit may be charged with investigating frauds, and although the external auditors will want to see them resolved, they are mainly concerned with those that materially affect the final accounts. While there is a growing recognition of the external audit role in fraud investigations, the truth is that tackling fraud is not only hard work but also very resource intensive. Referring matters to internal audit is one good way of managing this issue if it comes about. Accordingly,

some internal auditors tend to claim this area as their own. In the public sector where probity is seen as a key issue, there is generally a need to investigate all occurrences and/or allegations of fraud even where they go back some time. In the private sector this type of work will tend to be at the behest of the board of directors. In some cases the fraud aspects of organizational affairs will fall under specially designated security officers.

- Internal auditors cover all the organization's operations whereas external auditors work primarily with those financial systems that have a bearing on the final accounts. This point should not be underestimated since if external audit spends a great deal of time on financial systems it may result in the internal audit function dealing primarily with managerial/operational areas. If this is the case the internal auditor may well commit only a small level of resources to the financial arena. Although this type of arrangement does depend on a close cooperation of the two audit functions, it also creates a clear differentiation in the two work areas that will tend to move them further apart in the long term. It also moves away from the alternative model where internal audit work is used primarily to allow a reduction in the level of external audit cover in designated areas. Reverting to the previous example, an exaggeration of the separation of systems into financial and others, in line with the different roles of external and internal audit, may allow the latter function to assume a fuller identity in its own right.

- Internal audit may be charged with developing value-for-money initiatives that provide savings and/or increased efficiencies within the organization. Interestingly, this may also apply to the external auditor under the consultancy head (although the level of consultancy provided by the external auditor is restricted so as not to provide a conflict of interests). It also applies to some external auditors in the public sector (e.g. the UK's National Audit Office). Generally speaking, however, internal audit will be concerned with operational efficiency while the external audit function has no remit to delve into these areas of organizational activities.

- The internal auditor reviews systems of risk management and internal control in contrast to the external auditor who considers whether the state of controls will allow a reduced amount of testing. As such, external audit work is directed at the transactions that occurred within a past period in contrast to the future impact of good systems. As an example, the internal auditor may be concerned with the efficiency and effectiveness of the organization's marketing systems whereas there is no clear role for external audit in this area.

- Internal audit works for and on behalf of the organization whereas the external auditor is technically employed by and works for a third party, the shareholders. This is an important difference in that the client base has a great deal of influence on the audit role and reporting arrangements. The external auditor is clearly reporting on the organization's management as a fundamental part of their role. It is the board who approve the accounts and society views the external audit function as a direct check over the figures on the basis that it is not ideal to rely on the unchecked accounts as they stand. The internal auditor does not have this distinct philosophy for protection as it is management who decides to employ an internal auditor, not to check on them, but to seek improvements to risk management systems. The point though is that, having identified weaknesses, the internal auditor has no third party to go to if there is a lack of effective action to remedy these weaknesses. The internal auditor reports to the people in front of him/her, not some unseen force that periodically convenes as a group of shareholders watching over the organization with interest and ultimate authority. The theory is that an audit committee of NEDs fulfils this role, although the executive directors and chief executive do tend to have a great influence on this forum and so diminish its capacity as an ultimate control over the organization. This difference in reporting lines in turn creates a contrasting type of independence in that the external auditor is independent from the organization while internal audit is independent from the operations being reviewed. There are pressures on the external auditor, particularly for owner-run registered companies, that can impair the level of audit independence. There are also time pressures that can lead to junior staff doing limited work in poorly managed firms of auditors, although the drive for quality assurance procedures does diminish the frequency of this type of scenario.

- The internal audit cover is continuous throughout the year but the external audit tends to be a year-end process even though some testing may be carried out during the year. Having said this, some larger organizations have a permanent external audit presence who provide year-round coverage of account verification and substantiation. For smaller companies one might imagine the external auditor arriving at the finance department after the accounts have been closed and producing a suitable report after the requisite period of audit work. This is very different from the full-time internal auditor who is consumed by the organizational culture as the years pass by, and colleagues across all departments become personal friends. We may be tempted to argue that the internal auditor is as such 'playing at auditing' as the years grow closer to retirement, if this did not expose a complete misunderstanding of the internal audit role.

## Nonaudit Services

There is an ongoing debate over the provision of nonaudit services by the external auditor and their effect on independence, which means these services tend to have to be approved by the audit committee, while in the US rules prohibit:

- Acting temporarily or permanently as a director or employee of the audit client or performing any decision making, supervisory or ongoing monitoring function for the audit client.
- Recruitment activities.
- Broker dealer, investment adviser or investment banking services.
- Legal services where the service requires a licensed, admitted or otherwise qualified law practitioner.
- Expert services unrelated to an audit.
- Tax services related to planning, or opining on the tax treatment of a transaction that is a listed or confidential transaction or where a significant purpose is tax avoidance.
- Tax services for an officer in a financial reporting oversight role.

While the following services can be provided if it is reasonable to conclude that the results of these services will not be subject to audit procedures during an audit of the client's financial Statements:

- Bookkeeping.
- Financial information systems design and implementation.
- Appraisal and valuation services.
- Actuarial services.
- Internal audit outsourcing services.

## Coordinating Internal and External Audits

The cooperation between internal audit and external audit is important and better coordination should be encouraged. Harmonization of the planning task is fundamental in this respect and there are several levels to which audit planning may be interfaced, as Figure 2.5 suggests.

**STAGE ONE**

Copies of plans exchanged when complete

**STAGE TWO**

A joint meeting where plans are discussed
and harmonized – issued separately

**STAGE THREE**

Regular meetings where fully integrated
plans are issued as one composite document

**FIGURE 2.5**    Interfaced audit planning.

The stages move from one through to three to reflect an increasingly greater degree of interface between internal and external audit. At the extreme it can result in one planning document being prepared for the organization. This is more relevant in the public sector where external audit tends to assume a role in securing value for money. Stage one consists of a common courtesy where plans are exchanged, which in fact involves two sublevels where draft plans are given (which can as a result be altered). This is in contrast to the less integrated stance where finalized plans only are provided.

A swap of resources creates further cooperation as the available audit skills base is added to as and when required. This can allow as an example an external information systems auditor to run interrogation software to support the internal auditor's review of a large financial system. Internal audit may in turn complete a suitable testing programme that enables external audit to substantially reduce work in the area in question. Exchanging reports is a simple method of keeping each side informed, although it is more relevant within a public sector environment. Unfortunately what at first appears straightforward may involve an amount of political manoeuvring where each side applies special rules for confidential reports or reports that have not reached final report status. A more explicit statement of cooperation occurs where pre-report stage material, such as the agreed terms of reference for the ensuing audit, is also exchanged.

## 2.7   The Audit Committee

The topic of audit committees has an interesting background. The audit committee (AC) is a standing committee of the main board and tends to consist of a minimum of three nonexecutive directors (NEDs). Most audit committees meet quarterly and they are now found in all business and government sectors for larger organizations. The format is normally that the NEDs sit on the audit committee and the CFO, external audit, CEO and CAE attend whenever required. The committee will have delegated authority to act in accordance with its set terms of reference and also investigate areas that again fit with their agenda. The CAE will present reports to most regular committee meetings and will prepare an annual report to cover each financial year in question. This simple format hides many complicated and fundamental issues that cause many difficulties. In short, the audit committee is increasingly seen as one of the cornerstones of corporate governance. Many argue that the success of an organization's corporate governance arrangements relies in part on the success of the established audit committee. Failings in the membership, format, role, competence and commitment of this forum blast a hole in the organization's defined system of corporate governance. The Special Committee of Enron Corporation's Board of Directors report stated that: 'The Board assigned the Audit and Compliance Committee an expanded duty to review the transactions, but the committee carried out the reviews only in a cursory way. The board of directors was denied important information that might have led them to take action.' We would hope that the audit committee is now providing another layer of stakeholder comfort in the search for good corporate governance and allows us to add to our growing model in Figure 2.6.

**FIGURE 2.6**  Corporate governance (5).

Groundbreaking work was performed in the US by the Blue Ribbon Committee in 1998 who prepared 10 key recommendations on improving the effectiveness of ACs:

1. NYSE and NASD adopt a definition of independent directors – not employed by (last 5 years) associate, family contact, partner, consultant, executive on company whose executives serve on the Remuneration committee, etc. No relationship with the company that will impair independence.
2. NYSE and NASD listed companies with market capitalization over $200 m have an AC of only NEDs.
3. NYSE and NASD listed companies with market capitalization over $200 m have an AC minimum of 3 directors each of whom is financially literate and at least one member has accounting or related financial management expertise.
4. NYSE and NASD listed companies have an AC charter reviewed annually. Details of the charter disclosed in the company's proxy statement to annual shareholders' meeting.
5. SEC rules – statement that AC has satisfied its responsibilities under its charter.
6. NYSE and NASD charters of listed companies specify that external audit is accountable to the board and AC who have the ultimate authority to select, evaluate and replace the external auditor.
7. NYSE and NASD AC charter requires that the AC receive a formal statement detailing relationship between external audit and company, the AC should discuss EA independence and take or recommend to the board action to ensure independence of the external auditor.
8. GAAP revised to require external audit to discuss the auditor's judgement about the quality of accounting principles and financial reporting with the AC.

9. SEC adopt rules that the AC make a Form 10-K Annual Report covering: management has discussed quality of accounting principles, discussions with EA, discussed by AC members, AC believes financial statements are fairly presented and conform with GAAP.

10. SEC adopt rules that external audit conduct a SAS 71 Interim Financial Review before filing Form 10-Q and discuss the financial statements with the AC before filing the Form.

Staying with the US, each audit committee for companies listed on the NYSE, Nasdaq and AMEX must have a charter that shows:

- The scope of the AC responsibilities and how it carries them out.
- Ultimate accountability of the independent auditor to the board and AC.
- Ultimate authority of the board and AC to select, evaluate, and replace the independent auditors.
- The AC responsibilities re the independent auditor's independence.

The role of the audit committee is now firmly entrenched in business culture and they are mandatory for most international stock exchanges including London and New York. Even in smaller companies, their presence is recommended by many businesses – which some see as a substitute for an internal audit function.

## The Role of the Audit Committee

An audit committee will be established by the main board to perform those duties that the board decides should be properly allocated to this specialist forum. There has been a long fight to get the audit committee accepted by all as there was a view that the audit committee would blur the lines between boardroom executives' responsibilities and the interventions made by nonexecutives who may have a poor understanding of the business. The absence of good NEDs was another reason behind the slow growth of this type of business forum. The new-look audit committee has several distinct features, but will have a format that suits the organization in question, which means each audit committee will be completely different and there is no set standard that may be employed to define the role. We have already suggested that a 'one size fits all' approach to corporate governance structures is unrealistic, which is why most codes are both voluntary and fairly general in the way they define set standards. There is still scope to prepare best practice guides, even though they cannot be too specific. The Institute of Internal Auditors suggests that the audit committee responsibilities include:

- Ensuring that financial statements are understandable, transparent, and reliable.
- Ensuring the risk management process is comprehensive and ongoing, rather than partial and periodic.
- Helping achieve an organization-wide commitment to strong and effective controls, emanating from the tone at the top.
- Reviewing corporate policies relating to compliance with laws and regulations, ethics, conflicts of interest, and the investigation of misconduct and fraud.
- Reviewing current and pending corporate governance-related litigation or regulatory proceedings to which the organization is party.
- Continually communicating with senior management regarding status, progress, and new developments, as well as problematic areas.
- Ensuring the internal auditors have access to the audit committee and encouraging communication beyond scheduled committee meetings.

- Reviewing internal audit plans, reports, and significant findings.
- Establishing a direct reporting relationship with the external auditors.
- Balancing their role as advisor and counselor to management with their fiduciary duty to monitor and oversee management is challenging for most audit committees.[38]

## 2.8    Internal Audit

*The Essential Guide to Internal Auditing* is primarily about the role, responsibilities and performance of the internal audit function. This section simply provides a brief account of where internal audit fits into the corporate governance jigsaw. The IIA have prepared Performance Standard 2110 on this issue which says:

The internal audit activity must assess and make appropriate recommendations for improving the governance process in its accomplishment of the following objectives:

- Promoting appropriate ethics and values within the organization;
- Ensuring effective organizational performance management and accountability;
- Communicating risk and control information to appropriate areas of the organization; and
- Coordinating the activities of and communicating information among the board, external and internal auditors, and management.

This enables us to place internal audit into our agency model in Figure 2.7.

**FIGURE 2.7**    Corporate governance (6).

In fact the agency model in Figure 2.7 has become what we can now call our corporate governance model and the remaining components are explained in the remainder of this chapter. The IIA prepared a position statement entitled Organizational Governance; Guidance for Internal Auditors in 2006 that established the dual nature of the audit role in organizational governance, which suggests that:

Internal auditing typically operates in two capacities. First, auditors provide independent, objective assessments on the appropriateness of the organization's governance structure and the operating effectiveness of specific governance activities. Second, they act as catalysts for change, advising or advocating improvements to enhance the organization's governance structure and practices. In an organization, management and the board establish and monitor companywide systems.

This split between assurance work and consulting advice will be discussed at some length throughout the book.

## 2.9   The Link to Risk Management and Internal Control

We have said that the role of internal auditing incorporates coverage of risk management (RM), control and governance processes. It is a good idea briefly to establish the links between these three ideas so that while each chapter deals with each of the three concepts, they can be appreciated both separately and together. Figure 2.8 may help explain the links.

**FIGURE 2.8**   Linking RM to internal control.

We will look at each part of the model in turn:

**Corporate governance codes**   These are essentially the codes, guides, regulations and standards that, apart from family-run concerns, cover most larger organizations.

**Corporate structures**   The governance structures and processes include all those arrangements to ensure compliance with the governance codes. This includes boardroom arrangements, splitting the CEO's and chair's roles, codes of conduct, audit committees, NEDs, internal and external audit and so on.

**Disclosure arrangements**   The matters that have to be included in the annual report including the audited accounts, external audit report, notes to the accounts, directors' report and operational review. This also includes disclosures on compliance with corporate governance codes, risk management arrangements and a statement on internal control.

**Internal control framework**   We will deal with internal control in Chapter 4. For our model, we argue that all large organizations should adopt a control framework that sets out its vision of control. This provides a road map regarding the control environment, how people relate to each other and communicate, corporate structures and governance processes, mentioned above.

**Risk management** Within the context of the control framework, the organization should employ a process for identifying, assessing and managing risk. Note that risk management is covered in Chapter 3.

**Internal controls** After having assessed key risks, they will need to be managed in line with a defined risk management strategy. One major component of this strategy is appropriately derived internal controls that seek to mitigate unacceptable levels of risk. Each control will address a defined risk or be part of a regulatory requirement that in turn addresses the risk of breaching law, procedures and rule.

**Corporate strategies and review** The strategy for managing risk and ensuring controls do the job in hand should then be incorporated into an overall strategy that drives the organization towards the achievement of its objectives. The entire process should be directed, assessed, reviewed and improved in conjunction with a formal performance measurement system.

By considering the above components, we can see how corporate governance is the umbrella concept that drives a control and reporting framework, which in turn depends on risk management and an efficient system of internal control. The three big parts – governance, risk management and control – form an entire system that provides for effective performance and stakeholder accountability.

## 2.10  Reporting on Governance, Risk and Internal Controls

Sir Adrian Cadbury has said that corporate governance is about the way an organization is directed and controlled. If the board is in control of their business and they are adhering to all appropriate standards then stakeholders can take comfort in this fact. Meanwhile, being in control means that all foreseeable risks to the success of the business have been anticipated and addressed, as efficiently as possible. This alone does not guarantee success, but it does mean that there is a reasonable chance that the organization will maintain, if not exceed, market expectations. To underline the need to be in control, the published annual report for companies listed on the relevant stock market and most public sector bodies should include a statement of internal control. This statement is a bottom line item, which is derived from the complicated arrangement of systems, processes and relationships established within the organization. If these controls drive the organization forward and also tackle all known risks that threaten this positive direction, then there is a good system of internal control in place. A well-governed organization must have good controls and the statement of internal control represents a crucial vote of confidence from the board to the shareholders and other stakeholders. In an extract from the 2009 Corporate Governance Statement of a UK retail company, Tesco relate to their statement on Internal Control and Risk Management as follows:

### INTERNAL CONTROL & RISK MANAGEMENT

### Accountabilities

Accepting that risk is an inherent part of doing business, our risk management systems are designed both to encourage entrepreneurial spirit and also provide assurance that risk is fully understood and managed. The Board has overall responsibility for risk management and internal control within the context of achieving the Group's objectives. Executive management is responsible for implementing and maintaining the necessary control systems. The role of Internal Audit is to monitor the overall internal control systems and report on their effectiveness to Executive management, as well as to the Audit Committee, in order to facilitate its review of the systems.

## Background

The Group has a five-year rolling business plan to support the delivery of its strategy of long-term growth and returns for shareholders. Every business unit and support function derives its objectives from the five-year plan and these are cascaded to managers and staff by way of personal objectives. Key to delivering effective risk management is ensuring our people have a good understanding of the Group's strategy and our policies, procedures, values and expected performance. We have a structured internal communications programme that provides employees with a clear definition of the Group's purpose and goals, accountabilities and the scope of permitted activities for each business unit, as well as individual line managers and other employees. This ensures that all our people understand what is expected of them and that decision-making takes place at the appropriate level. We recognise that our people may face ethical dilemmas in the normal course of business so we provide clear guidance based on the Tesco Values. The Values set out the standards that we wish to uphold in how we treat people. These are supported by the Group Code of Business Conduct which was launched this year, replacing the Code of Ethics, and offers guidance on relationships between the Group and its employees, suppliers and contractors.

We operate a balanced scorecard approach that is known within the Group as our Steering Wheel. This unites the Group's resources around our customers, people, operations, community and finance. The Steering Wheel operates at all levels throughout the Group. It enables the business to be operated and monitored on a balanced basis with due regard for all stakeholders.

## Risk management

The Group maintains a Key Risk Register. The Register contains the key risks faced by the Group including their impact and likelihood, as well as the controls and procedures implemented to mitigate these risks. The content of the Register is determined through regular discussions with senior management and reviewed by the Executive Committee and the full Board. A balanced approach allows the degree of controllability to be taken into account when we consider the effectiveness of mitigation, recognising that some necessary activities carry inherent risk which may be outside the Group's control. Where our risk management process identifies opportunities to improve the business these are built into our future plans.

The risk management process is cascaded through the Group with operating subsidiary boards maintaining their own risk registers and assessing their own control systems. The same process also applies functionally in those parts of the Group requiring greater oversight. For example, the Audit Committee's Terms of Reference require it to oversee the Finance Risk Register. The Board assesses significant Social, Ethical and Environmental (SEE) risks to the Group's short-term and long-term value, and incorporates SEE risks on the Key Risk Register where they are considered material or appropriate.

We recognise the value of the ABI Guidelines on Responsible Investment Disclosure and confirm that, as part of its regular risk assessment procedures, the Board takes account of the significance of SEE matters to the business of the Group. We recognise that a number of investors and other stakeholders take a keen interest in how companies manage SEE matters and so we report more detail on our SEE policies and approach to managing material risks arising from SEE matters and the KPIs we use at www.tesco.com/cr2010. To provide further assurance, the Group's Corporate Responsibility KPIs are audited on a regular basis by Internal Audit.

## Internal controls

The Board is responsible for the Company's system of internal control and for reviewing the effectiveness of such a system. We have a Group-wide process for clearly establishing the risks and responsibilities assigned to each level of management and the controls which are required to be operated and monitored. The CEOs of subsidiary businesses are required to certify by way of annual governance returns that appropriate governance and compliance processes have been adopted. For certain joint ventures, the Board places reliance upon the internal control systems operating within our partners' infrastructures and the obligations upon partners' boards relating to the effectiveness of their own systems.

Such a system is designed to manage rather than eliminate the risk of failure to achieve business objectives and can only provide reasonable and not absolute assurance against material misstatement or loss. The Board has reviewed the effectiveness of internal controls and is satisfied that the controls in place remain appropriate.

## Monitoring

The Board oversees the monitoring system and has set specific responsibilities for itself and the various committees as set out below. Both Internal Audit and our external auditors play key roles in the monitoring process, as do several other committees including the Finance Committee, Compliance Committee and Corporate Responsibility Committee. The Minutes of the Audit Committee and the various other committees (Finance, Compliance and Corporate Responsibility Committees) are distributed to the Board and each Committee submits a report for formal discussion at least once a year. These processes provide assurance that the Group is operating legally, ethically and in accordance with approved financial and operational policies.

## Audit Committee

The Audit Committee reports to the Board each year on its review of the effectiveness of the internal control systems for the financial year and the period to the date of approval of the financial statements. Throughout the year the Committee receives regular reports from the external auditors covering topics such as quality of earnings and technical accounting developments. The Committee also receives updates from Internal Audit and has dialogue with senior managers on their control responsibilities. It should be understood that such systems are designed to provide reasonable, but not absolute, assurance against material misstatement or loss.

## Internal Audit

The Internal Audit department is fully independent of business operations and has a Group-wide mandate. It undertakes a programme to address internal control and risk management processes with particular reference to the Turnbull Guidance. It operates a risk-based methodology, ensuring that the Group's key risks receive appropriate regular examination. Its responsibilities include maintaining the Key Risk Register, reviewing and reporting on the effectiveness of risk management systems and internal control with the Executive Committee, the Audit Committee and ultimately to the Board. Internal Audit facilitates oversight of risk and control systems across the Group through risk committees in Asia and Europe and audit committees in a number of our international businesses and joint ventures. The Head of Internal Audit also attends all Audit Committee meetings.

## External Audit

PricewaterhouseCoopers LLP, who have been the Company's external auditor for a number of years, contributes a further independent perspective on certain aspects of our internal financial control systems arising from its work, and reports to both the Board and the Audit Committee. Our policy in relation to the reappointment of the external auditors is to consider their engagement and independence annually.

The Committee has satisfied itself that PricewaterhouseCoopers LLP is independent and there are adequate controls in place to safeguard its objectivity. One such measure is the non-audit services policy that sets out criteria for employing external auditors and identifies areas where it is inappropriate for PricewaterhouseCoopers LLP to work. Non-audit services work carried out by PricewaterhouseCoopers LLP is predominantly the review of subsidiary undertakings' statutory accounts, transaction work and corporate tax services, where their services are considered to be the most appropriate. PricewaterhouseCoopers LLP also follows its own ethical guidelines and continually reviews its audit team to ensure its independence is not compromised.

## Finance Committee

Membership of the Finance Committee includes Non-executive Directors with relevant financial expertise, Executive Directors and members of senior management. The Committee is chaired by Sir Terry Leahy, CEO. The Committee usually meets twice a year and its role is to review and agree the Finance Plan on an annual basis, review reports of the Treasury and Tax functions and to review and approve Treasury limits and delegations.

## Compliance Committee

Membership of the Compliance Committee includes three Executive Directors and members of senior management. The Committee is chaired by Lucy Neville-Rolfe, Corporate and Legal Affairs Director. The Committee normally meets six times a year and its remit is to ensure that the Group complies with all necessary laws and regulations and other compliance policies in all of its operations world-wide. The Committee has established a schedule for the regular review of operational activities and legal exposure. Each business in the Group has a Compliance Committee designed to ensure compliance with both local and Group policies, and each Compliance Committee reports to the Group Compliance Committee at least once a year.

## Corporate Responsibility Committee

The Corporate Responsibility Committee is chaired by the Corporate and Legal Affairs Director, Lucy Neville-Rolfe and membership is made up of senior executives from across the Group. It meets at least four times a year to support, develop and monitor policies on SEE issues and to review threats and opportunities for the Group. Progress in developing Community initiatives is monitored by the use of relevant KPIs for the businesses within the Group. The Board formally discusses the work of the Committee on a regular basis, including progress in implementing our Community Plan.

The Corporate and Legal Affairs department and the Trading Law and Technical department provide assurance and advice on legal compliance, health and safety, and SEE matters. These functions report on their work on a regular basis and escalate matters as appropriate.

## Whistleblowing

The Group operates a whistleblowing policy and has a confidential 'Protector Line' service accessible to concerned employees where they can report, anonymously if necessary, on issues of malpractice within the business. Such issues include illegal and unethical behaviour such as fraud, dishonesty and any practices that endanger our staff, customers or the environment.

Complaints made are treated as confidential and are investigated. Where appropriate, matters will be escalated to the Director of Group Security for further action.

## Management

In our fast moving business, trading is tracked on a daily and weekly basis, financial performance is reviewed weekly and monthly and the Steering Wheel is reviewed quarterly. Steering Wheels are operated in business units across the Group and reports are prepared of performance against target KPIs covering the five segments of the Steering Wheel (Customer, Operations, Community, People and Finance) on a quarterly basis, enabling management to measure performance. All major initiatives require business cases normally covering a minimum period of five years.

Post-investment appraisals, carried out by management, determine the reasons for any significant variance from expected performance. [39]

# 2.11   New Developments

After the WorldCom, Enron and Parmalat fiascos, the new millennium saw a new high in corporate malfunction with an array of amazing corporate headliners, which included:

## Société Générale

The French bank Société Générale uncovered 'an exceptional fraud' by a trader that would cost it nearly €5 billion. The fraud had been committed by a Paris-based trader in charge of 'plain vanilla' hedging on European index futures.

## Madoff

A major ponzi-type fraud was perpetrated by Bernard L. Madoff, where he swindled wealthy investors and banks of huge amounts.

## Parmalat

A fraud by Parmalat, an Italian dairy giant, could be as much as $16.8 billion (far more than WorldCom) and may have been the result of more than a decade of fraudulent accounting.

## Stanford

Sir Allen Stanford, the Antigua-based American billionaire, philanthropist and cricket promoter and enthusiast, was accused of a massive, $8 billion fraud by the US Securities and Exchange Commission (SEC).

## Lehman Brothers

During 2008, three of the largest US investment banks either went bankrupt or were sold at knock-down prices to other banks as part of the now infamous 'Credit Crunch'. Just before Lehman Brothers went under, plunging investor confidence in Lehman shares meant huge stock losses, with no bail-out plans forthcoming. As the crisis deepened some Lehman executives suggested that they would forgo million dollar bonuses as an example to their employees, but this was dismissed as unnecessary. Footage of Lehman staff removing their files and personal effects from HQ were beamed across the world as the reality of the Credit Crunch in action.

## Merrill Lynch

Towards the end of 2007 Merrill Lynch announced it would write down $8.4 billion in losses because of the national subprime housing crisis and removed its CEO and looked for the Bank of America to step in and buy it out.

## Morgan Stanley/Goldman Sachs

Meanwhile, investment banks Morgan Stanley and Goldman Sachs responded to the financial crisis by embracing more rigorous regulations as they became commercial banks.

## Fannie Mae/Freddie Mac

World-famous government-sponsored enterprises (GSEs), Fannie Mae and Freddie Mac, found themselves with trillions of dollars in mortgage obligations that were not supported by a weakened capital base, before being placed into receivership.

## Northern Rock

In the UK, people queued outside Northern Rock branches to withdraw their savings as the knock-on effect hit the rest of the world, while highly leveraged financial sector companies across the world were being bailed out by their governments or had to merge with stronger companies as credit dried up. Northern Rock used to be a building society before it demutualized so that it could be floated on the London Stock Exchange and proceeded to buy up smaller building societies. Towards the end of 2007, the bank sought support from the Bank of England, which caused customers to panic and form long queues to withdraw their savings. After dipping their toes into the US subprime mortgage market and failing, and with no clear takeover bids in place, they were effectively nationalized. At the start of 2009 Northern Rock announced that they would be offering £14 billion worth of new mortgages over the next two years, as a part of their new business plan.

## Consequences

Bank CEOs resigned amid a frantic search to find merger partners and government bailouts to keep the banking sector from going under. Meanwhile, over 100 billion dollars were withdrawn from US money funds, which meant the Credit Crunch brought the banking sector to the verge of a collapse. During the last quarter of 2008, central banks purchased US$2.5 trillion of government debt and troubled private assets from banks.

The 2007/08 Credit Crunch brought home the contrast between rapid short-term spurts of new business and steady growth that could be sustained in the long term. This point is brought home by the ACCA, who submitted comments to the Financial Reporting Council (FRC):

> In the current challenging economic conditions there is an even greater need on the part of shareholders and, indeed, society as a whole to be able to have confidence in corporate reporting. A reliable audit, carried out by a properly competent firm, should be a key component contributing to this confidence. It is important that audit firms are, and are seen to be, well governed. We recognise, therefore, the importance of this project and we support its objectives. We support the Combined Code and the 'comply or explain' approach for listed companies. However, as we have suggested in the past to the FRC, we consider the application of the Combined Code's principles to be at least as important as its provisions and so prefer what we refer to as an 'apply, comply or explain' approach. The current crisis affecting the banking sector has raised difficult questions about how well some organisations have applied the Combined Code's principles. In particular, there have been concerns about how shareholders engage with boards and boards engage with management. It would seem that such engagement to date has not been entirely in the long-term interest of companies or their shareholders and other stakeholders and may even have encouraged the short-termist behaviour which has jeopardised the financial system.[40]

There is an ongoing debate about the way companies disclose information to their stakeholders. Reporting on specific disclosure issues does not always provide a rounded picture of how well the business is coping with material risks. The Financial Reporting Council has raised these concerns:

> Regulations are written with the best of intentions – but there is sometimes a difference between intended and actual outcomes. For example, a number of interviewees, both users and preparers, expressed concern that disclosures made in accordance with the minimum requirements of IFRS 7 Financial Instruments: Disclosures are not as useful as they might be. Part of the issue here is that the minimum disclosure requirements focus on specific instruments rather than the bigger picture, so meeting these requirements does not provide a good understanding of the risk management strategies used by management. This is interesting, because the standard is actually underpinned by the principle that information should be provided 'through the eyes of

management'. Including a list of minimum disclosures in the standard has encouraged companies to comply with this list rather than providing information through the eyes of management; the result, according to many interviewees, is less useful information.[41]

Most agree that the task of achieving good governance in larger companies is an ongoing challenge. The UK's Combined Code tends to be reviewed by the FRC every two years or so and the 2009 review, taking on board the ramifications of the Credit Crunch, assessed the impact and effectiveness of the Code. Meanwhile the review by Sir David Walker was asked by the then Prime Minister to review corporate governance, risk management and remuneration incentives in UK banks (then extended to other financial institutions) while the FRC would want to consider the extent to which the resulting recommendations may be considered best practice for all listed companies. The FRC have made it clear that they now wish to increase the overall level of prescription in the Code and to preserve its principles-based style.

The Walker review called for the risk management process to be given a much higher profile with greater independence in the group risk management function and the chief risk officer having a clear enterprise-wide authority and independence, with tenure and remuneration determined by the board.[42]

Over in the US there has been a concerted effort to strengthen corporate governance for US publicly traded companies, based around important sets of principles, as one such version demonstrates:

I. Board Responsibility for Governance: Governance structures and practices should be designed by the board to position the board to fulfil its duties effectively and efficiently.

II. Corporate Governance Transparency: Governance structures and practices should be transparent – and transparency is more important than strictly following any particular set of best practice recommendations.

III. Director Competency & Commitment: Governance structures and practices should be designed to ensure the competency and commitment of directors.

IV. Board Accountability & Objectivity: Governance structures and practices should be designed to ensure the accountability of the board to shareholders and the objectivity of board decisions.

V. Independent Board Leadership: Governance structures and practices should be designed to provide some form of leadership for the board distinct from management.

VI. Integrity, Ethics & Responsibility: Governance structures and practices should be designed to promote an appropriate corporate culture of integrity, ethics, and corporate social responsibility.

VII. Attention to Information, Agenda & Strategy: Governance structures and practices should be designed to support the board in determining its own priorities, resultant agenda, and information needs and to assist the board in focusing on strategy (and associated risks).

VIII. Protection Against Board Entrenchment: Governance structures and practices should encourage the board to refresh itself.

IX. Shareholder Input in Director Selection: Governance structures and practices should be designed to encourage meaningful shareholder involvement in the selection of directors.

X. Shareholder Communications: Governance structures and practices should be designed to encourage communication with shareholders.[43]

There is a widely held view that we do not need more regulation, but we need better regulation. The trend to requiring more levels of disclosure looks good on paper, but the excessive amounts of information could cloud annual reports and make them even more confusing. The Financial Reporting Council has indicated that more information does not always make for clearer information:

> One widely acknowledged problem is that reports currently aim to please too many types of user. There is a need to refocus them on their primary purpose: providing investors with information that is useful for making their resource allocation decisions and assessing management's stewardship. We suggest that regulators and companies should reconsider how they address the needs of other stakeholders – for example, those with specialist interests in environmental and employee diversity issues.[44]

Transparency underpins good governance and companies are starting to report big picture issues as well as the detailed commentary that appears in the increasingly long and cumbersome annual reports. The UK's Financial Reporting Council has developed four principles for effective communication when developing reports, which are set out as follows:

> The lessons learned from the UK ASB's work on the Operating and Financial Review (OFR) should be extended to cover corporate reporting in its entirety. Reports should be:
>
> 1. **Focused;** Highlight important messages, transactions and accounting policies and avoid distracting readers with immaterial clutter.
> 2. **Open and honest;** Provide a balanced explanation of the results – the good news and the bad.
> 3. **Clear and understandable:** Use plain language, only well defined technical terms, consistent terminology and an easy-to-follow structure.
> 4. **Interesting and engaging:** Get the point across with a report that holds the reader's attention.[45]

Meanwhile, the New York Stock Exchange pushed the governance agenda forwards by creating a Commission on Corporate Governance in 2009. They issued their 10 principles of corporate governance on 23 September 2010:

> **Principle 1:** The board's fundamental objective should be to build long-term sustainable growth in shareholder value for the corporation, and the board is accountable to shareholders for its performance in achieving this objective.
>
> **Principle 2:** While the board's responsibility for corporate governance has long been established, the critical role of management in establishing proper corporate governance has not been sufficiently recognized. The Commission believes that a key aspect of successful governance depends upon successful management of the company, as management has primary responsibility for creating an environment in which a culture of performance with integrity can flourish.
>
> **Principle 3:** Shareholders have the right, a responsibility and a long-term economic interest to vote their shares in a thoughtful manner, in recognition of the fact that voting decisions influence director behavior, corporate governance and conduct, and that voting decisions are one of the primary means of communicating with companies on issues of concern.
>
> **Principle 4:** Good corporate governance should be integrated with the company's business strategy and objectives and should not be viewed simply as a compliance obligation separate from the company's long-term business prospects.

**Principle 5:** Legislation and agency rule-making are important to establish the basic tenets of corporate governance and ensure the efficiency of our markets. Beyond these fundamental principles, however, the Commission has a preference for market-based governance solutions whenever possible.

**Principle 6:** Good corporate governance includes transparency for corporations and investors, sound disclosure policies and communication beyond disclosure through dialogue and engagement as necessary and appropriate.

**Principle 7:** While independence and objectivity are necessary attributes of board members, companies must also strike the right balance between the appointment of independent and non-independent directors to ensure that there is an appropriate range and mix of expertise, diversity and knowledge on the board.

**Principle 8:** The Commission recognizes the influence that proxy advisory firms have on the market, and believes that such firms should be held to appropriate standards of transparency and accountability. The Commission commends the SEC for its issuance of the Concept Release on the U.S. Proxy System, which includes inviting comments on how such firms should be regulated.

**Principle 9:** The SEC should work with the NYSE and other exchanges to ease the burden of proxy voting and communication while encouraging greater participation by individual investors in the proxy voting process.

**Principle 10:** The SEC and/or the NYSE should consider a wide range of views to determine the impact of major corporate governance reforms on corporate performance over the last decade. The SEC and/or the NYSE should also periodically assess the impact of major corporate governance reforms on the promotion of sustainable, long-term corporate growth and sustained profitability.

A full copy of the report is available on nyx.com.

One issue that is starting to hit the corporate agenda is the need to ensure that the governance machine is driven by sound business ethics. There is little point viewing regulatory requirements as burdens on large companies that need to be 'got around' whenever possible. Ethical governance is based more on wanting to be transparent to shareholders rather than grudgingly adhering to the rules. Moreover, sound internal controls are seen as good business over and beyond a mere compliance reporting requirement that does not have much business value. Corporate transparency is about inviting external audit to review the accounts and looking forward to their opinion and any ideas they may have to strengthen financial reporting controls. For internal audit, this positive view is so important; it means being invited to the top table, rather than listening in at the door.

## Summary and Conclusions

The corporate governance debate is ongoing. The various codes and guidance that have been prepared throughout the world tend to build on what is already available. New codes have the advantage of recent information on what is working well and where there are still problems matching the theory with real life. As soon as we present the latest position on codes of practice, they are overtaken by a new version that is more inclusive and generally more comprehensive. International codes are starting to come together to form a common understanding of how corporate, commercial and public life should be conducted. The tremendous pressures created by environmental groups and global activists place the conduct of large organizations in the spotlight, where people are beginning to define acceptable as opposed to unacceptable corporate behaviours. The fully built model of corporate governance that we have been developing in this chapter is set out in Figure 2.9.

**FIGURE 2.9**   Corporate governance (7).

Many of the components of our model have already been referred to, but for completeness we can list them all and spend a little more time on the new additions:

- **Stakeholders**   They should understand their stewardship role of the organization and what they get from it, and be discerning in demanding information on the system of corporate governance in place and how major risks are identifed and managed. Institutional investors and pension fund managers should have an active role in managing their investments as long-term holdings that need to match the requisite risk appetite of their clients.
- **Legislation, rules and regulations**   These should all contribute to protecting people and groups who have invested in the organization or who have a direct interest in either the services or products provided or any partnering arrangements. The regulatory framework should also ensure a level playing field for competitors and inspire substance over form. Most governance codes promote 'comply or explain' where nothing is forced on companies, but any variation can be challenged by stakeholders. Perhaps if boards were asked to 'apply or explain' they would perceive governance principles as less of a compliance issue and more as a set of ideals that should be applied to the way corporations behave.
- **Final accounts**   The annual report and accounts should contain all the information that is required by users and be presented in a true and fair manner (in conjunction with international accounting standards). It should act as a window between the outside world and the organization so that interested users can peer through this window and get a clear view of the way management behave and their performance, with no chance of skeletons being hidden

in the closet. The focus is now on user-friendly reports that discuss strategy, risk management and how the company fits into the wider society. Complete openness is an attractive buzzword, although market confidentialities must always be protected.

- **External audit**    There should be a truly independent, competent and rigorous review of the final accounts before they are published, without the distraction of the need to attract large amounts of nonaudit fees from the company in question. This is why lead partners are being periodically rotated to ensure they do not get sucked too far into company politics.
- **The board**    The board should be a mix of executives and nonexecutives balanced so as to represent the interests of the shareholders in a professional and responsible manner, chaired by a respected NED. Their responsibilities should be fully defined and assessment criteria should be in place that ensure fair rewards are available for effective performance (via a remunerations committee). Chuck Prince, the former CEO of Citigroup, is reporting as saying as a way of explaining the events that led up to the Credit Crunch: 'When the music stops, in terms of liquidity, things will be complicated. But as long as the music is playing, you've got to get up and dance. We're still dancing.'[46] The role of the board and the directors is crucial to ensuring sensible behaviour in larger organizations. The chairman has to lead the board and make sure it delivers its agenda through both the executive and nonexecutive directors. Good boards have a robust self-evaluation process so that each member is seen to be properly contributing and shareholders can make informed decisions on electing board members along with good succession planning. Most governance codes see the role of nonexecutives as one of constuctive challenge so that, just because the music starts playing, the board is not always forced to dance.
- **Audit and compensation and risk committees**    The audit committee of nonexecutives should provide an oversight of the corporate governance process and have a direct line to the shareholders via a separate report in the annual report. A major development is the increased spotlight on the role of the compensation committee, as the Credit Crunch was partly caused by the failure of banks and other financial services companies to stop excessive bonuses leading to excessive risk taking. Likewise the trend now is to develop powerful risk committees so that the risk management processes that failed to stop excessive risk taking are given a new lease of life. These committees should also seek to ensure that management are equipped to install effective governance, risk management and controls in the organization. Competent and experienced people should sit on the committees and ensure they are able to commit sufficient time and effort to the task of guiding and monitoring the accounting, audit, accountability, ethical values and governance arrangements, with no conflicts of interest – real or perceived.
- **Performance, conformance and accountability**    These three concepts should form a framework for corporate behaviour where the spirit of the ideals is embraced (as part of organizational culture) in contrast to a list of rules that is studied by legal and accounting technicians with a view to 'getting around' them.
- **Key performance indicators (KPIs)**    Organizational effort should be formed around a clear mission, vision and set of values that fall into a balanced range of performance measures that ensure risks to effective performance are understood and properly managed. KPIs are being integrated with key risk indicators (KRIs) so that performance efforts are directed at the high-risk parts of the business.
- **Internal audit**    This should be professional, independent and resourced to perform to the professional standards enshrined in the new focus on risk management, control and governance – with a healthy balance of assurance and consulting effort.

- **Risk management**   There should be a robust system of risk management in place that is embedded into the organizational systems and processes and that feeds into an assurance reporting system (normally based on risk registers).
- **Managers, supervisors and operational and front line staff**   They should all understand the corporate governance framework and live up to the demands of their defined responsibilities (for performance, conformance and accountability) in this respect.
- **Systems of internal control**   This should exist throughout the organization and be updated to take account of all material risks that have been assessed, and should be owned and reviewed by the people who are closest to the associated operations. The published annual report should comment on the systems of internal control in place to manage internal and external risk.
- **Performance management**   The response to corporate governance ideals should be fully integrated into the way people are set targets and assessed in respect of their performance against these targets. Performance should be measured and managed in a balanced and meaningful manner.
- **Ethical standards**   These should form the platform for all organizational activities and should be given priority for all important decisions that are made. They should also underpin the human resource management systems (e.g. selection, training, appraisal, disciplinary, etc.) and be part of clear and consistent messages and values from top management. All employees should be encouraged to report material actual and potential risks to the business, customers and stakeholders, and positive action should be taken by management as a result.
- **Commitment and capability**   These are two further concepts that have been added to performance, conformance and accountability. Commitment is the embodiment of corporate governance values into the hearts and minds of everyone connected with the organization. Capability relates to the training, budgets, time and understanding that are needed to make any new arrangements, such as control self-assessment, work. There are many organizations who send bold statements on the need for, say, better risk management but then fail to provide training, resources or space to enable people to do something about any gaps. Performance, conformance, accountability, commitment and capability are the key drivers for ensuring effective corporate governance.

The private sector is engaged in a constant struggle to gain and hold the trust of society – to represent the acceptable face of capitalism. Meanwhile, the need to maintain public confidence in the corporate sector and credibility in government and not-for-profit sectors has never been stronger. There are calls from all quarters to maintain this pressure to improve, develop and progress corporate governance arrangements as far as possible. The internal audit task of reviewing the governance process sets a tremendous challenge as this has to be about assessing governance processes.

## Endnotes

1. *The Irish Times*, Tiarnan O'Mahoney (www.ireland.com, 21 November 2001).
2. Tonge, Andrew, 'Keeping better company'. *Accountancy Age*, 23 April 1999, pp. 16–17.
3. Chambers, Andrew (2002) 'Stakeholders – the court of public opinion', in *Corporate Governance Handbook*, Tolley's, Reed Elsevier (UK) Ltd, p. 627.
4. *Daily Mail*, 17 January 2002, p. 75, 'Rough diamond of the finance world', City and Finance, The City Interview by Cliff Feltham, p. 5.

5. *Evening Standard*, 22 March 2002, Business Day, 'Dark secrets of the boardroom bonus pay plans', Anthony Hilton, p. 73.

6. Weait, Mathew, 'The workplace ethic – is it a crime'. *Management Today*, January 2001, pp. 53–55.

7. Stilltow, John, *Internal Auditing*, May 1999, pp. 12–13.

8. www.oecd.org.

9. www.bodyshop.com.

10. 'Rearranging the board'. *Internal Auditing and Business Risk*, April 2002, pp. 28–29.

11. Cadbury Report, Report of the Committee on the Financial Aspects of Corporate Governance, 1992.

12. 'Corporate governance failures and their impact: in the Institute of Internal Auditors UK and Ireland Study Text'. *Corporate Governance and Risk Management*, October 2002, p. 17.

13. Lever, Lawrence (1992) *The Barlow Clowes Affair*, Macmillan London Ltd, p. 1.

14. 'Corporate governance failures and their impact: in the Institute of Internal Auditors UK and Ireland Study Text'. *Corporate Governance and Risk Management*, October 2002, p. 18.

15. www.guardian.co.uk/Archive/Article, visited 15 December 2002.

16. 'Corporate governance failures and their impact: in the Institute of Internal Auditors UK and Ireland Study Text'. *Corporate Governance and Risk Management*, October 2002, p. 18.

17. 'Corporate governance failures and their impact: in the Institute of Internal Auditors UK and Ireland Study Text'. *Corporate Governance and Risk Management*, October 2002, p. 18.

18. Weekes, Tim, 'The £5m lesson in swindling'. *Accountancy Age*, 22 June 1995.

19. *Daily Mail*, 15 June 1996, 'Fall of King Copper', Jason Burt, p. 19.

20. www.guardian.co.uk/business, visited 15 December 2002.

21. www.guardian.co.uk/business, visited 15 December 2002.

22. *Financial Mail on Sunday*, 18 October 1998, 'Inland Revenue "failures" in corruption case prompt call for whistleblowers' charter – taxman under fire over bribes scandal', p. 15.

23. www.news.bbc.co.uk/1/hi/world/Americas, visited 15 December 2002.

24. Cooper Cathy, 'Management blasted at nuclear plant'. *People Management*, 16 March 2000, p. 16.

25. *Daily Mail*, 25 July 2001, 'Equitable Life: a sad catalogue of chaos', Tony Hazell and Charlotte Beugge, p. 41.

26. *Daily Mail*, 31 January 2001, 'Agony of parents in babies scandal', William David and Jenny Hope, p. 2.

27. 'Corporate governance failures and their impact: in the Institute of Internal Auditors UK and Ireland Study Text'. *Corporate Governance and Risk Management*, October 2002, p. 19.

28. 'Corporate governance failures and their impact: in the Institute of Internal Auditors UK and Ireland Study Text'. *Corporate Governance and Risk Management*, October 2002, p. 19.

29. 'Corporate governance failures and their impact: in the Institute of Internal Auditors UK and Ireland Study Text'. *Corporate Governance and Risk Management*, October 2002, p. 19.

30. www.news.bbc.co.uk/1/hi/business, visited 15 December 2002.

31. www.news.bbc.co.uk/1/hi/business, visited 15 December 2002.

32. www.news.ft.com/servlet, visited 15 December 2002.

33. Kemeny, Lucinda, 'Turnbull faces review'. *Accountancy Age*, 30 September 1999.

34. *Global Principles of Accountable Corporate Governance*, March 2009, The California Public Employees' Retirement System (CalPERS).

35. *Corporate Governance Principle and Recommendations*, 2nd Edition, 2007, ASX Corporate Governance Council.

36. *OECD Principles of Corporate Governance*, 2004, Organisation for Economic Co-Operation and Development

37. *21st Century Governance and Financial Reporting Principles*, Corporate Governance Center, Kennesaw State University, 26 March 2002, www.ksumail.kennesaw.edu.

38. 'A global perspective on risk', in *The Tone at the Top*, Issue 43, May 2009, The Institute of Internal Auditors Exclusively for Senior Management, Boards of Directors, and Audit Committees.

39. Tescopic.com/plc/ir/corpgov/riskmanagement, viewed 8 September 2010.

40. Audit Firm Governance, Evidence Gathering Consultation Paper issued by The Audit Firm Governance Working Group in a project for The Financial Reporting Council, Comments from ACCA, January 2009.

41. 'Principles and actions for making corporate reports less complex and more relevant', in *Louder Than Words*, Financial Reporting Council, 2009, p. 20.

42. The Walker Review, 'A review of corporate governance in UK banks and other financial industry entities, recommendations', 16 July 2009.

43. National Association of Corporate Directors (NACD), October 2008, Set of principles to guide corporate leaders as they make boardroom decisions, known as the Key Agreed Principles to Strengthen Corporate Governance for U.S. Publicly Traded Companies (Principles).
44. 'Principles and actions for making corporate reports less complex and more relevant', in *Louder Than Words*, Financial Reporting Council, 2009, p. 5.
45. 'Principles and actions for making corporate reports less complex and more relevant', in *Louder Than Words*, Financial Reporting Council, 2009, p. 7.
46. Chuck, Prince, *Financial Times*, 10 July 2007.

# Chapter 3

# MANAGING RISK

## Introduction

The formal IIA definition of internal auditing is repeated here as follows:

> Internal auditing is an independent, objective assurance and consulting activity designed to add value and improve an organization's operations. It helps an organization accomplish its objectives by bringing a systematic, disciplined approach to evaluate and improve the effectiveness of risk management, control and governance processes.

We need to understand risk and we need to appreciate the importance of risk management to an organization. Good corporate governance codes require the board to install a system of risk management and tell their shareholders about this system. This chapter addresses the concept of risk. We consider some of the material that has been written about risk and introduce a risk model that is developed throughout the chapter to illustrate how risk management works. We touch on important aspects of the risk management system relating to risk policies and tools such as enterprise-wide risk management and control self-assessment. The breakthrough by most larger organizations in utilizing business risk management across all aspects of the business has impacted the internal auditor's work and an important account of this move into a new phase of internal auditing was provided in 1998 by David McNamee and Georges Selim, who defined three stages in the development of internal auditing:

1. counting and observing;
2. systems of internal control;
3. auditing the business process through a focus on risk.

They go on to describe the paradigm shift that enables this leap from stage 2 to stage 3, and argue that:

> The implications of this paradigm shift are enormous. It turns the focus of the audit away from the past and present and toward the present and future. Focusing on controls over transactions buried the internal auditor in the details of the past, limiting the value from any information derived. By focusing on business risks to present and future transactions, the auditor is working at a level above the details and dealing with the obstacles for organisation success. The information derived from such exploration has great value to the management governance team.[1]

The emphasis on risk management now underpins most larger organizations, not as a reporting requirement but as a powerful business tool that, used properly, improves performance. Note that all references to IIA definitions, code of ethics, IIA attribute and performance standards, practice advisories and practice guides relate to the International Professional Practices Framework (IPPF) prepared by the Institute of Internal Auditors in 2009. In an attempt to get to grips with risk management we cover the following ground in this chapter:

Internal auditors have derived key messages about the internal audit product based on the growing demand for suitable risk management in all organizations. Many view the new challenges from risk management as raising the bar for the internal auditor. This has been described in *Internal Auditor* magazine:

> 'This movement away from compliance toward proactive involvement in risk management and governance will necessarily change the emphasis of audit shops and increase awareness of the types of activities they should engage in,' says Larry Rittenberg... 'the change in focus may represent a challenge for some, but for many the new standards will simply reflect the leading edge activities they already practice'.... By mandating involvement in risk management and governance processes, the rewritten standards elevate the internal audit activity to a more strategic level within the organization.... The revised standards name consulting services along with assurance as a key raison d'être for internal auditing, making it clear that aiding management should be a significant part of internal auditing's focus.[2]

## 3.1  What is Risk?

We need go no further than the work of the late risk guru, Peter L. Bernstein, to get an insight into the quality of risk:

> The word 'risk' derives from the early Italian risicare, which means 'to dare'. In this sense, risk is a choice rather than a fate. The actions we dare to take, which depend on how free we are to make choices, are what the story of risk is all about. And that story helps define what it means to be a human being.[3]

This immediately introduces the concept of choice when it comes to risk. Not simply being subject to risks as a part of life, but being in charge of one's destiny, as there is much that we can control if we have the time and inclination to do so. The stewardship concept underpinning corporate governance that we discussed in Chapter 2 forces management to seek out risks to the business and address them, where appropriate. Peter L. Bernstein goes on to suggest:

> The capacity to manage risk, and with it the appetite to take risk and make forward-looking choices, are the key elements of energy that drive the economic systems forward.[4]

For those that are not convinced, we can turn to an article on risk taking that includes an interesting point:

> The best-paid man in Britain was revealed yesterday as a 52 year old investment manager who works from a small nondescript office. He earned an estimated £50 million last year for taking high risk bets predicting the movement of the interest rates and the path of the US dollar and Japanese yen on behalf of well heeled investors.[5]

The point is that success in business and the public sector is intimately tied into the act of risk taking. Risk arises from uncertainty and controls are based on reducing this uncertainty where both possible and necessary. HM Treasury defines risk as: 'the uncertainty of outcome within a range of exposures arising from a combination of the impact and probability of potential events', while the IIA Glossary defines risk as: 'the uncertainty of an event occurring that could have an impact on the achievement of objectives. Risk is measured in terms of consequences and likelihood.'

Throughout the chapter we will develop a model to consider risk and risk management. The first part of our first model appears as shown in Figure 3.1.

**FIGURE 3.1**    Risk management model (1).

There are risks out there and they impact on our existence. Many of these risks arise in totally unexpected ways and can have a major effect on key aspects of our lives, as shown in this simple example:

> Scientist Barry Mathews went to the North Pole and back without mishap. But when it came to getting his photographs developed, the expedition ended in disaster. The store lost all the pictures the climate expert took on his Arctic journey – and Dr Mathews is now suing for £30,000, the cost of a return trip.[6]

## 3.2    The Risk Challenge

We now move into the field of seeing risk as a dynamic force that can be understood, considered and then acted on. Before we get there it is as well to note an example of what happens when serious risks run out of control:

> Thousands of patients' lives are being put at risk because many operations are carried out by unsupervised trainee doctors, a report revealed. The study found that one in five operations carried out between 6pm and midnight were performed by trainee doctors. Almost half the operations involved trainee anaesthetists.[7]

The popular press is full of stories where things have gone terribly wrong. It seems that the mere act of walking out of one's door, or getting into a car, or jumping into a swimming pool can mean disaster, injury or even death. We have said that controls are ways of minimizing risk and uncertainty and turning once again to Bernstein we can obtain a perspective of this concept of control:

> But if men and women were not at the mercy of impersonal deities and random chance, they could no longer remain passive in the face of an unknown future. They had no choice but to begin making decisions over a far wider range of circumstances and over far longer periods of time than ever before.[8]

We arrive now at the view that risk represents a series of challenges that need to be met. Also, the key feature of this challenge is that it appears when a major decision has to be made. Risk has no real form unless we relate it to our aims; what are we trying to achieve? It is the risks to achieving objectives that affect us in that they detract from the focus on success and stop us getting to the intended result. We may add to the risk model and incorporate this feature into the existing dimensions in Figure 3.2.

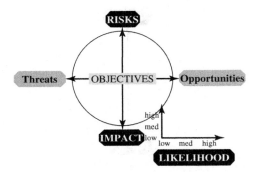

**FIGURE 3.2**    Risk management model (2).

In this way the impacts become the effect the risks have on the objectives in hand. Good systems of risk management keep the business objectives firmly in mind when thinking about risk. Poor systems hide the objectives outside the model or as something that is considered peripheral to the task of assessing the impact of the risks. In reality it is not as simple as this. The act of setting objectives in itself is based on real and perceived risks, i.e. some uncertainty about the future. Eileen Shapiro brought home this point in her book on *Fad Surfing in the Boardroom*:

> Most organisations create a vision but they cannot create one based on a 20/20 understanding of the future as this is impossible. Better to create the vision in steps, as the future changes one adapts and flexes and so capitalise on opportunities as they arise and respond to threats. Mission statements then communicate the vision of itself and its future. In the perfect world of plans, a blueprint can be laid out, with timetables and responsibilities. In the messy world of bets, circumstances shift unexpectedly and odds change – not an environment in which inviolable plans and rigid schedules will necessarily be helpful.[9]

In recognition of this, we have included a further addition concept that needs to be considered is that risk, in the context of achieving objectives, has both an upside and a downside. In our model we call these threats and opportunities, i.e. it can relate to forces that have a negative impact on objectives, in that they pose a threat. Upside risk, on the other hand, represents opportunities that are attainable but may be missed or ignored, and so mean we do not exceed expectations. This is why risk management is not really about building bunkers around the team to protect them from the outside world. It is more about moving outside of familiar areas and knowing when and where to take risks. This is quite important in that if we view controls as a means of reducing risk, we can now also view them as obstacles to grasping opportunities. Therefore risk management is partly about getting in improved controls where needed and getting rid of excessive controls where they slow proceedings down too much – in other words, making sure controls are focused, worth it and make sense.

Having established the two aspects of risk, we can start to think about which risks are not only material, in that they result in big hits against us, but also whether they are just around the corner or kept at bay – i.e. how likely they are to arise. Measuring risk tends to involve the Impact/Likelihood scale that is located on the right-hand bottom of the risk model. Since risk is based on uncertainty, it is also based on perceptions of this uncertainty and whether we have enough information to hand. Where the uncertainty is caused by a lack of information then the question turns to whether it is worth securing more information or examining the reliability of the existing information. Uncertainty based on a lack of information that is in fact readily available points to failings in the person most responsible for dealing with the uncertainty. There is much that we can control if we have time to think about it and the capacity to digest the consequences.

## 3.3   Risk Management Process

Risk management is a dynamic process for taking all reasonable steps to find out and deal with risks that impact our objectives. It is the response to risk and decisions made in respect of available choices (in conjunction with available resources) that is important and the IIA have made the pertinent point that:

> Although organisations use the term risk management frequently (and it is used here for lack of better terminology), it too is misleading, because risk is never actually managed. It is the organisation that is managed in anticipation of the uncertainty (and opportunities) presented by risk in the environment.[10]

Organizational resources and processes should be aligned to handle risk wherever it has been identified. We are close to preparing a risk management cycle and incorporating this into our original risk model. Before we get there we can turn to project management standards for guidance on the benefits of systematic risk management, which include:

- More realistic business and project planning.
- Actions implemented in time to be effective.
- Greater certainty of achieving business goals and project objectives.
- Appreciation of, and readiness to exploit, all beneficial opportunities.
- Improved loss control.
- Improved control of project and business costs.
- Increased flexibility as a result of understanding all options and associated risks.
- Fewer costly surprises through effective and transparent contingency planning.[11]

Remember, however, that some risks are so unusual that they are hard to anticipate, as another example illustrates:

> The stewardesses were used to dealing with the odd first-time flier suffering from anxiety. But this was something no amount of training could have prepared them for. As BA 837 reached its cruising height of 33,000 ft en route from Birmingham to Milan, the co-pilot began getting the jitters. Looking out through the cockpit window to the ground six miles below, he confessed to his astonished fellow crew members that he was afraid of heights. Initial attempts to calm him down failed and the plane – operated by Maersk Air on behalf of British Airways – was forced to divert to Lyon so he could get medical treatment.[12]

Before we can delve into business risk management we need to make a further point, i.e. that risk management is mainly dependent on establishing the risk owner, or the person most responsible for taking action in response to a defined risk, or type of risk, or risk that affects a particular process or project. The Turnbull report (see Chapter 2) on corporate governance for listed companies contains the following provisions regarding risk management:

> The reports from management to the board should, in relation to the areas covered by them, provide a balanced assessment of the significant risks and the effectiveness of the system of internal control in managing those risks. Any significant control failings or weaknesses identified should be discussed in the reports, including the impact that they have had, could have had, or may have, on the company and the actions being taken to rectify them. It is essential that there be openness of communication by management with the board on matters relating to risk and control (para. 30).

The risk cycle is now added to the model as set out in Figure 3.3.

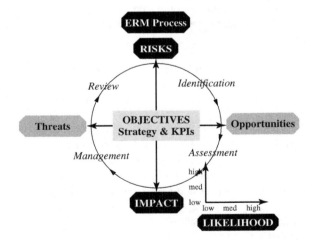

**FIGURE 3.3**    Risk management model (3).

The stages of risk management are commonly known as:

**Identification**    The risk management process starts with a method for identifying all risks that face an organization. This should involve all parties who have expertise, responsibility and influence over the area affected by the risks in question. All imaginable risks should be identified and recorded. In 1999 Deloitte & Touche carried out a survey of significant risks in the private sector, with each risk scored from 1 (low level of concern) to 9 (high level of concern) with the following summary results:

|  | *Score* |
|---|---|
| failure to manage major projects | 7.05 |
| failure of strategy | 6.67 |
| failure to innovate | 6.32 |
| poor reputation/brand management | 6.30 |
| lack of employee motivation/poor performance | 6.00[13] |

Business risk is really about these types of issues, and not just the more well-known disasters, acts of God or risks to personal safety.

**Assessment**   The next stage is to assess the significance of the risks that have been identified. This should revolve around the two-dimensional Impact/Likelihood considerations that we have already described earlier. Management need to be careful in the way they assess risk and there has been some criticism of overly optimistic positions that has been noted by some:

> The Traditional Approach has many useful features. It provides structure, governance standards and an intuitive approach to risk identification and assessment. But it also has some drawbacks. It is based on a conception of risk which is inconsistent with that used in the actuarial and risk management disciplines. One major discrepancy is that under the Traditional Approach risk is associated with the average loss. Yet, in the actuarial and risk management disciplines, risk represents uncertainty with respect to loss exposure or the worst case loss.[14]

**Management**   Armed with the knowledge of what risks are significant and which are less so, the process requires the development of strategies for managing high-impact, high-likelihood risks. This ensures that all key risks are tackled and that resources are channelled into areas of most concern, which have been identified through a structured methodology.

**Review**   The entire risk management process and outputs should be reviewed and revisited on a continual basis. This should involve updating the risk management strategy and reviewing the validity of the process that is being applied across the organization.

The above cycle is simple and logical and means clear decisions can be made on the types of controls that should be in place and how risk may be kept to an acceptable level, notwithstanding the uncertainty inherent in the nature of external and internal risks to the organization. In practice, the application of this basic cycle does cause many difficulties. Most arise because we impose a logical formula on an organization of people, structures and systems that can be complicated, unpredictable, vaguely defined and perceived, emotive and in a state of constant change. Most risk management systems fail because the process is implemented by going through the above stages with no regard to the reality of organizational life. Managers tick the box that states the stages have been gone through and eventually the board receives reports back stating that risk management has been done in all parts of the organization. Our risk models will have to be further developed to take on board the many intricacies that have to be tackled to get a robust and integrated system of risk management properly in place.

The IIA have sponsored work by PwC through the IIA Research Foundation in 2000, which was published as a booklet entitled *Corporate Governance and the Board: What Works Best* (pages 12–13). This has made clear the importance of risk management to the board and confirmed that organizations should have in place: 'an effective, ongoing process for identifying risk, measure its impact against a varied set of assumptions and do what's necessary to proactively manage it'. They go on to argue that:

> Second, the board also must be certain it is apprised of the most significant risks, and determine for each whether the right actions are being taken.... A director of one company laments, 'Our board isn't dealing with risk in a systematic, broad manner and isn't addressing the entire universe of risk associated with strategy, culture, and people.' ... Rather, it should be integrated within the way management runs the business, enriching that process and making it risk-focused. When done well, an enterprise-wide risk management architecture ensures risks are properly managed, assets secured, reputation protected and shareholder value enhanced.

## 3.4    Mitigation through Controls

We have suggested that risk management is an important part of the risk cycle, as it allows an organization to establish and review their internal controls and report back to the shareholders that these controls are sound. The internal control framework consists of all those arrangements and specific control routines and processes that drive an organization towards achieving objectives. In terms of risk management we need to add to our risk model to set out the types of response to risk that ensure we can remain in control. Borrowing from the thinking of Peter Drucker, these responses consist of specific controls over processes and overall control over the delivery of the agreed strategy. The way controls fit in with risk management is explained in the British standard on risk management:

> Those managing risk should prioritize changes to controls, taking into account the impact on other activities and the availability of resources. The control changes selected should be allocated to risk response owners and a schedule for their implementation should be prepared. Progress towards implementation of control changes should be monitored. The controls implemented should be documented. After control changes have been implemented and it becomes possible to gather data on the actual residual risk, the level of residual risk should be assessed. The same decision process should be used to decide whether to retain the residual risk or whether pursuing further control changes is worthwhile. The process should be repeated until the level of residual risk is within the risk appetite and pursuing further control changes does not seem worthwhile.[15]

Our latest risk model becomes Figure 3.4.

We have developed 10 measures for addressing risks that have already been assessed for impact and likelihood, in the bottom left box of our model. Each of the 10 responses (five Ts and five Cs) can be located within the appropriate part of the Impact/Likelihood grid in the bottom right of the risk model. For example, where we have assessed a risk as high impact but low likelihood, we may want to transfer (or spread) some of this risk, to an insurer as a suitable response. The responses are further described:

1. **Terminate**    Here, where the risk is great and either cannot be contained at all or the costs of such containment are prohibitive, we would have to consider whether the operation should continue. Sending sales reps to overseas countries may be common practice for enterprises that have a global growth strategy. Where certain locations are politically volatile then we may have to take precautions in the way they conduct business in these countries and the type of security arrangements for high-risk sites. Where the costs of adequate security measures are not only sky high but also cannot give reasonable assurance that the sales people would not be attacked,

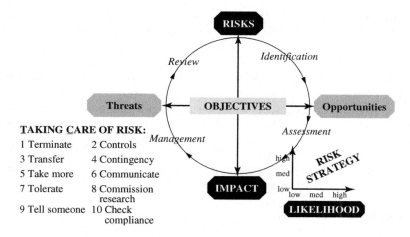

**FIGURE 3.4**   Risk management model (4).

kidnapped or simply caught up in dangerous situations, then we must decide whether to continue sending people to the country (or dangerous parts of the country); i.e. we may need to consider terminating the activity.

2. **Controls**   One of the principal weapons for tackling risks is better controls. Note that this is the subject of the next chapter. Building on our example of overseas sales staff, after having assessed certain locations as high personal risk, we would go on to consider what measures we currently have in place and decide whether we are doing enough. Controls may cover local surveys, security personnel, formal guidance on socializing, say in the evenings, procedures for travelling and use of drivers or guides, awareness seminars on ways of reducing the chances of becoming a target, a good personal communications set-up and so on. The degree of measures adopted may depend on the assessment of risk levels and changes in states of alert. The key question would be: Are we doing enough, bearing in mind what we know about this location?

3. **Transfer**   Where the risks are assessed as high impact but low likelihood, we may wish to adopt a strategy of spreading risk, wherever possible. High likelihood risk will be hard to transfer because all parties involved will want to be fully recompensed to the value of the impact of the risk. It is only where there is some uncertainty that transfers are more appropriate. Turning again to the running example, we may spread the impact of the risk by having an insurance policy that covers overseas staff or we may employ an international firm or local agency to perform the sales role in high-risk countries.

4. **Contingencies**   A useful response to risk that is again high impact, low likelihood is based around making contingency arrangements in the event the risk materializes. The contingencies would focus on impacts that affect the continued running of the business, so that even after having installed preventive controls there is still the chance that the risk may materialize. The overseas sales team may be covered by an evacuation procedure in the event that the risk of civil unrest materializes. This may involve access to a special charter plane that can be made available very quickly. The contingency plan may also cover business continuity for the sales lines that may be disrupted by the unrest. Many laypeople view risk management as essentially to do with contingency planning; i.e. their rather narrow view of risk does not attach to the achievement of strategic business objectives and the need for processes to handle all material risks.

5. **Take more**    One dimension of the risk management strategy is derived from the upside risk viewpoint. Where the impact/likelihood rating shows operations located down at low/low for both factors, this does not necessarily mean all is well. Risk management is about knowing where to spend precious time and knowing where to spend precious resources. Low/low areas are ripe for further investment (for commercial concerns) or ripe for further innovative development (for public sector services). In the overseas sales example, we may wish to send out teams to countries that had a reputation for instability, but are slowly settling down and are open for business. Peter Bernstein has provided a view on this need to exploit opportunities to stay ahead of the game:

> The essence of risk management lies in maximising the areas where we have some control over the outcome while minimising the areas where we have absolutely no control over the outcome and the linkage between effect and cause is hidden from us.[16]

6. **Communicate**    One aspect of risk management that is often missed relates to high impact and either medium or high likelihood, where controls may not address the risk to an acceptable level, i.e. a strategy to communicate this risk to stakeholders and make them aware that this impairs the organization's ability to be sure of success (at all times). Communicating risk is a completely separate discipline and sensitive stock markets and high-profile public services have a difficult task in managing expectations, handling price-sensitive information and keeping politicians and the media happy. Some argue that the financial misstatement scandals in 2002 were fuelled by markets that demanded rapid and linear profit growth and resented bad news. Success in communicating risk is mainly based on a trust relationship between the giver and receiver and the degree of consistency in the messages given. For our overseas sales people we may simply publish the national statistic on trouble spots and rates of infectious diseases, and tell people about the known risks before they accept assignments. This is particularly helpful where there is little scope to establish robust controls in the area in question, where matters may be outside of our control.

7. **Tolerate**    The low/low risks that come out of our assessment will pose no threat and as such can be tolerated. This stance may also relate to high-rated risks where we really have no option but to accept what is in front of us. At times where we install more controls over an area to increase the level of comfort, people adjust other controls so they fall back to what they see as a comfortable position. Extra checking installed in one part of a system can lead to a slackening of checks in another as people make this adjustment. Going back to the work of Peter Bernstein, we can see this very point illustrated:

> Finally, the science of risk management sometimes creates new risks even as it brings old risks under control. Our faith in risk management encourages us to take risks we would not otherwise take. On most counts, that is beneficial, but we must be wary of adding to the amount of risk in the system. Research reveals that seatbelts encourage drivers to drive aggressively. Consequently, the number of accidents rises even though the seriousness of injury in any one accident declines.[17]

For our sales reps, this may mean that the risks of communicable disease in parts of the world that they travel to may be low impact (because the sales team have had all the jabs) and low likelihood (because the areas visited have good sanitation infrastructures). Any remaining risk may simply be tolerated.

8. **Commission research**    We have argued that risk revolves around uncertainty as to the future. Gamblers are well versed in this and believe that they can beat the odds or simply enjoy

placing bets because of nonfinancial reasons. Many risk management systems are too rigid, in that they depend on quick assessments and a risk register that shows the agreed strategy for action. More developed systems will allow some thinking time, where one decision may be to go and find out more about the risk, its impact and whether is will probably materialize – i.e. to commission further research. For the overseas sales team we may ask an international consultant to travel to a possible 'hot spot' and report back on the local conditions and risks therein. Alternatively, we may ask the experts since the Foreign and Commonwealth Office (FCO) in its published *Risk Management Framework 2002* states that the FCO's aim is to promote internationally the interests of the UK and to contribute to a strong world community, and the FCO also has a specific responsibility to help identify and manage risks to British citizens abroad.

9. **Tell someone**    Some high/high risks create a blockage in that they can only really be resolved by parties outside those participating in the risk management exercise. Many such exercises grind to a halt as the responsibility for managing the risk in question does not reside with the people who are designing the risk strategy. A better response is to set out the unguarded risk and work out a strategy for relaying this position to the party who can tackle it and also refer the result up through the line. At times, if outside parties do not realize that their inaction has stopped progress in another area, they have no reason to address the problem. Using our sales team example, we may argue that the sales drive is affected by unreliable communications between head office and an assessment of business risk may make this a key barrier to successfully getting orders placed and turned around. The management strategy may suggest that there is nothing that can be done as communications networks are run by the country in question. A better response is to relay this information to the board and note that there is a danger of missing strategic growth objectives if it is left unattended. The board may be able to lobby the government in question or support bids to international development agencies for projects that improve global communications. While these moves may not lead to improvements straight away, it may over time facilitate progress.

10. **Check compliance**    The final weapon in the arsenal of risk responses is often overlooked. This is to focus on areas where controls are crucial to mitigating significant risks, and to ensure that they are actually working as intended. Controls that counter more than one material risk are particularly important. These controls may be reviewed and tested by internal auditors or a specialist compliance team at the behest of management. We can make a final visit to our sales team example: a key control over the team may be a regional coordinator who ensures smooth transport between countries and keeps everyone in touch with product developments. It may be essential that the coordinator sticks to their terms of agreement and any shortfalls will lead to significant exposure. The risk management response may be based on reliance on a key control that, so long as it works, means the risk is mitigated – the strategy then is to focus on the existing control and strengthen it where possible, and ensure it does what it is meant to do. In this case, review the regional coordinators and check they are discharging their responsibilities properly.

The 5Ts and 5Cs model provides a wide range of techniques for developing a suitable risk management strategy.

## 3.5  Risk Registers and Appetites

The basic risk model has to be made more dynamic to incorporate the next risk tool, which is the risk register shown in Figure 3.5.

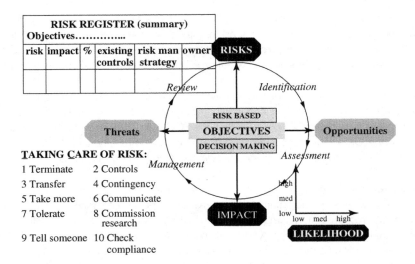

**FIGURE 3.5**    Risk management model (5).

The subject of risk registers (some call them risk logs) has a very interesting past. Project managers have used them for a long time as they assess risks at an early stage in a large project and enter the details in a formal record that is inspected by the sponsors or project board. The insurance industry again is well used to documenting assumptions about risk and using this to form judgements on where to offer insurance cover and what aspects of an operation are included in this cover. More recently, they have come to the fore as an important part of general business risk management used by many large private and public sector organizations. Risk registers act as a vehicle for capturing all the significant assessment and business decisions made in respect of identified risks to operational objectives. Moreover, the registers may form part of the assurance process, where they can be used as evidence of risk containment activity, which supports the management reports on the state of their internal controls. We have suggested that risk management is simply the task of defining risk, identifying risks, assessing this risk for impact and materiality, and then devising suitable ways of dealing with more significant risks. Risk registers can be attached to this process to record the above stages and end up with both a record and action plan that feeds into the defined risk strategy. The register in our latest model is a basic version that details the key objectives in question, the risks that have been identified by those closest to the action, their impact and likelihood and overall score. It is then possible to define a set of actions required to reflect the adopted risk strategy, which is then the responsibility of the appropriate risk owner. The register should be frequently updated to reflect changes in the objectives, external and internal risks and controls, as a result of changes in the environment within which the business operates. What goes in the register and what is documented as significant as opposed to immaterial risk depends on the risk appetite that is in place. An elementary diagram forms the basis for a consideration of risk appetite in Figure 3.6.

The risk appetite defines how inherent risk is perceived and whether there is an aggressive or more passive growth strategy in place. Risk tolerance is what is acceptable after appropriate controls have been put in place to mitigate risk, through an appropriate risk management strategy. Deciding on what is appropriate depends on how the business stands on whether risks need to

**FIGURE 3.6**  Risk management model (6).

be contained through more controls or accepted as just about right whether more risky strategies are in place to exploit opportunities.

The concept of risk appetite is very tricky to get around. The contrasting positions are that the board sets a clear level and tells everyone inside the organization or that people are empowered to derive their own levels based around set accountabilities. These accountabilities mean defined people are responsible for getting things right and also must explain where this has not happened and things are going wrong. HM Treasury (Strategic Risk Management), suggest that:

> Risk appetite is the amount of risk to which the organisation is prepared to be exposed before it judges action to be necessary . . . Risk appetite may be very specific in relation to a particular risk, or it may be more generic in the sense that the total risks which an organisation is prepared to accept at any one time will have a limit . . . Any particular organisation is unlikely to have a single risk appetite. The tolerable extent of risk will vary according to the perceived particular risks . . . . The most significant issue is that it is unlikely, except for the most extreme risk, that any particular risk will need to be completely and absolutely obviated . . . . Identification of risk appetite is a subjective . . . issue . . . (para. 6.1).

If an organization gets the risk appetite wrong then key stakeholders may well misunderstand the extent to which their investment is insecure, and, conversely, where corporate risk tolerance is low, returns on investment may be likewise restrained. Funds will move in accordance with the level of risk that they are attracted to, so long as this level has been properly communicated to all interested parties as the following case suggests:

> Merrill Lynch court battle with Unilever involved a £130 m claim from Unilever alleging that Merrill had pursued a too-high risk strategy was settled for around £75 m. During the trial a metaphor was used: Fund management and risk is like driving a car – If you can see the road, you drive faster; if it is foggy you slow down . . . . One witness said: 'If you think you can see clearly, you should go faster . . . ' to which the judge said, 'The better the driver, the more justifiable it is for him to go at 90 rather than 70 mph?'[18]

Risk appetite varies between organizations, between departments, between sections, teams and, more importantly, between individuals and the types of activites they are involved in. People go for jobs that suit their risk preference and a list of the most dangerous jobs around suggests that there are those that thrive on danger, and possibly achieve higher salaries than others:

| | |
|---|---|
| formula one driver | bomb disposal officer |
| test pilot | member of the SAS |
| circus entertainer | film stuntman |
| commercial driver | oil rig worker |
| scaffolder | miner[19] |

For each of the jobs listed above, the normalization equation means that the riskier the job the more detailed the controls over the task. Therefore a high risk appetite may encourage someone to become a test pilot, but at the same time a low risk tolerance means that so many controls are put in place over fighter jets that the chances of random accidents is very low. Of all these jobs it may be that the scaffolder has the less-developed control arrangements and the net risk may make this job the most dangerous of all. If risk tolerance throughout an organization hovers at different levels with no rational explanation, then we may well experience problems. Key performance indicators need to be set to take on board acceptable risk tolerances so that the organization is pulled in a clear direction and not subject to fits and starts as different parts of the organization slow things down while others are trying to speed them up. Where the entire organization has a high risk tolerance, then it will tend not to install too many controls, particularly where these controls are expensive.

Returning to the IIA Research Foundation's *Corporate Governance and the Board* (page 20), they confirm that risk appetite is a crucial concept for both the board and the CEO:

> One director's view – 'If the board isn't comfortable with the strategy that management has set, it should tell management to rethink it, and come back with something better. But, the board shouldn't be involved in developing strategy. That is, noses in fingers out' (page 1) .... Although employees typically know what's going on before a crisis strikes, and 95 percent of CEOs say they have an open door policy and will reward employees who communicate bad news, half of all employees believe the bad news messenger runs a real risk of being seriously damaged.... The 'tone at the top' establishes the true expectations for behavior. And the right behavior must be practiced consistently by management – through good times and bad.

The need for a clear message on risk acceptability appears again in the IIA UK&Ireland's Professional Briefing Note Thirteen on Managing Risk, which states that: 'The assessment of risk and the determination of acceptable, or tolerable, levels of risk together with suitable control strategies are key management responsibilities' (para. 5.1). The majority of risk management guides refer to tolerance, acceptance, appetite and other such measures of what we have called unmanaged residual risk. The problem is that there is very little guidance on how to put this concept into action on the ground. Risk assessment is based on logic, measures and gut feeling. The gut feeling component is what makes it hard to set standards that, say, 10% level of risk is acceptable or that a £100 000 is okay or that 1000 errors per month will be tolerated. It is easier to say that major decisions shall not be made without having conducted a formal appraisal of risks and a determination of the optimal way of managing these risks. An even better stance would be to add that the context of risk assessment is based on transparency, integrity and accountability, which is good corporate governance. Therefore keeping within these values while applying competence and robust approaches to measuring and managing risk takes us closer to a risk tolerance level, albeit somewhat implicit. The Institute of Risk Management (in conjunction with the National Forum for Risk Management in the Public Sector (ALARM) and the Association of Insurance and Risk Managers (AIRMIC)) prepared a risk management standard in 2002, which states that:

> When the risk analysis process has been completed, it is necessary to compare the estimated risks against risk criteria which the organisation has established. The risk criteria may include associated costs and benefits, legal requirements, socio-economic and environmental factors, concerns of stakeholders, etc. Risk evaluation, therefore, is used to make decisions about the significance of risk to the organisation and whether each specific risk should be accepted or treated.

Attitudes to risk tolerance become even more important when we consider the responsibilities of an organization to its stakeholders. The board members have a fiduciary duty to act in a reasonable manner and shareholders have a right to receive any announced dividends and to have their investment managed adequately. However, they will also need to understand the way the organization behaves towards risks. The ICAEW has commented on this very point:

> Enterprises in the same industry, facing similar risks, will often choose different risk management actions because different managements have different risk strategies, objectives and tolerances. It is therefore important that investors are made aware of the key business risks and how each risk is managed rather than given simply an assessment of the net risk.[20]

The British standard on risk management has set out guidance on risk appetites and the risk profile that is mentioned below:

> Considering and setting a risk appetite enables an organization to increase its rewards by optimizing risk taking and accepting calculated risks within an appropriate level of authority. The organization's risk appetite should be established and/or approved by the Board (or equivalent) and effectively communicated throughout the organization. The organization should prepare a risk appetite statement, which may:
>
> - Provide direction and boundaries on the risk that can be accepted at various levels of the organization, how the risk and any associated reward is to be balanced, and the likely response;
> - Consider the context and the organization's understanding of value, cost effectiveness of management, rigour of controls and assurance process;
> - Recognize that the organization might be prepared to accept a higher than usual proportion of risk in one area if the overall balance of risk is acceptable;
> - Define the control, permissions and sanctions environment, including the delegation of authority in relation to approving the organization's *risk acceptance*, highlighting of escalation points, and identifying the escalation process for risk outside the acceptance criteria, capability or capacity;
> - Be reflected in the organization's risk management policy and reported upon as part of the organization's internal risk reporting system;
> - Include qualitative statements outlining specific risks the organization is or is not prepared to accept; and
> - Include quantitative statements, described as limits, thresholds or key risk indicators, which set out how certain risks and their rewards are to be judged and/or how the aggregate consequences of risks are to be assessed and monitored.[21]

## 3.6    The Risk Policy

Our risk model has taken a clear form with many components that form the basis of effective risk management. In some organizations, risk assessment workshops are set up for key teams as a response to the trend towards Control Risk Self-Assessment (CRSA) programmes, often on the back of recommendations from the auditors or an external consultant. Teams get together, talk about risk and how it is being managed in their outfit and come out with a risk register that is filed and action points given to nominated managers. This annual exercise appears to be enough to satisfy the auditors and someone within the organization attempts to place the risk registers on to a database and eventually prepares summary reports for top management and the board. Better models use a key to highlight high impact, high likelihood (perhaps indicated in red), which then triggers a rapid response from the board, who will want to know that action is being taken to handle key exposures. The board then reports that it has reviewed the system of internal control, partly through the use of the risk management process as described.

This fairly typical arrangement has a number of shortcomings:

- Many staff do not know why they are engaged in the workshops and simply see it as a one-off exercise for the auditors.
- Many managers are reluctant to spend time on the workshops as they are busy doing 'real work'.
- Many workshops operate completely outside the important strategic realignment, restructuring and other change initiatives that are a feature of most large organizations.
- Many workshops are seen as clumsy devices for getting more work out of fewer staff.
- Many of the programme workshops result in masses of information that are impossible to coordinate or make into a whole.
- A lot of the action points that come out of the workshops are superseded by subsequent events and new developments.
- Most workshops are developed outside of the performance management system and there is little incentive to take on additional tasks that do not hit any key performance indicators (KPIs).
- Many see control self-assessment as relating only to the financial aspects of operations.
- Many workshop participants have already carried out risk assessment in their specialist fields of health and safety, security, project management, legal compliance and other areas of the business.
- Often the workshop facilitator introduces the event as a discrete exercise with no links to the organization's strategic direction.
- Many participants suffer the fallout from initiative overload and have spent much time in teambuilding events, performance review meetings, change programmes, budget reduction exercises, diversity training, e-business projects and so on.
- Many participants have experienced a culture where good ideas from staff never go anywhere and motivation levels are fairly low.

We could go on, where risk workshops or risk reviews based on survey or interviews are derived from an incomplete model of the risk management system. As a result, we have developed our risk model to incorporate further dimensions that seek to counter the negatives listed above, as Figure 3.7 demonstrates. The amended model has built in three new factors (based around the risk policy), i.e. the board sponsor, people buy-in and a chief risk officer (CRO). Each one is discussed briefly below.

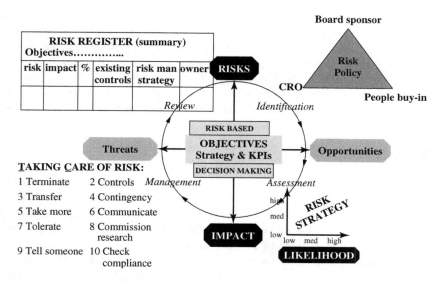

**FIGURE 3.7**   The risk management model (7).

## Board Sponsor

Where there is no board member driving the risk management process it will tend to fail. The board makes a statement on the systems of internal control in the annual report and it is the board that reports that this system has been reviewed. The original King report (from South Africa) makes this point crystal clear:

> The board is responsible for the total process of risk management, as well as for forming its own opinion on the effectiveness of the process. Management is accountable to the board for designing, implementing and monitoring the process of risk management and integrating it into the day-to-day activities of the company (para. 3.1.1). The board should set the risk strategy policies in liaison with the executive directors and senior management. These policies should be clearly communicated to all employees to ensure that the risk strategy is incorporated into the language and culture of the company (para. 3.1.1).

We are engaged in a continual search for better business practice. Meanwhile, the first cornerstone of the risk management policy rightly sits at the board, as the highest part of the organization. The board may in turn establish a risk management committee or look to the audit committee for advice and support, in respect of ensuring there is a reliable system for managing risks, or the audit committee may be more inclined to provide an independent oversight of the risk management and whether the arrangements are robust and focused. Regardless of the set-up, the board remains responsible for ensuring management have implemented proper risk management. Some organizations have gone all the way and appointed a director of risk management, particularly in sectors such as banking, where the risk agenda is also driven by regulators. The board sponsor will direct the risk management activity and ensure that it is happening and makes sense. One way of mobilizing the board and audit committee is to get them to participate in a facilitated risk assessment around the corporate strategy. Many risk consultants suggest that the board arrive at the top 10 or so risks to achieving the corporate strategy and make this information known to the management. A more dynamic approach is to suggest that the Chief Executive Officer should be the board sponsor as this person should have the highest level view of risks to the businesses success and how these risks should be handled.

The board come back into the frame when reviewing the risk management process and ensuring it stands up to scrutiny. They would also consider the reports that come back from their management teams that isolate key risks and whether these are being contained adequately.

## People Buy-In

Another problem with many risk management systems is that they do not mean anything to the people below middle management level. They are seen as another management initiative that is 'done' to employees along with the multitude of other tools and techniques for improving performance and driving down costs. At worst, the employees are squeezed in between performance and costs in an attempt to work harder for less or the same recompense. In one risk management policy the organization had prepared a detailed diagram covering roles, responsibilities and relationships in the risk management system with committees, boards, risk manager, facilitators, auditors and stakeholder analysis. At the bottom of the diagram is the word 'individuals' with no further detail. The impression is that the risk management process is something that happens to them. The individual is really the foundation of risk management, since it is what people do and how they behave that determines whether an organization succeeds or fails. It would have been more apt to start with the individual and work through how they fit into the risk management process or, better still, how risk management can be made part of the way they work in future. This point has not been lost on the people who prepare guides to risk management and several extracts demonstrate the significance of 'people buy-in' for successful risk management.

The Institute of Risk Management's standard on risk management suggests that the focus of good risk management is the manager and employee responsible for the identification and treatment of these risks. The result of people buy-in is that we can get closer to a risk managed culture where people around the organization take responsibility for isolating risks and making sure they provide criteria for making key decisions. If buy-in works for risk management, then the spin-off is that people build their own controls.

## Chief Risk Officer

The next leg of the risk policy stool relates to the need for a person responsible for coordinating risk effort around the organization. This person proactively directs the effort and sets up systems that embed the risk policy into everyday activities. There needs to be an in-house expert who can drive through the risk policy and make it work in practice. Their role may include:

- Translating the board's vision on risk management.
- Helping to develop and implement the corporate risk policy.
- Ensuring the people buy-in mentioned earlier.
- Providing training and awareness events where appropriate.
- Helping respond to requirements from regulators that impact on risk management systems.
- Establishing a strategic approach to risk management across the organization with programmes, the appropriate approaches, tools and reporting arrangements.

- Ensuring that the business is responding properly to changes and challenges that create new risks on a continuous basis.
- Establishing a risk reporting system from managers in the organization that can be used to provide assurances that support the board review of internal control.
- Helping facilitate risk management exercises and programmes.
- Becoming a centre of excellence on risk management and going on to develop an on-line support infrastructure, based on the latest technology that can be used by all parts of the organization.
- Helping coordinate risk management activities such as health and safety, security, insurance, product quality, environmental matters, disaster recovery, compliance teams and projects and procurement.
- Providing advice on sensitive issues such as perceptions of risk tolerance and the consistency of messages in different parts of the organization.
- Seeking to implement enterprise-wide risk management as an integrated part of existing processes such as decision making, accountability and performance management.

We could go on, and there is a shortcut to defining the role of the CRO – it is to make good all aspects of our risk model and ensure that together they provide an effective system of risk management that is owned by all employees and integrated into the way the organization works. No risk policy will work without a commitment to resource the necessary process and ensure there is someone who can help managers translate board ideals into working practices. The IIA Research Foundation's booklet on *Corporate Governance and the Board: What Works Best* suggests that the chief risk officer: '... acts as line managers' coach, helping them implement a risk management architecture and work with it ongoing. As a member of the senior management team the CRO monitors the company's entire risk profile, ensuring major risks identified are reported upstream.' Each organization will develop a formula that suits and government bodies may well turn to the HM Treasury *Strategic Risk Management* guide for help as they argue that: 'The designated risk owners can be formed into a RM committee which reports to the Accounting Officer or acts as a subcommittee to the senior management board.'

## Risk Policy

We have defined the main aspects that support the risk policy as board sponsorship, people buy-in and a source of expertise and assistance (the CRO). To close, it is possible to list the items that may appear in the published risk policy and strategy itself:

1. Define risk and state the overall mission in respect of risk management.
2. Define risk management and the difference between upside and downside risk.
3. Make clear the objectives of the risk policy – mention why we need a defined position on risk management.
4. Stakeholders and where they fit in – and the need to communicate a clear and reliable message.
5. Background to regulators and their requirements for risk management (and note on corporate governance code).
6. Position on appetite and whether the aim is risk avoidance, risk seeking or a measured balance.
7. Why bother? Whether to create a list of benefits behind risk management, better controls and better performance and better accountability and the impact on corporate reputation.

8. Background to the RM process (the risk cycle) and how it is integrated into decision making and planning, and performance management.
9. Risk responses and strategies leading to better certainty of achieving goals.
10. Internal controls – what this means with brief examples. The right control means putting in controls where risk is evident and getting rid of them where they are not required.
11. Training and seminars – importance and use.
12. Roles and responsibilities of all staff and specialist people such as board, CRO, internal audit, external audit and technical risk-based functions. Importance of the business unit manager.
13. Structures including board, audit committee, any risk committee and links to the CRO, quality teams and auditors.
14. Risk classifications or categories used in the risk management process.
15. Tools and techniques – guidance on the Intranet including a short guide to CRSA workshops (method, tools and principles involved).
16. Links to the overall internal control model that is applied with particular reference to the need for a good control environment to underpin the risk process.
17. Links to established risk assessment practices built into projects, security, contingency planning and so on.
18. Assurance reporting – giving overall responsibilities, review points, validation of reports and the use of risk registers, including regular updates.
19. Need for integration into existing management systems such as performance management.
20. Glossary of terms.
21. Where to go to for help.

The policy may be a brief document that gives an overview of the organization's position of risk management with clear messages from the board. The risk strategy will go into more detail and develop more guidance on how to put the policy into action. The British Standard on risk management has described the importance of the risk management policy:

> The risk management policy should provide a clear and concise outline of the organization's requirements for risk management as an integral part of the organization's overall approach to governance. To achieve consistency of risk management activities across the organization, with appropriate variations in detail, the policy should contain a high level overview and description of the risk management process. The risk management policy should be:
>
> • Owned by a manager, preferably at Board (or equivalent) level;
> • Developed in consultation with key stakeholders;
> • Developed with consideration of how the organization will monitor adherence to the policy and reference any relevant standards, regulations and policies that have to be included or taken into account; and
> • Subject to quality assurance practices, e.g. document, change and version control.

## Content of the risk management policy

The organization's risk management policy may include:

- **Governance**, outlining how risk management is governed;
- **Policy scope**, describing the purpose of the policy and who it is aimed at; describing the high level principles and the benefits of implementing risk management; setting out the objectives, including legal and regulatory requirements, and what it intends to achieve; and providing an explanation of the relationship with other policies;

- **Policy applicability**, setting out to whom and to what the policy applies;
- **Risk management process**, providing a high level overview and description of the risk management process adopted by the organization;
- **Risk appetite**, outlining the organization's risk appetite, thresholds and escalation procedure;
- **Reporting**, describing the purpose, frequency and scope of reporting;
- **Roles, accountabilities and responsibilities**, describing the high level roles, accountabilities and responsibilities in respect of risk management; and
- **Variations and dispensations**, stating whether variations or dispensations from the policy are allowed and, if they are allowed, describing the process for requests for this.[22]

## 3.7  Enterprise-Wide Risk Management

Enterprise-wide risk management or enterprise risk management (ERM) is simply the extension of risk management across the organization in an integrated fashion. This is in contrast to the old approach where specialist pockets of dedicated processes such as contingency planning were risk assessed but only at a local level for the process in question. Jim Deloach, Global Leader of Strategic and Enterprise Risk Consulting, Arthur Andersen, has said that:

> There is no one size fits all approach to ERM. That said, we do believe that any ERM project must begin with five essential actions:
>
> 1. establishing an oversight structure;
> 2. defining a common language and framework;
> 3. targeting risks and processes;
> 4. establishing goals, objectives, and a uniform process; and
> 5. assessing risk management capability. [23]

ERM has not yet fully arrived in many organizations and research in the US by the Certified Public Accountants clearly demonstrated this point:

> Almost 57% of our respondents have no formal enterprise-wide approach to risk oversight, as compared to 61.8% in our 2009 report with no formal ERM processes in place. Only a small number (11%) of respondents believe they have a complete formal enterprise-wide risk management process in place as compared to 9% in the 2009 report. Thus, there has been only a slight movement towards an ERM approach since our 2009 report.[24]

Before we delve into ERM further there is a related point to clarify with the risk model we have been using throughout this chapter. The new risk model is amended in Figure 3.8. In the middle box we have added **Strategy** and **KPIs** to the original factor, **Objectives**. We started with objectives as the driver for risk management and this viewpoint stands. What we are working towards is for risk management to be part of the strategic planning process and therefore integrated within the performance measurement system. This can be best illustrated with another model (Figure 3.8) that considers the role of risk assessment and where it fits into the organization's strategic analysis.

Starting with the black boxes first, these additions are explained below:

***ERM/CRSA*** As discussed above, there should be a process that ensures risk is understood, identified and managed at grassroots level, ideally through a form of control risk self-assessment programmes. Meanwhile, there should be a further process for ensuring risk assessment is

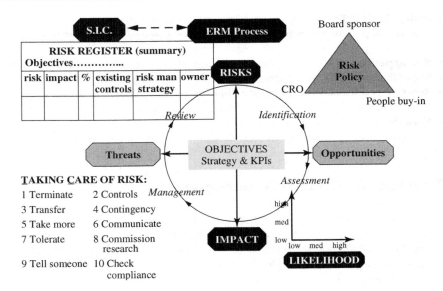

**FIGURE 3.8**   Risk management model (8).

undertaken throughout key parts, if not all, of the organization and that it is driven from the top and runs down, across and throughout all levels of management. The chief risk officer (CRO) would help coordinate these efforts.

**SIC**   The risk efforts and ensuring controls should feed into the statement of internal control (SIC) that each larger organization should formally publish. The inputs to the annual SIC should arrive from a suitable assurance reporting system (perhaps revolving around local and aggregated risk registers). The organization should have a formal process for communicating with stakeholders the efforts of the risk management system and any information that gives value to various interested parties. The risk management system should address the concept of risk tolerance and make clear what areas are likely to pose a threat to the organization, or the general public where appropriate, and the extent to which strategies and performance targets are likely to be fully achieved. Much use can be made of the Internet web site to communicate risk publicly.

ERM is fully defined by the Committee of Sponsoring Organizations (COSO) in their ERM framework, which was published in September 2004 and can be viewed in full at www.coso.org. In their executive summary COSO defines ERM as:

A process, effected by an entity's board of directors, management and other personnel, applied in strategy setting and across the enterprise, designed to identify potential events that may affect the entity, and manage risk to be within its risk appetite, to provide reasonable assurance regarding the achievement of entity objectives.

COSO goes on to suggest that ERM encompasses:

- *Aligning risk appetite and strategy*   Management considers the entity's risk appetite in evaluating strategic alternatives, setting related objectives and developing mechanisms to manage related risks.

- *Enhancing risk response decisions*   Enterprise risk management provides the rigour to identify and select among alternative risk responses – risk avoidance, reduction, sharing and acceptance.
- *Reducing operational surprises and losses*   Entities gain enhanced capability to identify potential events and establish responses, reducing surprises and associated costs or losses.
- *Identifying and managing multiple and cross-enterprise risks*   Every enterprise faces a myriad of risks affecting different parts of the organization, and enterprise risk management facilitates effective response to the interrelated impacts and integrated responses to multiple risks.
- *Seizing opportunities*   By considering a full range of potential events, management is positioned to identify and proactively realize opportunities.
- *Improving deployment of capital*   Obtaining robust risk information allows management to effectively assess overall capital needs and enhance capital allocation.

## 3.8  Control Self-Assessment

The success of enterprise-wide risk management depends on an integrated process for ensuring that risks are assessed and managed across an organization in a dynamic and meaningful way. There are many techniques for reaching all parts of an organization so that self-assessment by front line staff becomes the norm. Some argue the widespread use of questionnaires that are completed by key employees as a way of assessing whether there are operations that are at risk and whether controls are addressing these risk areas properly. Another technique is the use of interviews with managers in particular business units to gauge whether the area is under control or not. A further approach is to commission comprehensive reviews of risk in high-profile parts of the organization normally by the use of external consultants, who would report back on any problems found. These three techniques are fairly straightforward in that they involve a process superimposed on the normal business operations and support services. Unfortunately they reinforce the ad hoc silo approach and appear as one-off exercises carried out by a special purpose head office team. A more popular approach is the use of control self-assessment workshops, or what some call control and risk self-assessment (CRSA) workshops. Proponents of CRSA are convinced that the only way to get risk management into the heart and minds of the organization is to get everyone involved in a participative manner. CRSA may be called many different things in different organizations. In some companies the terms *risk* and *control* do not inspire people and other more friendly terms are applied to the workshops. Note that the technique is dealt with in Chapter 7 on the audit approaches. Here we simply mention the key principles relating to CRSA as part of the risk management system. An article by Paul Makosz in *CSA Sentinel* outlined the development of the CRSA approach:

> While I was at Gulf Canada Resources, we began to recognize that the heart of many problems lies in a corporate culture that could directly affect the bottom line; but we unfortunately had no tools to help us in identifying major risks before they became problems. Bruce McCuaig, my predecessor at Gulf Canada Resources, originated the CSA idea. He had been studying Watergate related issues at the parent company, Gulf Corp. About the same time, a serious management fraud had been discovered in a Gulf Canada subsidiary, although the internal auditors had been there only recently. Bruce kept asking, 'What's the point of auditing the little things if the culture is wrong-headed?' Gulf was going through some team productivity exercises at the time, so Bruce wanted to teach teams about internal control and have them self-assess their position. The rest is history. Bruce and I wrote about it in 'Ripe for Renaissance,' an article that appeared in the December 1990 edition of Internal Auditor.[25]

## 3.9   Embedding Risk Management

We now arrive at the pinnacle of risk management best practice – the much-sought-after 'embedded risk management'. Again, like much of the theory of risk management, it sounds simple as an ideal and Turnbull includes among the criteria to assess the internal control framework (monitoring arrangements) the following question:

> Are there ongoing processes embedded within the company's overall business operations, and addressed by senior management, which monitor the effective application of the policies, processes and activities related to internal control risk management? (Such processes may include control self-assessment, confirmation by personnel of compliance with policies and codes of conduct, internal audit reviews or other management reviews.)

Meanwhile the Treasury's *Strategic Risk Management* guide recognizes a similar need to integrate risk into the organization by suggesting that: 'The embedding of risk management is in turn critical to its success; it should become an intrinsic part of the way the organisation works, at the core of the management approach; not something separated from the day to day activities.'

We could go on. Most risk standards, guides, aids and commentary contain the phrase (or an equivalent term) *embedded risk management*. Gordon Hill warns about trying to do too much too quickly:

> Integration with existing process is as important but presents different challenges purely because the process will be operational. You could embark on a programme of reviewing all processes for risk. However, I would guard against this approach on the basis of 'if it ain't broke don't fix it'. Wait until there is a problem within a process that suggests changes are needed; this is the time to introduce risk assessment and this will ensure the greatest value is delivered. If benefit is provided then staff will understand the value of risk intervention .... Attacking everything at once is not a practical solution. Organizations need a way of deciding where to integrate and when. Using a properly prioritized risk register to focus on the biggest issues is the most effective way of targeting effort. This way the organization will achieve the fastest payback and the greatest commitment and will have in its grasp a route map to the managed risk culture.[26]

There are many ways of categorizing risks across an organization and each executive team will have their own way of defining different types of risk. The British risk standard acknowledges that each organization will have its own classification influenced by regulatory provisions and provides the following categories that are in general usage:

- strategic risk
- programme risk
- project risk
- financial risk and
- operational risk.[27]

## 3.10   The Internal Audit Role in Risk Management

This chapter has so far provided a brief introduction to risk management – the growing trend towards recognizing risk as a key driver for all the systems that underpin a successful organization.

We now have to touch on the way internal audit fits into the risk equation. As a start the IIA Attribute Standard 1220.A3 states that internal auditors must have regard to key risks and that:

Internal auditors must be alert to the significant risks that might affect objectives, operations, or resources. However, assurance procedures alone, even when performed with due professional care, do not guarantee that all significant risks will be identified. The internal auditors should be alert to the significant risks that might affect objectives, operations, or resources. However, assurance procedures alone, even when performed with due professional care, do not guarantee that all significant risks will be identified.

Back in 1999, Gill Bolton issued a warning to internal auditors that they were in danger of fighting against effective risk management because they:

- Tend to recommend highly risk averse processes and procedures.
- Are not aware of the organisational preferences for risk taking (also known as risk appetite or risk tolerance). They are not alone in this as few organisations have properly defined risk taking preference.
- Make recommendations on a fairly ad hoc basis, often without considering the organisational impact of their recommendations.
- Fail to get sufficiently close to the strategic opportunities and challenges that their organisations are working on and working towards.
- Add an administrative burden at a time when speed and flexibility are critical.
- Do not become actively involved in major organisational change programmes.

… In conclusion I do not believe that internal auditors should aim to change their role to that of the risk manager. Rather, they should work together with all other risk management and monitoring functions in their organisation to help achieve aligned and streamlined total risk management.[28]

It is clear that the rapid drive towards risk management arose partly because of prescribing codes, partly fuelled by scandals across sectors and organizations and also because successful businesses understood and addressed their key risks. This movement towards embracing risk should in no way be hindered by the internal auditor. The IIA Handbook Series on *Implementing the Professional Practices Framework* (page 92) suggests that: 'The idea that risk must be both embraced and eliminated by the organization runs contrary to traditional internal auditing thought. In the past internal audit practitioners have often sought only to eliminate risk.' The definition of internal auditing makes it clear that we must be concerned with risk and risk management. Moreover, there are several IIA professional standards that drive home the importance of internal audit involvement in the organization's system for managing risk. Performance Standard 2120 makes it clear that: 'The internal audit activity must evaluate the effectiveness and contribute to the improvement of risk management processes.' The performance standard on risk management states that:

The internal audit activity must evaluate the effectiveness and contribute to the improvement of risk management processes.

***Interpretation:***   *Determining whether risk management processes are effective is a judgment resulting from the internal auditor's assessment that:*

- *Organizational objectives support and align with the organization's mission;*
- *Significant risks are identified and assessed;*

- *Appropriate risk responses are selected that align risks with the organization's risk appetite; and*
- *Relevant risk information is captured and communicated in a timely manner across the organization, enabling staff, management, and the board to carry out their responsibilities.*

*Risk management processes are monitored through ongoing management activities, separate evaluations, or both.*

**2120.A1** – The internal audit activity must evaluate risk exposures relating to the organization's governance, operations, and information systems regarding the:

- Reliability and integrity of financial and operational information;
- Effectiveness and efficiency of operations;
- Safeguarding of assets; and
- Compliance with laws, regulations, and contracts.

A ground-breaking Professional Briefing Note Thirteen issued by the IIA UK&Ireland (1998) addressed the internal audit's role in managing risk. Some of the key points made in the briefing note have been summarized below:

It is increasingly recognised, however, that internal audit needs to add value to the organisation by closely aligning itself with the major concerns of senior management and focusing on those issues that are critical to success. An internal auditor's responsibilities are similar to those of a consultant. They are responsible for the technical quality of the advice that they give. But it is management's decision whether, or not, to accept that advice in the light of its fuller understanding of the situation. Internal auditors' involvement in assessing risk or identifying controls includes:

- Facilitators enabling and guiding managers and staff through the process . . .
- Team members who are a part of broader based groups . . .
- Risk and control analyst providing manager with expert advice . . .
- Proving tools and techniques used by internal audit to analyse risks and controls.
- Becoming a centre of expertise for managing risk.

The problem of how the need for audit objectivity and independence can be squared with the demands of management for professional advice and assistance, as well as the necessity for internal audit to be perceived as value-adding is not, in itself, new.[29]

The need to balance independence and the assurance and consulting roles of internal audit is a growing feature of the new-look internal auditor. The value-add equation means we cannot ignore the need to help as well as review. Some argue that internal audit needs to reposition itself at the heart of the risk dimension and drive through the required changes. In a recent study funded by IIA Inc. titled 'Enterprise Risk Management (ERM): Trends and Emerging Practices', Tim Leech asks the profession to get to grips with ERM and has questioned whether internal audit departments will help or hinder the enterprise risk management movement:

We believe ERM will become an integral part of the management process for organisations of the 21st century. It will influence how organisations are structured, with some appointing a chief risk officer that reports to the CEO or board of directors. It will influence how strategic planning is done. And it will certainly influence how internal auditing is performed. This conclusion may come as a shock to many internal auditors who do not even know what the term ERM means, let alone play a significant role helping their clients implement ERM systems. Numerous other studies released over the last few years are unanimous – ERM is vastly superior to traditional 'silo based' approaches to risk and assurance management.... Traditionalists defend the status quo on the grounds that the silo approach to audit is necessary to maintain 'auditor independence'. As long as internal auditors think their job is to decide what constitutes 'adequate' control on a fraction of the risk universe, instead of reporting on the quality of the risk assessment processes and the reliability of management representations on risk status to the board, true audit independence will not exist. I encourage internal auditors to consider whether they are helping or hindering the adoption of ERM. What is becoming increasingly obvious is that internal audit practitioners that do not get behind the ERM movement may soon see it roll right over them. Make sure you are on the right side as the ERM movement gathers momentum.[30]

This viewpoint represents an important challenge for the internal auditor who has been asked to champion the risk movement while retaining the independent assurance role. Models are available to help in the key decisions underpinning the new look internal audit role. Practice Advisory 2120-1 on Assessing the Adequacy of Risk Management Processes gives an interpretation of Standard 2120 (The internal audit activity must evaluate the effectiveness and contribute to the improvement of risk management processes):

- Determining whether risk management processes are effective is a judgment resulting from internal auditor's assessment that:
- Organizational objectives support and align with the organization's mission.
- Significant risks are identified and assessed.
- Appropriate risk responses are selected that align risks with the organization's risk appetite.
- Relevant risk information is captured and communicated in a timely manner across the organization,
- Enabling staff, management, and the board to carry out their responsibilities.

Risk management processes are monitored through ongoing management activities, separate evaluations, or both.

Internal auditors must add value to an organization and IIA Performance Standards 2110 covers the nature of internal audit work:

The internal audit activity must evaluate and contribute to the improvement of governance, risk management, and control processes using a systematic and disciplined approach.

## 2110 – Governance

The internal audit activity must assess and make appropriate recommendations for improving the governance process in its accomplishment of the following objectives:

- Promoting appropriate ethics and values within the organization;
- Ensuring effective organizational performance management and accountability;
- Communicating risk and control information to appropriate areas of the organization; and
- Coordinating the activities of and communicating information among the board, external and internal auditors, and management.

**2110.A1 –** The internal audit activity must evaluate the design, implementation, and effectiveness of the organization's ethics-related objectives, programs, and activities.

**2110.A2 –** The internal audit activity must assess whether the information technology governance of the organization sustains and supports the organization's strategies and objectives.

**2110.C1 –** Consulting engagement objectives must be consistent with the overall values and goals of the organization.

## 3.11   New Developments

In terms of risk management, the Walker review (a review of corporate governance in UK banks and other financial industry entities, 16 July 2009) made several major observations on risk management that are relevant to all larger companies. One major recommendation was that the bank's board should establish a board risk committee separately from the audit committee with responsibility for oversight and advice to the board on the current risk exposures of the entity and future risk strategy. The board risk committee should, like the audit committee, be a committee of the board and should be chaired by an NED with a majority of nonexecutive members, but additionally with the finance director (FD) as a member or in attendance and with the CRO invariably present. This risk committee would advise the board on risk appetite and tolerance for future strategy, taking account of the board's overall degree of risk aversion, the current financial situation of the entity and – drawing on assessment by the audit committee – its capacity to manage and control risks within the agreed strategy.

The Walker recommendations may well have profound implications for internal audit as the chief risk officer assumes a much higher status in many companies and, alongside increased independence and a remit to report to a powerful risk committee, the CRO may end up with more status than the chief audit executive. The strains on risk management in banks and other financial institutions were obvious when the Credit Crunch traumatized the financial system in most developed economies. These strains were clearly described by KMPG when they addressed the question: 'Is risk management permanently broken?':

> In some ways, it is not surprising that organizations are struggling. The number and the complexity of the risks that investment funds have to manage today are vast and growing all the time. Against such a backdrop, many organizations' risk management systems have become overcomplicated, cumbersome, confused, inefficient, ineffective, and expensive. All too often, it is difficult for organizations to 'see the forest for the trees.' KPMG believes that a single, consistent risk framework, wherein all functions have a coherent, integrated view of both risk and return, is required to meet business needs and external requirements while adding value to the management process. In light of the current crisis, the question at the top of senior executives' minds is 'where do we start?' One central aim of any reassessment of risk management must therefore be to simplify the system so that the three essential elements of an effective risk regime – governance, reporting and data, and processes and systems – are in place.[31]

However, the United States Proxy Exchange provided their own strong views on proposals to penalize excessive risk taking – that much of what happened during the Credit Crunch can be put down to good old-fashioned abuse:

> In the midst of the most recent market crisis, Congress and other branches of our government didn't wait for hearings to embrace Wall Street's excuse that 'excessive risk' was to blame. We believe this shifting of blame from abuse, where the blame correctly belongs, to excessive risk, where it does not, is forestalling appropriate legislative and regulatory initiatives that might prevent future market panics. We believe the current administration's proposal to form a systemic-risk regulator is, regretfully, misguided. What our economy needs is a systemic-abuse regulator. Excessive risk taking is one form of abuse, and it may be motivated by perverse incentive compensation schemes, but it is not the only one:
>
> • Putting low-income families into mortgages they cannot afford is 'predatory lending.' It is a form of abuse unrelated to 'excessive risk taking.'

- Routinely falsifying those families' mortgage applications to ensure they are approved is 'fraud.' It too is a form of abuse unrelated to 'excessive risk taking.'
- Bundling those structured-to-fail mortgages into CDOs and giving them investment grade ratings is 'deception.' It too is a form of abuse unrelated to 'excessive risk taking.'
- Parking the toxic CDOs in affiliated hedge funds and providing those hedge funds inflated valuations to hide the losses is 'collusion.' It too is a form of abuse unrelated to 'excessive risk taking.'
- Foisting those hedge funds on unsuspecting institutional investors and charging them '2 and 20' for the privilege is 'manipulative sales practices.' It too is a form of abuse unrelated to 'excessive risk taking.'[32]

The search for more effective risk management is now the norm in all but the smallest of organizations. External assessment agencies are now seeking better ways of assessing entities as is clear from an account of the way Standard & Poor undertake corporate analysis:

GAMMA (Governance, Accountability, Management Metrics & Analysis) is Standard & Poor's new emerging markets equity product, designed for equity investors in emerging markets and specifically focusing on non-financial risk assessment. Good corporate governance creates shareholder value and reduces risks for investment. Independent opinions on corporate governance, management, and accountability practices of individual companies are particularly valuable in emerging markets.... Standard & Poor has developed criteria and methodology for assessing corporate governance since 1998 and has been actively assessing companies' corporate governance practices since 2000. In 2007, the methodology of stand-alone governance analysis underwent a major overhaul to strengthen the risk focus of the analysis based on the group's experience assigning governance scores. GAMMA analysis focuses on a number of risks that vary in probability and expected impact on shareholder value. Accordingly, our analysis seeks to determine the most vulnerable areas prompt to potential losses in value attributable to governance deficiencies. Recent developments in the international financial markets emphasize the relevance of enterprise risk management and the strategic process to governance quality. GAMMA methodology incorporates two new elements, addressing these areas of investor concern. It also promotes the culture of risk management and long-term strategic thinking among companies.[33]

The emergence of risk management as a powerful way of enhancing corporate performance means that we must start with strategic risk before we drill down into the various specific risks that face most management teams. One huge issue that is now emerging as an obstacle to effective risk management is the role of the audit committee and the fact that many organizations assign the majority of risk-related tasks to their audit committees, which can lead to a dangerous overload. The National Association of Corporate Directors (NACD) has warned of this heavy burden on audit committees:

The combination of risk oversight with other mandated responsibilities can be overwhelming. While risk events may ultimately find their way to the audit committee because of its responsibility for oversight of financial reporting, other committees as well as the full board should participate. Many risks (e.g., technological obsolescence, product quality, mergers/acquisitions, and sales practices) lie outside the audit committee and require other committees – if not the full board – to oversee. The full board may want to consider assigning oversight of risks to certain committees to help ensure adequate coverage. Currently, only one out of four boards uses the full board for their risk oversight, while an even slimmer 6 percent use a risk committee. Boards can benefit from weighing the pros and cons of these different oversight paradigms for their companies.

Whether directors use the full board or committees, they must devote greater attention to the primary duty of vigorously probing and testing management's assumptions. Risk oversight is a full board responsibility. However, certain elements can be best handled at the committee level with the governance committee coordinating those assignments. Similarly, the board must ask management: 'Who is the owner of each risk area?' Management should identify the personnel responsible to manage and mitigate specific risk areas. Assignment of senior level responsibility will improve the accountability and reliability of information coming from management.[34]

The National Association of Corporate Directors go on to call for improved risk identification procedures and mention the importance of internal auditors as a crucial function in this respect:

Management has the primary responsibility for the identification of risk. In a recent NACD member poll, a large majority (76.3 percent) of directors indicated that management provides directors with the information they need to effectively execute their risk governance role. However, those same directors said that two of the top challenges in providing risk oversight are: 1) management's capacity to define and explain the organization's risk management structure and process, and 2) the organization's capacity to identify and assess risks. Directors are increasingly concerned about risk oversight and will become more actively engaged in supporting the company's efforts to manage risk. Boards can prepare by selecting directors who have broad experience as well as industry expertise. Directors must then utilize their internal and external sources of information. Internal auditors can serve a crucial function because they are often on the front lines in identifying the likelihood of risk events and can raise these issues to the board level. Externally, outside sources of information, such as consultants or even D&O insurance agents, can provide new insight beyond what management supplies. Directors should also be aware that in some of the recent corporate meltdowns, the high-risk behaviors occurred in relatively small pockets of large companies. Therefore, understanding smaller high-risk operations is an important element. These changes in board behavior will likely improve the overall effectiveness of identifying risks for the company.[35]

The Walker Review highlighted the basic role of the board in governing the risk management process:

The focus in this Review is on how governance of risk by the boards of BOFIs can be made more effective alongside such enhanced regulation and supervision. In the past, some boards may have seen risk oversight as a compliance function essentially designed to meet regulatory capital requirements at minimum constraint on leveraged utilisation of the balance sheet. There has probably also been an element of 'disclosure fatigue', leading to some sense that a large part of the board's obligations in respect of risk in the entity can be discharged through full disclosures. Such attitudes should have no place in the proper governance of risk in future. In essence, the obligation of the board in respect of risk should be to ensure that risks are promptly identified and assessed; that risks are properly controlled; and that strategy is informed by and aligned with the board's risk appetite.[36]

Walker went on to describe the key principles underpinning a board risk committee report that he felt should be included in the annual report and accounts, as follows:

- **Strategic Focus** – the report should seek to put the firm's agreed strategy into a risk management context; this should include information on the inherent risks to which the strategy exposes the firm.

- **Forward Looking** – the report should provide information to the reader that indicates the impact of potential risks facing the business – it should be clear for example whether a firm would be materially exposed to a fall in property prices for example. If the firm carries out stress testing, the report should reveal high level information on this stress testing programme. This should include the nature of the stresses, the most significant stresses and how the significance has changed during the reporting period.
- **Risk Management Practices** – the report should provide a brief description of how risk is managed in the business, ideally using examples of material risks that arose in the previous reporting period. In particular this should focus on the role of the Committee in the management of that risk. In addition the report should provide a brief statement on the number of meetings in the reporting period, an attendance record and whether any votes were taken. The report should cover the key responsibilities of the board risk committee and whether these have changed in the reporting period. Finally the report should briefly record the key areas that the committee has considered in the reporting period.[37]

Another ongoing debate revolves around the distinction between conformance and performance. Therefore regulations that say each enterprise should have a sound risk management process exist to ensure there is a process and it is adhered to because the rules say so, or that they exist to ensure the enterprise can create and protect its core business. Deloitte make clear their position in this debate:

> At many organizations, risk governance and value creation are viewed as opposed or even as mutually exclusive, when in fact they are inseparable. Every decision, activity, and initiative that aims to create or protect value involves some degree of risk. Hence, effective risk governance calls for Risk Intelligent governance – an approach that seeks not to discourage appropriate risk-taking, but to embed appropriate risk management procedures into all of an enterprise's business pursuits.[38]

There is growing pressure on companies to say more about their risk management process in their published reports and indicate how they deal with their major risks. However, the disclosure of key corporate risks may be seen as giving away sensitive information to competitors and the auditors review of whether risk management is working or not can add to this dilemma, if it were publicized. There is so much that is happening in the business risk management field and the internal auditor needs to be totally involved in these developments to make sure the professional audit role is preserved and enhanced.

## Summary and Conclusions

Risk management is not really a management fad. It provides a platform for corporate governance by giving comfort to shareholders and other stakeholders that the risks to their investment (or public services) are understood by their representatives, the board and systematically addressed by the management. True risk management is about changing the culture of the organization to get people to embrace their responsibilities knowing that this tool will help them get around problems and drive the business forward in a considered manner. Let us go over a revised version of the risk model that we have developed throughout the chapter (see Figure 3.9).

We end up with only a few of the components of the risk model in Figure 3.9, but there is a new focus on the main factor and that is *risk-based decision making*. We will go through each item once again.

**FIGURE 3.9**   Risk management model (9).

## The Board

The term Enterprise Risk Management (ERM) is replaced by the board. ERM is a process that drives risk management but the new model suggests that it is the board that drives ERM and not a separate and removed process. In this way, the board becomes the risk management forum and the CEO becomes the chief risk officer as high-impact risks, if they spiral out of control, will damage the corporate reputation of the business. In fact, one view of the CRO is that it should stand for the Corporate Reputation Officer. One handy way of describing respective risk management roles comes from Deloitte who, in their first installment of the principles of risk intelligence, considered some of the practical steps that should be considered for incorporating the concept of risk intelligence into an organization:

> In sum, it needs to be a harmonious collaboration. Here's what the score looks like:

- The board sets the tone.
- The executive wields the baton.
- The business units play the music.
- Certain functions (HR, finance, IT, tax, legal) support the concert backstage.
- Other functions (internal audit, risk, and compliance) monitor the performance.[39]

## Threats and Opportunities

The twofold aspects of risk are retained in the model to ensure there is balance in the way ERM is applied. KPMG has something important to say on this:

> Focusing on opportunities can also lead to greater ERM program buy-in from risk owners by having ERM personnel operate as risk advisors, rather than risk compliance police. Standard processes can provide risk owners with an opportunity to think through risks, see market opportunities as the 'flip-side' of risk, and paint a more balanced picture for potential business strategies.[40]

The perception of threats and opportunities across the workplace is related to the type of risk appetite that is in place at the top. A survey by PricewaterhouseCoopers on what keep directors awake at night gives an insight into the way threats are perceived at the top:

| | |
|---|---|
| Unknown risks | **59%** |
| Ability of the CEO to manage through the current challenges | **25%** |
| Personal liability | **13%** |
| Unacceptable business practices coming to light | **12%** |
| Possibility of fraud | **9%** |
| Possibility of need to declare bankruptcy | **4%**[41] |

## Risk-Based Decision Making

We have already said that business risk management should never be just a process. What we can go on to say is that it should really be a culture change technique to encourage 'risk smart' behaviour that underpins 'risk smart' decision making. The old view of ERM is that it entails lots of:

- Paperwork.
- Workshops and meetings.
- Policy statements.
- Risk registers.
- Training days.
- Risk assessment tools.
- Quality checks by risk officers.
- Compliance checks by inspectors and regulators.
- Increased performance targets.

More importantly, it is a view that nothing can ever go wrong, or if it does each manager needs to make sure there is a risk register to cover their backs. A better approach is to view risk management as an attempt to ensure all employees understand the board's position on risk, understand the threats and opportunities that impact their aims and objectives and are fully equipped to handle their business responsibilities in a smart way. The aim is to allow the organization to respond to risk in an efficient manner that works and that can be integrated into the business strategy. In this way the business strategy may be driven by and informed by the internal and external risks that face the business.

## Risk Strategy

Risk strategy is important as it should underpin business strategy to describe the way risk-based decisions are captured and incorporated into the way plans are devised and actioned. As a refinement we could call this the Risk-Based Business Strategy, to reinforce the fact that it should be integrated into business strategy and business activity. The Securities and Exchange Commission has made it clear that the board's role in the risk management process should be disclosed, which means describing how the board has established and oversees their risk management process.

## SIC

The board needs to report to its shareholders and wider stakeholders on arrangements for ensuring everything is under control through a statement on internal control; this is dealt with in the next chapter. We will only note here that the statement on internal control along with details of governance arrangements and risk management ensures that the investment community can monitor current and prospective investments. There is one weakness in relying on control compliance routines such as those required for Sarbanes–Oxley, as noted by Ernst and Young:

> Due to the recent turmoil in the financial sector, it is easy to lose sight of the fact that risk management at many non-financial companies is not sufficiently effective either. All too often, and in all sectors of our economy, efforts in risk management are dispersed, isolated and unrelated to the wider company strategy. Many organizations would benefit greatly from a more comprehensive and integrated risk management approach that takes into account strategic, operational, financial and compliance risks. It is perfectly possible for a company to be fully SOX compliant but suffer from clearly inadequate risk management, with flaws that can prove fatal. In fact, more shareholder value has been destroyed as a result of strategic mismanagement and poor execution than in all the financial reporting scandals combined.[42]

Our new risk model is based on the argument that the risk cycle, risk registers and the risk policy should not represent part of a separate risk management process but should be assimilated into the way people make strategic, operational and day-to-day decisions in an organization. By weighing up the pros and cons, the strengths, weaknesses, opportunities and threats, people are able to think through the impact of risk for this type of activity – what is acceptable compared to what would be a step too far. The internal auditor has traditionally been asked to audit each of the components that together form the risk management process. This audit may result in the auditor being able to tick off most of the items that have been noted on the standard risk model and the board may be able to confirm that it has a risk management process in place. However, what is more important is the way executives, managers and work teams behave at work and this is more to do with the way *risk-based decision making* occurs. This means that the internal auditor may have to be concerned about reviewing behaviour and the way people in the organization are working together, as well as the set components of the risk management process. A case study of auditing risk management is documented in the Appendix.

# Endnotes

1. McNamee, David and Selim, Georges, IIA Research Foundation, 'Risk management: changing the internal auditor's paradigm'. *Internal Auditing*, December 1998, pp. 6–9.
2. Chapman, Christy, 'Raising the bar'. *Internal Auditor*, April 2001, p. 56.
3. Bernstein, Peter L. (1996) *Against the Gods*, New York: John Wiley & Sons, Inc., p. 8.
4. Bernstein, Peter L. (1996) *Against the Gods*, New York: John Wiley & Sons, Inc., p. 3.
5. *Daily Mail*, 2 Oct.ober 1996, 'Financial wizard's reward for risk-taking'.
6. *Daily Mail*, 10 December 1996, 'Explorer goes up the pole at Boots'.
7. *Daily Mail*, 1 October 1997, 'Trainee doctors "put lives at risk" ', p. 33.
8. Bernstein, Peter L. (1996) *Against the Gods*, New York: John Wiley & Sons, Inc., p. 20.
9. Shapiro, Eileen. C. (1996) *Fad Surfing in the Boardroom*, Capstone Publishing Ltd.
10. *Tone at the Top*, IIA, Issue 11, September 2001, 'Risk or opportunity – the choice is yours', para. 20.
11. BS 6079-3:2000 *Project Management Part 3 – Guide to the Management of Business Risk*.
12. *Daily Mail*, 12 September 1996, 'Pilot who found he hated heights – at 33,000ft', p. 3.
13. *Top Risks in the Private Sector* (1999) Deloitte & Touche Survey of Significant Risks.
14. *A New Approach for Managing Operational Risk Addressing the Issues Underlying the 2008 Global Financial Crisis*. Sponsored by Joint Risk Management Section Society of Actuaries Canadian Institute of Actuaries Casualty Actuarial Society, December 2009, Society of Actuaries

15. British Standards Institute, *Risk Management 21 21, Code of Practice*, BS 31100: 2008, pp. 20–21, BSi 2008, iCS 03.100.01.
16. Bernstein, Peter, L. (1996) *Against the Gods*, New York: John Wiley & Sons, Inc., p. 197.
17. Bernstein, Peter, L. (1996) *Against the Gods*, New York: John Wiley & Sons, Inc., p. 335.
18. *Daily Mail*, 7 December 2001, Sunderland, Ruth, p. 81.
19. *Mail on Sunday*, 30 May 1999, 'Night and Day, Most dangerous jobs', p. 18.
20. ICAEW Website, www.icaew.co.uk, Thursday 8 September 2002.
21. British Standards Institute, *Risk Management – Code of Practice*, BS 31100: 2008, p. 12, BSi 2008, iCS 03.100.01.
22. British Standards Institute, *Risk Management – Code of Practice*, BS 31100: 2008, pp. 7–8, BSi 2008, iCS 03.100.01.
23. Chapman, Christy, 'The big picture'. *Internal Auditor*, June 2001, pp. 30–37.
24. *AICPA Research Study 2 18 2010, Report on the Current State of Enterprise Risk Oversight*, 2nd edition, 2010.
25. Makosz, Paul, *Sentinel*, No. 1, January 1997, IIA and the IIA Control Self-Assessment Center.
26. Hill, Gordon, 'Embedding Turnbull, achieving a managed risk culture'. *Internal Auditing and Risk Management*, 1999, p. 30.
27. British Standards Institute, BS 31100:200, BSi 2008, iCS 03.100.01.
28. Bolton, Gill, 'Organisational risk management'. *Internal Auditing*, October 1999, p. 6.
29. Professional Briefing Note Thirteen, Managing Risk, IIA UK, *Internal Audit's Role In Managing Risk*, 1998.
30. 'Getting to grips with ERM'. *Internal Auditing and Business Risk*, August 2002, p. 11.
31. *Risk Management. Is It Permanently Broken? An Investment Management Perspective*, 2009, p. 3, KPMG LLP, a US Limited Liability Partnership.
32. Comments of the United States Proxy Exchange, September 2009, pp. 3–4, File S7-13-09, *Proxy Disclosure and Solicitation Enhancements*.
33. *Standard & Poor, a Division of The McGraw-Hill Companies, Inc.*, 2008, The McGraw-Hill Companies, p. 4.
34. White Papers: Series, *Risk Oversight/Transparency/Strategy/Executive Compensation*, 2009, National Association of Corporate Directors, pp. 8–10.
35. White Papers: Series, *Risk Oversight/Transparency/Strategy/Executive Compensation*, 2009, National Association of Corporate Directors, pp. 8–10
36. *The Walker Review*, 'A review of corporate governance in UK banks and other financial industry entities', para 6.3, 16 July 2009.
37. *The Walker Review*, 'A review of corporate governance in UK banks and other financial industry entities', annex 10, 16 July 2009.
38. *Risk Intelligent Governance, A Practical Guide for Boards*, Risk Intelligence Series, Issue 16, 2009, Deloitte Development LLC, Member of Deloitte Touche Tohmatsu, p. 2.
39. *First Installment in Deloitte's Series on the Fundamental Principles of Risk Intelligence*, 2009, Deloitte Development LLC.
40. *Placing a Value on Enterprise Risk Management*, KPMG Advisory, 2009, KPMG LLP.
41. 2009 Special Supplement, *What Directors Think*, 2009, TK Kerstetter, President and CEO, Corporate Board Member, Catherine L. Bromilow, Partner, Corporate Governance, PricewaterhouseCoopers LLP.
42. *A New Balanced Scorecard, Measuring Performance and Risk*, EYG AU0227, 2009, Ernst & Young.

# Chapter 4

# INTERNAL CONTROLS

## Introduction

We have referred to corporate governance and risk management; internal control forms the third component of this stool. Good governance is dependent on a management that understands the risks it faces and is able to keep control of the business. *Brink's Modern Internal Auditing* suggests that internal control is the most important and fundamental concept that an internal auditor must understand.[1]

Note that all references to IIA definitions, code of ethics, IIA attribute and performance standards, practice advisories and practice guides relate to the International Professional Practices Framework (IPPF) prepared by the Institute of Internal Auditors in 2009. This chapter covers the following areas:

We will build a model of control that is used to capture most of the key features of a sound system of internal control. Much is dependent on the control environment and there is a view that, if an organization can get this right, the rest will tend to follow. The trend towards risk management as the way forward for ensuring objectives are achieved does not mean that controls, as a fundamental aspect of risk management, are any less important. The control framework covers the risk management process and the use of tailored control mechanisms is a fundamental aspect of business life. We try to demonstrate why a good understanding of internal control is important in achieving sound corporate governance.

## 4.1   Why Controls?

The Committee of Sponsoring Organizations (COSO) of the Treadway Commission have suggested that (www.coso.org):

> Senior executives have long sought ways to better control the enterprises they run. Internal controls are put in place to keep the company on course toward profitability goals and achievement of its mission, and to minimize surprises along the way. They enable management to deal with rapidly changing economic and competitive environments, shifting customer demands and priorities, and restructuring for future growth. Internal controls promote efficiency, reduce risk of asset loss, and help ensure the reliability of financial statements and compliance with laws and regulations. Because internal control serves many important purposes, there are increasing calls for better internal control systems and report cards on them. Internal control is looked upon more and more as a solution to a variety of potential problems.

Where there are risks to the achievement of objectives, which mean failure is a strong possibility, controls have to be put in place to address these risks. If not, failure becomes likely. At the same time, controls cost money and they have to be worthwhile. A lot depends on the risk appetite and what is considered acceptable as opposed to unacceptable to the organization and its stakeholders.

Poor controls lead to losses, scandals and failures and damage the reputation of organizations in whatever sector they are from. Where risks are allowed to run wild and new ventures are undertaken without a means of controlling risk, there are likely to be problems. Internal control is nothing new and back in 1949 the AICPA argued that internal control comprises the plan of the organization and all the coordinate methods and measures adopted within a business to safeguard its assets, check the accuracy and reliability of its accounting data, promote operational efficiency and encourage adherence to prescribed managerial practices. Internal auditors throughout the ages have argued the cause for good controls and the regulators have appreciated the need for control. It has been said that there is no substitute for internal control. It is the responsibility of management, and the reason for the existence of internal auditors.[2]

The control banner is being waved by many authorities and regulators. For example, the US Stock Exchange Commission (SEC) regulations require organizations to devise and maintain a system of internal accounting control, while in the UK, the Turnbull report (see Chapter 2) suggests that:

> A company's system of internal control has a key role in the management of risks that are significant to the fulfilment of its business objectives. A sound system of internal control contributes to safeguarding the shareholders' investment and the company's assets (para. 10). Internal control . . . facilitates the effectiveness and efficiency of operations, helps ensure the reliability of internal and external reporting and assists compliance with laws and regulations (para. 11).

The UK's 2008 Combined Code makes clear the need for good controls:

> The board should maintain a sound system of internal control to safeguard shareholders' investment and the company's assets. The board should, at least annually, conduct a review of the effectiveness of the group's system of internal controls and should report to shareholders that they have done so. The review should cover all material controls, including financial, operational and compliance controls and risk management systems.[3]

The original King report (para. 3.2.1) from South Africa continues this drive to keep controls on the board room agenda and reasons that a comprehensive system of control should be established by the board to ensure that risks are mitigated and that the company's objectives are attained. The control environment should also set the tone of the company and cover ethical values, management's philosophy and the competence of employees. Control is everything that is in place to move successfully from the present to the future. The IIA take this wide view and state that control is:

Any action taken by management, the board, and other parties to manage risk and increase the likelihood that established objectives and goals will be achieved. Management plans, organizes, and directs the performance of sufficient actions to provide reasonable assurance that objectives and goals will be achieved.

We can build on the view that control is about achieving objectives, dealing with risk and keeping things in balance by introducing our basic first model of control in Figure 4.1.

**FIGURE 4.1** The control model (1).

An organization will set clear objectives and then assess the inherent risks to achieving these objectives. Before it can reach the black achievements box, there needs to be a control strategy to deal with the inherent risks and provide a reasonable expectation of getting there. The risk control strategy will be derived from a wider risk management strategy, but having, as a key component, focused and effective systems of internal control. Effective controls are measures that work and give a reasonable probability of ensuring that operations are successful and resources protected. Where these controls contain obvious loopholes, there is a chance that this will be exploited:

A woman bank executive was jailed for four-and-a-half years yesterday for stealing £ 1.75 million from her employers. Ms x, who earned £ 55,000 a year at the Dunbar Bank, took cash from the tills and walked out with it in her pockets. After her arrest, she told police: 'It was so simple and easy to do. It was easy to spend thousands of pounds during my lunch hour, which I did frequently.' . . . She also stole by making transfers to a third party and by writing cheques and falsifying the information on the stubs.[4]

The Institute of Internal Auditors is the professional body that has real expertise in the subject of organizational control. The IIA has described the control environment as:

The attitude and actions of the board and management regarding the significance of control within the organization. The control environment provides the discipline and structure for the achievement of the primary objectives of the system of internal control. The control environment includes the following elements:

- Integrity and ethical values.
- Management's philosophy and operating style.
- Organizational structure.
- Assignment of authority and responsibility.
- Human resource policies and practices.
- Competence of personnel.

The system of internal control needs to be adequate and we can turn again to the IIA for an understanding of what adequacy means. They suggest that adequacy is present if:

Management has planned and organized (designed) in a manner that provides reasonable assurance that the organization's risks have been managed effectively and that the organization's goals and objectives will be achieved efficiently and economically.

Control is not only about installing a range of procedures to ensure staff can get from A to B; it is also a process. Viewing internal control as a dynamic concept that runs across an organization as opposed to a series of basic procedures takes the topic to a higher level. Turnbull (see Chapter 2) provides some background as to what makes up a sound system of internal control:

An internal control system encompasses the policies, processes, tasks, behaviours and other aspects of a company that, taken together:

- facilitate its effective and efficient operation by enabling it to respond appropriately to significant business, operational, financial, compliance and other risks to achieving the company's objectives. This includes the safeguarding of assets from inappropriate use or from loss and fraud, and ensuring that liabilities are identified and managed;
- help ensure the quality of internal and external reporting. This requires the maintenance of proper records and processes that generate a flow of timely, relevant and reliable information from within and outside the organisation;
- help ensure compliance with applicable laws and regulations, and also with internal policies with respect to the conduct of business (para. 20).

## Management's Responsibilities

Turnbull has made clear where control responsibility lies in an organization:

The board of directors is responsible for the company's system of internal control. It should set appropriate policies on internal control and seek regular assurance that will enable it to satisfy itself that the system is functioning effectively. The board must further ensure that the system of internal control is effective in managing risks in the manner which it has approved (para. 16).

While the board sets overall direction, it is management who must implement good controls by considering the following:

**Determine the need for controls**  Managers must be able to isolate a situation where there is a need for specific internal controls where there is an unacceptable level of risk and respond appropriately. For example, when designing a new computer system, they must consider controls over both the development process and the resulting system at an early stage as part of their overall responsibility to promote the welfare of the organization. The determination of need precedes the design stage as there is little point in resourcing a control routine that is not really required. Another good example of this principle is where a previously in-house service is contracted out to an external provider. Here the contract specification along with suitable contract management procedures constitute key controls over the contract where it is monitored and compliance checked. Management must consider the need for additional controls over and above the contract compliance issue. This may include a review of the database for, say, a debtors system where accounts that are left out may simply be ignored and so not collected. Checks over the completeness of this database may be required to protect the organization where there would be no other way of knowing whether the database was being properly maintained. The decision on whether to install extra controls is obviously relevant here and this must be placed at the foot of management. A simple story demonstrates how the need for controls may not always be recognized:

> In the space of 92 minutes Stephen Humphries brought Sussex Futures to its knees. The rogue city trader ran up losses of £ 750,000 on the London International Financial Futures Exchange, effectively betting other people's money against a change in US interest rates.... Last week, a year later, he was imprisoned for three years and two months; Sussex Futures, having racked up debts of £ 2.3 m went into liquidation earlier this year. The story has 'Barings' stamped all over it, albeit not quite the same scale or the same length of time, but the principles are the same; one rogue trader, trying to conceal his position, failing to trade out of his unauthorised position, then fleeing the crime scene.[5]

**Design suitable controls** Once the need for controls has been defined, management must then establish suitable means to install them. This is not a simple process that relies solely on doing what was done in the past. It involves much more, including a formal process of assessing relative risks and seeking to guard against the types of problems that might arise if controls are not firmly in place. We have already outlined the criteria that should be considered when devising controls, and this and much more should be taken on board in the design process. Managers know their staff, work environment and type of culture they operate within better than anyone else, which makes them well placed for this task. Consultants, auditors, project teams and other sources of advice may be employed in the search for improved control, but, notwithstanding this, responsibility still lies with the managers themselves.

**Implement these controls** Managers are then duty bound to ensure that the control processes are carefully implemented. This entails at a minimum the provision of suitable guidance on how they should be used, ideally in written format, and a mechanism by which staff can be coached in the application of the underlying actions. We may care to move back a step and suggest that managers have to think about the basic skills necessary to effect these controls and whether they are employing the right calibre of staff in this respect. Remember it is the responsibility of management to deem that defined posts attract certain minimum qualifications and experience. If these are not asked for, then there is no point then blaming staff for poor performance. It is generally the managers' fault that their subordinates are not able to discharge the requirements of their post. Training and development are the other techniques that seek to support basic performance standards. This must be fully applied in the pursuit of success in line with the control arrangements that underpin this search.

**Check that they are being applied correctly** Management and not internal audit is responsible for ensuring that control mechanisms are not being bypassed but are fully applied as they were originally intended. One cannot wait for the auditors for information on how controls are working as this defeats this important principle. Management should seek to set control as a highly regarded discipline that deserves the respect of all staff and not an unnecessary set of rules that impair performance. All these things lead to an environment where control is fostered and publicized, again leading to the chance of greater compliance. It therefore becomes more and more difficult for managers to shrug their shoulders and declare that poor control is caused by junior staff and not them. Once we have arrived at this acceptance we have great scope for a well-controlled organization.

**Maintain and update the controls** This feature is also important in that securing control is a continuous task that should be at the forefront of management concerns. The need to define control implications must be revisited as we reinforce the view that management must acknowledge this issue in a vigorous way. This includes the need to discard outdated control wherever necessary so as to avoid the unmanageable situation where controls are perceived as patchy, with some being applied while others have fallen into disuse, and also to avoid excessive debate on the question of updating control.

**Include the above noted matters within any appraisal scheme that seeks to judge management's performance** We would expect management to consider the application of controls as part of management skills and training. Furthermore, if this were built firmly into employee performance appraisal mechanisms then managers would be in the enviable position whereby they receive suggestions from their staff on how to better effect good control over the resources under their command.

## Internal Audit's Role

The internal auditor has to be concerned about the state of control in the organization. The pace has been set by the IIA whose Performance Standard 2130 goes straight to the point: 'The internal audit activity must assist the organization in maintaining effective controls by evaluating their effectiveness and efficiency and by promoting continuous improvement.' The auditor's role regarding systems of internal control is distinguished from management's in that it covers:

- Assessing those areas that are most at risk in terms of the key control objectives that we have already mentioned (i.e. MIS, compliance, safeguarding assets and VFM).
- Defining and undertaking a programme for reviewing these high profile systems that attract the most risk.
- Reviewing each of these systems by examining and evaluating their associated systems of internal control to determine the extent to which the five key control objectives are being met.
- Advising management whether or not controls are operating adequately and effectively so as to promote the achievement of the system's/control objectives.
- Recommending any necessary improvements to strengthen controls where appropriate, while making clear the risks involved for failing to effect these recommended changes.
- Following up audit work so as to discover whether management has actioned agreed audit recommendations.

The IIA's Performance Standard 2130.A1 provides four key aspects of the scope of controls by indicating that the internal audit activity must evaluate the adequacy and effectiveness of controls in responding to risks within the organization's governance, operations and information systems regarding the:

- Reliability and integrity of financial and operational information;
- Effectiveness and efficiency of operations;
- Safeguarding of assets; and
- Compliance with laws, regulations, and contracts.

The IIA go on to make quite clear that the nature of internal audit's work means that even when internal audit is working on consulting engagements, there is still the need to consider whether controls are sound so that efforts from consulting engagements can inform assurance work:

**2130.C1** – During consulting engagements, internal auditors must address controls consistent with the engagement's objectives and be alert to significant control issues.

**2130.C2** – Internal auditors must incorporate knowledge of controls gained from consulting engagements into evaluation of the organization's control processes.

## Building the Control Model

One important feature of control relates to the need to contain activity within set limits or boundaries. We can amend our model to incorporate these limits in Figure 4.2.

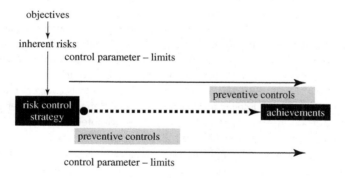

**FIGURE 4.2**   The control model (2).

Therefore activity moves an organization towards achieving its objectives, by keeping the activities within prescribed standards. The dotted black line moves dead straight to the achievement box and preventive controls are set to ensure that everything is contained within the upper and lower control parameters. Constraining, containing and restricting controls are applied at the boundaries to ensure that only the right people get in the organization, they only do the right things and they cannot access anything that falls outside their remit. Note that Section 4.6 provides more detail about different types of controls. The trend towards devolved organizations where each business unit is pretty well autonomous depends on a series of boundaries set at local levels throughout the organization. Each local unit has their own perception of how these boundaries should be set and how much leeway is given on either side of the limits. There is some move towards recentralizing some of the support services and so making corporate alignment much easier.

## Making Controls Work

Control may be seen as one of the single most important topics that the auditor needs to master. The main justification for the internal auditing function revolves around the need to review systems of internal control with all other audit activities being to an extent subsidiary to this task. A good understanding of the concept of control and how controls may be applied in practice is an important skill that takes many years to fully acquire. There are a number of issues that underlie the concept of controls:

- Controls are all means devised to promote the achievement of agreed objectives. This is an extremely broad interpretation of the control concept that in theory brings into play everything that management does in pursuing its objectives. We will return to this issue later.
- All controls have a corresponding cost and the idea is that the ensuing benefits should be worth the required outlay. Costs may be defined to include actual additional expenditure as in the case of a security officer employed to enhance controls over the safety of portable, moveable equipment held in offices. On the other hand, costs may simply relate to the increased efforts applied by management in seeking compliance with, for example, a new document signing procedure that makes it easier to find out who was involved in a certain transaction. The types of controls that spring to mind during a typical systems audit must be set within the cost context if the ensuing recommendations are to have any real use. Moreover, we must remember that these additional costs are borne by management and not the auditor.
- Controls belong to those who operate them and should not be viewed in isolation. In this respect management is responsible for the controls and the success of its operations will be linked to the degree to which controls work. There is a view that there are certain 'audit requirements' that have to be acted on when considering controls over operations. This term is in reality a fallacy since it implies that certain control criteria are not under management's responsibility but are in some way under the purview of internal audit. Thus, for example, audit may state that managers must install a mechanism that enables them to know the whereabouts of portable PCs at all times. To suggest that this is an audit requirement rather than a management procedure is to relieve management of this responsibility, and so distort the control orientation. The temptation to issue 'audit instructions' should be resisted as it will bring this inconsistency into play.
- Internal control is all about people since controls work well only if they are geared to the user's needs in terms of practicality and usefulness. What appears sound on paper may be very difficult to put into practice. One may recall the newly appointed auditor who asks the cashier to record all cheques posted out each day, only to be told that it would take a certain type of individual to be able to log thousands of items daily. Again a detailed user manual that explains how a computerized system may be operated is of little use where the staff using the system have no real IT competence. Likewise controls that involve an officer monitoring staff by observing their every movement may be very difficult to apply in practice. Where an auditor comes across staff who are not at all motivated then he/she may find a level of noncompliance that may be difficult to explain. The 'people factor' must be properly recognized. This comes to the fore when a change programme is being developed and new systems and procedures

are installed within a short time frame. The principle may be taken to the extreme where we might argue that if the right people are employed, then they will seek to develop their own controls as part of their everyday responsibilities. Unfortunately the converse would be true where inadequate staff are taken on.

- Overcontrol is as bad as undercontrol in that it results in an impression that someone, somewhere, is monitoring activity whereas this may not be the case in reality. Burdensome controls reduce the efficiency of operations and create an atmosphere of extreme bureaucracy where everything has to be signed for in triplicate. We have all read novels where the fictional police detective makes all the important arrests by refusing to 'do things by the book'. The other danger with overcontrol stems from a view that someone else will provide the necessary checks and balances. This appears where accounts fail to reconcile but because so many parties become involved in the balancing process, differences are left in suspense on the basis that they will be corrected somewhere along the line. Where front line managers do not take responsibility for controlling their areas of work, but rely on a whole army of control teams, we again have a recipe for disaster.

- Entropy is the tendency to decay and all control systems will underachieve where they are not reviewed and updated regularly. This is a quite straightforward concept that simply means that controls fall out of date as risks change and systems adapt to the latest environmental forces. Control routines fall into disuse over time while new developments call for a change in control orientation. Most organizations have devolved their support functions to the business unit level where what used to be corporate controls now fall under the remit of local business managers. The traditional control disciplines over, say, hiring and firing staff are no longer relevant in this new climate where local management has much devolved power. If the control orientation (say, better corporate standards) does not alter to reflect these types of developments then problems can ensue. Returning to the micro level, we can suggest that every time a form falls into disuse this represents a symptom of entropy at work. There is an argument for getting management to consult with internal audit on all material proposals for restructuring and new systems installations, so that these issues may be considered. An alternative would be to educate management in the various control techniques as part of an ongoing development programme. Here we would expect all feasibility studies to contain a section covering 'risk assessed implications' that addresses any shift in balance of control as a mandatory consideration.

- The organizational culture affects the type of control features that are in place, which may be bureaucratic or flexible in nature. There is no one right answer since each activity will have its own control policies.

One way of viewing the control system is to consider that each operation must be accompanied by a corresponding control system that is superimposed on the operation itself. In this way control should not be an alien concept that impinges on the activity being performed, but as a way of managing risks to the operation. A system's objectives should be dependent on the underlying control objectives with each working in harmony to ensure that activities are undertaken in a controlled fashion. We can argue that assets can be acquired so long as they are used for authorized purposes, reports prepared so long as they are accurate and useful, and operations managed so long as this is done in an efficient fashion. In this way control follows risk to the activity. The only way to make managers responsible for control is to incorporate the key concerns within their objectives. Therefore an objective to achieve something must also incorporate a requirement to do so, while having due regard to matters of regularity, efficiency, compliance with procedure and overall control.

## 4.2  Control Framework – COSO

The wide view of controls means that internal controls cover all aspects of an organization and there is a clear need for a way of pulling together control concepts to form an integrated whole, i.e. a control framework. The Committee of Sponsoring Organizations (COSO) of the Treadway Commission devised one such model that has international recognition as a useful standard. All larger organizations need a formal control framework as a basis for their systems of internal control and IIA Performance Standard 2120.A4 notes the importance of a set of organizational criteria that the auditor can use to review control systems (www.coso.org):

> Adequate criteria are needed to evaluate controls. Internal auditors should ascertain the extent to which management has established adequate criteria to determine whether objectives and goals have been accomplished. If adequate, internal auditors should use such criteria in their evaluation. If inadequate, internal auditors should work with management to develop appropriate evaluation criteria.

In the past the silo approach has been to consider whatever individual system we were auditing at the time. Systems were defined and audited, while the resultant report detailed the weak areas and how they could be improved. There is no possible way the aggregation of separate internal audit reports over a period could be used to comment on the overall state of controls in an organization. It is only by considering the adopted control model that the internal auditor is able to make board level declarations concerning internal control. In fact we can develop our control model to reflect the valuable platform provided by the control framework in Figure 4.3.

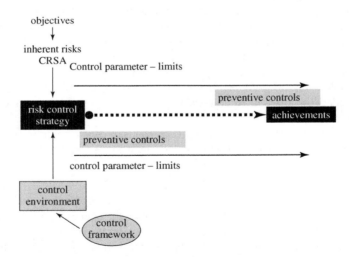

**FIGURE 4.3**   The control model (3).

The control framework needs to be in place to promote the right control environment. Some might argue that the control environment in turn inspires an organization to build a suitable framework, although we will see that our first framework, COSO, incorporates the control environment as a separate component. The framework drives the environment, which in turn enables an organization to develop its control strategy in response to the assessment of various risks to achieving objectives. Risk assessment and control design is fragmented when not attaching to a clear control framework and any audit effort not directed at the big picture will itself be less valuable. The next areas to cover are based around the COSO components and the entire model is shown in Figure 4.4 before we describe each part.

**FIGURE 4.4**   The COSO control model.

The COSO website (www.coso.org) gives the official background to their work:

In 1985 the National Commission of Fraudulent Financial Reporting, known as the Treadway Commission, was created through the joint sponsorship of the AIPCA, American Accounting Association, FEI, IIA and Institute of Management Accountants. Based on its recommendations a task force under the auspices of the Committee of Sponsoring Organisations conducted a review of internal control literature. The eventual outcome was the document *Internal Control – Integrated Framework* in 1992. COSO emphasised the responsibility of management for internal control.

The idea is to arrive at a commonly understood definition of internal control since, in the words of COSO: 'internal control means different things to different people'. Each component of the COSO model is dealt with next.

## Control Environment

Turning once again to the COSO website (www.coso.org), their summary of the control environment follows:

The control environment sets the tone of an organization, influencing the control consciousness of its people. It is the foundation for all other components of internal control, providing discipline and structure. Control environment factors include the integrity, ethical values and competence of the entity's people; management's philosophy and operating style; the way management assigns authority and responsibility, and organizes and develops its people; and the attention and direction provided by the board of directors.

The control environment is the main platform upon which the rest of the control framework is built. In fact, there is a strong argument that if we can get the control environment right then everyone at whatever level they sit in the organization will construct the rest of the COSO framework themselves.

## Risk Assessment

The COSO website (www.coso.org) provides a summary of where risk assessment fits into the control equation:

> Every entity faces a variety of risks from external and internal sources that must be assessed. A precondition to risk assessment is establishment of objectives, linked at different levels and internally consistent. Risk assessment is the identification and analysis of relevant risks to achievement of the objectives, forming a basis for determining how the risks should be managed. Because economic, industry, regulatory and operating conditions will continue to change, mechanisms are needed to identify and deal with the special risks associated with change.

The risk assessment stage arises naturally from the control environment where people want to get their control right by focusing on prioritized risks.

## Control Activities

The COSO website (www.coso.org) provides a summary of where this aspect fits into their model:

> Control activities are the policies and procedures that help ensure management directives are carried out. They help ensure that necessary actions are taken to address risks to achievement of the entity's objectives. Control activities occur throughout the organization, at all levels and in all functions. They include a range of activities as diverse as approvals, authorizations, verifications, reconciliations, reviews of operating performance, security of assets and segregation of duties.

The COSO model requires controls to be designed to counter unacceptable levels of risk that have been identified during the risk assessment stage. Note that a later section will cover detailed control mechanisms or activities as they are termed here.

## Information and Communication

The COSO website (www.coso.org) provides a summary of where this aspect fits into their model:

> Pertinent information must be identified, captured and communicated in a form and timeframe that enable people to carry out their responsibilities. Information systems produce reports, containing operational, financial and compliance-related information, that make it possible to run and control the business. They deal not only with internally generated data, but also information about external events, activities and conditions necessary to informed business decision-making and external reporting. Effective communication also must occur in a broader sense, flowing down, across and up the organization. All personnel must receive a clear message from top

management that control responsibilities must be taken seriously. They must understand their own role in the internal control system, as well as how individual activities relate to the work of others. They must have a means of communicating significant information upstream. There also needs to be effective communication with external parties, such as customers, suppliers, regulators and shareholders.

Information should be recorded and communicated to management and others within the organization who need it and in a form and within timeframes that enables them to carry out their internal control and other responsibilities.

## Monitoring

The COSO website (www.coso.org) provides a summary of where this aspect fits into their model:

> Internal control systems need to be monitored – a process that assesses the quality of the system's performance over time. This is accomplished through ongoing monitoring activities, separate evaluations or a combination of the two. Ongoing monitoring occurs in the course of operations. It includes regular management and supervisory activities, and other actions personnel take in performing their duties. The scope and frequency of separate evaluations will depend primarily on an assessment of risks and the effectiveness of ongoing monitoring procedures.

Internal control monitoring should assess the quality of performance over time and ensure that the findings of audits and other reviews are promptly resolved:

- Everyone should have a clear responsibility for monitoring their work and the work of others as a natural consequence of the way work is organized.
- Staff should assess risks to achieving their objectives and monitor the way controls act to mitigate these risks.
- There should be clearly defined roles for staff with supervisory responsibilities, with examples of the types of checks that should be made, ongoing support that should be given to front line staff and care taken to ensure compliance with procedure.
- The use of inspections and random checks should be applied to high-risk areas and there should be regular contact between head office and local units. Management by walking around is highly recommended.
- Management should seek to secure independent evidence that controls are working as prescribed in a fair and positive manner. Staff should be told that these checks will be made and cooperate fully. Problem areas should be given greater attention.
- Formal lines of communication to address concerns that need to be accelerated upwards, including a whistleblowing line for unresolved problems and control weaknesses.
- Random checks made on use of information systems to isolate unauthorized activity as well as routine monitoring of computer interactions to check consistency with organizational policies.
- Regular communication with the board to help them discharge their role to oversee the system of internal control.
- Formal monitoring role located at board level, which may be resourced through a defined compliance officer, charged with ensuring standards are adhered to and people know what is required to meet regulatory and legal obligations. Compliance may have an educational role but must also have enough teeth to act in case of serious breaches and negligence.

- Formal reporting lines for support activities such as human resources to ensure poor practices in business units can be isolated and remedied.
- Constant scanning to determine whether aspects of supervision and review can be discarded or reduced without any adverse effects.
- Professional and dynamic internal audit process that seeks to support self-assessment and review among managers and their teams.
- Formal review mechanisms built into project management to ensure progress is considered and quality issues resolved.
- Careful consideration of complaints from customers and others to assess implications for the functioning of internal controls.
- Robust use of exception reporting where variances in budgeting systems, performance measures, quality targets and planning systems to highlight problems and ensure action-oriented solutions are devised.
- Formal system of assurance reporting where internal control statements are signed by senior management based on their monitoring activities over internal controls.
- All new systems designed with suitable controls and mechanisms to allow monitoring and authorizations for material transactions.
- Efficient process for addressing gaps in controls and failures that have been identified by stakeholders (e.g. customers, suppliers, etc.), employees or auditors and consultants.
- Careful consideration of different sources of information so that discrepancies can be followed up and addressed.
- Good use of reconciliations of records for physical resources such as stores, cash, equipment and speedy follow-up of discrepancies.
- Dynamic audit committee with a role in ensuring that monitoring systems work well and high-risk problems are made known to senior management. The audit committee will also want to see that the control framework is working well.
- Awareness training for managers and supervisors on the techniques available to monitor and inspect routines and the need to install competencies in all staff relating to this aspect of control.
- Performance evaluation systems that involve monitoring of KPIs and whether they are likely to be achieved.
- Integration of monitoring arrangements with initiatives to empower people to take decisions and drive the business forward. All new initiatives should have an associated process for monitoring use or resources, success criteria and whether policies and procedures are being followed.

The COSO model is quite dynamic in that it covers most aspects of structures and processes that need to be in place to provide control. It is difficult to know how a board can state that it has reviewed its systems of internal control without reference to a comprehensive model or criteria for evaluating these controls at a corporate level. COSO simply asks five key questions:

1. Do we have the right foundations to control our business? (control environment)
2. Do we understand all those risks that stop us from being in control of the business? (risk assessment)
3. Have we implemented suitable control activities to address the risks to our business? (control activities)
4. Are we able to monitor the way the business is being controlled? (monitoring)
5. Is the control message driven down through the organization and associated problems and ideas communicated upwards and across the business? (communication and information)

If we can assess the quality of the responses to these five questions, we are on the way to achieving control and being able to demonstrate to all parties that their business concerns are in safe hands, even though no absolute guarantees are possible.

## 4.3   Control Framework – CoCo

The COSO framework is a powerful tool in that it allows an organization to focus on key structures, values and processes that together form this concept of internal control, far outside the narrow financial focus that used to be the case. The individual is part of the process but it can be hard to get a corporate solution down to grassroots. The criteria of control (CoCo) is a further control framework that can mean more to teams and individuals and includes an interesting learning dynamic. CoCo was developed by the Canadian Institute of Chartered Accountants (CICA) and is now an international standard. The CICA website (www.cica.ca) gives an account of their understanding of control as a platform for the criteria that was developed:

> Control needs to be understood in a broad context. Control comprises those elements of an organization (including its resources, systems, processes, culture, structure and tasks) that, taken together, support people in the achievement of the organization's objectives. The effectiveness of control cannot be judged solely on the degree to which each criterion, taken separately, is met. The criteria are interrelated, as are the control elements in an organization. Control elements cannot be designed or evaluated in isolation from each other. Control is as much a function of people's ethical values and beliefs as it is of standards and compliance mechanisms. Control should cover the identification and mitigation of risks. These risks include not only known risks related to the achievement of a specific objective but also two more fundamental risks to the viability and success of the organization:
>
> 1. failure to maintain the organization's capacity to identify and exploit opportunities;
> 2. failure to maintain the organization's capacity to respond and adapt to unexpected risks and opportunities, and make decisions on the basis of the telltale indications in the absence of definitive information.
>
> *The board of directors should assess the effectiveness of control – CoCo principles of assessment:*
>
> - The assessment focuses on significant objectives of the organization and the management of risks related to such objectives.
> - The assessment is from the perspective of the organization as a whole.
> - The assessment is the responsibility of the chief executive officer.
> - The assessment uses a thorough and trustworthy process that incorporates the perspective of people from throughout the organization.
> - The assessment is based on the CICA criteria of control framework.
> - The assessment is conducted by people with the appropriate skills, knowledge, qualities and perspectives.
> - The assessment includes reporting the results of the assessment to the board of directors.
> - The assessment process is reviewed to learn how the assessment might have been improved.

The principles may be organized according to the four groupings of the CICA criteria of control framework as illustrated in Figure 4.5. The main components are explained below.

**Purpose** The model starts with the need for a clear direction and sense of purpose. This includes objectives, mission, vision and strategy; risks and opportunities; policies; planning; and performance targets and indicators. It is essential to have a clear driver for the control criteria and, since controls

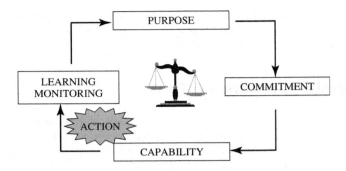

**FIGURE 4.5**   The CoCo control model.

are about achieving objectives, it is right that people work to the corporate purpose. Much work can be done here in setting objectives and getting people to have a stake in the future direction of the organization. To make any sense at all, the crucial link between controls and performance targets is established here as controls must fit in with the way an organization measures and manages performance.

**Commitment** The people within the organization must understand and align themselves with the organization's identity and values. This includes ethical values, integrity, human resource policies, authority, responsibility and accountability, and mutual trust. Many control systems fail to recognize the need to get people committed to the control ethos as a natural part of the way an organization works. Where people spend their time trying to 'beat the system', there is normally a lack of commitment to the control criteria. The hardest part in getting good control is getting people to feel part of the arrangements.

**Capability** People must be equipped with the resources and competence to understand and discharge the requirements of the control model. This includes knowledge, skills and tools, communication processes, information, coordination and control activities. Where there is a clear objective, and everyone is ready to participate in designing and installing good controls, there is still a need to develop some expertise in this aspect of organizational life. Capability is about resourcing the control effort by ensuring staff have the right skills, experience and attitudes not only to perform well but also to be able to assess risks and ensure controls make it easier to deal with these risks. Capability can be assisted by training and awareness seminars, either at induction or as part of continuing improvement programmes.

**Action** This stage entails performing the activity that is being controlled. Before employees act, they will have a clear purpose, a commitment to meet their targets and the ability to deal with problems and opportunities. Any action that comes after these prerequisites has more chance of leading to a successful outcome.

**Monitoring and learning** People must buy into and be part of the organization's evolution. This includes monitoring internal and external environments, monitoring performance, challenging assumptions, reassessing information needs and information systems, follow-up procedures and assessing the effectiveness of control. Monitoring is a hard control in that it fits in with inspection, checking, supervising and examining. Challenging assumptions is an important soft control in that it means people can develop and excel. Each activity is seen as part of a learning process that lifts an organization to a higher dimension. Some organizations employ people who have tried and failed to start their own high-risk venture, on the basis that they have had invaluable experiences that, if they have learnt lessons from, will make them stronger and much more resilient in growing a new business. Organizations that are based around blame cultures will not encourage positive learning experiences and will interpret controls as mechanisms for punishing people whose performance slips. The CoCo criteria encourages a positive response to feedback on activities.

This emphasis on 'soft controls' as well as more traditional ones is an important aspect of CoCo.

## 4.4   Other Control Models

COSO and CoCo are well-known control frameworks and they provide most of what is needed for an organization to consider when developing its own framework. There are, however, other sources of information to assist this task of getting control understood, addressed and reported.

### Control Objectives for Information and Related Technology (CobiT)

This control standard, known as CobiT, covers security and control for information technology (IT) systems in support of business processes and is designed for management, users and auditors. Several definitions are applied to this standard including:

- **Control**   The policies, procedures, practices and organizational structures designed to provide reasonable assurance that business objectives will be achieved and that undesirable events will be prevented or detected and corrected.
- **IT control objective**   Statement of the desired results of purpose to be achieved by implementing control procedures in a particular IT activity.
- **IT governance**   A structure of relationships and processes to direct and control the enterprise in order to achieve the enterprise's goals by adding value while balancing risk versus returns over IT and its processes.

The standard argues that there are certain critical success factors to reflect the critical importance of IT systems. The success factors cover the following areas:

- IT governance activities are integrated into the enterprise governance process and leadership behaviours.
- IT governance focuses on the enterprise goals, strategic initiatives, the use of technology to enhance the business and on the availability of sufficient resources and capabilities to keep up with business demands.
- IT governance activities are defined with a clear purpose, documented and implemented, based on enterprise needs and with unambiguous accountabilities.
- Management practices are implemented to increase efficient and optimal use of resources and increase the effectiveness of IT processes.
- Organizational practices are established to enable: sound oversight; a control environment/culture; risk assessment as standard practice; degree of adherence to established standards; monitoring and follow-up of control deficiencies and risks.
- Control practices are defined to avoid breakdowns in internal control and oversight.
- There is integration and smooth interoperability of the more complex IT processes such as problem, change and configuration management.
- An audit committee is established to appoint and oversee an independent auditor, focusing on IT when driving audit plans, and review the results of audits and third-party review.

CobiT has four main components (domains) and for these domains there are a further 34 high-level control processes:

- Planning and organization
- Acquisition and implementation
- Delivery and support
- Monitoring.

## Basle Committee on Banking Supervision

This committee reflects the work on internal controls for banking organizations developed by the Basle Committee on Banking Supervision, which is a committee of banking supervisory authorities established by the central bank governors of the group of 12 countries in 1975. It consists of senior representatives of bank supervisory authorities and central banks from Belgium, Canada, France, Germany, Italy, Japan, Luxembourg, the Netherlands, Sweden, Switzerland, the United Kingdom and the United States. It usually meets at the Bank for International Settlements in Basle, where its permanent secretariat is located. The Basle Committee view a system of effective internal controls as a critical component of bank management and a foundation for the safe and sound operation of banking organizations. While the Committee has adopted COSO in that it assesses internal control under the five main headings of the COSO model, it is nonetheless an important source of advice on control, particularly for the banking and financial services sectors. The committee describes the five COSO areas as:

1. Management oversight and the control culture
2. Risk recognition and assessment
3. Control activities and segregation of duties
4. Information and communication
5. Monitoring activities and correcting deficiencies.

They argue that internal control is a *process* effected by the board of directors, senior management and all levels of personnel. It is not solely a procedure or policy that is performed at a certain point in time, but rather it is continually operating at all levels within the bank. The board of directors and senior management are responsible for establishing the appropriate culture to facilitate an effective internal control process and for monitoring its effectiveness on an ongoing basis; however, each individual within an organization must participate in the process. They also note several common causes of control breakdowns in banks that suggest a failing of internal controls including:

- Lack of adequate management oversight and accountability, and failure to develop a strong control culture within the bank.
- Inadequate recognition and assessment of the risk of certain banking activities.
- Whether on- or off-balance sheet.
- The absence or failure of key control structures and activities, such as segregation of duties, approvals, verifications, reconciliations, and reviews of operating performance.
- Inadequate communication of information between levels of management within the bank, especially in the upward communication of problems.
- Inadequate or ineffective audit programs and monitoring activities.

Each organization must decide what to do about its system of internal control. There are several options:

1. Do nothing. On the basis that individual controls are in place and working and that this is good enough to satisfy stakeholders.
2. Document the existing control arrangements and develop them further to reflect an agreed corporate internal control framework.
3. Invent a model. Each organization may develop a unique perception of its controls and have this as its corporate internal control framework.
4. Adopt an existing published framework. Here the organization will simply state that it has adopted COSO, or CoCo or some version that the regulators promote.
5. Adapt an existing framework to suit the context and nuances of the organization in question. An international control framework may then be used as a benchmark to develop a tailored framework that fits the organization in question.
6. Selectively use all the available published material as criteria to develop a control framework that suits. This is similar to option 5 above but draws from all available sources of published guidance.

Whatever the chosen solution, each organization should publish a policy on internal control, and in developing the policy it will become clear that decisions have to be made along the lines suggested by options 1 to 6.

## 4.5   Links to Risk Management

We may expand our control model to include two more features. The first is CRSA, where inherent risks are considered and assessed in a workshop setting to ensure any controls that need updating are firmly related to the risks that have been debated. The second addition is the corporate governance arrangements involving the role and responsibilities of the main board and audit committee. Control models that fail to link their mission to the governance structures will flounder. In fact, it is the governance arrangements that drive the risk assessments, which in turn drives the adopted processes and controls put in place. In this way the model assumes some depth and links the control effort back to the main board in Figure 4.6.

As suggested by the Basle Committee, there are many things that can go wrong where suitable controls are not firmly in place. Where accountabilities are wrongly located, and excessive power is not held in check by balancing and checking forces, and where security is ignored and there is pressure to take convenient short cuts to accounting for income and expenditure, then there are likely to be problems. Moreover, where controls do not work, or they can be overridden at a whim, then what looks good on paper may be useless in practice. Where the focus is on getting business done whatever the fallout and whoever gets hurt, there will always be the type of scandals that were discussed in Chapter 2.

The equation is quite simple. Controls are needed if they guard against an unacceptable risk to the business or if they are part of a legal or regulatory compliance regime. In fact, these later controls guard against the risk of failing to comply with the regime. Controls that do not pass these two tests may well be discarded, since they in turn cause a risk to the business by increasing costs and/or slowing down the organization.

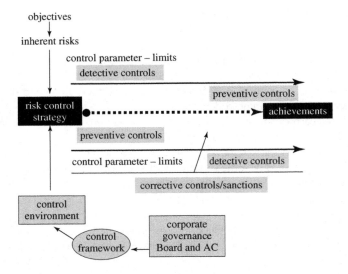

**FIGURE 4.6**   The control model (4).

## 4.6  Control Mechanisms

Control mechanisms are all those arrangements and procedures in place to ensure the business objectives may be met. They consist of individual mechanisms used by people and processes throughout the organization and they should exhibit certain defined attributes:

1. They should be clearly defined and understood by all users.
2. Mechanisms should be established to monitor the extent to which control is being applied in practice.
3. Their use should be agreed by management and the staff who operate them.

### Types of Controls

Principal controls may be categorized in a number of different ways. One way is to view them as being classified as follows:

- Administrative
- Informational
- Managerial
- Procedural
- Physical.

Another way is to break them down into:

1. **Directive**   To ensure that there is a clear direction and drive towards achieving the stated objectives. These are positive arrangements to motivate people and give them a clear sense of direction (and the ability) to make good progress. In terms of emergency fire procedures, directive controls may consist of staff awareness training where the importance of guarding against fire, in line with a formal policy, should direct staff to mitigate the effects of this risk.

2. **Preventive**   To ensure that systems work in the first place. These may include employing competent staff, high moral standards, segregation of duties and generally establishing a good control environment. Physical and access controls such as lock, passwords and security personnel are all designed to stop people breaching the system. Banning unauthorized electrical appliances is designed to prevent fire in the first place.

3. **Detective**   These controls are designed to pick up transaction errors that have not been prevented. They cover controls such as supervisory review, internal checks, variance reporting, spot checks and reconciliations. Fire alarms are detective controls in that they will be activated in the event of a fire or release of smoke.

4. **Corrective**   The final category of controls ensures that where problems are identified they are properly dealt with. These include management action, correction and follow-up procedures. Fire appliances and fire extinguishers are designed to deal with an emergency if and when it arises and, as best as possible, correct the situation.

A combination of the above types of controls is essential to address the four key questions:

1. How do we get the right culture and drive to ensure these risks are appreciated and anticipated?
2. How do we install specific measures to prevent the risks that we now understand?
3. How can we find out if, despite our best efforts, things are still going wrong?
4. How can we plan in advance to address problems that we detect, particularly when they represent a significant risk to our business?

Many feel that a heavy dependence on detective and corrective controls may suggest an imbalance where upfront direction and prevention have not been adequately resourced.

## General Controls Mechanisms

Controls need to work well. There is one view that they should be smart, in that they should be:

- Specific
- Measurable
- Achievable
- Results oriented
- Timely.

Some of the more traditional control mechanisms that may be applied in practice include:

**Authorization**   The act of authorizing something brings with it the process of granting permission on behalf of the organization. This is normally associated with a signature from the authorizing officer that records this decision. There is a move to drive empowerment down the organization and so the relative risk of problems such as fraud and error should be weighed against the disadvantages in passing too many items to senior management and bogging down the organization with excessive bureaucracy. In this environment excessive authorization routines will result in more rubber stamping, or blank forms signed or signing on behalf of someone else.

**Physical access restrictions**   Physical access measures should be applied to information through, say, passwords, access restrictions to desktop computers and an overall policy covering buildings security. It is based on two principles. The first principle is the 'need to know/have' policy that provides information or assets only where this is necessary for the performance of one's work. The second principle is based on the view that there is little point in leaving cash on a desk and so testing the resolve of people to resist temptation. Access restrictions only work where there is careful consideration given to the control of keys/passwords and access rights. CCTV, alarms, links with local police stations and a full-blown security policy and resource are now standard in many organizations. Where different states of alert can be defined depending on the circumstances, then there can be grades of security assigned to each level. September 11 has meant a complete rethink of security arrangements, international alerts, response plans and contingency arrangements in the event of a terrorist attack. A robust response is now expected as the norm, because the risk has been seen to be real and not just perceived.

**Supervision**   This control tends to have a dual nature whereby staff are observed at first hand by their line managers, while at the same time these supervisors are available to help and assist their subordinates. Supervision will not really work unless these two features are firmly in place. When reviewing the success of supervision it is not enough simply to have line managers located with their staff but we must also consider what is achieved through the relationship. Where a supervisor ignores blatant breaches of procedure (say, abuse of the telephones) then this impairs control.

**Compliance checks**   We have already discussed compliance as a fundamental component of the control systems and the way it is part of the process of doing things properly. Here we consider compliance in the context of special steps taken to check on whether authorized procedures are being applied as prescribed. This is a support control that seeks independent confirmation that staff are performing in the way that was originally intended. Control teams with a remit to carry out regular compliance checks are one way of doing this. Remember that compliance checks cannot be part of a quality assurance programme unless there is an in-built way of tracing identified problems back to their underlying cause and so correcting them. Straightforward compliance checks simply provide a device for making sure procedures are used. A mechanism should be in place whereby the organization is made aware of new legislation or regulations, such as changes to employment laws, and that it can respond by changing its systems and ensuring compliance. It may be necessary to appoint a legal officer or an employment lawyer, or health and safety specialist.

**Procedures manuals**   As a high-level control, the organization should set corporate standards that cover at least the following areas:

- Financial regulations covering income, expenditure, cash, banking, general accounting, contracts and related matters.
- Staff handbook covering recruitment, training and development, performance, discipline and so on.
- Purchasing code of practice on goods and services acquired by the organization.
- Code of personal conduct with guidance on gifts and hospitality.
- Computer standards on the use of computer systems and security procedures.

**Recruitment and staff development practices**   We have indicated that most controls are based around what people do and the people factor cannot be ignored. The successful operation of basic controls presupposes that the staff involved are competent, motivated, honest and alert so that they are both able and willing to perform. While much of this is dependent on good management practices based around communication and team building, the foundation is derived from using the right people in the first place. This in turn is wholly dependent on sound recruitment practices.

**Segregation of duties**   This control brings into play more than one individual during any one transaction, which can lead to an actual gain or benefit. The idea is to stop one person from undertaking a transaction from start to finish. There are obvious examples, such as a payments systems where the preparation, authorization, processing and dispatching of the cheque should each be done by different people. The idea is not only to act as a check on each other's work but also to help prevent fraud. An internal check is a related procedure whereby the work of one person is checked by another so as to minimize fraud and error. As such, reliance is not placed solely on the work of one person in recognition of the human frailty that allows mistakes to occur.

**Organization**   The way an organization is structured can promote or impair good control. Clear reporting lines that establish links between accountability, responsibility and authorization is a good starting place. Sensible location of specialist staff and general managers so that the functional and line management structures complement each other rather than compete for resources is a prerequisite to good control. Some organizations appoint an internal control officer to ensure all aspects of risk mitigation and control are addressed. There is also legislation such as the New York Government Accountability and Internal Control Act 1987 – updated in 1999 (www.osc.state.ny.us) – which details the need to establish and maintain guidelines for internal control policies, awareness and reviews for agency managers.

**Sequential numbering of documents and controlled stationery**   Valuable documents such as orders, cheque requisitions and cheques themselves have an in-built control in terms of the sequential numbers. All controlled stationery should meet this criterion. The ability to check and report on these sequences creates a useful control technique where missing, duplicated or inconsistent items may be readily isolated. Transactions sequencing can be applied to many situations where we wish to monitor what is going through a system and/or what documents are being used.

**Reconciliations**   The act of balancing one system with another does in itself engender control. As a principle this should be applied to all systems that have an association in terms of data from one relating to data from another.

**Project and procurement management**   Most organizations have established ongoing change programmes to push ahead or simply keep up with the competition and heightened expectations from stakeholders. Where these programmes are supported by efficient projects based on project management principles, they have more chance of being successful. Procurement and contracting are other related areas that should be subject to the best practice standards developed by the relevant professional bodies.

**Financial systems controls**   Most of the well-known specific controls over basic payments, income, sales, purchasing, inventory and other financial-based systems should be firmly in place. This is in spite of the move towards more devolvement of financial management to business unit managers and less head office central control. Risk tolerance for key financial systems that can be abused and defrauded should be set quite high and the corresponding controls geared into ensuring that we only process the right transactions in the right manner and are able to account for them in accordance with accounting standards and procedures. There are many well-known specific controls such as access controls, specialist finance staff, financial regulations, segregation of duties, reconciliations, exception reports, coding to budget heads, ratio analysis, retention rules on documentation, financial controller checks, external audit and so on that help protect the financial systems and transactions.

*IT security* All organizations use information systems and these will tend to be automated with internal networks and links to the Internet. The risks from unauthorized access, unauthorized use of data, systems crashes and poor information and reports can cause an organization to fail altogether. An IT security policy and contingency plan should be in place and be assigned to a designated officer with links up to board level. There are numerous specific controls such as off-site documents, data encryption, automated dial back, passwords, security personnel, CCTV and data profiling that are available to tackle computer abuse. In terms of information systems CobiT provides a useful way of analyzing the types of controls that may be applied:

- Application controls. These relate to the transactions and standing data appertaining to each computer-based application system and are therefore specific to each such application.
- Control risk. This is the risk that an error that could occur in an audit area, and could be material, individually or in combination with other errors, will not be prevented or detected and corrected on a timely basis by the internal control system.
- Detailed IS controls. These are controls over the acquisition, implementation, delivery and support of IS systems and services. They are made up of application controls plus those general controls not included in pervasive controls.
- General controls. These are controls other than application controls, which relate to the environment within which computer-based applications are developed, maintained and operated, and which therefore are applicable to all the applications.
- Internal control. The policies, procedures and organizational structures, designed to provide reasonable assurance that business objectives will be achieved and that undesired events will be prevented or detected and corrected.
- Pervasive information systems controls. Those controls that are designed to manage and monitor the IS environment and therefore affect all IS-related activities.

*Performance management* Another key control that should be firmly in place is related to a process whereby outputs and overall performance are examined by line management. This may involve reviewing reconciliations, working papers, reports, physical products, achievements (e.g. a new contract agreed with the client) and assessment of key performance indicators (KPIs) and so on. The point being made is that some form of check is made on what staff produce. If the task of setting performance standards and measuring the extent to which KPIs are properly resourced is checked there will be a much better chance of operational success. Some argue that the entire control concept is based on comparing actuals with a set standard (set to ensure objectives are achieved) and that the organization can be sure of doing the right things at the right time, and cost. All important information systems are geared into this process and reports help direct attention towards problems that interfere with the drive to attain these set standards. The performance system should be integrated with the risk management systems and target factors critical to business success.

## The Suitability of Controls

In terms of assessing the suitability of systems of internal control, there are some danger signs that should be looked for that might lower the efficiency of the control environment as follows:

*Ability of senior management to override accepted control* Many quite acceptable procedures constitute good control over staff activities so long as they are being applied. Furthermore, compliance checks may help isolate staff who do not use prescribed procedures and action taken to remedy this. Informal groups with decision-making powers are also able to form a pressure group that may be able to overrule control routines. Formal control procedures that are written up and applied by all staff lead to good control. However, where there are matters that fall outside the norm, vague contingency arrangements may be in place that are in practice unwritten and in part simply made up. Where this happens, controls may break down and it may be very difficult to discover who made what decisions. The problem arises where managers are able to suspend controls at will, so as to expedite a required activity. The difficulty arises where staff feel unable to challenge senior managers who are bypassing a standard control. Where controls can be suspended for emergencies this must be agreed and written into the procedure, and ideally subject to special checks when the emergency is over.

**Lack of staff and vacant posts**  Control relating to authorization, internal check, segregation and supervision can suffer where there are insufficient staff to enact the agreed procedure. For example, a procedure for enveloping cheques that requires two people being present is very hard to apply where there simply are not enough staff. There needs to be a level of flexibility in designing controls so that unusual circumstances, where staff are not available, may be catered for. To compensate for this, it is essential that a management trail is present that allows one to ascertain who initiated a transaction for later review and consideration. Moreover, management must assume responsibility for failing to fill vacant posts or not arranging suitable cover, thus allowing controls to be impaired. They cannot simply ignore this issue or blame it on budget restrictions.

**Poor control culture**  The types of controls mentioned above depend on managers and staff doing things properly. It normally takes longer and can be more cumbersome to perform these control arrangements, which in turn takes a level of all-round discipline from staff. The aggregation of these views on discipline from all levels in the organization constitutes what we may call the 'control environment' or alternatively the 'control culture'.

**Staff collusion**  Many controls depend on two or more staff members' involvement as a form of a check over each other's activities. The idea is that while one person could be corrupt, this would be a rare occurrence, which is catered for by not allowing an individual sole authority over one routine. This unfortunately does not take on board research that suggests many people are only as honest as controls require them to be. Therefore, where dishonest staff conspire to defeat controls they can do a great deal of damage. When reviewing transactions, the fact that there are two signatures attached to a document does not mean that it is necessarily correct and proper. In practice, there are some systems that can be wholly bypassed through well-planned collusion by key personnel.

**Reliance on a single performance indicator**  We have agreed that controls are in place to ensure that management is able to achieve its objectives. Where these objectives are centred on performance indicators then we would expect the associated controls to recognize this factor. The problem arises where management is given one basic indicator to work to, which is regularly reported. The temptation to base one's activities around one key factor can lead to many distortions that do not necessarily promote organizational objectives. A bottom-line ratio can have unforeseen side-effects that make many controls redundant as they do not contribute to the requisite figure.

**Reliance on memory**  There are some controls that are dependent on knowledge held only in the minds of employees. This may relate to identity and/or signature of authorizing officers, procedures used for dealing with various activities, levels of delegated authority, key contacts, roles of respective officers and so on. While on the one hand this gives well-deserved responsibility to long-serving employees, and as a result places them in a special position, it can also have many disadvantages. One is a lack of clarity as to precisely what actions the organization has authorized.

**Retrospective transaction recording** There are many managers who feel that documentation that records and/or authorizes a transaction is a matter of pure bureaucracy, which interferes with the day-to-day running of their work area. There are times when orders are placed over the phone with the associated paperwork compiled many weeks later. There are records that are written up as and when there is time available, where in many cases the relevant detail is based mainly on memory.

**Uncontrolled delegation of tasks** The idea of controls is linked to various management principles that include accountability and responsibility. Having someone in charge of an operation and responsible for the end result is the best way of ensuring that there is a driving force that directs resources towards the defined goals of the organization. This principle is fundamental to the business world as experience shows that consensus rules through various committees blurs the decision-making process and leads to excessive bureaucracy. Responsibility does not mean that tasks cannot be delegated to various levels under a manager's command and again this is generally good practice. The danger lies in excessive delegation that has not been controlled in any sense.

## Soft Controls

These are best described by Jim Roth, who wrote about the importance of understanding soft controls:

> If we think our job is to evaluate compliance with policies and procedures, it leaves us nowhere. However, that's not what our organizations need. As managements move into empowerment modes, they need help with the transition. Most of all, they need us to be an independent, objective observer who will give them the kind of realistic, honest, substantial feedback that most people in the organization won't provide. So our job, I think, increasingly is going to involve evaluating these soft, intangible areas . . . . In addition, all the major developments I see in internal auditing somehow relate to soft controls . . . . So what do internal auditors do, other than create the audit routines? We do what helps management control an organization that is much looser, freer, and potentially more chaotic . . . . To effectively evaluate the soft side of controls, auditors must demonstrate different mindsets than those of the traditional auditors. This visioning process is the right way to go about changing the auditor's mindset. Mostly, it helps the whole department focus on the specific things that need to be done. I've learned that when it comes to the softer sides of control, there is no 'one size fits all' solution. Everything has to be tailored.[6]

From our discussion so far, it should be clear that there is no such thing as an audit control. There are only management controls. In this context we should restate that management should establish business objectives and for each business objective there will be underlying control objectives to ensure that the information is adequate, compliance occurs, assets are protected and value for money is promoted. Sufficient control mechanisms should be designed, installed and reviewed to ensure that these control objectives are achieved. These controls should form a system to cover control at a corporate, managerial and operational level.

## 4.7   Importance of Procedures

The previous section on control mechanisms outlined the different types of controls that are available when designing a suitable system of controls. We can now refine our control model to incorporate the additional features that have been described, as shown in Figure 4.7.

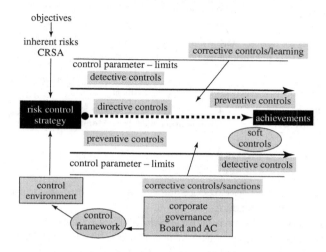

**FIGURE 4.7**   The control model (5).

The preventive controls were already on our model and they revolve around the upper and lower control parameters, above and below the achievements line. We then set additional levels outside the two parameters and locate detective controls outside the control parameters. These detective controls will pick up transactions and activity that fall outside the acceptable limits (parameters) or appear likely to go outside these limits. The detective controls will tend to be information-based and will ring alarms when management intervention is needed to deal with activity that either has gone or appears to be going haywire. Corrective controls, as we have already discussed, are measures designed to put right any deviations that have been detected and hence the arrowed lines start at the corrective control and then go back inside the control parameters. The final addition is soft controls that focus on the hearts and minds of people to encourage them to take responsibility for their controls and to take action where appropriate. There is a complicated view of control and a more simple version. The complicated view is based around our control model and recognizes the wide variety and range of controls that can be applied to getting the job done. The simple view is that most risks to operations can be mitigated through better procedures – ways of doing the job. Hence the importance of good procedures is a major arm of the risk management strategy. We can base our discussion of procedures around an amended version of a model (in Figure 4.8) first used in the book *Internal Control: A Manager's Journey.*[7]

Once the operational risk assessment has identified the need for tighter procedures, the task is then set to make and issue an improved version for staff. By going through the nine-stage model, there is a better change to get procedures correct, understood and accepted in the operation in question. Taking each stage of the model in turn:

1. **Development**   This involves reviewing the underlying processes, simplifying them and working with users and then drafting an agreed document that reflects the required activities.

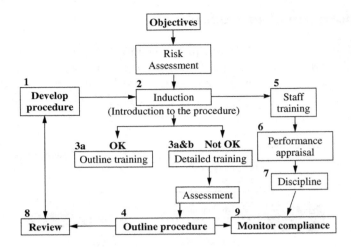

**FIGURE 4.8**    The procedures model.

2. **Induction**    It is important to introduce the procedure to new starters and show existing staff a new or improved procedure.
3. **The training manual**    This may be broken down into two levels. Where staff are assessed as able to apply procedures, an outline manual ('a') can be provided. Where this is not the case, a more comprehensive package ('a&b') with exercises can be given to them to work through.
4. **Outline**    After the training or induction period, it is possible to turn to a shortcut outline document with key tasks and processes summarized for use thereafter.
5. **Training**    The skills of staff affect the degree to which procedures are successful. The training on procedures is mainly about knowledge and, to supplement this, we should also seek to develop the underlying skills and the appropriate attitudes as a parallel training initiative.
6. **Appraisal**    Link the way staff are using procedures in their performance appraisal framework. In this way, it is seen to have some meaning for the work people do and their individual development programmes.
7. **Discipline**    This is a fall-back position, where if all else fails staff may need to be disciplined for breach of procedure.
8. **The review process**    This should be straightforward in that it entails keeping the procedure relevant, vibrant and up to date.
9. **Compliance**    This stage deals with compliance and it is the line manager's responsibility to ensure that staff comply with procedure. This is best done by getting staff to understand how they can monitor themselves, and supporting them in this task.

There is a lot to the simple view of better control, which is based on better procedures. Because procedures are so important to the business it is worthwhile resourcing efforts to get them focused on known risks and integrated into the way people work.

## 4.8    Integrating Controls

The control model comes back into the frame with a few additional features covering performance, communications, and policy, competence and training, as shown in Figure 4.9.

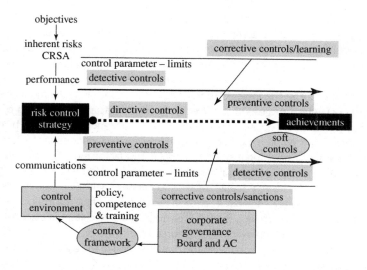

**FIGURE 4.9**   The control model (6).

Each of these is now explained:

**Performance**   The process of assessing risk must fit and be integrated with the performance management system. Dealing with risk properly is part of good management and should therefore be a task that is measured along with other obligations for managers and teams throughout the organization. Any other way of viewing risk activities is rather pointless. Therefore the control strategy that is applied to dealing with known and anticipated risks to our current and future plans is in turn aligned to the performance system that is in place for all operational areas and support services. This is the start to integrating controls into the work ethos.

**Communications**   The control model is improved by the addition of good communications in the organization. This factor fits between the control environment and the adopted control strategy, but is also important through all aspects of the model. Communication is the main way of achieving assent from all the players in the operation and is a key consideration when devising control solutions. Poorly controlled organizations are normally held back by poor communications.

**Policy, competence and training**   The crucial pivot for the control model is the policy on internal control. This sets standards, roles and key messages on what internal control means and what mechanisms are available to help promote good control and so turn aspirations into achievements. The control policy may be located in the risk policy as a component within the overall risk assessment and management regime. The next item to note is the links to competence, i.e. that employees should have an understanding of internal controls and the ability to recognize and apply suitable techniques and mechanisms to address unacceptable risks. Having the right staff competencies (i.e. knowledge, skills and attitudes) is a useful start to getting proficient internal controls in place. After this, training and development are required to ensure the set competencies are obtained and applied to the workplace. Induction training and refresher courses and ongoing advanced seminars can all be used to bring home the message that everyone is responsible for ensuring control and that suitable internal controls need to be in place to discharge fiduciary obligations to the organization's stakeholders.

One further point is to reconsider the corrective controls that have appeared in the control model. The upper version has an add-on (learning), which suggests that people need to learn from their experiences where controls have failed, or they do not respond to changes in risk profiles or there have been near-misses that suggest a problem. This ongoing learning and improvement is based on the assumption that most problems experienced by an organization can be traced to a failing in control of sorts. The lower version of corrective controls in the model has a different add-on (sanctions), which suggests that corrective controls that address a failing of directive or preventive controls may be the result of a breach of procedure and/or negligence by one or more employees. Here an organization must be firm and determine whether control failure is a learning opportunity or the result of outright staff misconduct. This factor must be built into the control model to deal with those rare circumstances where people have failed to live up to the standards expected from them with no reasonable excuse. Sanctions may include warning, demotion and transfers, as well as ultimately dismissal. If sanctions are used as a first resort and are the norm in dealing with avoidable control failure, there is likely to be a blame culture in place and the control model will be seen by most employees as an enforced constraint that creates stress, tension and unfair practices. This is the opposite to what the model is seeking to achieve. If, on the other hand, the control model acts as a corporate interpretation of the means to manage risk and ensure the business is successful, it reverts to the positive footing for control that it is intended to be.

## 4.9  The Fallacy of Perfection

There is a great deal of material around on internal control. Any Internet search on 'internal controls' will bring up hundreds if not thousands of individual devices (control mechanisms) that relate to many of the key business systems like procurement, income, transport, stores and so on. The searcher may take the view that anything and everything can be controlled with the right set of measures and this position leads us to the fallacy of perfection. The more measures put in place to achieve objectives, the better the chances of success. Or to put it another way, the greater the uncertainty of achieving objectives, the more measures are needed to reduce this uncertainty. However, the measures will normally cost money and time and will tend to involve doing more work, to get to the end result. In business, time, additional work and cost are all factors that run counter to success, in that most organizations try to generate business quickly, cheaply and with the least effort. Therefore control measures may appear to run counter to business success but, at the same time, many of these control measures are needed to give the organization its best chance of achieving success. To sum up, it may be suggested that:

- Controls tend to cost money and slow an organization down.
- Controls are needed to help manage risks to an organization's business.
- Controls cannot guarantee success.
- Control is effected through people and dependent on the way they behave and relate to each other.
- Even the best-managed organization can fail.

The fallacy is that controls will ensure success and it is just a question of how many measures are needed and how they should be best implemented. While internal control can help an entity achieve its objectives, it is not a panacea. Turning to the UK, Turnbull has reinforced this point:

A sound system of internal control reduces, but cannot eliminate, the possibility of poor judgement in decision-making; human error; control processes being deliberately circumvented by employees and others; management overriding controls; and the occurrence of unforeseeable circumstances (para. 23). A sound system of internal control therefore provides reasonable, but not absolute, assurance that a company will not be hindered in achieving its business objectives, or in the orderly and legitimate conduct of its business, by circumstances which may reasonably be foreseen. A system of internal control cannot, however, provide protection with certainty against a company failing to meet its business objectives or all material errors, losses, fraud, or breaches of laws or regulations (para. 24).

This is a fundamental point that runs across the whole concept of risk management. The extent to which controls should guard against risks depends on the risk appetite of the organization and its managers. In some parts of an organization (say, marketing and communications), risk seeking is rewarded, while in others (say, finance and production) it is frowned on. In some parts of an organization people are encouraged to go ahead and try out new approaches to their business while in others the adage 'just repeat what we did last year' rules and basic routine is the norm. Moreover, where there is ownership of the controls by the work teams, then there is more chance of a positive environment that helps drive the organization forward, while overcontrol tends to slow an organization down. Sawyer has issued a warning about the effects of overcontrol:

One fear that followed passage of the U.S. Foreign Corrupt Practices Act of 1977 was the possibility of excessive, redundant, useless, and/or inordinately expensive controls. When a difficulty arises, the tendency sometimes is to throw money at it and hope that it will subside. But too much control can be as bad as too little. Expensive, restrictive controls can stifle performance and initiative. Protection is bought at the price of repression.[8]

## 4.10   The Complete Control Model

If everyone had a clear understanding of internal controls and they were motivated to establish good controls in line with risk-assessed operations and functions within an organization, then controls are more likely to work. Staff awareness training is one way of getting the message across the organization, and is often missed out of the CRSA exercises that are now becoming popular. We can refer to the final version of our control model and use this as the basis for awareness seminars. The final version appears in Figure 4.10.

The additional items to complete the model are described:

**Audit of inherent risk** Superimposed on the control model is the role of internal audit and external audit. External audit will want to see that the underlying financial systems and accounting policies applied do not lead to any material misstatement of the financial accounts. They will also want to see that there is no fraud or noncompliance that has a material impact on the accounts. Their audit tests will provide a reasonable expectation that these types of inherent risks are not present and much hinges on the definition of material and the reliance placed on published financial statements by various users. Internal audit will want to help management deal with inherent risk in a professional manner by providing advice and consulting input to management's efforts to deal with business risk.

**Audit of residual risk** Internal audit will also be concerned that the risks that remain after controls have been applied are fully understood and acceptable. The focus on residual risk needs an audit approach that drills down in the way controls are working in practice and considers evidence that either supports or challenges this view. This mainly revolves around the internal

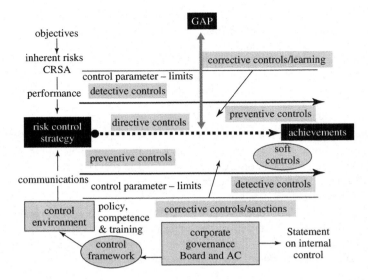

**FIGURE 4.10**    The control model (7).

audit's assurance role. Since residual risk is that which remains after controls are put in place, the scale of this risk depends on the success of the control regime, which may not always be what it appears, as one article demonstrates:

> Desperate health chiefs 'hid' seriously ill patients waiting for admission to hospital to try to distort a survey of the NHS, it was claimed yesterday. Senior nurses were 'pressured' into clearing out accident and emergency departments just hours before a spot-check across England and Wales. In one instance, a ward was re-opened at the last minute. At another hospital, patients waiting in casualty were distributed around the building and 'placed in beds irrespective of needs'.[9]

**Statement of internal control**  One important constituent of the control model is the feed into the published statement on internal control. Turnbull makes it clear that the board should report on its internal controls:

> The board should define the process to be adopted for its review of the effectiveness of internal control. This should encompass both the scope and frequency of the reports it receives and reviews during the year, and also the process for its annual assessment, such that it will be provided with sound, appropriately documented, support for its statement on internal control in the company's annual report and accounts (para. 29).

**Gap**  The final part of the control model consists of a single 'gap' that breaks through the upper and lower control parameters. This gap may be defined as 'an extra capacity to allow for growth and the potential to reach outside the norm, challenge existing assumptions and search for new corporate inspiration'. This is important so that control frameworks don't just contain activities but also allow for some experimentation and innovation, that break the rules but still sit within the constitution. An enterprise may give someone a budget and tell them to go away for a month and come back with new ideas, in any way they deem appropriate. This person may be allowed to break the normal project management rules, so long as they stay within the spirit of the overall value system.

This gap may be crucial to survival. There are many who see the business of the future revolving around the Internet, where instead of selling to customers, the tables are turned and the customer simply sets out what they need (a personal specification) and sends this proposal to their favourite suppliers and waits to see which one provides the best, cheapest and quickest response. Flexibility and responsiveness become the bywords for future business success and controls that stop this from happening will have to be discarded; i.e. there has to be a gap in control constraints that allows such versatility. Now that the control model is complete the components can be turned into staff control awareness seminars.

## 4.11   New Developments

In most developed countries, the system of internal control has to be reviewed in listed companies as part of regulatory provisions. Moreover, public sector agencies tend to have a similar requirement to design and review suitable controls. Regulatory codes can get quite complex, but a simple way of viewing the controls oversight concept is set out below:

- The board set the policy on internal control on behalf of their shareholders and oversee the results, with help from their audit committee.
- Management implements this policy to ensure the business is properly controlled. In fact, the new perspective is that management itself will want to ensure controls work and that staff can give them assurances that controls are in place and adhered to.
- Various compliance, risk, financial control and internal performance and assurance teams will each contribute to the pool of knowledge on the state of controls and where they need to be improved. These teams may be brought together in one governance, risk and compliance function.
- Internal audit review controls and provide independent assurances to the management and the audit committee. Under their consulting arm, the internal auditor may well help improve risk management processes and specific controls.
- External audit assess key controls over the financial reporting system to reduce the amount of testing they need to carry out to form an opinion on the accounts. As well as carrying out testing routines, external audit are starting to form opinions on the adequacy of financial controls as part of the overall system of internal control.
- The board report on arrangements to ensure sound controls, which depends on an effective risk management process.
- The shareholders will need to satisfy themselves that the above arrangements work, and one way is to consider the views of the audit committee and risk management committee.

### Sarbanes–Oxley (SOX)

We discussed the catastrophic company failures of Enron and WorldCom in Chapter 2 and, following these corporate scandals, the US introduced the Sarbanes–Oxley Act in 2002 to tighten up company regulation. Moreover, the external auditors had to move away from self-regulation with the creation of the Public Company Accounting Oversight Board (PCAOB) to oversee their activities. One huge implication was the use of SOX internal control certification over financial reporting systems. SOX led to amended SEC annual filing requirements, which meant that a registrant's annual report had to include a report on internal control over financial reporting, which has to contain the following:

- Statement of management's responsibility for establishing and maintaining adequate internal control over financial reporting.
- Statement identifying the framework used by management to evaluate the effectiveness of internal control over financial reporting.
- Management's assessment of the effectiveness of the registrant's internal control over financial reporting.
- A statement that the registered public accounting firm on management's assessment of the registrant's internal control over financial reporting.

The assessment by management of its internal controls had to be done in conjunction with a suitable internal control framework that is free from bias and allows qualitative and quantitative measurements of internal control to be made in a consistent manner. The 1992 COSO *Internal Control–Integrated Framework*, the Canadian CoCo framework and the UK Turnbull guidance were all deemed adequate in meeting the SEC requirements.

In the UK, the Financial Reporting Council explained the current controls disclosure requirements and the effect of the 2006 Companies Act:

> Section C.2 of the Combined Code states that companies should maintain a sound system of internal control, the effectiveness of which should be reviewed at least annually with the review being reported on in the annual report. Further guidance on this subject, including recommendations on disclosure, is set out in the Turnbull Guidance, which was last revised in 2005.

> Listed companies are also required under the Companies Act 2006 to include in the Business Review a description of the principal risks and uncertainties facing the company, and under the FSA's Disclosure and Transparency Rules to describe the main features of the internal control system as it relates to financial reporting. In addition, IFRS 7 requires companies to set out in their audited accounts how they manage financial risks and a summary of the information that key operating decision makers use to manage those risks. All of these disclosures are monitored by the Financial Reporting Review Panel (FRRP), which is part of the FRC.[10]

One new development occurred in 2008, when COSO released a document, *Guidance on Monitoring Internal Control Systems*, to help organizations monitor the quality of their internal control systems. Eddie Best has provided an outline of the COSO guidance in providing broad direction to help:

- Identify and leverage good monitoring practices.
- Reduce redundancies.
- Recognise inefficiencies and weaknesses.
- Embed effective monitoring into everyday practices.

Here are the three steps:

1. **Establish a foundation:** Is monitoring currently a priority in your organisation? Set a tone from the top that conveys the importance of monitoring. Consider the roles of management and the board with respect to monitoring and the use of evaluators. Identify who oversees which areas of control and any potential impairment of objectivity. Ensure that your organisation has a baseline understanding of your internal control system's effectiveness.

2. **Design and execute:**   The crux of monitoring is designing and executing procedures that evaluate important controls over meaningful risks.

- **Prioritise risks:**   Understand and prioritise risks to organisational objectives
- **Identify controls:**   Identify key controls that address those prioritised risks
- **Identify information:**   Identify information that will persuasively indicate whether the internal control system is operating effectively
- **Implement monitoring:**   Develop and implement cost-effective procedures to evaluate that persuasive information. Choose the right information for the given circumstances

3. **Assess and report:**   The final step is assessing and reporting results. Prioritise deficiencies by significance and the likelihood a deficiency will result in an error, giving due consideration to the effectiveness of other compensating controls. By evaluating your internal control system in this way, deficiencies can be identified and addressed before they materially affect the organisation. Management, the board and internal auditors all play important roles in the monitoring process and should take a proactive approach in its implementation.

The ultimate efficacy of this guidance, as with many aspects of effective management, hinges on sound judgement. Integrating the objective examination of monitoring processes and preventative measures being exercised into organisational management will promote successful delivery of strategic objectives.[11]

## Summary and Conclusions

The internal control concept is crucial to business success. There are models and guidance and hundreds of specific control measures that can be used to develop and maintain a good system of internal control. There are reporting standards that ask the board to report on internal control and ensure that this is linked to a suitable system for assessing risk and formulating a wider risk management strategy. Controls tend to form a major component of the risk management, and there are some controls that are standard requirements – implicitly or explicitly. There has been some criticism of COSO's framework as, with the passing of time, some feel it is dated and does not reflect current practices and the complex risk landscape facing most larger entities. However, COSO have worked hard to establish a workable control framework and pose a strong argument that (www.coso.org):

> Internal control can help an entity achieve its performance and profitability targets, and prevent loss of resources. It can help ensure reliable financial reporting. And it can help ensure that the enterprise complies with laws and regulations, avoiding damage to its reputation and other consequences. In sum, it can help an entity get to where it wants to go, and avoid pitfalls and surprises along the way.

If there is a sound system of corporate governance in place and if this underpins a robust control environment then an organization may develop a control policy, perhaps as part of the risk policy. Where these considerations have been addressed then control awareness training may be carried out to turn ideas into practice. The internal auditor needs to be able to assess the organization in terms of these types of issues before any useful internal audit work can begin. The consulting role of internal audit argues that the auditor may help set up the necessary infrastructure (control framework) while the assurance role suggests that internal audit can go on to make sure the framework is owned by managers and that it makes sense and works well. It is difficult to talk about risk management without talking about internal control, as they are both necessary aspects of ensuring the business succeeds. For the private sector, control is really about survival. For public sector services, a wonderful summary of the importance of internal control is found in the guidance issued by the State of New York, Office of the State Comptroller, who explained that:

> Citizens demand and deserve cost effective government programs. They also expect to receive value for their tax dollars. Over the years, my auditors have been able to trace almost every major shortcoming they have identified in government programs, from lack of program accomplishment or results to wasteful or fraudulent activity, to a breakdown on some component of the systems of internal control. If government organizations are to be effective, we must establish and maintain a system of internal control to protect government resources against fraud, waste, mismanagement or misappropriation. Employees often underestimate the importance of internal controls, or think internal controls amount to merely separating duties. However, internal controls encompass a comprehensive system that is critical to helping an organization achieve its goals and mission. A good system of internal control can do this because it helps you manage risk and run your agency's programs and administrative activities effectively and efficiently.[12]

## Endnotes

1. Moeller, Robert and Witt, Herbert (1999) *Brink's Modern Internal Auditing*, 5th edition, New York: John Wiley & Sons, Inc.
2. Flesher, Dale (1996) *Internal Auditing: A One-Semester Course*, Florida: The Institute of Internal Auditors, p. 127.
3. *The Combined Code on Corporate Governance*, June 2008, Financial Reporting Council.
4. *Daily Mail*, 10 November 2001, 'Jail for woman banker who stole £ 1.75 million', p. 35.
5. Smith, Philip, 'Reining in the rogue traders'. *Accountancy Age*, 12 October 2000, p. 6.
6. Interview with Roth, Jim, 'A hard look at soft controls'. *Internal Auditor*, February 1998, pp. 31–33.
7. Pickett, K. H. Spencer and Pickett, Jennifer M. (2001) *Internal Control: A Manager's Journey*, New York: John Wiley & Sons, Inc.
8. Sawyer, Lawrence B. and Dittenhofer, Mortimer A. assisted by Scheiner, James H. (1996) *Sawyer's Internal Auditing*, 4th edition, Florida: The Institute of Internal Auditors.
9. Rawstome, Tom, *Daily Mail*, 3 February 2000, 'Cover-up in casualty', p. 41.
10. Financial Reporting Council, *Review of the Effectiveness of the Combined Code*, July 2009, Progress Report and Second Consultation.
11. Best, Eddie, 'Internal auditing'. *Internal Auditing & Business Risk*, IIA Magazine, October 2008, p. 35.
12. State of New York, Office of the State Comptroller, US, February 1999 (www.osc.state.ny.us).

# Chapter 5

# THE INTERNAL AUDIT ROLE

## Introduction

This chapter covers the role of internal auditing and describes what it takes to become a good auditor.

Note that all references to IIA definitions, code of ethics, IIA attribute and performance standards, practice advisories and practice guides relate to the International Professional Practices Framework (IPPF) prepared by the Institute of Internal Auditors in 2009. The areas covered are:

5.1  Defining Internal Audit
5.2  The Four Main Elements
5.3  The Audit Charter
5.4  Audit Services
5.5  Independence
5.6  Audit Ethics
5.7  Police Officer versus Consultant
5.8  Managing Expectations through Web Design
5.9  Audit Competencies
5.10  Training and Development
5.11  New Developments
     Summary and Conclusions

The challenges for the internal audit profession are found in the early chapters of the book, i.e. reviewing corporate governance, risk management and control. These developments set the context for the audit role and we need now to explore how such challenges may be met.

## 5.1   Defining Internal Audit

The starting place for internal audit theory is the definition of internal audit. A standard definition is made up of important issues that form the basic framework of internal audit principles. The divergence of interpretation of the audit role is explored since internal auditing may be performed in a variety of ways, each with its own approach and style. Accordingly, it is important that a formal definition is devised and agreed since it will have a vital impact on the perceived role of the audit function. Management often asks auditors exactly what they are responsible for, and a variety of responses may be received. Some auditors feel that they should police the organization while others are convinced they must check the accuracy of accounting records. Still others feel obliged to search out poor value for money or new and improved ways of using resources or focus on high-level reviews of the corporate risk management process. Much depends on the audit charter, the chief audit executive's (CAE) views and management expectations. One must have a model developed by the profession that represents the true scope of internal auditing. In

:nt is clearly responsible for controlling risks to ensure objectives are met,
Jit work is based on reviewing risk management and controls.

## ernal Auditors' (IIA) Definition

ιn independent, objective assurance and consulting activity designed to add
ιn organisation's operations. It helps an organisation accomplish its objectives
by bringing a systematic, disciplined approach to evaluate and improve the effectiveness of risk
management, control and governance processes.

Although brief, it contains the basic principles on which internal auditing is based. Meanwhile IIA
Performance Standard 2100 deals with the nature of internal audit's work and says that:

> The internal audit activity must evaluate and contribute to the improvement of governance, risk
> management, and control processes using a systematic and disciplined approach.

We can analyze the IIA's formal definition in detail by examining each of the material concepts:

**'Internal auditing'** The service is provided within the organization and is distinct from the
external audit role. The concept of internal audit is well known and is reflected in many regulatory
codes throughout the world. Note that some organizations use outside resources to provide the
internal audit service, in contrast to the more prevalent in-house teams.

**'Independent'** The concept of independence is fundamental. Internal auditing cannot survive if
it is not objective. All definitions of internal audit feature an element of independence, although
its extent, and how it is achieved, is a topic in its own right. The audit function must have sufficient
status and be able to stand back from the operation under review for it to be of use. If this is not
achieved, then this forms a fundamental flaw in the audit service and some internal audit functions
may not be able to subscribe to the standards.

**'Assurance and consulting'** This part of the definition refers to the fundamental shift in the
role of internal audit. The shift makes clear that the past tinkering with the advice and consulting
aspect of auditing is now a full-blown additional consultancy arm of the function. Internal audit
may provide advice and assistance to management in a way that best suits each manager's needs.
Even consulting work should take on board the impact of risks, and IIA Performance Standard
2120.C1 says that:

> During consulting engagements, internal auditors must address risk consistent with the engage-
> ment's objectives and be alert to the existence of other significant risks.

Meanwhile, the primary role of internal audit is to provide independent assurances that the
organization is, or is not, managing risk well. Internal audit can provide assurance on the extent to
which controls are able to address risks but cannot give any absolute guarantees.

**'Activity'** The fact that the internal audit function is an activity is important. This means it is a
defined service, although as we have already noted it may not necessarily be located within the
organization. However, it must be a defined activity with a team, a budget and led by a senior
figure – the CAE.

**'Designed to add value'** As a service, auditing has to form a client base and understand the needs of the organization. Here the service role should lead to a defined benefit to the organization rather than internal audit working for its own mysterious goals. Adding value should be uppermost in the minds of chief audit executives and this feature should drive the entire audit process.

**'And improve an organization's operations'** This brings into play the notion of continuous improvement. The auditors are really there to make things better and not to inspect and catch people out. In one sense, if the CAE cannot demonstrate how the auditors improve the business, there is less reason to resource the service.

**'It helps an organization accomplish its objectives'** The task of internal audit is set firmly around the organization's corporate objectives. Making an organization successful is the key driver for corporate governance (a badly governed organization will not be successful), for risk management (where risks to achieving objectives is the main focus) and for internal controls (that seek to ensure objectives are realized). Moreover, it is the search for long-term corporate success that must steer the internal audit shop, or there is little point setting up the team.

**'Systematic, disciplined approach'** Internal audit is a now a full-blown profession. This means it has a clear set of professional standards and is able to work to best practice guidelines in delivering a quality service. One measure of this professionalism is that the organization can expect its auditors to apply a systematic and disciplined approach to its work. Be it consulting or assurance work, IIA Performance Standard 2040 requires that:

> The chief audit executive must establish policies and procedures to guide the internal audit activity.

**'Evaluate and improve'** We have mentioned the need to focus on making improvements in the organization and part of this search for improvement entails making evaluations. Internal audit sets what is found during an audit against what should be present to ensure good control. This necessarily entails the use of evaluation techniques that are applied in a professional and impartial manner to give reliable results. Many review teams leave out the evaluation aspect of review work and simply ask a few questions or check a few records and their results are not robust. Internal audit, on the other hand, has built into its definition the formal use of evaluation procedures to support steps to improve operations.

**'Effectiveness'** Effectiveness is a bottom-line concept based on the notion that management is able to set objectives and control resources in such a way as to ensure that these goals are in fact achieved. The link between controls and objectives becomes clear, and audit must be able to understand the fundamental needs of management as it works to its goals. The complexities behind the concept of effectiveness are great, and by building this into the audit definition, the audit scope becomes potentially very wide.

**'Risk management, control and governance processes'** These three related concepts have been covered in early chapters of the book and set the parameters for the internal audit role. Organizations that have not developed vigorous systems for these matters will fail in the long run and fall foul of regulators in the short term. The internal auditors are the only professionals who have these dimensions of corporate life as a living and breathing component of their role. They should therefore be the first port of call for anyone who needs to get to grips with corporate governance. IIA Performance Standard 2120 states:

> The internal audit activity must evaluate the effectiveness and contribute to the improvement of risk management processes. Determining whether risk management processes are effective is a judgment resulting from the internal auditor's assessment that:
>
> - Organizational objectives support and align with the organization's mission;
> - Significant risks are identified and assessed;
> - Appropriate risk responses are selected that align risks with the organization's risk appetite; and
> - Relevant risk information is captured and communicated in a timely manner across the organization, enabling staff, management, and the board to carry out their responsibilities.
>
> Risk management processes are monitored through ongoing management activities, separate evaluations, or both.

The assurance role of internal auditing needs to be understood. Assurance implies a form of guarantee that what appears to be the case is in fact the case, based on a reliable source of confirmation that all is well. The more impartial and professional the source of these assurances the more reliable they become.

## 5.2   The Four Main Elements

Let us return to the scope of internal auditing, which is found in the Institute of Internal Auditors' Performance Standard 2110.A1 and states that:

> The internal audit activity must evaluate risk exposures relating to the organization's governance, operations, and information systems regarding the:
>
> - Reliability and integrity of financial and operational information;
> - Effectiveness and efficiency of operations;
> - Safeguarding of assets; and
> - Compliance with laws, regulations, and contracts.

Let us take a closer look at these elements.

**Reliability and integrity of financial and operational information**  Internal auditors review the reliability and integrity of financial and operating information and the means used to identify, measure, classify and report such information.

**Effectiveness and efficiency of operations**  Internal auditors should appraise the economy and efficiency with which resources are employed. They should also review operations or programmes to ascertain whether results are consistent with established objectives and goals and whether the operations are being carried out as planned.

**Safeguarding of assets**  Internal auditors should review the means of safeguarding and, as appropriate, verifying the existence of such assets.

**Compliance with laws, regulations and contracts**  Internal auditors should review the systems established to ensure compliance with those policies, plans, procedures, laws, regulations and important contracts that could have a significant impact on operations and reports, and should determine whether the organization is in compliance.

Internal audit reviews the extent to which management has established sound systems of internal control so that objectives are set and resources applied to these objectives in an efficient manner. This includes being protected from loss and abuse. Adequate information systems should be established to enable management to assess the extent to which objectives are being achieved via a series of suitable reports. Controls are required to combat risks to the achievement of value for money (VFM) and it is these areas that internal audit is concerned with. Compliance, information systems and safeguarding assets are all prerequisites to good value for money. There is a fundamental link between quality assurance and VFM as it is the quality systems that underpin the achievement of VFM. It may then be possible to re-state the control objectives to read that controls are required for the achievement of organizational objectives in an efficient manner, ensuring that:

• Information systems and published reports are adequate.
• Policies, procedures, laws and regulations are complied with.
• Assets, including the corporate reputation, are protected.

## Implications of the Wide Scope

The wide scope of internal audit has several implications:

1. **Expertise**    Great expertise is required from auditors to enable them to provide advice on the wide range of key control objectives. Since we are charged with auditing anything and everything, we need some knowledge of almost all organizational activities. The ideal internal auditor may be the most experienced employee of the organization in terms of an overall knowledge of the different areas, second only to the chief executive. While this ideal is unrealistic it represents a major challenge for the auditor. Unfortunately traditional internal audit departments who are locked into a never-ending annual cycle of checking the output from basic accounting systems will find it impossible to achieve the high standards that underpin this wide scope of audit work. A useful test is to ensure that audit reports interest the chief executive officer (CEO) as well as the director of finance. Resources directed at anything less than this may be of little use to the organization. Whereas the CEO assumes a risk and control orientation the CAE must assume an educational role in promoting the right culture. This is easy if one considers that controls ensure that organizational objectives are achieved. Once high standards have been established, this raises expectations that must be met. It can be achieved by implementing quality auditing systems, as shown in Figure 5.1.

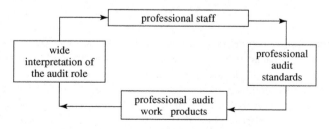

**FIGURE 5.1**    The internal auditing role.

2. **Safeguarding assets**    It is necessary to establish who is responsible for investigating frauds since this is resource intensive. Where internal audit is wholly responsible for investigating fraud,

error and irregularities, this may become a drain on audit resources. Adopting a wide scope of work and having the necessary skills to operate at this level will be of little use where most of the available time is spent responding to management referrals on matters of regularity. High-level fraud investigations do require an associated level of skills and there is potential for major impact on the organization. There is a defensive stance that may be assumed to preserve audit resources that will be effective in the short term. This is to plan a comprehensive programme of compliance checks and verification routines to protect organizational assets. It is then possible to calculate the minimum resources to fund such a programme and it is in this way that the audit budget may be preserved. The main drawback is the need to deploy armies of junior resources to carry out the basic checks of compliance work, which militates against working to high professional standards. Balancing is required and this is the CAE's task. Management is, in the final analysis, responsible for safeguarding assets.

3. **The compliance role**   Controls over compliance may include an inspection routine and audit's role in this should be clearly defined. Do we provide a probity-based service on behalf of management and visit all relevant locations or merely provide an advisory function to management on promoting compliance? Many larger organizations have established a separate compliance team to ensure that the rules and regulations the company is supposed to adopt are fully adhered to and that there is no legal exposures resulting from ongoing business activities.

4. **Information systems**   The audit of management information systems (MIS) is crucial since this may involve reviewing MIS as part of operational audits, or these systems can be audited separately. MIS cannot be tackled without expertise. Auditing MIS may follow two main routes. We may review information systems as a concept in terms of looking at the way they are applied to enhancing the overall efficiency of operations. The assessment of MIS must be related to business objectives. The advantage is that one can concentrate expertise on the specific application that will almost certainly be computerized. Alternatively, it is possible to incorporate the assessment of MIS into all audits so that this becomes a fundamental feature of general audit work. This not only builds an appreciation of the importance of MIS by general auditors but also allows expertise to be acquired. It is easier to link MIS into business objectives when this information is viewed in conjunction with the wider elements of the audit. Moreover, information systems cannot be ignored, and is wholly within the scope of audit work.

5. **Value for money**   The concept of economy, efficiency and effectiveness (or VFM) is another sensitive issue. Auditors can assist management's task in securing good arrangements for promoting VFM or alternatively undertake a continual search for waste and other poor VFM. These two different perspectives of the audit role will continue to arise in many different areas as it is based on the fundamental distinction between systems audits and investigations. A systems approach considers the managerial systems for addressing risks to VFM and judges whether this is working. Investigatory work, on the other hand, furnishes management with suggestions as to alternative operational methods. In terms of defining the scope of audit work, the former approach is purist auditing work that falls within our definition. The investigatory stance is more akin to a consultancy approach that, while in line with the scope of work, falls closer to a management role. VFM is relevant to audit work whatever the adopted approach.

6. **Management needs**   A wide scope requires a good understanding of the operations being reviewed and it is necessary to include management's needs in the terms of reference by adopting a more participative style. Unlike the narrow approach that underpins traditional probity

auditing, this depends on getting inside management objectives. It is then impossible to operate as outsiders and work primarily from documentation and records. This will hinder the ability to achieve high-level results. Close working arrangements with management are essential.

7. **Specialists**   The four elements of the key control objectives may require specialists in each of the defined areas and the level of expectation may place great demands on the audit service. One might imagine that the audit function will eventually be broken down into defined fields with experts specializing in different ones. This point is explored below in the section on resourcing the wide scope of audit work.

## 5.3   The Audit Charter

The audit charter sets the agreed role and position of internal auditing in an organization, and is defined in the IIA's glossary of terms as:

> The internal audit charter is a formal document that defines the internal audit activity's purpose, authority, and responsibility. The internal audit charter establishes the internal audit activity's position within the organization; authorizes access to records, personnel, and physical properties relevant to the performance of engagements; and defines the scope of internal audit activities . . . .

IIA Attribute Standard 1000 says that the:

> Purpose, authority, and responsibility of the internal audit activity must be formally defined in an internal audit charter, consistent with the Definition of Internal Auditing, the Code of Ethics, and the Standards. The chief audit executive must periodically review the internal audit charter and present it to senior management and the board for approval.

This also applies to all types of internal audit work as per Attribute Standards 1000.A1 and 1000.C1 respectively, which state that:

> The nature of assurance services provided to the organization must be defined in the internal audit charter. If assurances are to be provided to parties outside the organization, the nature of these assurances must also be defined in the internal audit charter. And that the nature of consulting services must be defined in the internal audit charter. If assurances are to be provided to parties outside the organization, the nature of these assurances should also be defined in the charter. The nature of consulting services should be defined in the charter.

The audit charter may be used in a positive fashion to underpin the marketing task that is discharged by audit management. It can also be used to defend audit services in the event of a dispute or an awkward audit. The charter formally documents the *raison d'être* of the audit function. It is important that all audit departments both develop and maintain a suitable charter. The Institute of Internal Auditors has issued a statement of responsibilities that covers the role of internal auditing and this document may be used to form the basis of such a charter.

### Role of the Audit Charter

The audit charter constitutes a formal document that should be developed by the CAE and agreed by the highest level of the organization. If an audit committee exists then it should be agreed in this forum although the final document should be signed and dated by the chief executive officer. The IIA's Attribute Standard 1000 covers the purpose, authority and responsibility of internal audit:

> The purpose, authority, and responsibility of the internal audit activity must be formally defined in an internal audit charter, consistent with the Definition of Internal Auditing, the Code of Ethics, and the Standards. The chief audit executive must periodically review the internal audit charter and present it to senior management and the board for approval.

The audit charter establishes audit's position within the organization and will address several issues:

1. **The nature of internal auditing**   This should cover the general concept of auditing and the fact that it comprises the impartial assurance regarding systems of internal control by providing that they are subject to formal review. In addition, internal audit may provide an associated consulting service.

2. **The audit objectives**   The precise definition of internal audit should be set out. This will be in formal words and include references to the objectives of internal audit. There should be a clear link to organizational objectives and the way that the internal audit role contributes to these. The consultancy-based services from internal audit should be specifically provided for. It may be possible to use the formal definition of internal audit applied by a professional auditing body such as the Institute of Internal Auditors.

3. **The scope of audit work**   The main areas that internal audit covers should be a feature of the audit charter, which, as mentioned before, will relate to:

- Reliability and integrity of financial and operational information.
- Effectiveness and efficiency of operations.
- Safeguarding of assets.
- Compliance with laws, regulations and contracts.

4. **Audit's responsibilities**   It is important that the role of internal audit is clearly set out and that this is distinguished from management's responsibilities. For each of the components of the scope of audit (see above) the expectation of audit's role should be defined. This will include the audit role in respect of coverage of fraud, compliance matters and value for money. In the main one would expect management to be wholly responsible for addressing these matters while audit would review the risk management, control and governance systems that ensure these objectives are achieved. It is possible to provide further detail by outlining internal audit's duty to prepare plans and undertake the required work to professional auditing standards.

5. **Audit's authority**   The audit charter will have to refer to the rights of internal audit and the fact that they are confirmed through the charter itself. This will include unimpaired access to all information, explanations, records, buildings and so on that are required to complete audit work. It may be possible to insert a crucial clause that provides that this access be available without undue delay (perhaps within 24 hours). This is because the time factor can be controversial with some of the more difficult audits.

6. **Outline of independence**   No charter would be complete without a clear reference to the concept of independence. This must be perceived as a high-profile, prioritized factor that underpins all audit work. While it is necessary in practice to strike a realistic balance, the intention to secure a high level of audit independence will be specifically documented in the charter.

The audit charter may be seen as the mission statement of internal audit and a clear definition may be documented to form the basis of later explanations that auditors may apply when describing their role to management. It may also come to the CAE's aid in the event of a dispute with management, which is why it should be formulated by the CAE and agreed with the utmost care and consideration.

## 5.4   Audit Services

The role of internal auditing is wide. Within the context of improving risk management, control and governance processes, the type of work undertaken to add value to an organization will vary greatly. Organizations with rigid regulatory requirements in an industry where scandals are common may find that compliance reviews are the best way to add value to the business. Enterprises in rapid growth sectors where speed in delivering new products is the key to success may find that consulting advice on controlling programmes and projects may be the most appropriate value-add proposition. Public bodies in developing countries may want their audit effort directed at helping to build better controls and deal with corruption issues. Companies and bodies that are embarking on a long-term reform programme may want their auditors to help build a capacity to self-assess risk and controls in line with awareness events and facilitated self-assessment programmes. Organizations that are spread across the world and linked by associates, joint ventures and partnering deals may want their auditors to keep head office informed about local systems and arrangements and whether risks are being managed properly. It all depends on the context and best use of resources. Internal audit shops that focus on the corporate governance arrangements, rather than take on any work that comes its way, will tend to have a better direction. The remit is the audit charter, the parameters are the professional standards, while the context is the success criteria that is set by the organization. Within these factors will fall the range of audit products that are on offer. These may include one or more of the following possible interpretations of the audit role. Note the following are listed internal audit services selected at random from various websites that feature internal audit shops from both private and public sector organizations:

- Cyclical audit (stock, petty cash, payroll).
- Investigations into specific problems.
- Responding to requests by management.
- Operational efficiency and effectiveness reviews.
- Internal control reviews.
- Fraud investigations.
- Compliance reviews.
- Reviewing controls over revenue, contracts administration and operational expenses.
- Acting as a contact point for allegations of fraud, waste and abuse.
- Information system reviews.
- Financial and compliance audits.
- Performance audits.
- Internal control reviews and testing poor areas.
- Investigative audits into reported irregularities.
- Verify assets and review safeguards.
- Evaluation of reporting systems and procedures.
- Cost-saving reviews.

- Review of administration and accounting controls.
- Financial and performance audits.
- Revenue audits.
- Management studies into cost savings, problems in technical support and performance.
- Special reviews of projects.
- Control self-assessment facilitation.
- Environmental audits.
- Auditing the change management process.
- Operational audits.
- Computer audits.
- Control self-assessment questionnaire design and analysis.
- Issuing guidance to staff on internal control.
- Value-driven internal consultancy, acting as change agents.
- Business process analysis.
- Supporting business risk assessments.
- Quality advocates and reviews.
- Providing measures to strengthen mechanisms to achieving objectives.
- Evaluation of corporate governance processes.
- Working with management on their risk management practices.
- Advising clients on risk exposures and measures to remedy.
- Review risk management arrangements.
- Provide practical solutions and supporting management in implementing them.
- Participating in major information systems projects.
- Reviews to improve quality of management processes.
- Communicate risk information to clients.
- Operational auditing (or management audits).
- Financial systems audits, accounting and financial reporting.
- Compliance auditing on adherence to laws, regulations, policies and procedures – concentrating on improved controls to help compliance.
- Computer auditing during the systems development stage.
- Advice to managers when making changes to procedure.
- Training in risk and control awareness.
- Provision of independent assurance on internal controls.
- General advice and guidance on control-related issues.
- Operate follow-up system for outstanding audit recommendations.
- Evaluate action plans made in response to audit recommendations.
- Liaison and joint projects with external audit.
- Special projects as requested by management.
- Management reviews of new or existing programmes, systems, procedures.
- Control consciousness seminars.
- Recommendations for enhancing cost-effective control systems.
- Monitoring financial information and reporting results.
- Reviews of fixed assets, cash receipts, budgets, purchasing and accounting routines.
- Surprise audits over cash funds, accounting records, employee records, observation of operations and inventory records.
- Accountability and fraud awareness training.
- Projects to improve the quality of information or its context for decision making.
- Reviews of e-commerce arrangements and security.

- Audits of internal control structures, efficiency and effectiveness and best practice.
- Safeguarding assets (and information) using verification of asset registers, inventories and the adopted security policy.

There is clearly an abundance of related services on offer from the many internal audit shops in existence. Some are built around the compliance model and others focus more on consulting projects.

## 5.5  Independence

All definitions of internal audit contain the word 'independence' and this is an important component of the audit role. It is both a concept and an ideal. One could assume that since internal audit is located within the organization it cannot be independent. The counterargument suggests that internal audit has to be totally independent or it has little use. The real position falls somewhere between. There are degrees and a quality of independence that have to be earned to ensure that audit is sufficiently distanced from the particular operation being reviewed. IIA Standard 1100 covers independence and objectivity:

The internal audit activity must be independent, and internal auditors must be objective in performing their work.

**Interpretation:**  Independence is the freedom from conditions that threaten the ability of the internal audit activity or the chief audit executive to carry out internal audit responsibilities in an unbiased manner. To achieve the degree of independence necessary to effectively carry out the responsibilities of the internal audit activity, the chief audit executive has direct and unrestricted access to senior management and the board. This can be achieved through a dual-reporting relationship. Threats to independence must be managed at the individual auditor, engagement, functional, and organizational levels.

Objectivity is an unbiased mental attitude that allows internal auditors to perform engagements in such a manner that they believe in their work product and that no quality compromises are made. Objectivity requires that internal auditors do not subordinate their judgment on audit matters to others. Threats to objectivity must be managed at the individual auditor, engagement, functional, and organizational levels.

Standard 1110 deals with the need to achieve a degree of organizational Independence:

The chief audit executive must report to a level within the organization that allows the internal audit activity to fulfill its responsibilities. The chief audit executive must confirm to the board, at least annually, the organizational independence of the internal audit activity.

**1110.A1** – The internal audit activity must be free from interference in determining the scope of internal auditing, performing work, and communicating results.

### 1111 – Direct Interaction with the Board

The chief audit executive must communicate and interact directly with the board.

### 1120 – Individual Objectivity

Internal auditors must have an impartial, unbiased attitude and avoid any conflict of interest.

**Interpretation:**    *Conflict of interest is a situation in which an internal auditor, who is in a position of trust, has a competing professional or personal interest. Such competing interests can make it difficult to fulfill his or her duties impartially. A conflict of interest exists even if no unethical or improper act results. A conflict of interest can create an appearance of impropriety that can undermine confidence in the internal auditor, the internal audit activity, and the profession. A conflict of interest could impair an individual's ability to perform his or her duties and responsibilities objectively.*

Standard 1130 addresses the need to deal with any impairment to independence or objectivity:

If independence or objectivity is impaired in fact or appearance, the details of the impairment must be disclosed to appropriate parties. The nature of the disclosure will depend upon the impairment.

**Interpretation:**    Impairment to organizational independence and individual objectivity may include, but is not limited to, personal conflict of interest, scope limitations, restrictions on access to records, personnel, and properties, and resource limitations, such as funding.

The determination of appropriate parties to which the details of an impairment to independence or objectivity must be disclosed is dependent upon the expectations of the internal audit activity's and the chief audit executive's responsibilities to senior management and the board as described in the internal audit charter, as well as the nature of the impairment.

There are several other aspects of the main 1130 standard that should also be noted:

**1130.A1** – Internal auditors must refrain from assessing specific operations for which they were previously responsible. Objectivity is presumed to be impaired if an internal auditor provides assurance services for an activity for which the internal auditor had responsibility within the previous year.

**1130.A2** – Assurance engagements for functions over which the chief audit executive has responsibility must be overseen by a party outside the internal audit activity.

**1130.C1** – Internal auditors may provide consulting services relating to operations for which they had previous responsibilities.

**1130.C2** – If internal auditors have potential impairments to independence or objectivity relating to proposed consulting services, disclosure must be made to the engagement client prior to accepting the engagement.

## The Meaning of Independence

Independence means that management can place full reliance on audit findings and recommendations. *Brink's Modern Internal Auditing* makes clear the crucial role of audit independence: 'internal audit is the one function in the modern organization that is completely detached from both the operational components and functional staff groups'.[1]

There are many positive images that are conjured up by this concept of independence:

1. **Objectivity**    Behind this word is a whole multitude of issues that together form a complex maze. The main problem is that the whole basis of objectivity stems from a human condition of correctness and fair play. Any models that involve a consideration of the human condition have to deal with many psychological matters, and at times irrational behaviour. Although objectivity is

located in the mind, it is heavily influenced by the procedures and practices adopted. The ACCA guide to *Ethics and the Accountant in the Public Sector* defined objectivity in the following way:

> Objectivity can be described as a state of mind which allows the individual to make judgements, based upon all the available evidence relating to the situation, in a state of emotional and psychological detachment from the situation or decision.[2]

2. **Impartiality**   Objectivity may be seen as not being influenced by improper motives while impartiality is not taking sides. The question of impartiality is important because there is a view that internal audit, like all other units, will work in a politically advantageous way. This may result in audit taking the side of the most powerful party in any work that impacts on the political balances within an organization. If this is allowed to occur unchecked then the audit evidence that supports any audit report may be secured with a view to assisting one side only. An absence of impartiality will undermine the audit process. If audit plans are changed, reports withdrawn and audits aborted because this suits certain parties in the organization, this reputation will stay with the audit function and give it a poor image.

3. **Unbiased views**   When an audit report states that 'the audit view is . . . ', this should provide a comment on the state of internal controls. Where used to provide an advantage for the audit function, credibility is risked. The other aspect of audit bias is where certain officers/sections have been earmarked as 'poor, uncooperative or suspect . . . '. We go into an audit looking for any material that supports our original contentions. If taken to the extreme, the audit function will become a hit squad, conjuring up cases against people it does not like.

4. **Valid opinion**   Readers of audit reports require the auditors to complete work to professional standards with the audit opinion properly derived from this work. This opinion must make sense having reference to all relevant factors. The audit role is not to please nominated parties or simply maintain the status quo; it is to present audit work in a professional and objective manner. The temptation to keep certain individuals happy may well result in a distorted audit opinion, which in turn will make the underlying audit work unreliable. Managers will issue hundreds of reports during the course of their careers, each taking a stance that is derived from their position within the organization. Internal audit, on the other hand, depends wholly on a reputation for reviewing an area, or performing an investigation, and producing an opinion that is valid. This is not to suggest that this opinion will be supported by all levels of management, but it should be accepted as a fair representation of the facts.

5. **No spying for management**   Professional objectivity means that audit does not fall into the trap of acting as spies for management, particularly where managers feel that their staff are not performing. Most general problems with staff can be related to a failure by management to install effective controls and this is a point that the auditor will return to time and time again. The latest definition of internal audit suggests that audit serves the organization as a whole rather than targeting specific officers. This means that the welfare of the organization is paramount as the audit role rises above the in-fighting that goes on in both private and public sector bodies. There is an issue surrounding the provision of audit consultancy services that makes this a complicated area, which is dealt with later.

6. **No 'no-go' areas**   There are senior managers who adopt a particularly aggressive stance to managing their areas of responsibility. All outsiders are treated with great suspicion. In fact, there

is a correlation between professional incompetence and this threatening posture; i.e. the less able the manager the more aggressive he/she becomes. If this results in certain areas being deemed out of bounds to internal audit then this means that audit's independence is impaired and they will have a lesser role. If audit can be kept away from certain areas then this restricts the audit field, and if this trend is allowed to continue it could set a damaging precedent. The net result may be that the audit field becomes relegated to defined parts of the organization only. This is playing at auditing far removed from the demands of any professionally based audit practice.

7. **Senior management audited**   There is a view that system controls are primarily located within the management processes that underpin the operations. Where audit fails to incorporate this factor into the scope of audit work, a great deal will be missed. The problem is that managers may not wish to be audited, particularly where this exposes gaps in their responsibility to establish sound controls. The CAE will have a quiet life where he/she works only at a detailed operational level and ignores the whole management process. Again this restricts the audit role and so adversely impacts on the auditor's independence.

8. **No backing-off**   We do not expect auditors to back down without a valid reason when confronted by an assertive manager. This is not to say that auditors march unchecked across the organization, unaware of any disruption they might be causing to front line operations. It does, however, mean that they will pursue audit objectives to the full in a diplomatic and professional manner. If this is not the case then audit will be vulnerable to criticism from all sides. Audit reports would then reflect what managers allowed the auditor to do rather than the work required to discharge the terms of reference for the audit. In this instance audit can claim very little real independence.

The above provides a foundation for the audit practice at the heart of the audit role. This distinguishes it from management consultancy and other review agencies who provide professional review services but only to the terms of reference set by management. These factors must be in place for the audit function to have any real impact on the organization. If managers are able to pick and choose which audit reports to believe, then this represents a major flaw in the audit service. It will eventually lead to its downfall, as well as a failure to meet professional internal auditing standards.

## Freedom from Line Operations

This is very important. Most audit units have now moved away from direct line functions such as certifying contractors' interim and final accounts before payment. However, a new trend has arisen where audit departments seek to discharge management's responsibilities for designing suitable systems and guarding against frauds. This results from mixing consultancy-based work with audit work so that the lines of responsibility become blurred. Management no longer needs to think about the adequacy of their control systems as this role has been passed over to audit. These systems have no real owners and so drift into disrepair. The consultancy debate is outlined later. This vexed issue has been the subject of IIA Practice Advisory 1130.A2-1: *Internal Audit's Responsibility for Other (Non-audit) Functions*. Standard 1130.A2 states:

> Assurance engagements for functions over which the chief audit executive has responsibility must be overseen by a party outside the internal audit activity.

The advisory 1130.A2-1 states that internal auditors are not to accept responsibility for nonaudit functions or duties that are subject to periodic internal audit assessments. If they have this responsibility, then they are not functioning as internal auditors.

## Objectivity

The CAE should continuously seek out ways to improve the level of objectivity throughout audit and some of the relevant matters have been mentioned earlier. A great deal of this hinges on installing suitable policies and procedures. The aim is to remove any potential barriers to the auditor's ability to perform fair and unbiased work. IIA Standard 1120 covers individual objectivity and says that:

Internal auditors must have an impartial, unbiased attitude and avoid any conflict of interest.

Practice Advisory 1120-1 provides some guidance on this topic:

- Individual objectivity means the internal auditors perform engagements in such a manner that they have an honest belief in their work product and that no significant quality compromises are made. Internal auditors are not to be placed in situations that could impair their ability to make objective professional judgements.
- Individual objectivity involves the chief audit executive (CAE) organizing staff assignments that prevent potential and actual conflict of interest and bias, periodically obtaining information from the internal audit staff concerning potential conflict of interest and bias, and, when practicable, rotating internal audit staff assignments periodically.
- Review of internal audit work results before the related engagement communications are released assists in providing reasonable assurance that the work was performed objectively.
- The internal auditor's objectivity is not adversely affected when the auditor recommends standards of control for systems or reviews procedures before they are implemented. The auditor's objectivity is considered to be impaired if the auditor designs, installs, drafts procedures for, or operates such systems.
- The occasional performance of nonaudit work by the internal auditor, with full disclosure in the reporting process, would not necessarily impair objectivity. However, it would require careful consideration by management and the internal auditor to avoid adversely affecting the internal auditor's objectivity.

## Organizational Status

There are some internal audit units that are located within the director of finance's (DF) department. Politicians, when considering legislation on accountability, view the internal audit role as primarily concerned with promoting financial accountability on behalf of the chief financial officer. This is a fundamental misunderstanding of the true audit role as it fails to recognize that we cover systems at a corporate, managerial and operational level that includes the financial implications therein. It is nonetheless impossible to ignore forces (i.e. legislation) directed at expanding the audit role and profile. We will, however, have to address two basic questions when reporting to the DF:

- Can we be truly independent in auditing the financial systems?
- If we were in dispute with the DF on an audit-related issue how would this be resolved?

Being in the pocket of the DF is an unfortunate situation that the CAE may experience as a result of the political forces of the day and the assumed reporting line. Where this arises one's only real option for retaining professional integrity may be to resign on principle. Having support from the board is important in balancing out the power relationships and extracts from Practice Advisory 1110-1 (Organizational Independency – for Standard 1110) give some practical advice. Standard 1110 states:

The chief audit executive must report to a level within the organization that allows the internal audit activity to fulfill its responsibilities. The chief audit executive must confirm to the board, at least annually, the organizational independence of the internal audit activity.

Advisory 1110-1 goes on to suggest:

Support from senior management and the board assists the internal audit activity in gaining the cooperation of engagement clients and performing their work free from interference.

The chief audit executive (CAE), reporting functionally to the board and administratively to the organization's chief executive officer, facilitates organizational independence. At a minimum the CAE needs to report to an individual in the organization with sufficient authority to promote independence and to ensure broad audit coverage, adequate consideration of engagement communications, and appropriate action on engagement recommendations.

Functional reporting to the board typically involves the board:

- Approving the internal audit activity's overall charter.
- Approving the internal audit risk assessment and related audit plan.
- Receiving communications from the CAE on the results of the internal audit activities or other matters that the CAE determines are necessary, including private meetings with the CAE without management present, as well as annual confirmation of the internal audit activity's organizational independence.
- Approving all decisions regarding the performance evaluation, appointment, or removal of the CAE.
- Approving the annual compensation and salary adjustment of the CAE.
- Making appropriate inquiries of management and the CAE to determine whether there is audit scope or budgetary limitations that impede the ability of the internal audit activity to execute its responsibilities.

Administrative reporting is the reporting relationship within the organization's management structure that facilitates the day-to-day operations of the internal audit activity. Administrative reporting typically includes:

- Budgeting and management accounting.
- Human resource administration, including personnel evaluations and compensation.
- Internal communications and information flows.
- Administration of the internal audit activity's policies and procedures.

## 5.6   Audit Ethics

The auditing profession is charged with providing a high standard of audit services to each employing organization and the audit charter forms a contract with the organization in this respect. An extension of this concept is the view that audit professionals are also charged with performing their work with the highest of moral standards that one would expect from people in this position. Moreover, the code of ethics (or code of conduct) forms a contract to cover the auditor's moral obligations. The organization may therefore rely on this code for guiding the conduct of members of the audit department. The IIA consider that the purpose of the IIA code of ethics is:

> To promote an ethical culture in the profession of internal auditing. A code of ethics is necessary and appropriate for the profession of internal auditing, founded as it is on the trust placed in its objective assurance about risk management, control and governance. The Institute's Code of Ethics extends beyond the Definition of Internal Auditing to include two essential components:
>
> 1   Principles that are relevant to the profession and practice of internal auditing; and
>
> 2   Rules of Conduct that describe behaviour norms expected of internal auditors. These rules are an aid to interpreting the Principles into practical applications and are intended to guide the ethical conduct of internal auditors.
>
> The Code of Ethics provides guidance to internal auditors serving others. 'Internal auditors' refers to Institute members and those who provide internal auditing services within the Definition of Internal Auditing.

## Relevant Factors

The IIA Code of Ethics is reproduced below:

## Principles

Internal auditors are expected to apply and uphold the following principles:

### 1. Integrity
The integrity of internal auditors establishes trust and thus provides the basis for reliance on their judgment.

### 2. Objectivity
Internal auditors exhibit the highest level of professional objectivity in gathering, evaluating, and communicating information about the activity or process being examined. Internal auditors make a balanced assessment of all the relevant circumstances and are not unduly influenced by their own interests or by others in forming judgments.

### 3. Confidentiality
Internal auditors respect the value and ownership of information they receive and do not disclose information without appropriate authority unless there is a legal or professional obligation to do so.

### 4. Competency
Internal auditors apply the knowledge, skills, and experience needed in the performance of internal audit services.

## Rules of Conduct

### 1. Integrity

Internal auditors:

1.1. Shall perform their work with honesty, diligence, and responsibility.

1.2. Shall observe the law and make disclosures expected by the law and the profession.

1.3. Shall not knowingly be a party to any illegal activity, or engage in acts that are discreditable to the profession of internal auditing or to the organization.

1.4. Shall respect and contribute to the legitimate and ethical objectives of the organization.

## 2. Objectivity

Internal auditors:

2.1. Shall not participate in any activity or relationship that may impair or be presumed to impair their unbiased assessment. This participation includes those activities or relationships that may be in conflict with the interests of the organization.

2.2. Shall not accept anything that may impair or be presumed to impair their professional judgment.

2.3. Shall disclose all material facts known to them that, if not disclosed, may distort the reporting of activities under review.

## 3. Confidentiality

Internal auditors:

3.1. Shall be prudent in the use and protection of information acquired in the course of their duties.

3.2. Shall not use information for any personal gain or in any manner that would be contrary to the law or detrimental to the legitimate and ethical objectives of the organization.

## 4. Competency

Internal auditors:

4.1. Shall engage only in those services for which they have the necessary knowledge, skills, and experience.

4.2. Shall perform internal audit services in accordance with the International Standards for the Professional Practice of Internal Auditing.

4.3. Shall continually improve their proficiency and the effectiveness and quality of their services.


A code of ethics is necessary and appropriate for the profession of internal auditing, founded as it is on the trust placed in its objective assurance about risk management, control and governance. The Institute's Code of Ethics extends beyond the definition of internal auditing to include two essential components:

1. Principles that are relevant to the profession and practice of internal auditing.
2. Rules of conduct that describe behaviour norms expected of internal auditors. These rules are an aid to interpreting the Principles into practical applications and are intended to guide the ethical conduct of internal auditors.

The Code of Ethics, together with the rest of the Institute's IPPF and other relevant Institute pronouncements, provides guidance to internal auditors serving others. 'Internal auditors' refers to Institute members, recipients of or candidates for IIA professional certifications and those who provide internal auditing services within the definition of internal auditing.

There is an expection from each and every internal auditor that they should be:

- Honest and diligent.
- Not get involved in illegal activity.
- Contribute to the ethical objectives of the organization.
- Preserve an unbiased assessment.
- Does not accept gifts that would impair professional judgement.
- Confidential material not disclosed.
- Compliance with standards.
- Seek continuous improvement.

If auditors abide by the Code of Ethics then all uncertainty is removed. Impairment is defined by the IIA as:

> Impairment to organizational independence and individual objectivity may include personal conflict of interest, scope limitations, restrictions on access to records, personnel, and properties, and resource limitations (funding).

## 5.7   Police Officer versus Consultant

Most audit textbooks make reference to the impact that internal audit has not only on business systems but also on people, and stress the importance of understanding human behaviour. This is sometimes extended by the view that auditors face various complicated issues because of their special position in the organization. The alternatives to the word 'Audit' from a standard thesaurus include the following terms:

> *examination*      *review*
>
> *investigation*    *inspection*
>
> *scrutiny*

These terms do not conjure up the concept of a helpful, value-add service and here we tackle the fallout of negativity and the need to manage this problem by adopting the stance that merely being genuine is not enough. One has seriously to consider one's position and the impact of the applied audit policies on the behavioural aspects of this role, to uncover any actual or potential barriers to good performance. Alan Marshall outlines his approach when asked by someone 'So what do you do for a living?': 'The word "audit" has negative connotations, fostering the image of tick and turn.... When announcing that I work as internal auditor... perhaps the most frustrating reaction is "Ah! You're an accountant. You check people's books, don't you?"'[3]

### Audit Relationships

Internal audit cannot be done in the audit office with no contact with management and operatives. The audit objective is based on providing sound advice to management on their systems of risk and control. Here, the auditor requires a good understanding of the client's systems as a necessary prerequisite to effective audit work. It has been argued that internal control is really about people and if the people factor is missed then little useful work will ensue. The truly effective auditor is one who is able to extract all the required information from whatever source in an efficient manner. This requires talking to people, asking questions and securing assistance throughout the audit process, and human relation skills may here be skilfully applied. Contacts the auditor may experience include:

| | |
|---|---|
| Audit management | Corporate managers |
| Operational managers | Operatives |
| Delegates at audit conferences | Government officials |
| Officials and lawyers | Finance and computer specialists |
| External auditors | Staff from other internal review agencies |
| Members of the public and customers | The organization's clients |
| Local police and the fraud squad | Auditors from other organizations |

Each of these groups may require a different mode of communication and the auditor has to be flexible in meeting their expectations and at the same time satisfying the audit objective.

## Dealing with People

There are certain obstacles that the internal auditor may come across when carrying out audit work, many of which relate to the behavioural aspects of work. Many auditors are seen as checkers who spend their time ticking thousands of documents and records. In this way management may treat the auditor as someone who has an extremely limited role that requires little skill and professionalism. At the extreme, managers may view audit staff with disdain and greet their presence with what can only be termed ridicule. This position can account for the strained atmosphere that many an auditor has faced when meeting with client managers at the outset of an audit. The perception that operational management is very busy doing important work while the auditor is simply checking some of the basic accounting data that relates to the area can create a great imbalance. This sets the auditor at a disadvantage from day one of the audit. Client expectations of traditional internal audit services typically consist of:

- A check on remote establishments to ensure that they are complying with procedures.
- The investigation of frauds where they have been detected within the organization.
- Investigations into employees who cause concern to management in terms of breaching procedure.
- A continuous programme of checks over the output from various financial systems to assess whether these are correct.
- On-the-spot advice as to whether proposed management decisions are acceptable in terms of compliance with procedure and best practice.
- Ad hoc investigations requested by members of the corporate management team.
- Additional resources for computer system development projects.

The above expectations create a major problem for internal audit in that, on the one hand, we have to market audit services and as such define what the client wants. On the other hand, we have to retain the right to provide a professional audit service, which means essentially advising on systems of risk management and internal control as a result of an agreed programme of audits. If we fail to respond to management expectations then this will put us at risk in the long term, while if we carry out the above work, this turns us into management consultants. The rules to be applied to managing this situation may be set out as:

1. Isolate two ranges of clients. The audit committee who will be the client for audit work (risk-based systems auditing) and managers who can receive additional consultancy services.
2. Make sure the audit committee understands the concept of planned systems audits and that a basic block of resources must be reserved for this task.
3. Provide consultancy as additional services that are clearly distinguished from audit work. Ensure that management understands that they are responsible for compliance, information systems, fraud investigations and achieving value for money.
4. Publicize the audit role through suitable brochures, website presentations and correspondence.
5. Encourage managers to take a long-term view in promoting sound controls and so avoid the many problems that are derived from poor arrangements. This is a long process but is assisted by oral presentations in control that audit may provide to management.

## 5.8   Managing Expectations through Web Design

This section gives a brief review of some of the material that is being set up on internal audit websites. Most larger organizations have developed corporate websites that provide an open communications link between them and the outside world. Many of these websites drill down into separate areas for sections within the organization, including internal audit. The website material is also part of a more extended internal Intranet. The CAE needs to consider carefully how to use this mechanism to communicate with stakeholders and internal customers, and help break down some of the mystique behind internal auditing. The internal audit website may be used to establish the role of the function and assist the task of managing expectations from people who may have a distorted perception of the audit role: as a basic checking function that examines the work of the finance staff and occasionally looks at operational records. A consideration of a sample of the websites of various internal audit shops makes for interesting reading. Some of the material that is being posted on these websites includes the following frequently asked questions (the reader may wish to choose some of these for their own website):

1. **Why this guide?**   It is an idea to say why this information is being provided. Some audit shops suggest that the word 'audit' usually elicits some discomfort and we need to ensure there is no need for worry since audit aims to make a positive contribution. In years gone by internal audit used to look for mistakes and report these to senior management.
2. **What is internal audit?**   Provide a formal definition of internal auditing that makes sense and fits the organization. Perhaps the IIA definition, then a short, user-friendly explanation of some of the components.
3. **Overall mission statement?**   This may be a short statement that has been agreed as the overall mission – perhaps linked to promoting good corporate governance and risk management in all levels across the organization and providing independent assurances.
4. **Vision?**   Some audit shops develop a vision of what they would like to be in the future as, say, having helped develop a committed workforce who have got to grips with the demands of good corporate governance.
5. **What is the audit objective?**   This part will say what internal audit is trying to achieve and may be a mix of consulting roles in helping management understand and manage their risks, along with an assurance role of providing impartial assurances to the board and audit committee that controls are in place and working.
6. **Why do we have internal audit?**   This provides an opportunity to note the benefits from internal auditing without going over the top. Some measure the success of internal audit in terms of the development of a sound control environment within the organization.

7. **Who are the internal auditors?**   It may be possible to say who exactly works in internal audit along with thumbnail photographs.

8. **How are we organized?**   Provide the authority mandate (laws, regulations, listing rules and so on) and then the organization chart with the CAE, reporting lines and then make reference to the audit charter. Specialist areas such as financial, information system audits, fraud, CSA, other consultancy services and so on may be listed.

9. **Difference between the audit and management role?**   It may be possible to describe management's responsibility for ensuring sound systems of internal control that mitigate unacceptable risks and then the internal audit role in adding value to this task and providing independent assurances. Mention management's responsibilities to cooperate with the internal audit process.

10. **Difference between external and internal audit?**   Make clear these differences and explain that we try to coordinate efforts wherever possible. It may also be an idea to mention other review and inspection teams that may visit parts of the organization. Advise a protocol for clarifying which team the visitor comes from by suggesting that the manager ask questions to determine which team is carrying out the review. Suggest a reporting procedure where the manager feels there are too many different review teams visiting and therefore excessive duplication and interruption. Make clear that internal audit is a high-level function that also audits other review and compliance teams.

11. **Why do we need internal audit?**   Describe some of the advantages in having good risk and compliance systems and an overall sound system of internal control; the internal auditors are a source of expertise in these somewhat complicated areas. We are all on the same side in seeking to ensure there are no material weaknesses in systems of internal control.

12. **How is internal audit independent?**   Outline the concept of independence (status and objectivity) and that internal audit work can be relied on as professional, impartial and reliable.

13. **How does the audit committee come in?**   Outline the role of the audit committee and the types of support, plans and reports that are provided by internal audit to help then discharge this role.

14. **Where does internal audit authority come from?**   State the source and explain where the audit charter can be viewed. Make it clear that internal audit operates to professional standards. Say that internal audit has access to all information, explanation, records, files and buildings to perform audit work.

15. **Scope of audit work?**   Describe the components of value for money, information, safeguarding assets and ensuring compliance. Mention corporate governance, risk management and internal control, along with other aspects such as fraud, IT audits, CRSA and staff awareness seminars and guides.

16. **What does internal audit do?**   List in more detail the services that are provided by internal audit, including ongoing advice and assistance. Make it clear that auditors spend a lot of time interviewing staff and analyzing records and information. They are not checking on what staff do, they are checking on the system for managing risks to the operation. Although audit standards tend to mean anything that is presented to the auditor, these may need to be confirmed before being accepted as evidence.

17. **How are areas selected for audit?**   Set out the risk-based planning process and the way audit plans are aligned to the risk exposures in all parts of the organization. Define the role of the board and audit committee in agreeing these plans and the consultation process involved before the annual audit plan is adopted. Essentially we focus on high-risk areas. If cyclical audits are still undertaken then describe the areas covered, such as cash, payroll. It may be possible to mention the key audit priorities for the current year.

18. **How does this fit in with risk management?**   Make clear how internal audit fits in with overall risk management. An audit is not responsible for managing business risk but will have various degrees of involvement from setting up the systems to facilitating risk workshops to reviewing the process in hand – whatever the format, internal audit will still give formal assurances on the system and report any gaps and weaknesses.

19. **What is CRSA and do we not do our own audit using this tool?**   Tell the reader about CSA (or CRSA – or whatever it is called in the organization). It is a good idea to have a guide (two to three pages) on the Intranet, or available in hardcopy form. Some internal audit shops will present the guide to group meetings of staff annual conferences on request. CSRA does not replace an audit but it is an attempt to get business risks understood, assessed and then managed by those responsible for the process in question. Internal audit may help with this process or may use the results as a head start into their independent review based on sound evidence.

20. **Does management have any involvement in setting audit terms of reference?** Make it clear that the audits are taken from the audit plans and advance notice is provided (say, one to four weeks in advance) and that the auditor will do some preliminary work before the initial meeting. The manager's views will be taken into consideration before finalizing the audit terms of reference, and this will happen after the opening meeting (which may also involve touring the facilities and considering the manager's risk register).

21. **What if you feel you do not need to be audited?**   The preliminary survey will help determine the terms of reference and in rare cases it may not be necessary to go ahead with the audit. Where the client feels that there is no need, it is unlikely that the audit will be cancelled, but the audit work may be reduced where there is sufficient reason.

22. **How can you facilitate the progress of the audit?**   Internal audit work in partnership with management and their staff and the audit will go smoothly if there is good cooperation. Making time, space and information available to the auditor beforehand will help progress the work. Assigning a staff member to deal with requests from the auditor is another good idea. The auditor is used to working with busy people and will try to minimize disruption. The audit policy suggests that the real benefits from the audit will mean it is seen as worth spending time on.

23. **Do we have any set values?**   Mention any agreed values such as integrity, honesty, excellent service, respecting clients and others. Also that audit will be conducted with due regard to set protocols (refer the reader to a separate paper on the audit process).

24. **Professional standards?**   Mention the fact that internal audit subscribes to professional standards (e.g. IIA) and that the audit manual reflects the way the requirements of these standards will be discharged.

25. **What takes place during an audit?**   Define the audit process, e.g.:
    1. Notification
    2. Entrance conference
    3. Terms of reference confirmed via risks that have been identified
    4. Fieldwork and data gathering and testing
    5. Discussion of findings as they arise
    6. Quality review of audit work
    7. Closing conference – all findings discussed in outline
    8. Draft report
    9. May make formal presentation to your management team
    10. Response to report within 15 days – we will take on board points raised
    11. Action plan

12. Final report
13. Customer survey – feedback on how you found the audit in terms of performance and end result
14. Follow-up within 12 months of the audit
15. Quarterly summary report to audit committee.

An alternative approach will be to carry out a CSA workshop at stage 3 to determine operational objectives and assess the risks that need to be addressed. These risks are considered during fieldwork through a clear testing strategy. Then discuss audit findings at stage 7 and work with the management team on a sensible outline action plan.

26. **How long do audits last?**    This depends on the type of audit, significance of risks and what is found. It can last between (put in a figure), for example, one and two weeks, two and four weeks, etc.

27. **What is audit testing?**    Describe the testing approach and how audits have moved away from blanket testing to risk-based audits and very selective testing. Explain that audit findings should be based on sound evidence.

28. **What occurs after the audit?**    Describe the report clearance process from draft to final and that comments will be incorporated into the report or added as an annex. Discuss the follow-up audit and what happens to the audit report. The main thing that happens after an audit is action to put right any weaknesses and the receipt of formal assurances from the internal audit where controls are sound. All agreed audit recommendations need to be implemented unless there is good reason not to.

29. **Where do the reports go?**    Explain the protocols and who receives copies of the report, such as directors, board members, audit committee on request, external audit, management team, etc. Less material matters may go into a memo to the line manager. Public bodies may post the audit report on the organization's website. External parties such as regulators may have access to the reports if required.

30. **Follow-up procedures?**    Describe the follow-up procedures and that more work will be carried out on more significant findings to address outstanding risk. Crucial recommendations may have to be acted on urgently.

31. **Do we accept requests from management?**    Describe the criteria for deciding whether or not to perform any formal consulting projects that are requested by management. This may include assessment of the following:
   - Material risks involved
   - Previous efforts to address concerns
   - Related to risk, control and governance issues
   - No audits scheduled in the areas for a while
   - Audit has expertise and time available
   - Board (or senior management) endorse the request
   - Major impact on achievement of corporate (or department) objectives
   - Problem impacts on reputation of organization
   - Previous audit work on similar problems has proved successful
   - Audit has access needed for this type of work
   - High level of sensitivity required
   - Importance of impartiality of reviewer
   - Other special factors.

32. **What do managers need to know about risk and controls?**    Some audit shops prepare a guide to internal control that can be downloaded for use by managers and work

teams. Other audit shops offer staff awareness seminars on risk management and internal control.

33. **Do we conduct surprise audits?**   If this rather old-fashioned technique is still used explain why and how it is conducted for, say, cash funds, accounting records, employee records, observation of operations, inventory records and so on. If surprise audits are no longer used make this clear because many people do not realize that internal audit has generally moved on from being a hit squad.

34. **What do we do about fraud?**   Describe the fraud policy, audit's role in respect of fraud and the reporting system for suspicions. This should all be in the separate fraud policy, available to staff. Make it clear that management is responsible for dealing with fraud but may seek help from specialist staff.

35. **What does internal audit not do?**   List some of the line roles that audit used to do but has since dropped. Some say that audit will not tell management how to do its job, but simply use audit expertise to help management discharge its obligations in respect of risk management, control and governance processes.

36. **Who audits the auditors?**   Outline the quality assurance regimes of internal and external review, supervision of audits and setting and reporting on performance measures. Mention that the audit committee monitors the work of internal audit and each auditor accounts for their time and performance through a highly developed management information system (time recording and accounting).

37. **Complaints procedure?**   Describe the complaints procedure and say that internal audit works to the highest professional standards in adding value to the organization and that we welcome comments and suggestions. Give the reader a contact point.

## 5.9  Audit Competencies

We have covered the role and responsibilities of the internal auditor and the tremendous challenges facing the new-look auditor in the continual search for better and more effective corporate governance arrangements. One aspect of these challenges that is often overlooked is the need to ensure that the audit staff are equipped to work at sub-board level, i.e. right near the top of huge international organizations. The new-look internal auditor has to be totally competent or they will fail miserably. IIA Standard 1200 deals with proficiency and due professional care by stating that:

> Engagements must be performed with proficiency and due professional care.

Standard 1210 covers proficiency in more detail:

> Internal auditors must possess the knowledge, skills, and other competencies needed to perform their individual responsibilities. The internal audit activity collectively must possess or obtain the knowledge, skills, and other competencies needed to perform its responsibilities.

> **Interpretation:**   *Knowledge, skills, and other competencies is a collective term that refers to the professional proficiency required of internal auditors to effectively carry out their professional responsibilities. Internal auditors are encouraged to demonstrate their proficiency by obtaining appropriate professional certifications and qualifications, such as the Certified Internal Auditor designation and other designations offered by The Institute of Internal Auditors and other appropriate professional organizations.*

## What Makes Good Internal Auditors?

The first thing that needs to be in place to ensure good internal auditors is effective human resource policies and practices. Here we are concerned with the attributes of successful internal auditors. The IIA Practice Advisory 1210-1 deals with proficiency and requires that each internal auditor should possess certain knowledge, skills, and other competencies:

- Proficiency in applying internal audit standards, procedures, and techniques in performing engagements. Proficiency means the ability to apply knowledge to situations likely to be encountered and to deal with them appropriately without extensive recourse to technical research and assistance.
- Proficiency in accounting principles and techniques if internal auditors work extensively with financial records and reports.
- Knowledge to identify the indicators of fraud.
- Knowledge of key information technology risks and controls and available technology-based audit techniques.
- An understanding of management principles to recognize and evaluate the materiality and significance of deviations from good business practices. An understanding means the ability to apply broad knowledge to situations likely to be encountered, to recognize significant deviations, and to be able to carry out the research necessary to arrive at reasonable solutions.
- An appreciation of the fundamentals of business subjects such as accounting, economics, commercial law, taxation, finance, quantitative methods, information technology, risk management, and fraud. An appreciation means the ability to recognize the existence of problems or potential problems and to identify the additional research to be undertaken or the assistance to be obtained.
- Skills in dealing with people, understanding human relations, and maintaining satisfactory relationships with engagement clients.
- Skills in oral and written communications to clearly and effectively convey such matters as engagement objectives, evaluations, conclusions, and recommendations.

The new look creates a very demanding role. It includes all those aspects that make a good traditional auditor with a hard nose and deep concern with getting to the truth, and the new approach of being a top-flight consultant on risk and control issues. A job advertisement for European Commission–Deputy Director for Audit includes the following extracts:

Have the necessary professional competencies and in particular have a social auditing background as well as a sound knowledge of internal control frameworks, and management techniques. Be able to demonstrate:

- The necessary personal qualities and excellent management skills for a complex multicultural environment.
- Excellent intellectual, communication and interpersonal skills.
- Proven ability to take a leading role in developing and supporting an active, strategic and modern Internal Audit Service.

## Continuous Professional Development

Having got the right audit staff in post, it is then a question of getting them to perform and ensuring that they continue to develop. The IIA Attribute Standard 1230 on continuing professional development requires that:

Internal auditors must enhance their knowledge, skills, and other competencies through continuing professional development.

The IIA Practice Advisory 1230-1 continues this theme and suggests that:

Internal auditors are responsible for continuing their education to enhance and maintain their proficiency. Internal auditors need to stay informed about improvements and current developments in internal audit standards, procedures, and techniques, including the IIA's International Professional Practices Framework guidance. Continuing professional education (CPE) may be obtained through membership, participation, and volunteering in professional organizations such as the IIA; attendance at conferences, seminars, and in-house training programs; completion of college and self-study courses; and involvement in research projects.

Internal auditors are encouraged to demonstrate their proficiency by obtaining appropriate professional certification, such as the Certified Internal Auditor designation, other designations offered by the IIA, and additional designations related to internal auditing.

Internal auditors are encouraged to pursue CPE (related to their organization's activities and industry) to maintain their proficiency with regard to the governance, risk, and control processes of their unique organization.

Internal auditors who perform specialized audit and consulting work – such as information technology, tax, actuarial, or systems design – may undertake specialized CPE to allow them to perform their internal audit work with proficiency.

Internal auditors with professional certifications are responsible for obtaining sufficient CPE to satisfy requirements related to the professional certification held.

Internal auditors not presently holding appropriate certifications are encouraged to pursue an educational program and/or individual study to obtain professional certification.

## 5.10 Training and Development

Training is an important aspect of developing internal auditors and has to be carefully planned in line with a career developmental programme. Several issues should be noted.

### Common Body of Knowledge

The IIA has developed 20 disciplines in order of overall perceived importance:

|     |                      |     |                      |
| --- | -------------------- | --- | -------------------- |
| 1.  | Reasoning            | 2.  | Communications       |
| 3.  | Auditing             | 4.  | Ethics               |
| 5.  | Organizations        | 6.  | Sociology            |
| 7.  | Fraud                | 8.  | Computers            |
| 9.  | Financial accounting | 10. | Data gathering       |
| 11. | Managerial accounting| 12. | Government           |
| 13. | Legal                | 14. | Finance              |
| 15. | Taxes                | 16. | Quantitative methods |
| 17. | Marketing            | 18. | Statistics           |
| 19. | Economics            | 20. | International        |

## Training Auditors

1. **Specialist skills training via internal or external skills workshops**   These can be extremely efficient in terms of auditor development as long as the following rules are adhered to:

- They are tailored to the exact requirements of the internal audit department in question and not framed as general developmental courses. There is little point having a trainer stand in front of an audit team who has no idea what specialist work this team is involved in.
- They form part of an individual auditor's career development programme and can be geared towards tackling known weaknesses, identified from the performance appraisal scheme.
- They are based around a needs analysis that has formally identified the training needs of the department.
- The matters set out in the course are immediately put to use in a practical way in current audit work. This is a major benefit in that the real training goal is achieved not when participants listen to a trainer but when they actually perform the new techniques learnt.
- There is a clear link into the performance standards as set out in the audit manual. Skills workshops may be used to reinforce the standards required by the audit manual, which will encompass the defined working methodologies that have been adopted by the audit unit in question.
- They form part of a formal ongoing programme that falls within the strategic goals of the audit department, as a way of ensuring that staff understand and work within the frame established by the strategy.
- The workshops may be supported by audit management who may assume a key role in delivering the training modules.
- The policy may be to utilize all available in-house skills before external sources are applied to this programme. This is why the skills database that was discussed earlier is useful in isolating in-house skills and ensuring that they are shared.
- If the skills workshops are performed by external resources, they should be based on a tailored programme specifically designed by audit management.
- The CAE takes a personal interest in these programmes and ensures that they are given a high profile in the audit strategy. One major benefit of the skills workshop approach is that they may be contained within the working day. For example, we would expect audit management to introduce a two-hour session to cover a new development that will consume very little audit hours or interfere with ongoing audit work. This means there is no reason why this type of training should not be undertaken frequently, whenever there is a need.
- Value for money is achieved from them in terms of their transition from classroom to their successful application to audit work.

2. **Professional training**   This may be based on passing examinations of a defined professional body such as the Institute of Internal Auditors, which is a completely different form of training from skills-based courses. Therefore the rules here are different:

- This must form part of a long-term strategy underpinning the entire staffing policy of the audit department. It takes years to put staff through professional courses and a long-term approach is essential for this policy to become successful.
- A formal budget must attach to this programme that caters for subscription fees, books, travelling, college fees, time off, exam fees and so on. The CAE must be wary about depending on corporate training budgets as these tend to suffer in times of budget reduction exercises. Therefore the CAE may wish to set aside a separate fund for this activity, financed by fees from additional areas such as consultancy services.

- The requirement to secure a professional qualification should form part of the staffing policy. Real success is achieved when auditors are required to pass the internal audit qualification, to remain with the organization or at least obtain internal promotion. Unfortunately it is only by placing this severe pressure over the career auditor that one can guarantee that studies will be prioritized, so making success in the ensuing exams more probable. Without this pressure much is left to chance and many auditors will not study sufficiently hard to pass the exams.
- Professional exams cannot replace skills workshops for a number of reasons. First, they are based on general concepts and not geared towards any particular audit methodology. Second, they do not train individual auditors based on their special training needs but simply convey the basic principles of best audit practice. Lastly, an auditor who is well versed in 'question spotting' can pass a variety of exams without really understanding much about the topic in question.
- Audit management must have a mechanism to enable any elements of best professional practice, which is learnt in a classroom and brought back to work, to be considered and catered for within the audit department. An example may be statistical sampling, which may or may not be applied by the CAE, but cannot simply be ignored.
- The policy on audit textbooks should ensure that they are acquired for the department and not the individual, and sufficient copies are made available to all audit staff. This applies equally to research papers and other relevant material.

3. **The training coordinator**   Appointing a training coordinator is a positive way of promoting various training programmes, particularly where the coordinator can undertake some of the actual training. All larger internal audit departments should designate an audit manager as having responsibility for staff training. If this responsibility is extended to cover auditors' career development in line with a suitable programme of individual SWOT analysis then one is well on the way towards quality training. In fact, it is a good idea to make one audit manager responsible for implementing all human resource management policies and procedures. Where this manager is able to carry out in-house skills training personally, great progress may be made with audit training. Whatever the adopted format, it is clearly essential that all training is properly coordinated, or one might fall into the trap of staff attending a variety of courses with the sole objective of making themselves more marketable so that they might leave the organization for a better paid job. The other problem is where training has no relevance to the audit work being performed and is not being applied once learnt. The final drawback in not resourcing a training coordinator is that this might lead to a low pass rate for professional exams because insufficient support is made available.

4. **Directed reading**   This is one way of encouraging auditors to research aspects of internal audit. The department should subscribe to all relevant journals and publications. It is possible to assign specific topics to auditors so that each member of the department will research designated audit topics via the world wide web as a contribution to the audit information database. The auditor responsible for (as an example) 'systems interrogation' will research any articles or material that impact on this subject. This falls under 'training' since it involves the assimilation of new information.

5. **Training through work**   Programmed audits enable audit management to ensure auditors are rotated and exposed to a variety of audits and experiences. It is possible to designate smaller audits as 'training audits' where they form part of the auditors' personal development programme. This applies to all audits to an extent. For a training audit, additional budgeted hours will be assigned and extra assistance made available. This is the best type of on-the-job training so long as high standards have been adopted, supervision is good and monitoring and feedback are properly used.

6. **The audit review**   The audit review process enables audit managers and team leaders to direct the work of junior staff and also provides experience in staff management. The process should form part of the training programme by building in the concept of staff development. Therefore we are not looking for errors and/or poor performance, but merely providing advice to junior staff on how they might comply with the requirements of auditing standards. This allows a positive interface between audit management and more junior staff and should be seen as such. The review process also provides some training in management techniques primarily based around communication skills where the audit work that has been performed is considered and discussed. A good manager will use the review as an opportunity to provide vital on-the-job training. While being wholly relevant to the task in hand, it should also make reference to best audit practice and the underlying principles. This obviously depends on the presence of 'good' audit managers.

7. **Professional affiliations**   These can be part of CPD and stimulate group discussions. Membership of professional working groups should be encouraged as another way of keeping up to date. Seminars, meetings and presentations all contribute to bringing new thinking into the audit department as long as participants provide feedback once they return to work.

8. **The audit manual**   This sets out the defined methods and procedures required to discharge the audit mission. To feed into the auditor's personal development, this should be assimilated with accompanying skills workshops and training programmes. It is possible to compile a training manual that represents a basic minimum level of expertise required across the department. The manual defines how these skills will be applied. The audit manual has a wider role in addressing human resource policies on audit training and links into individual career development.

## 5.11   New Developments

So much is happening in the corporate governance arena and these pressures are impacting the internal audit role. The Institute of Internal Auditors has also made clear its views on the expanding role of internal auditing in organizational governance:

> Internal auditing will often be most effective in dealing with governance activities by doing more than performing discrete audits of specific processes. An internal auditor's unique position in an organization allows him or her to observe governance structure and design, while not having direct responsibility for them. Often, internal auditors can assist organizations better by advising the board of directors and executive management on needed improvements and changes in structure and design, not just whether established processes are operating. This is different, however, from providing objective assessment of specific governance activities through discrete audits. Ultimately, internal audit assessments regarding governance activities are likely to be based on information obtained from numerous audit assignments over a period of time. Optimally, internal auditors should aim to provide assessments on the effectiveness of key organizational governance elements, either separately from, or combined with, assessments on the effectiveness of risk management and key controls. These governance activity assessments should take into account:
>
> - Provide advice that focuses on the organization's governance structure to meet compliance requirements and addresses basic organization risks.
> - Perform audits of design and effectiveness of specific governance-related processes.

- Evaluate best practices and their adaptation to the organization by focusing on the optimization of governance practices and structure.
- Allocation of Audit Effort.
- Less Structured More Structured.
- Specific governance assignments.
- The results of specific board-level governance review work.
- Governance issues arising out of myriad audit assignments performed during a specific period of time.
- Other information available to or known by the internal auditor.

Internal auditors may operate most effectively for the board as an agent of the board who provide independent, objective information and evaluation. The board would then own internal auditing, fostering a mutually supportive internal audit–board relationship. To gain a complete understanding of the organization's operations, it is essential that the board consider the internal auditor's work. For instance, internal auditors can inform the board on matters such as culture, tone, ethics, transparency, and internal interactions. In addition, contemporary internal auditing is based on the organization's framework for identifying, responding to, and managing the different strategic, operational, financial, and compliance risks facing the organization. As a result, internal auditors can provide objective assurance on the effectiveness of the framework as a whole, including management's monitoring and assurance activities, and on management of individual key risks. This role of supporting the board, however, can create tensions because internal auditing also may be positioned as a partner to management. Internal auditors will need to manage the needs and expectations of both constituents carefully.[4]

In their blueprint for the internal audit profession, the Institute of Internal Auditors suggest that internal audit functions should undertake four main tasks:

1. Work more closely with senior management to ensure the key risks to their organisation are identified.
2. Identify skills gaps which stop them providing assurance over key risks and work with management to plug those gaps.
3. Take care that they move into new areas only if they can agree with management that this will be valuable in providing assurance over key risks and if they are confident they have the required skills.
4. Coordinate assurance activities over these key risks. [5]

Internal audit's role in the risk management agenda has been given a boost by the Institute of Internal Auditors in their significant guidance covering 10 risk management imperatives that internal auditors should be considering:

### 1. Assess the Organization's Current Processes and Capabilities
To strengthen organizational risk management, internal auditing should first conduct a detailed assessment of the organization's risk management processes, many of which might be undocumented and informal. The assessment should help build an inventory of risk processes and serve as a foundational baseline. It should also help determine the organization's ability to identify, analyze, monitor, and mitigate significant risks that could impede achievement of organizational objectives.

### 2. Coordinate with Other Risk and Control Functions
Look for opportunities to partner with other risk and control functions while maintaining your functional independence and objectivity. For example, consider involving other risk and control

functions in the assessment of risk management processes recommended in Imperative No. 1. Also consider how the functions can collaborate on an enterprisewide assessment of risk management processes. Roundtable participants agreed that most organizations would benefit from a common, single risk assessment developed by internal auditing in concert with other governance, risk, and control (GRC) functions in addition to a single risk profile. It's also important to establish communication protocols and procedures to share risk knowledge and information on an enterprisewide basis.

### 3. Participate in Summits with Key Stakeholders

To many observers, risk oversight is the No. 1 priority for directors and management alike in today's post-meltdown business environment. It's critical for CAEs to facilitate in-depth discussions with senior management and directors about risk management issues and priorities to ensure that internal auditing and other key risk players understand their chief stakeholders' expectations. Ideally, such an effort would be conducted jointly by internal auditing and any other key risk and control players, such as the chief risk officer, in addition to senior financial officers. Plan to brief members of the audit committee and senior management on a regular basis and consider holding a series of educational seminars with directors to provide an ongoing vehicle for two-way communication on this essential topic.

### 4. Help the Organization Develop Near-term Strategies

After assessing current risk management processes, and revisiting stakeholder expectations, try to facilitate the development of near-term organizational risk management strategies. Discussions at the roundtable point to the benefits of organizations taking a step-by-step approach to risk management. Accordingly, facilitate a plan to achieve the organization's next step in terms of risk management maturity as opposed to the final stage in the developmental process. Although internal auditing should refrain from any decision-making role in the development of risk management strategies, the CAE can serve as a valuable adviser to both senior management and the board of directors. If your organization lacks an ERM strategy, suggest options for consideration. Scope out the benefits of a step-by-step approach to ERM and suggest what these steps might be. Also consider delineating the roles of the various risk and control functions relative to risk management.

### 5. Strengthen Top-level Communications

As the organization steps up its focus on risk management, keep executive management and the audit committee well-informed of the organization's progress and strategic direction. Explore how to enhance risk reporting to the committee and seek to make risk considerations a central discussion item on the audit committee's agenda.

### 6. Define Internal Auditing's Role

After facilitating a strategic reassessment of the organization's approach to risk, work with chief stakeholders to develop an appropriate role and strategy for internal auditing related to risk management. If the organization's risk management processes are in the developmental stage, internal auditing might prefer to adopt a consulting role. Conversely, if risk management processes are developed sufficiently to audit, then internal auditing can play an assurance role. Practitioners should recognize that internal auditing's role will likely evolve along with the organization's risk management processes.

### 7. Audit Risk Management Incrementally

Roundtable CAEs spoke enthusiastically about the benefits of taking a step-by-step approach to auditing risk management. 'You can't audit all of your company's ERM activities but you can evaluate parts of them and look at how they get their data,' said one CAE. 'Bite off manageable chunks; audit risks in a given area,' said another. 'Don't try to be world-class all at once,' said a third CAE. When it comes to setting priorities, audit committees and executive management want internal auditing to concentrate on areas posing the greatest risks – those that could impact achievement of major corporate objectives. Make sure to identify and monitor key strategic, operational, and business risks, advised one roundtable CAE. Another recommended singling out the three to five risks that could destroy the organization, including the types of high-impact, low-probability risks that contributed to the subprime mortgage crisis.

## 8. Assess Audit Skills and Capabilities

One of the challenges facing internal auditors seeking to expand their scope of risk management activities is the perception that risk management is beyond the scope and capabilities of internal auditing. 'Many auditors think control first and lack an adequate business perspective,' said one roundtable CAE. 'Internal auditing needs to provide value beyond compliance, and it's hard to add value when you've been focusing on Sarbanes–Oxley,' said another.

## 9. Execute the Audit Strategy with Appropriate Reporting

Effective reporting is central to successful internal auditing and risk management. Determine the type of reporting that best suits your particular internal audit function. For organizations with more formal or maturing risk management processes, it might be appropriate to perform audits and then issue assurance reports. For organizations that are just developing risk processes, internal auditing might play a more consultative role and issue consulting reports. If the organization has yet to produce any risk reports, internal auditing should consider other types of reporting that could provide management and directors with important updates on the organization's risk profile or other risk-related changes. Auditors should also consider providing the audit committee with periodic updates on the implementation of management's risk management strategy.

## 10. Keep up with Evolving Practices

As risk management practices and processes continue to evolve, it's important for CAEs to keep abreast of relevant internal audit practices and to ensure the organization benefits from their up-to-date insights and perspectives. For example, credit rating agency Standard & Poor's has begun to include ERM assessments in its ratings of nonfinancial companies. In addition, the National Association of Corporate Directors, The Committee of Sponsoring Organizations of the Treadway Commission, and other leading organizations are producing numerous studies and papers focusing on risk management practices that offer useful information and insights for internal auditors. [6]

Risk imperative 2 is interesting as it calls for building bridges with other risk and control functions. This idea takes us further into our discussion of the respective responsibilities of the chief audit executive and the chief risk officer. It is only a question of time before the audit committee or the risk committee calls for the integration of the risk and control functions along with an integrated approach to reviewing and reporting back the assurances arising from these teams. The call for enterprise-wide risk management, enterprise-wide risk reporting and the same approach to the assurance process means that organizations may be able to simplify the way risk is managed and reviewed by everyone within the organization.

There is no escaping the fallout from scandals such as Enron, WorldCom and Xerox and the IIA has issued guidance in the wake of these high-impact corporate financial scandals that impact the internal audit role:

The key lessons to be learned from the recent corporate scandals are centred on a better understanding of the need to realise the value of effective corporate governance.

- The role of the board must in future be significantly enhanced. Each board member needs to understand clearly their duties and obligations. There must be a better framework for the board to interact with other parties that have responsibility for independent assurance, such as internal audit and the audit committee. The effectiveness of the board must also be enhanced through an increased and better informed level of participation by non-executive directors. The board must have available to it all forms of reliable information to be in a position to properly understand the real business risks facing the organisation and to explore issues in sufficient depth. This requires that the board must commit sufficient time on a regular basis for meetings.

- The internal audit function must have the professionalism, profile and independence to fulfil its role effectively. It must be able to provide an environment of challenge, transparency and candid reporting to the highest level without fear and retribution. Internal audit must provide the focus on risk for the organisation. It must demonstrate a good understanding of the organisation's business operations together with communication and persuasion skills to get its message across. The IIA's International Standards are the benchmark against which effective internal audit functions can be measured.

Loyalty to the right stakeholders and serving the right interests. Executive management serve the organisation and exist to preserve and protect it from exposures to risks of any kind. Internal auditors provide independent assurance to executive management and the board about the adequacy and effectiveness of the risk management and control framework in operation and seek to improve that framework through the promulgation of best practice. Both parties should also be aware of all stakeholder interests in the organisation. External auditors serve the interests of the shareholders and investors in the company. Alarm bells should ring when there is a perceived shift in loyalties and priorities.[7]

The scandals continue with the 2007/08 Credit Crunch, where internal audit is being asked to redefine its role as the world calls out for more control over reckless behaviour from businesses that fail to fully understand the systemic risk that comes with global trading. Meanwhile, there are calls from around the world to make internal audit mandatory in all publicly quoted companies, or ensure that there is careful consideration for setting up such a team. The ICGN has added its voice to the debate in their global corporate governance principles:

Companies should establish and maintain an effective internal audit function that has the respect, confidence and co-operation of both the board and management. Where the board decides not to establish such a function, full reasons for this should be disclosed in the annual report, as well as an explanation of how adequate assurance has been maintained in its absence. The internal audit function should have a functional reporting line to the audit committee chair. The audit committee should be ultimately responsible for the appointment, performance assessment and dismissal of the head of internal audit or outsourced internal audit provider. The external auditor should not provide internal audit services to the company.[8]

## Summary and Conclusions

The challenge has been set by the corporate governance, risk management and control dimensions that now drive both the business world and public services. The role of internal auditing now reflects this factor, and audit charters are being torn up and rewritten to secure this important focus. These heightened expectations have impacted the competence demanded of the internal auditor. We can summarize this development by using the simple model shown in Figure 5.2.

We have already mentioned the corporate governance, risk management and control context of internal auditing. This is incorporated into the audit charter and in turn determines which audit

**FIGURE 5.2**   Audit competence cycle.

services are provided. The second part of the triangle is the audit processes and procedures, which is the way audit work is performed to provide risk-based assurance and consulting services. The third dimension is the people who are recruited and retained at audit manager level and below, to perform the actual services (using the set procedures). Internal audit competencies sit in the middle of the triangle as the key to ensuring the rest is achieved. So long as we have the right people doing the right things to set standards there is a good chance of success. If there is no focus on developing competencies to reflect the new expectations, then there is no real starting place for tackling the 'raised bar'. Raising the bar for the internal audit shop has been a key consideration for many standard setters and is uppermost in the minds of most CAEs. Note that Dan Swanson's book, *Raising the Bar*, published by IT Governance, August 2010, covers many of the key issues that now sit on the internal auditor's agenda.

## Endnotes

1. Moeller, Robert and Witt, Herbert (1999) *Brink's Modern Internal Auditing*, 5th edition, New York: John Wiley & Sons, Inc., para 1.7.
2. 'Ethics and the accountant in the public sector'. ACCA, March 1999, p. 51.
3. Marshall, Alan, 'So what do you do for a living?' *Internal Auditing*, May 1994, p. 17.
4. *Organizational Governance: Guidance for Internal Auditors*, July 2006, The Institute of Internal Auditors, Position Paper.
5. 'Towards a blueprint for the internal audit profession'. Research by the Institute of Internal Auditors, UK and Ireland in association with Deloitte, Deloitte & Touche and the Institute of Internal Auditors, UK and Ireland, 2008, p. 7–.
6. *10 Risk Management Imperatives for Internal Auditing*, 2009, The Institute of Internal Auditors and its Audit Executive Center.
7. *A New Agenda for Corporate Governance Reform*, IIA UK&Ireland, 2008, Corporate governance reforms recommended by the Institute of Internal Auditors, UK and Ireland (IIA), in the wake of recent high-impact corporate financial scandals such as Enron, WorldCom and Xerox.
8. ICGN Member Ratification of the *ICGN Global Corporate Governance Principles*, Revised 20 August 2009, 6.6 Internal Audit.

Chapter 6

# PROFESSIONALISM

## Introduction

The internal auditor must be professional in the way work is planned and performed. This basic requirement involves a great deal of effort to ensure it is achieved and there are many sources of information that we can turn to for guidance in this respect. The ACCA argue that the term 'profession' suggests a grouping of people who have made a study of an area of knowledge or expertise and have achieved a level of competence in their chosen field.[1]

Internal audit is now a full-blown profession that features in most large organizations, throughout all sectors. This entails the use of competent staff, a respected role in the organization and robust quality assurance arrangements that underpin the defined services that are provided. Note that all references to IIA definitions, code of ethics, IIA attribute and performance standards, practice advisories and practice guides relate to the International Professional Practices Framework (IPPF) prepared by the Institute of Internal Auditors in 2009. This chapter covers the following areas:

Note that the IIA International Standards for the Professional Practices of Internal Auditing is used extensively in *The Essential Guide to Internal Auditing*, since the IIA is the only professional body that is dedicated to the specialist field of internal auditing.

## 6.1 Audit Professionalism

Internal auditing needs defined standards and this contributes to the development of professional audit services.

## Hallmarks of Professionalism

Before studying the various standards attached to internal auditing we consider the main features of a professional discipline:

1. **Training programme**   A long specialized training programme that has to be undergone by the student before reaching practitioner status. This will typically last several years, covering topics that are dedicated to (or have a direct link with) the particular discipline.

2. **Common body of knowledge**   A common body of knowledge (CBOK) attaches to the discipline and has to be mastered. This represents a minimum level of knowledge that is studied and understood. Some feel that the practitioner need not memorize an extensive range of facts as in practice one would have access to reference material. There is, though, a level of knowledge that should be at the instant recall of the practitioner. The extent to which various subjects are relevant to the discipline will have to be addressed when defining the content of the CBOK. The process of setting the CBOK will partly determine the boundaries of the profession and the areas considered important.

3. **Code of ethics**   A code of ethics covering the required conduct expected from individual members of the profession. This is a fundamental requirement for all true professions in that it sets a moral framework within which individuals may practise. When one is acting as a professional, one in fact represents the entire profession. A suitable code of ethics will not only refer to the standards to which work will be performed, it will also set an overall code of conduct based around complete honesty and integrity as generalized concepts. This then sets the framework within which members are expected to conduct their affairs over and above mere compliance with the laws of the land. The invisible bond between the individual practitioner and the professional body allows a mutual trust that directs the respective activities of the two parties at all times.

4. **Sanctions**   The sanction of the community applies to ensure that members perform to the required standards to form a formal bond between the profession and society in general. If the profession is unable to regulate itself, then society will resort to legislation to ensure that these demands are achieved. This is due to the importance of the services in question, in terms of their impact on society. Nonprofessionals will tend not to attract this degree of attention from society.

5. **Control over services**   A professional person should be able to withdraw services where the situation is morally unacceptable. True professionals work to extremely high standards that cannot be compromised. If they were compromised, the individual should be in a position to withdraw from the situation.

6. **Qualified practitioners**   The practice should be limited to qualified practitioners who have mastered the common body of knowledge. Some form of licence would be issued. Licensed practitioners would be recognized by society as the only people allowed to carry out this type of work. This constitutes a formal barrier to the achievement of professional status as it is difficult to argue that a profession can be carried out by anyone without restriction.

7. **Morality**   The concept of morals over pure profits means that the discipline moves to a higher level above simple employment. Individuals should be practising through a desire to

develop the profession and a wish to make a positive contribution, and would not be expected to hold a second job (as opposed to voluntary work) that is in any way related to the main role. The professional would be asked to work within the formal moral framework and not seek profit making as an overriding objective.

8. **Technical difficulty**   The services provided should be technically difficult and this is linked to the concept of a common body of knowledge. There should be some level of technical difficulty that has to be mastered through extensive training and several years' practical experience. If anyone can do the required work there is no justification for deeming the area as meeting the requirements of professionalism.

9. **Examinations**   Formal examinations form part of the learning process in showing that the participant has acquired the various skills and techniques required. Although the extent to which examinations represent real-life situations that the practitioner will have to face is debatable, they remain an important component. The process of formulating the examinations syllabus is useful for it forces one to define the scope of work and level of competence demanded.

10. **Journals**   The publication of a journal and literature dedicated to the subject is another hallmark of professional status. One would expect to see a relevant monthly journal that contains technical updates and useful articles along with features on social meetings. Another main sign of professionalism is research studies that examine subjects of interest to members. These studies should result in changes to the direction and focus of the profession in specific areas. Textbooks play an important role, with major works representing academic standards in terms of providing a comprehensive coverage of relevant subject matter. It is difficult to visualize a profession unable to display a major range of associated textbooks.

11. **Professional body**   A professional body represents the interests of its members and this is a prerequisite for many of the matters outlined above.

12. **Compliance with rules**   The professional body would have to enforce various sanctions against members who failed to comply with any of the requirements of membership. One would wish to see a formal process (say with an ethics committee) to receive, consider and decide on cases referred to the professional body concerning the conduct of their members. There should be formal representation and an appeals process.

13. **Service to society**   A major feature of a profession is the overriding concept that its members are providing a service to society as opposed to individual clients. The ethos of the profession should be embodied in the view that it is there to fulfil an important role in society that is over and above the role it plays in servicing clients. Any conflict should be resolved by placing the duty of care to society first, which may serve to rule out many contenders who cannot show this.

Internal auditing is able to meet all of the above measures and is now firmly established as a professional discipline. This has been a huge achievement as 10 to 20 years ago it certainly was not the case. Having a firm professional base allows the internal audit community to plan for the future and track the way it needs to progress as its newly acquired high profile places it firmly on the boardroom agenda.

## 6.2   Internal Auditing Standards

### The Institute of Internal Auditors (IIA)

The IIA have described their original objectives in 1941 when they were first established (www.theiiaorg.com):

> To cultivate, promote, and disseminate knowledge and information concerning internal auditing and subjects related thereto; to establish and maintain high standards of integrity, honor, and character among internal auditors; to furnish information regarding internal auditing and the practice and methods thereof to its members etc.

Since then the IIA has moved on to develop their Professional Practices Framework (PPF), which contains the basic elements of the profession. It provides a consistent, organized method of looking at the fundamental principles and procedures that make internal auditing a unique, disciplined and systematic activity. The purpose of the standards is to:

1. Delineate basic principles that represent the practice of internal auditing as it should be.
2. Provide a framework for performing a broad range of value-added internal audit activities.
3. Establish the basis for the measurement of internal audit performance.
4. Foster improved organizational processes and operations.

The IPPF consists of International Standards for the Professional Practice of Internal Auditing, which have to be followed by all practising (IIA) internal auditors. Practice Advisories are pronouncements that are strongly recommended and endorsed by the IIA. Note that the revisions of 2009 reduced the number of practice advisories down from 83 to 42. Position Papers deal with specific aspects of the governance and risk management agenda, while Practice Guides cover detailed guidance for carrying out internal audit activities.

The 2009 standards now use the word 'must' to mean an unconditional requirement and the word 'should' where conformance is expected unless, when applying professional judgement, circumstances justify deviation.

The formal definition of internal audit is repeated for reference:

> Internal auditing is an independent, objective assurance and consulting activity designed to add value and improve an organisation's operations. It helps an organisation accomplish its objectives by bringing a systematic, disciplined approach to evaluate and improve the effectiveness of risk management, control, and governance processes.

A main part of the IPPF is attribute and performance standards. Attribute standards describe the defining character of organizations and individuals performing internal audit services, while performance standards describe the nature of internal audit services and provide quality criteria against which to measure performance, and the individual implementation standards are used to augment the attribute and performance standards by helping employ them in particular types of engagements. The 2009 International Standards for the Professional Practice of Internal Auditing cover both assurance services and client-based consulting and are reproduced below:

ATTRIBUTE STANDARDS

# 1000 – Purpose, Authority, and Responsibility

The purpose, authority, and responsibility of the internal audit activity must be formally defined in an internal audit charter, consistent with the Definition of Internal Auditing, the Code of Ethics, and the *Standards*. The chief audit executive must periodically review the internal audit charter and present it to senior management and the board for approval.

**Interpretation:**   *The internal audit charter is a formal document that defines the internal audit activity's purpose, authority, and responsibility. The internal audit charter establishes the internal audit activity's position within the organization; authorizes access to records, personnel, and physical properties relevant to the performance of engagements; and defines the scope of internal audit activities. Final approval of the internal audit charter resides with the board.*

**1000.A1** – The nature of assurance services provided to the organization must be defined in the internal audit charter. If assurances are to be provided to parties outside the organization, the nature of these assurances must also be defined in the internal audit charter.

**1000.C1** – The nature of consulting services must be defined in the internal audit charter.

# 1010 – Recognition of the Definition of Internal Auditing, the Code of Ethics, and the Standards in the Internal Audit Charter

The mandatory nature of the Definition of Internal Auditing, the Code of Ethics, and the *Standards* must be recognized in the internal audit charter. The chief audit executive should discuss the Definition of Internal Auditing, the Code of Ethics, and the *Standards* with senior management and the board.

# 1100 – Independence and Objectivity

The internal audit activity must be independent, and internal auditors must be objective in performing their work.

**Interpretation:**   *Independence is the freedom from conditions that threaten the ability of the internal audit activity or the chief audit executive to carry out internal audit responsibilities in an unbiased manner. To achieve the degree of independence necessary to effectively carry out the responsibilities of the internal audit activity, the chief audit executive has direct and unrestricted access to senior management and the board. This can be achieved through a dual-reporting relationship. Threats to independence must be managed at the individual auditor, engagement, functional, and organizational levels.*

*Objectivity is an unbiased mental attitude that allows internal auditors to perform engagements in such a manner that they believe in their work product and that no quality compromises are made. Objectivity requires that internal auditors do not subordinate their judgment on audit matters to others. Threats to objectivity must be managed at the individual auditor, engagement, functional, and organizational levels.*

## 1110 – Organizational Independence

The chief audit executive must report to a level within the organization that allows the internal audit activity to fulfill its responsibilities. The chief audit executive must confirm to the board, at least annually, the organizational independence of the internal audit activity.

**1110.A1** – The internal audit activity must be free from interference in determining the scope of internal auditing, performing work, and communicating results.

## 1111 – Direct Interaction with the Board

The chief audit executive must communicate and interact directly with the board.

## 1120 – Individual Objectivity

Internal auditors must have an impartial, unbiased attitude and avoid any conflict of interest.

**Interpretation:**    *Conflict of interest is a situation in which an internal auditor, who is in a position of trust, has a competing professional or personal interest. Such competing interests can make it difficult to fulfill his or her duties impartially. A conflict of interest exists even if no unethical or improper act results. A conflict of interest can create an appearance of impropriety that can undermine confidence in the internal auditor, the internal audit activity, and the profession. A conflict of interest could impair an individual's ability to perform his or her duties and responsibilities objectively.*

## 1130 – Impairment to Independence or Objectivity

If independence or objectivity is impaired in fact or appearance, the details of the impairment must be disclosed to appropriate parties. The nature of the disclosure will depend upon the impairment.

**Interpretation:**    *Impairment to organizational independence and individual objectivity may include, but is not limited to, personal conflict of interest, scope limitations, restrictions on access to records, personnel, and properties, and resource limitations, such as funding.*

*The determination of appropriate parties to which the details of an impairment to independence or objectivity must be disclosed is dependent upon the expectations of the internal audit activity's and the chief audit executive's responsibilities to senior management and the board as described in the internal audit charter, as well as the nature of the impairment.*

**1130.A1** – Internal auditors must refrain from assessing specific operations for which they were previously responsible. Objectivity is presumed to be impaired if an internal auditor provides assurance services for an activity for which the internal auditor had responsibility within the previous year.

**1130.A2** – Assurance engagements for functions over which the chief audit executive has responsibility must be overseen by a party outside the internal audit activity.

**1130.C1** – Internal auditors may provide consulting services relating to operations for which they had previous responsibilities.

**1130.C2** – If internal auditors have potential impairments to independence or objectivity relating to proposed consulting services, disclosure must be made to the engagement client prior to accepting the engagement.

## 1200 – Proficiency and Due Professional Care

Engagements must be performed with proficiency and due professional care.

## 1210 – Proficiency

Internal auditors must possess the knowledge, skills, and other competencies needed to perform their individual responsibilities. The internal audit activity collectively must possess or obtain the knowledge, skills, and other competencies needed to perform its responsibilities.

**Interpretation:** *Knowledge, skills, and other competencies is a collective term that refers to the professional proficiency required of internal auditors to effectively carry out their professional responsibilities. Internal auditors are encouraged to demonstrate their proficiency by obtaining appropriate professional certifications and qualifications, such as the Certified Internal Auditor designation and other designations offered by The Institute of Internal Auditors and other appropriate professional organizations.*

**1210.A1** – The chief audit executive must obtain competent advice and assistance if the internal auditors lack the knowledge, skills, or other competencies needed to perform all or part of the engagement.

**1210.A2** – Internal auditors must have sufficient knowledge to evaluate the risk of fraud and the manner in which it is managed by the organization, but are not expected to have the expertise of a person whose primary responsibility is detecting and investigating fraud.

**1210.A3** – Internal auditors must have sufficient knowledge of key information technology risks and controls and available technology-based audit techniques to perform their assigned work. However, not all internal auditors are expected to have the expertise of an internal auditor whose primary responsibility is information technology auditing.

**1210.C1** – The chief audit executive must decline the consulting engagement or obtain competent advice and assistance if the internal auditors lack the knowledge, skills, or other competencies needed to perform all or part of the engagement.

## 1220 – Due Professional Care

Internal auditors must apply the care and skill expected of a reasonably prudent and competent internal auditor. Due professional care does not imply infallibility.

**1220.A1** – Internal auditors must exercise due professional care by considering the:
- Extent of work needed to achieve the engagement's objectives;
- Relative complexity, materiality, or significance of matters to which assurance procedures are applied;
- Adequacy and effectiveness of governance, risk management, and control processes;
- Probability of significant errors, fraud, or noncompliance; and
- Cost of assurance in relation to potential benefits.

**1220.A2** – In exercising due professional care internal auditors must consider the use of technology-based audit and other data analysis techniques.

**1220.A3** – Internal auditors must be alert to the significant risks that might affect objectives, operations, or resources. However, assurance procedures alone, even when performed with due professional care, do not guarantee that all significant risks will be identified.

**1220.C1** – Internal auditors must exercise due professional care during a consulting engagement by considering the:

- Needs and expectations of clients, including the nature, timing, and communication of engagement results;
- Relative complexity and extent of work needed to achieve the engagement's objectives; and
- Cost of the consulting engagement in relation to potential benefits.

## 1230 – Continuing Professional Development

Internal auditors must enhance their knowledge, skills, and other competencies through continuing professional development.

## 1300 – Quality Assurance and Improvement Program

The chief audit executive must develop and maintain a quality assurance and improvement program that covers all aspects of the internal audit activity.

**Interpretation:** *A quality assurance and improvement program is designed to enable an evaluation of the internal audit activity's conformance with the Definition of Internal Auditing and the Standards and an evaluation of whether internal auditors apply the Code of Ethics. The program also assesses the efficiency and effectiveness of the internal audit activity and identifies opportunities for improvement.*

## 1310 – Requirements of the Quality Assurance and Improvement Program

The quality assurance and improvement program must include both internal and external assessments.

## 1311 – Internal Assessments

Internal assessments must include:

- Ongoing monitoring of the performance of the internal audit activity; and
- Periodic reviews performed through self-assessment or by other persons within the organization with sufficient knowledge of internal audit practices.

**Interpretation:** *Ongoing monitoring is an integral part of the day-to-day supervision, review, and measurement of the internal audit activity. Ongoing monitoring is incorporated into the routine policies and practices used to manage the internal audit activity and uses processes, tools, and information* considered necessary to evaluate conformance with the Definition of Internal Auditing, the Code of Ethics, and the Standards.

Periodic reviews are assessments conducted to evaluate conformance with the Definition of Internal Auditing, the Code of Ethics, and the Standards. Sufficient knowledge of internal audit practices requires at least an understanding of all elements of the International Professional Practices Framework.

## 1312 – External Assessments

External assessments must be conducted at least once every five years by a qualified, independent reviewer or review team from outside the organization. The chief audit executive must discuss with the board:

- The need for more frequent external assessments; and
- The qualifications and independence of the external reviewer or review team, including any potential conflict of interest.

**Interpretation:**   A qualified reviewer or review team consists of individuals who are competent in the professional practice of internal auditing and the external assessment process. The evaluation of the competency of the reviewer and review team is a judgment that considers the professional internal audit experience and professional credentials of the individuals selected to perform the review. The evaluation of qualifications also considers the size and complexity of the organizations that the reviewers have been associated with in relation to the organization for which the internal audit activity is being assessed, as well as the need for particular sector, industry, or technical knowledge.

An independent reviewer or review team means not having either a real or an apparent conflict of interest and not being a part of, or under the control of, the organization to which the internal audit activity belongs.

## 1320 – Reporting on the Quality Assurance and Improvement Program

The chief audit executive must communicate the results of the quality assurance and improvement program to senior management and the board.

**Interpretation:**   The form, content, and frequency of communicating the results of the quality assurance and improvement program is established through discussions with senior management and the board and considers the responsibilities of the internal audit activity and chief audit executive as contained in the internal audit charter. To demonstrate conformance with the Definition of Internal Auditing, the Code of Ethics, and the Standards, the results of external and periodic internal assessments are communicated upon completion of such assessments and the results of ongoing monitoring are communicated at least annually. The results include the reviewer's or review team's assessment with respect to the degree of conformance.

## 1321 – Use of 'Conforms with the International Standards for the Professional Practice of Internal Auditing'

The chief audit executive may state that the internal audit activity conforms with the International Standards for the Professional Practice of Internal Auditing only if the results of the quality assurance and improvement program support this statement.

## 1322 – Disclosure of Nonconformance

When nonconformance with the Definition of Internal Auditing, the Code of Ethics, or the *Standards* impacts the overall scope or operation of the internal audit activity, the chief audit executive must disclose the nonconformance and the impact to senior management and the board.

## PERFORMANCE STANDARDS

## 2000 – Managing the Internal Audit Activity

The chief audit executive must effectively manage the internal audit activity to ensure it adds value to the organization.

**Interpretation:**   *The internal audit activity is effectively managed when:*

- *The results of the internal audit activity's work achieve the purpose and responsibility included in the internal audit charter;*
- *The internal audit activity conforms with the Definition of Internal Auditing and the Standards; and*
- *The individuals who are part of the internal audit activity demonstrate conformance with the Code of Ethics and the Standards.*

## 2010 – Planning

The chief audit executive must establish risk-based plans to determine the priorities of the internal audit activity, consistent with the organization's goals.

**Interpretation:**   *The chief audit executive is responsible for developing a risk-based plan. The chief audit executive takes into account the organization's risk management framework, including using risk appetite levels set by management for the different activities or parts of the organization. If a framework does not exist, the chief audit executive uses his/her own judgment of risks after consultation with senior management and the board.*

**2010.A1** – The internal audit activity's plan of engagements must be based on a documented risk assessment, undertaken at least annually. The input of senior management and the board must be considered in this process.

**2010.C1** – The chief audit executive should consider accepting proposed consulting engagements based on the engagement's potential to improve management of risks, add value, and improve the organization's operations. Accepted engagements must be included in the plan.

## 2020 – Communication and Approval

The chief audit executive must communicate the internal audit activity's plans and resource requirements, including significant interim changes, to senior management and the board for review and approval. The chief audit executive must also communicate the impact of resource limitations.

## 2030 – Resource Management

The chief audit executive must ensure that internal audit resources are appropriate, sufficient, and effectively deployed to achieve the approved plan.

**Interpretation:** *Appropriate refers to the mix of knowledge, skills, and other competencies needed to perform the plan. Sufficient refers to the quantity of resources needed to accomplish the plan. Resources are effectively deployed when they are used in a way that optimizes the achievement of the approved plan.*

## 2040 – Policies and Procedures

The chief audit executive must establish policies and procedures to guide the internal audit activity.

**Interpretation:** *The form and content of policies and procedures are dependent upon the size and structure of the internal audit activity and the complexity of its work.*

## 2050 – Coordination

The chief audit executive should share information and coordinate activities with other internal and external providers of assurance and consulting services to ensure proper coverage and minimize duplication of efforts.

## 2060 – Reporting to Senior Management and the Board

The chief audit executive must report periodically to senior management and the board on the internal audit activity's purpose, authority, responsibility, and performance relative to its plan. Reporting must also include significant risk exposures and control issues, including fraud risks, governance issues, and other matters needed or requested by senior management and the board.

**Interpretation:** *The frequency and content of reporting are determined in discussion with senior management and the board and depend on the importance of the information to be communicated and the urgency of the related actions to be taken by senior management or the board.*

## 2100 – Nature of Work

The internal audit activity must evaluate and contribute to the improvement of governance, risk management, and control processes using a systematic and disciplined approach.

## 2110 – Governance

The internal audit activity must assess and make appropriate recommendations for improving the governance process in its accomplishment of the following objectives:

- Promoting appropriate ethics and values within the organization;
- Ensuring effective organizational performance management and accountability;
- Communicating risk and control information to appropriate areas of the organization; and
- Coordinating the activities of and communicating information among the board, external and internal auditors, and management.

**2110.A1** – The internal audit activity must evaluate the design, implementation, and effectiveness of the organization's ethics-related objectives, programs, and activities.

**2110.A2** – The internal audit activity must assess whether the information technology governance of the organization sustains and supports the organization's strategies and objectives.

**2110.C1** – Consulting engagement objectives must be consistent with the overall values and goals of the organization.


## 2120 – Risk Management

The internal audit activity must evaluate the effectiveness and contribute to the improvement of risk management processes.

**Interpretation:**   *Determining whether risk management processes are effective is a judgment resulting from the internal auditor's assessment that:*

- *Organizational objectives support and align with the organization's mission;*
- *Significant risks are identified and assessed;*
- *Appropriate risk responses are selected that align risks with the organization's risk appetite; and*
- *Relevant risk information is captured and communicated in a timely manner across the organization, enabling staff, management, and the board to carry out their responsibilities.*

*Risk management processes are monitored through ongoing management activities, separate evaluations, or both.*

**2120.A1** – The internal audit activity must evaluate risk exposures relating to the organization's governance, operations, and information systems regarding the:

- Reliability and integrity of financial and operational information.
- Effectiveness and efficiency of operations.
- Safeguarding of assets; and
- Compliance with laws, regulations, and contracts.

**2120.A2** – The internal audit activity must evaluate the potential for the occurrence of fraud and how the organization manages fraud risk.

**2120.C1** – During consulting engagements, internal auditors must address risk consistent with the engagement's objectives and be alert to the existence of other significant risks.

**2120.C2** – Internal auditors must incorporate knowledge of risks gained from consulting engagements into their evaluation of the organization's risk management processes.

**2120.C3** – When assisting management in establishing or improving risk management processes, internal auditors must refrain from assuming any management responsibility by actually managing risks.

## 2130 – Control

The internal audit activity must assist the organization in maintaining effective controls by evaluating their effectiveness and efficiency and by promoting continuous improvement.

**2130.A1** – The internal audit activity must evaluate the adequacy and effectiveness of controls in responding to risks within the organization's governance, operations, and information systems regarding the:
- Reliability and integrity of financial and operational information;
- Effectiveness and efficiency of operations;
- Safeguarding of assets; and
- Compliance with laws, regulations, and contracts.

**2130.A2** – Internal auditors should ascertain the extent to which operating and program goals and objectives have been established and conform to those of the organization.

**2130.A3** – Internal auditors should review operations and programs to ascertain the extent to which results are consistent with established goals and objectives to determine whether operations and programs are being implemented or performed as intended.

**2130.C1** – During consulting engagements, internal auditors must address controls consistent with the engagement's objectives and be alert to significant control issues.

**2130.C2** – Internal auditors must incorporate knowledge of controls gained from consulting engagements into evaluation of the organization's control processes.

## 2200 – Engagement Planning

Internal auditors must develop and document a plan for each engagement, including the engagement's objectives, scope, timing, and resource allocations.

## 2201 – Planning Considerations

In planning the engagement, internal auditors must consider:

- The objectives of the activity being reviewed and the means by which the activity controls its performance;
- The significant risks to the activity, its objectives, resources, and operations and the means by which the potential impact of risk is kept to an acceptable level;
- The adequacy and effectiveness of the activity's risk management and control processes compared to a relevant control framework or model; and
- The opportunities for making significant improvements to the activity's risk management and control processes.

**2201.A1** – When planning an engagement for parties outside the organization, internal auditors must establish a written understanding with them about objectives, scope, respective responsibilities, and other expectations, including restrictions on distribution of the results of the engagement and access to engagement records.

**2201.C1** – Internal auditors must establish an understanding with consulting engagement clients about objectives, scope, respective responsibilities, and other client expectations. For significant engagements, this understanding must be documented.

## 2210 – Engagement Objectives

Objectives must be established for each engagement.

**2210.A1** – Internal auditors must conduct a preliminary assessment of the risks relevant to the activity under review. Engagement objectives must reflect the results of this assessment.

**2210.A2** – Internal auditors must consider the probability of significant errors, fraud, noncompliance, and other exposures when developing the engagement objectives.

**2210.A3** – Adequate criteria are needed to evaluate controls. Internal auditors must ascertain the extent to which management has established adequate criteria to determine whether objectives and goals have been accomplished. If adequate, internal auditors must use such criteria in their evaluation. If inadequate, internal auditors must work with management to develop appropriate evaluation criteria.

**2210.C1** – Consulting engagement objectives must address governance, risk management, and control processes to the extent agreed upon with the client.

## 2220 – Engagement Scope

The established scope must be sufficient to satisfy the objectives of the engagement.

**2220.A1** – The scope of the engagement must include consideration of relevant systems, records, personnel, and physical properties, including those under the control of third parties.

**2220.A2** – If significant consulting opportunities arise during an assurance engagement, a specific written understanding as to the objectives, scope, respective responsibilities, and other expectations should be reached and the results of the consulting engagement communicated in accordance with consulting standards.

**2220.C1** – In performing consulting engagements, internal auditors must ensure that the scope of the engagement is sufficient to address the agreed-upon objectives. If internal auditors develop reservations about the scope during the engagement, these reservations must be discussed with the client to determine whether to continue with the engagement.

## 2230 – Engagement Resource Allocation

Internal auditors must determine appropriate and sufficient resources to achieve engagement objectives based on an evaluation of the nature and complexity of each engagement, time constraints, and available resources.

## 2240 – Engagement Work Program

Internal auditors must develop and document work programs that achieve the engagement objectives.

**2240.A1** – Work programs must include the procedures for identifying, analyzing, evaluating, and documenting information during the engagement. The work program must be approved prior to its implementation, and any adjustments approved promptly.

**2240.C1** – Work programs for consulting engagements may vary in form and content depending upon the nature of the engagement.

## 2300 – Performing the Engagement

Internal auditors must identify, analyze, evaluate, and document sufficient information to achieve the engagement's objectives.

## 2310 – Identifying Information

Internal auditors must identify sufficient, reliable, relevant, and useful information to achieve the engagement's objectives.

**Interpretation:** *Sufficient information is factual, adequate, and convincing so that a prudent, informed person would reach the same conclusions as the auditor. Reliable information is the best attainable information through the use of appropriate engagement techniques. Relevant information supports engagement observations and recommendations and is consistent with the objectives for the engagement. Useful information helps the organization meet its goals.*

## 2320 – Analysis and Evaluation

Internal auditors must base conclusions and engagement results on appropriate analyses and evaluations.

## 2330 – Documenting Information

Internal auditors must document relevant information to support the conclusions and engagement results.

**2330.A1** – The chief audit executive must control access to engagement records. The chief audit executive must obtain the approval of senior management and/or legal counsel prior to releasing such records to external parties, as appropriate.

**2330.A2** – The chief audit executive must develop retention requirements for engagement records, regardless of the medium in which each record is stored. These retention requirements must be consistent with the organization's guidelines and any pertinent regulatory or other requirements.

**2330.C1** – The chief audit executive must develop policies governing the custody and retention of consulting engagement records, as well as their release to internal and external parties. These policies must be consistent with the organization's guidelines and any pertinent regulatory or other requirements.

## 2340 – Engagement Supervision

Engagements must be properly supervised to ensure objectives are achieved, quality is assured, and staff is developed.

**Interpretation:** *The extent of supervision required will depend on the proficiency and experience of internal auditors and the complexity of the engagement. The chief audit executive has overall responsibility for supervising the engagement, whether performed by or for the internal audit activity, but may designate appropriately experienced members of the internal audit activity to perform the review. Appropriate evidence of supervision is documented and retained.*

## 2400 – Communicating Results

Internal auditors must communicate the engagement results.

## 2410 – Criteria for Communicating

Communications must include the engagement's objectives and scope as well as applicable conclusions, recommendations, and action plans.

**2410.A1** – Final communication of engagement results must, where appropriate, contain internal auditors' overall opinion and/or conclusions.

**2410.A2** – Internal auditors are encouraged to acknowledge satisfactory performance in engagement communications.

**2410.A3** – When releasing engagement results to parties outside the organization, the communication must include limitations on distribution and use of the results.

**2410.C1** – Communication of the progress and results of consulting engagements will vary in form and content depending upon the nature of the engagement and the needs of the client.

## 2420 – Quality of Communications

Communications must be accurate, objective, clear, concise, constructive, complete, and timely.

**Interpretation:**   *Accurate communications are free from errors and distortions and are faithful to the underlying facts. Objective communications are fair, impartial, and unbiased and are the result of a fair-minded and balanced assessment of all relevant facts and circumstances. Clear communications are easily understood and logical, avoiding unnecessary technical language and providing all significant and relevant information. Concise communications are to the point and avoid unnecessary elaboration, superfluous detail, redundancy, and wordiness. Constructive communications are helpful to the engagement client and the organization and lead to improvements where needed. Complete communications lack nothing that is essential to the target audience and include all significant and relevant information and observations to support recommendations and conclusions. Timely communications are opportune and expedient, depending on the significance of the issue, allowing management to take appropriate corrective action.*

## 2421 – Errors and Omissions

If a final communication contains a significant error or omission, the chief audit executive must communicate corrected information to all parties who received the original communication.

## 2430 – Use of 'Conducted in Conformance with the International Standards for the Professional Practice of Internal Auditing'

Internal auditors may report that their engagements are 'conducted in conformance with the *International Standards for the Professional Practice of Internal Auditing*' only if the results of the quality assurance and improvement program support the statement.

## 2431 – Engagement Disclosure of Nonconformance

When nonconformance with the Definition of Internal Auditing, the Code of Ethics or the *Standards* impacts a specific engagement, communication of the results must disclose the:

- Principle or rule of conduct of the Code of Ethics or *Standard(s)* with which full conformance was not achieved;
- Reason(s) for nonconformance; and
- Impact of nonconformance on the engagement and the communicated engagement results.

## 2440 – Disseminating Results

The chief audit executive must communicate results to the appropriate parties.

**Interpretation:**   *The chief audit executive or designee reviews and approves the final engagement communication before issuance and decides to whom and how it will be disseminated.*

**2440.A1** – The chief audit executive is responsible for communicating the final results to parties who can ensure that the results are given due consideration.

**2440.A2** – If not otherwise mandated by legal, statutory, or regulatory requirements, prior to releasing results to parties outside the organization the chief audit executive must:
- Assess the potential risk to the organization;
- Consult with senior management and/or legal counsel as appropriate; and
- Control dissemination by restricting the use of the results.

**2440.C1** – The chief audit executive is responsible for communicating the final results of consulting engagements to clients.

**2440.C2** – During consulting engagements, governance, risk management, and control issues may be identified. Whenever these issues are significant to the organization, they must be communicated to senior management and the board.

## 2500 – Monitoring Progress

The chief audit executive must establish and maintain a system to monitor the disposition of results communicated to management.

**2500.A1** – The chief audit executive must establish a follow-up process to monitor and ensure that management actions have been effectively implemented or that senior management has accepted the risk of not taking action.

**2500.C1** – The internal audit activity must monitor the disposition of results of consulting engagements to the extent agreed upon with the client.

## 2600 – Resolution of Senior Management's Acceptance of Risks

When the chief audit executive believes that senior management has accepted a level of residual risk that may be unacceptable to the organization, the chief audit executive must discuss the matter with senior management. If the decision regarding residual risk is not resolved, the chief audit executive must report the matter to the board for resolution.

## The IIA Code of Ethics

The purpose of the Institute's Code of Ethics is to promote an ethical culture in the profession of internal auditing. A code of ethics is necessary and appropriate for the profession of internal auditing, founded as it is on the trust placed in its objective assurance about risk management, control and governance. The Institute's Code of Ethics extends beyond the definition of internal auditing to include the principles that are relevant to the profession and practice of internal auditing and the Rules of Conduct that describe behaviour norms expected of internal auditors; which were discussed in Chapter 5.

## 6.3   Due Professional Care

Taking care during the audit process is becoming an increasingly onerous requirement for the internal auditor. The dismissal of two internal auditors by Allied Irish Bank's US subsidiary (Allfirst) in the wake of the activities of rogue trader John Rusnak provides a powerful illustration of the concept of due professional care. The need to take care is reinforced by Attribute Standard 1220 (Due Professional Care), which states that internal auditors must apply the care and skill expected of a reasonably prudent and competent internal auditor. Due professional care does not imply infallibility. Standard 1220.A1 goes on to say that the internal auditor should consider the:

- Extent of work needed to achieve the engagement's objectives.
- Relative complexity, materiality, or significance of matters to which assurance procedures are applied.
- Adequacy and effectiveness of risk management, control, and governance processes.
- Probability of significant errors, irregularities, or noncompliance.
- Cost of assurance in relation to potential benefits.

In determining whether standards have been met there is help at hand. IIA Standard 1200 covers proficiency and due professional care by stating that:

Engagements must be performed with proficiency and due professional care.

The IIA Practice Advisory 1220-1 (Proficiency and Due Professional Care) suggests that:

- Proficiency and due professional care are the responsibility of the chief audit executive (CAE) and each internal auditor. As such, the CAE ensures that persons assigned to each engagement collectively possess the necessary knowledge, skills, and other competencies to conduct the engagement appropriately.
- Due professional care includes conforming with the Code of Ethics and, as appropriate, the organization's code of conduct as well as the codes of conduct for other professional designations the internal auditors may hold. The Code of Ethics extends beyond the Definition of Internal Auditing to include two essential components:
  a. Principles that are relevant to the profession and practice of internal auditing: integrity, objectivity, confidentiality, and competency.
  b. Rules of conduct that describe behavioral norms expected of internal auditors. These rules are an aid to interpreting the principles into practical applications and are intended to guide the ethical conduct of internal auditors.

Consulting work is also covered by the need for care and Attribute Standard 1220.C1 argues that care in consulting work is exercised:

> The chief audit executive must decline the consulting engagement or obtain competent advice and assistance if the internal auditors lack the knowledge, skills, or other competencies needed to perform all or part of the engagement.

Due care is a duty that runs throughout the internal audit shop and also for work commissioned by the internal auditor. Where outsiders are used to support the internal audit work, the need to exercise care in managing the arrangement is reflected in IIA Practice Advisory 1210.A1-1 (Obtaining External Services to Support or Complement the Internal Audit Activity). Primary Standard 1210.A1 states that:

> The chief audit executive must obtain competent advice and assistance if the internal auditors lack the knowledge, skills, or other competencies needed to perform all or part of the engagement.

In addition, Practice Advisory 1210.A1-1 makes the following suggestions:

1. Each member of the internal audit activity need not be qualified in all disciplines. The internal audit activity may use external service providers or internal resources that are qualified in disciplines such as accounting, auditing, economics, finance, statistics, information technology, engineering, taxation, law, environmental affairs, and other areas as needed to meet the internal audit activity's responsibilities.

2. An external service provider is a person or firm, independent of the organization, who has special knowledge, skill, and experience in a particular discipline. External service providers include actuaries, accountants, appraisers, culture or language experts, environmental specialists, fraud investigators, lawyers, engineers, geologists, security specialists, statisticians, information technology specialists, the organization's external auditors, and other audit organizations. An external service provider may be engaged by the board, senior management, or the chief audit executive (CAE).

3. External service providers may be used by the internal audit activity in connection with, among other things:

- Achievement of the objectives in the engagement work schedule.
- Audit activities where a specialized skill and knowledge are needed such as information technology, statistics, taxes, or language translations.
- Valuations of assets such as land and buildings, works of art, precious gems, investments, and complex financial instruments.
- Determination of quantities or physical condition of certain assets such as mineral and petroleum reserves.
- Measuring the work completed and to be completed on contracts in progress.
- Fraud and security investigations.
- Determination of amounts, by using specialized methods such as actuarial determinations of employee benefit obligations.
- Interpretation of legal, technical, and regulatory requirements.
- Evaluation of the internal audit activity's quality assurance and improvement program in conformance with the Standards.
- Mergers and acquisitions.
- Consulting on risk management and other matters.

Each individual audit has to meet a set of baseline standards if it is to be of acceptable quality, and therefore the components outlined above will have to be firmly in place. If this is not the case then there is a strong argument to conclude that the audit has not been performed properly. We can go on to state that, where this is the norm for most audits, then the audit function itself can in no way be proficient. In this instance, the CAE, if a member of a professional auditing body, should be disciplined by the professional body. This simple formula should be firmly in place or there is little hope for developing the practice of internal auditing. In this sense it may be the case that all chief auditors need to be members of an appropriate professional auditing body. We have shown that there are mechanisms that must be in place to satisfy the auditing standards that cover the performance of audit work. One acid test is to ask whether the procedures covering this issue would stand up in a court of law that wished to consider whether an audit had been performed to acceptable standards. Although this point is more relevant to firms of external auditors, it should nonetheless be noted by internal auditors as more public sector internal audit functions are being contracted out. Professional standards emphasize a disciplined approach to the auditor's duties and work that is derived from best practice. In addition, the various requirements call for a professional approach to auditing where the work is planned, based on good evidence, reported and followed up. The move towards risk-based auditing has gained ground and it may be suggested that professional audit work should reflect this fact.

## 6.4   Professional Consulting Services

The definition of internal auditing makes it clear that it is an assurance and consulting activity. The IIA has defined an assurance service as:

> An objective examination of evidence for the purpose of providing an independent assessment of risk management, control, or governance processes for the organization. Examples may include financial, compliance, systems security, and due diligence engagements.

Consulting services are defined by the IIA as:

> Advisory and related client service activities, the nature and scope of which are agreed with the client, are intended to add value and improve an organization's governance, risk management, and control processes without the internal auditor assuming management responsibility. Examples include counsel, advice, facilitation, and training.

The primary players in assurance work are the auditor, the client and the third party to whom assurance is being provided, while for consulting work it is simply the auditor and the client. Assurance work is well understood by the internal audit community and over the years there has been 'creeping consulting', normally in the form of advice and information on request from the line managers. What has not happened before is the offer of a formal consulting service based around the corporate governance, risk management and control dimensions. Many auditors simply suggest that they will do more consulting work, but may not appreciate that this is an entire industry, with set standards and methods, many of which are similar to internal audit techniques. The IIA have helped with guidance on consulting to help set the scene. Consulting Standard 1130.C1 states:

> Internal auditors may provide consulting services relating to operations for which they had previous responsibilities.

Standard 1130.C2 goes on to say:

> If internal auditors have potential impairments to independence or objectivity relating to proposed consulting services, disclosure must be made to the engagement client prior to accepting the engagement.

Practice Advisory 1120-1 covers individual objectivity and there is advice on what does and what does not impair objectivity:

> The internal auditor's objectivity is not adversely affected when the auditor recommends standards of control for systems or reviews procedures before they are implemented. The auditor's objectivity is considered to be impaired if the auditor designs, installs, drafts procedures for, or operates such systems.

## What is Management Consulting?

IIA Attribute Standard 1000.C1 states that the nature of consulting services must be defined in the charter. But just what is the nature of this work? After considering several different definitions Milan Kubr came up with the following: 'Management consulting is an independent professional advisory service assisting managers and organisations to achieve organisational purposes and objectives by solving management and business problems, identifying and seizing new opportunities, enhancing learning and implementing changes'.[2]

Consulting work calls for different types of tools, techniques and approaches. The auditor will probably be well versed in process-based problem solving, but may be on less sure ground when dealing with the human dimension. Even where the internal auditor is only concerned with, say, risk management systems, there is still a need to address the people issues when developing risk workshops, questionnaires or awareness seminars, and also ensuring that any new systems (or better focused systems) do not throw existing processes out of balance. This in practice tends to come full circle, back to issues of interpersonal relationships. The question of independence is also more complicated than at first sight. It may be thought that consulting work is never independent because the primary consideration is the interests of the client. However, there is also the need to retain integrity, independence, and objectivity in meeting these requirements. The IIA see a crossover between consulting work and the assurance role, which is unique to the audit position where strict confidentiality may not be an absolute. Performance Standard 2120.C2 makes it clear that: 'Internal auditors must incorporate knowledge of risks gained from consulting engagements into their evaluation of the organization's risk management processes.'

One further point to note is that the internal auditor should not take on projects that cannot be undertaken competently. Attribute Standard 1210 says on this matter:

> Internal auditors must possess the knowledge, skills, and other competencies needed to perform their individual responsibilities. The internal audit activity collectively must possess or obtain the knowledge, skills, and other competencies needed to perform its responsibilities.

The CAE should decline the consulting engagement or obtain competent advice and assistance if the internal audit staff lack the knowledge, skills or other competencies needed to perform all or part of the engagement. Standards apply to consulting work as well as the more traditional assurance-based auditing. One point made by the guidance is that documentation used on assurance work may not be appropriate to consulting tasks and there are different techniques that may be applied, in particular to address the human dimension of consulting projects. There is some crossover between assurance and consulting work and one standard (2220.A2) suggests that:

> If significant consulting opportunities arise during an assurance engagement, a specific written understanding as to the objectives, scope, respective responsibilities, and other expectations should be reached and the results of the consulting engagement communicated in accordance with consulting standards.

## 6.5   The Quality Concept

The IIA's Attribute Standard 1300 (Quality Assurance and Improvement Program) states that:

> The chief audit executive must develop and maintain a quality assurance and improvement program that covers all aspects of the internal audit activity.

There is a lot being said about quality assurance (QA), as this appears to be one of the standard management buzzwords. Quality is about:

- Knowing your business.
- Knowing your customers and understanding how they see your business.
- Looking for and dealing with problems.
- Having a way of finding out what stakeholders think of the service.
- Relating all problems to systems that need to be improved. In other words, risks to success should be identified, assessed and managed.
- Being very concerned about the section's reputation and overall standing in the organization.
- A clear focus on value for money.
- Resourcing the drive for quality.
- Having efficient and effective procedures.
- Having the quality role built into all staff and ensuring audit managers review and supervise work with this in mind.
- Developing assessment models that can be used to judge whether quality standards are being met.
- Adopting a culture of getting things right and continually improving.

### The Quality Equation

Without going into great detail, the key point that emerges from the latest research is that checking done at the end of a system (i.e. an operation) is an inefficient way of promoting quality. What is more relevant is to ensure that the systems themselves are steeped in a culture of quality from start to finish. This concept is, in truth, not new as it should underpin the whole thrust of internal audit's efforts in promoting better systems and systems controls. Nonetheless, internal audit like any other activity must set and meet quality standards under the direction of the CAE. The other feature of the drive towards quality assurance is the principle of getting the client to set these quality standards, as the ultimate recipient of audit services. One might argue that the CAE is primarily responsible for quality assurance and procedures, and all the resources that should be directed towards the various related initiatives.

## Compliance with Code of Conduct and Standards

One further point to note in respect of quality assurance is the due reliance that is placed on professional standards. Quality systems must, above all, be able to distinguish noncompliance with professional standards, be they personal (i.e. relating to conduct) or operational. We would look to our systems to tell us whether internal audit is meeting the requirements of these standards. This entails the following:

1. Adopt suitable professional standards (e.g. IIA) as part of the formal mission statement that drives and directs the audit service.
2. Redefine the above as local standards via suitable enclosures in the audit manual. This creates an assimilation of outline standards into working practices as a necessary step towards fully integrating them into the audit role.
3. Implement them via a formal procedure whereby staff are advised as to the requirements of these standards and so understand all that this entails.
4. Train and develop staff to meet them.
5. Review compliance with standards via suitable control mechanisms.
6. Deal with any noncompliance as high-profile serious issues.
7. Review these standards to ensure that they make sense and fit with the audit work that is performed.
8. Seek to relate quality problems with these standards in terms of gaps therein or noncompliance. This is in full recognition of the systems approach to problem solving where all operational defects are related to deficiencies in the underlying systems.

## 6.6  Supervision

Auditors should be able to discharge their audit role in a professional manner and audit management will supervise this work in an appropriate manner. IIA Performance Standard 2340 (Engagement Supervision) states that:

> Engagements must be properly supervised to ensure objectives are achieved, quality is assured, and staff is developed.

The interpretation of this standard clarifies the requirement:

> The extent of supervision required will depend on the proficiency and experience of internal auditors and the complexity of the engagement. The chief audit executive has overall responsibility for supervising the engagement, whether performed by or for the internal audit activity, but may designate appropriately experienced members of the internal audit activity to perform the review. Appropriate evidence of supervision is documented and retained.

There should be supervision checks for compliance with agreed standards and procedures. The other factor is that they should be provided with sufficient guidance and advice from audit management, including clear terms of reference and any assistance where required. The team leader, audit manager and CAE each have a duty to ensure that they are available to direct staff as the audit is being conducted. The IIA Practice Advisory 2340-1 (Engagement Supervision) includes the following matters (extracts only):

1. The chief audit executive (CAE) or designee provides appropriate engagement supervision. Supervision is a process that begins with planning and continues throughout the engagement. The process includes:

- Ensuring designated auditors collectively possess the required knowledge, skills, and other competencies to perform the engagement.
- Providing appropriate instructions during the planning of the engagement and approving the engagement program.
- Ensuring the approved engagement program is completed unless changes are justified and authorized.
- Determining engagement working papers adequately support engagement observations, conclusions, and recommendations.
- Ensuring engagement communications are accurate, objective, clear, concise, constructive, and timely.
- Ensuring engagement objectives are met.
- Providing opportunities for developing internal auditors' knowledge, skills, and other competencies.

The CAE is responsible for all internal audit engagements, whether performed by or for the internal audit activity, and all significant professional judgments made throughout the engagement. The CAE also adopts suitable means to ensure this responsibility is met. Suitable means include policies and procedures designed to:

- Minimize the risk that internal auditors or others performing work for the internal audit activity make professional judgments or take other actions that are inconsistent with the CAE's professional judgment such that the engagement is impacted adversely.
- Resolve differences in professional judgment between the CAE and internal audit staff over significant issues relating to the engagement. Such means may include discussion of pertinent facts, further inquiry or research, and documentation and disposition of the differing viewpoints in engagement working papers. In instances of a difference in professional judgment over an ethical issue, suitable means may include referral of the issue to those individuals in the organization having responsibility over ethical matters.
- All engagement working papers are reviewed to ensure they support engagement communications and necessary audit procedures are performed. Evidence of supervisory review consists of the reviewer initialing and dating each working paper after it is reviewed. Other techniques that provide evidence of supervisory review include completing an engagement working paper review checklist; preparing a memorandum specifying the nature, extent, and results of the review; or evaluating and accepting reviews within the working paper software.

Reviewers can make a written record (i.e., review notes) of questions arising from the review process. When clearing review notes, care needs to be taken to ensure working papers provide adequate evidence that questions raised during the review are resolved. Alternatives with respect to disposition of review notes are as follows:

- Retain the review notes as a record of the reviewer's questions raised, the steps taken in their resolution, and the results of those steps.

- Discard the review notes after the questions raised are resolved and the appropriate engagement working papers are amended to provide the information requested.
- Engagement supervision also allows for training and development of staff and performance evaluation.

The audit review should be based around ensuring that the auditor complied with procedures. These procedures play the key role when audit management is considering the quality of an audit. The reviewer must ask questions such as:

1. What were the procedures relevant to this audit? The answer will vary according to the type of work performed and the experience of the auditor in question.
2. Have these procedures been fully communicated to the auditor who carried out the work?
3. Is there sufficient evidence of compliance with these procedures?
4. Is there any evidence of noncompliance with these procedures?
5. Is there any explanation for apparent noncompliance?
6. Has the audit been a success, i.e. achieved its objectives? If this is not the case, do procedures, or the way they are used (or not used) need revising in any way?

We should try to move to a position where a cause-and-effect relationship is established, so that poor performance can be related to the underlying procedures that form the basis of audit work.

## 6.7    Internal Review

Quality can be promoted by clear standards and effective supervision to ensure these standards are understood and employed throughout the audit shop. The CAE should also install a system of internal assessment to review whether everything is as it should be. The IIA's Attribute Standard 1311 requires the CAE to provide an internal assessment, which should include:

- Ongoing monitoring of the performance of the internal audit activity; and
- Periodic reviews performed through self-assessment or by other persons within the organization with sufficient knowledge of internal audit practices.

The interpretation of this standard says that:

> Ongoing monitoring is an integral part of the day-to-day supervision, review, and measurement of the internal audit activity. Ongoing monitoring is incorporated into the routine policies and practices used to manage the internal audit activity and uses processes, tools, and information considered necessary to evaluate conformance with the Definition of Internal Auditing, the Code of Ethics, and the Standards. Periodic reviews are assessments conducted to evaluate conformance with the Definition of Internal Auditing, the Code of Ethics, and the Standards. Sufficient knowledge of internal audit practices requires at least an understanding of all elements of the International Professional Practices Framework.

Internal reviews may operate at a number of levels, including reviewing the working papers and draft audit reports. One should develop a programme of audit reviews where audit management will carry out comprehensive reviews of, say, the bigger audits that have been completed. Spot checks may be undertaken at random on various audits to establish whether they are meeting acceptable standards. It is advisable to appoint one manager responsible for quality assurance throughout the audit department. This person will report periodically (say, annually) to the CAE on the overall position and indicate whether any changes to current practices are required. The internal review will consider various aspects of an audit that has been recently completed including:

- The source – how it came to be conducted.
- The preliminary survey and the way the terms of reference were established.
- The way the audit resources were assigned to the audit.
- The structure of the audit and whether it followed a logical approach to meet the set terms of reference.
- The way the documentation was put together and whether this was enough to meet the audit terms of reference but not excessive. The same reasoning applies to any testing carried out.
- The way the findings were gathered and placed into the report.
- The actual communication of findings and recommendations.
- The overall quality of the audit.
- Time management, budgets and the way audit hours were charged and accounted for.
- The extent of supervision and review and whether any potential and actual problems were dealt with.
- Whether the audit team demonstrated a good understanding of the audit standards in use.
- The extent to which the audit added value to the operation in question.
- The contribution the audit made to the annual assurance on internal controls provided by the CAE.
- And other considerations that impact on the quality of the audit.

The internal reviewer may also consider some of the wider issues, such as the risk-based planning procedures, use of tools such as CRSA, automated recording, performance management system, audit committee reporting. These issues may be difficult to address for people working within the audit shop as they will be too close to the action, and may be better addressed by the more wide-ranging external reviews. Internal reviews will tend to look at compliance issues with perhaps the occasional extra topic, such as reviewing the auditor time recording system in use or the extent to which automated data interrogation is applied or whether we can allow people to work at home at times.

## 6.8    External Reviews

The IIA's Attribute Standard 1312 deals with external assessments:

> External assessments must be conducted at least once every five years by a qualified, independent reviewer or review team from outside the organization. The chief audit executive must discuss with the board:
>
> - The need for more frequent external assessments; and
> - The qualifications and independence of the external reviewer or review team, including any potential conflict of interest.

This is interpreted as follows:

> A qualified reviewer or review team consists of individuals who are competent in the professional practice of internal auditing and the external assessment process. The evaluation of the

competency of the reviewer and review team is a judgment that considers the professional internal audit experience and professional credentials of the individuals selected to perform the review. The evaluation of qualifications also considers the size and complexity of the organizations that the reviewers have been associated with in relation to the organization for which the internal audit activity is being assessed, as well as the need for particular sector, industry, or technical knowledge. An independent reviewer or review team means not having either a real or an apparent conflict of interest and not being a part of, or under the control of, the organization to which the internal audit activity belongs.

External assessments, such as quality assurance reviews, should be conducted at least once every five years by a qualified, independent reviewer or review team from outside the organization. There are various options for commissioning this wide-ranging review:

- External audit. Here an overemphasis on financial systems and support for the external audit role may bias the work.
- Internal audit departments in groups of companies. An informal policy of not criticizing each other may invalidate the work, or fierce competition may make the review less than objective.
- Reciprocal arrangements. Here companies may review each other, although confidentiality may be a real problem.
- Other external auditors. Using other companies' external auditors helps reduce bias but they would still tend to have a financial orientation.
- Consultant. A consultant who specializes in internal audit reviews will probably be the best choice in terms of skills, independence and final result.

The CAE should use the results of the external review to help form a strategy for improving the audit function and producing an effective quality programme. We can use the model in Figure 6.1 to illustrate the more traditional view of quality, which starts at the end of the management cycle, i.e. at the end of the audit. The issues that arise as a result of the quality assurance process are then fed into the strategic analysis and staff development exercises whereby any problems may be resolved. An alternative way of dealing with quality is to try to ensure that these problems do not arise in the first place, by establishing sound management and operational practices within the entire audit function. We have explained the three-point procedure of supervision, internal review and the occasional external reviews that feed into the quality process. The QA programme should be built into the strategic development process as a high-profile item. In turn the strategy should then ensure that quality impacts directly on the staff development programme, in recognition of the far-reaching effects of moves in this direction, as illustrated in Figure 6.1.

Practice Advisory 1312-1 provides guidance on these external assessments and extracts from this advisory follow:

External assessments cover the entire spectrum of audit and consulting work performed by the internal audit activity and should not be limited to assessing its quality assurance and improvement program. To achieve optimum benefits from an external assessment, the scope of work should include benchmarking, identification, and reporting of leading practices that could assist the internal audit activity in becoming more efficient and/or effective. This can be accomplished through either a full external assessment by a qualified, independent external reviewer or review team or a comprehensive internal self-assessment with independent validation by a qualified, independent external reviewer or review team. Nonetheless, the chief audit executive (CAE) is to ensure the scope clearly states the expected deliverables of the external assessment in each case.

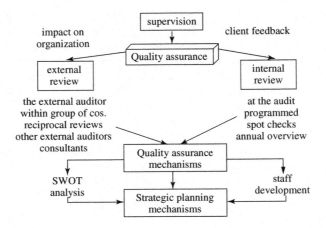

**FIGURE 6.1**    An audit quality assurance programme.

External assessments of an internal audit activity contain an expressed opinion as to the entire spectrum of assurance and consulting work performed (or that should have been performed based on the internal audit charter) by the internal audit activity, including its conformance with the Definition of Internal Auditing, the Code of Ethics, and the Standards and, as appropriate, includes recommendations for improvement. Apart from conformance with the Definition of Internal Auditing, the Code of Ethics, and the Standards, the scope of the assessment is adjusted at the discretion of the CAE, senior management, or the board. These assessments can have considerable value to the CAE and other members of the internal audit activity, especially when benchmarking and best practices are shared. On completion of the review, a formal communication is to be given to senior management and the board.

There are two approaches to external assessments. The first approach is a full external assessment conducted by a qualified, independent external reviewer or review team. This approach involves an outside team of competent professionals under the leadership of an experienced and professional project manager. The second approach involves the use of a qualified, independent external reviewer or review team to conduct an independent validation of the internal self-assessment and a report completed by the internal audit activity. Independent external reviewers should be well versed in leading internal audit practices.

The CAE involves senior management and the board in determining the approach and selection of an external quality assessment provider.

The external review or assessment represents a chance for the audit management team to receive a report that gives a wide-ranging view on some of the key strategies and procedures in place. It also helps answer the question: Who audits the auditors? The reviewer will challenge some of the assumptions made by the internal audit shop and consider the extent to which it has embraced the risk management systems in terms of giving assurances and providing proactive help and assistance. The review will be concerned that audit is equipped to handle any heightened expectations from customers and stakeholders. One way of establishing the terms of reference for the review is to get the audit team together and carry out a formal risk assessment process, which ends up with a list of key risks and associated key controls that are being relied on. This information may be used to drive the review, in that it would seek to tackle the key risks and also consider how robust the key controls are. Stakeholders such as the audit committee and the main board can input into the draft terms of reference in an attempt to ensure that the resulting report has value. The review will look at whatever is set in the agreed terms of reference, which as suggested could come from a risk workshop. However, it may well include some of the following areas:

1. Audit charter – mission and vision and buy-in from staff and stakeholders.
2. Organizational status.
3. Independence.
4. Codes of conduct and internal disciplinary mechanisms.
5. Mix between assurance and consulting activity.
6. Audit strategy and whether it fits with corporate strategy of organization.
7. Relations with the board, senior manager and general reputation.
8. Interface with the audit committee and whether best practice measures are used to keep the audit committee informed.
9. Links with external audit and internal review teams.
10. Performance measurement system and whether this makes sense – also links with performance reporting systems.
11. Communication and participation between auditors and also with external parties – whether use is made of web-based material.
12. Mix of specialists, such as fraud, IT, projects, contract and other areas.
13. Complaints procedure and whether this picks up all significant problems.
14. Structure and flexibility – in response to changes and strategies.
15. Staff competence, qualification and CPD.
16. Morale levels among auditors, and remuneration and retention rates – why do people leave internal audit?, policies on secondment, career auditors and short-term placements.
17. Formal training programmes.
18. Research into developing best practice and links with professional bodies, local universities, conferences and international developments. Do the audit staff keep themselves up to date?
19. Planning systems and the annual audit plan.
20. Budgets and budgetary control and also cost per audit day.
21. Extent to which audit is accomplishing its objectives.
22. Planning and control of audit assignments and supervision arrangements.
23. Working papers, standards and compliance (also extent of automation, protection, security, retention, back-up and confidentiality).
24. Level of equipment such as laptops, communication links, etc.
25. Balance work–life issues and use of flexible approaches such as working from home.
26. Measures to encourage diversity among staff.
27. Quality assurance systems and whether internal reviews are adequate – the review will start with considering outcomes of recent internal reviews.
28. Due professional care and measures taken to ensure professionalism and consistency, including the use of the audit manual.
29. Compliance mechanisms to ensure laws and regulations are adhered to.
30. The adopted value-add proposition and whether this is being achieved.

The list is, in one sense, open ended – it really depends on the risks that form the basis of the terms of reference for the review. Where the three-pronged approach of supervision, internal and/or external review uncovers a problem to do with noncompliance, this problem needs to be addressed. The audit committee and senior official need to be informed where this impacts the overall scope or operation of internal audit, including a lack of external assessment. Meanwhile, the chief audit executive must communicate the results of the quality assurance and improvement programme to senior management and the board, as required by IIA Standard 1320.

## 6.9   Marketing the Audit Role

There are those who argue that the unique feature of the internal audit function, which relates to its independence, in some way means that there is no need to adopt a market-based orientation in the way services are delivered. They may go on to suggest that if we let managers define the way internal audit works then we become little more than consultants. This view is misconceived as it fails to recognize that internal audit is a service to the organization and not to itself, although there are some considerations that impact on a purist view of marketing.

### Revisiting the Acid Test

This is one useful way of assessing whether our marketing efforts have interfered with the levels of independence that we should have achieved. A purist's view would have an acid test that insists that internal audit is not independent if their activities keep parts of the business from failing, since audit should be free from any operational involvement. The dilemma, from a marketing angle, is that this exposes the audit role and makes it akin to a dispensable commodity and there is an inherent conflict between the general marketing concept and the independence test that must be recognized and managed by the CAE.

### Different Approaches to Marketing

We move to marketing as it impacts on the internal audit role. This may be set within an illustration of the marketing approach contrasted with other managerial standpoints, shown in Figure 6.2.

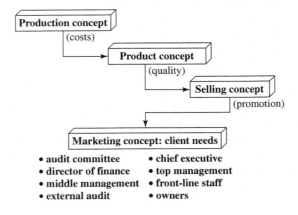

**FIGURE 6.2**   The marketing concept.

Let us go over the model. The *production concept* seeks to minimize the costs of the audit, which translates to the number of hours spent on each individual project. The *product concept* will, on the other hand, concentrate on the audit itself and suggests that so long as the work is good and the report is done to quality standards everything will be fine. The *selling concept* is particularly relevant to internal audit in that it suggests we need only ensure that the client pays for our services, which may be mandatory in most organizations who resource an audit function. The *marketing approach*, on the other hand, takes the view that we must first find out what is required by the organization and then seek to meet these requirements. No matter how efficient or professional the audit work is, so long as we have not fed our work into client expectations then our future is not assured. This may come as a surprise to many auditors who do not believe that they (or the CAE) work for anyone. Marketing audit services starts with being able to offer professional services. Services should be publicized and arrangements set out for first identifying and second addressing any concerns that clients may have with the quality and delivery of audit services. Marketing helps extend the audit role beyond the point where the final report is issued and brings home the undeniably important concept of effective client-based service delivery.

## 6.10 Creating the Audit Image

Audit needs to formulate and maintain an appropriate image and one auditor who breaches professional behaviour may tarnish the reputation of the whole department. The audit image is based around the standards set out in the audit manual and the auditor code of conduct. In addition, it requires the following features of the internal auditor:

- Politeness, having regard to the need to respect fellow officers at whatever grade.
- Being positive by building constructive working relations with management.
- Sensitivity to management's needs.
- Respect for confidentiality with an understanding of the damage that idle gossip can do.
- A team-based audit approach working with and alongside management.
- A hard-working attitude with a constant mission to encourage management to promote good controls.
- A desire to explain the role of audit and promote the audit service wherever possible.

It may be an idea to organize a series of seminars (or a slot at the corporate annual conference) and deliver the new-look internal audit approach.

### The Audit Brochure

This standing forum can be used to provide much of the detail that clients might require along with details of audit services and contact names. It should be a brief, colourful, foldable brochure, possibly with several photographs. Reference can be made to the published annual report for more comprehensive information, on the basis that a brochure with excessive detail will tend not to be read. It is also advisable to have a brochure produced professionally from a print shop where a glossy, conveniently sized pamphlet may be commissioned without appearing excessively flamboyant. It should be given to employees on those occasions when auditors feel this would be appropriate, covering:

- What is internal audit?
- What can internal audit do for you?
- Who do you contact?

The audit department should ideally follow a house style with an appropriate logo that projects the basic image that audit wishes to present. The audit name and logo will appear on all correspondence and reports, and a suitable 'house colour' will also be used for all published documents, including the brochure.

## Auditors' Business Cards

Each auditor may be issued with a business card that will set out:

- The auditor's name.
- The designation.
- Any professional/academic titles.
- Areas of responsibility.
- The contact information number.

Again the audit logo would appear on this document.

## Audit Feedback Questionnaire

One way of achieving a degree of feedback from the client is to obtain a response to a formal questionnaire that makes enquiries about the audit service. We have already outlined the survey of clients as part of the quality assurance programme and a major control that the CAE may use to assess the success of internal audit. The client survey also has a role in the marketing plan since it constitutes a formal mechanism for obtaining independent evidence of audit's successes and problems when dealing with clients. The survey has to be carefully administered since it should not give the impression that audit management does not trust its staff; neither should it be an opportunity for line managers to undermine the field auditors. Accordingly, the purpose of the survey should be explained in a covering memo from the CAE and the main objectives are:

- To obtain the client's view on the benefits secured from the audit.
- To isolate any communication problems that may have been experienced by the client.
- To assess whether the client's perceived needs have been met.
- To identify any adjustments to marketing strategy and audit methodologies that may be required.

The client surveys operate at two levels: one as an assignment follow-up while the other looks for more general comments that are not linked to any particular audit. An Audit Effectiveness Questionnaire, along with a covering memorandum from the CAE, may be given to the client by the lead field auditor and once the audit has been completed it will be returned direct to the CAE. It is felt that by allowing the field auditors to distribute and explain the survey, this dispels the view that the CAE does not trust them. The arrangement whereby the form is filled in by the client and returned direct to the CAE ensures that the client may be quite open in their views. Audit working papers will note any disagreement that the auditors may have had with the client and this point should be taken on board when reviewing the survey results. A wider survey may also be carried out from time to time, which can be used to provide feedback on audit's overall impact on management, for use in formulating audit marketing plans.

## A Complaints Procedure

A formal complaints procedure should be applied whereby management is advised of a clear process for submitting their concerns. The introductory memoranda to management may include the following paragraph:

> We trust that you will not experience any problems with the audit work since all auditors work to the highest professional standards. However, should you have any particular concerns please voice them to **X** who is the team leader for this project. In the event that you are still not satisfied please contact the CAE.

## The Published Annual Report

The internal audit department will publish an annual report after the confidential annual activity report has been considered by the audit committee. This will cover the work carried out and services provided, and has the role of a general information document. It should be written in a public relations style to communicate the services that audit may provide and how management may participate and incorporate its views into audit planning. Important concepts such as independence, behavioural aspects, audit approach, different perspectives of external audit and so on may also be mentioned. This should be sent to senior management and be available on request, and via the internal audit website to all employees.

## 6.11    New Developments

A major dilemma that has continued to rage for some time now relates to ways that the efficiency of the internal audit function can be assessed. There is an abundance of different measures in use and some are better than others. Bearing in mind the importance of efficiency in the way audit resources are applied means effective measures are always welcome, including those suggested by PwC:

- Internal audit department costs compared to budget.
- Number of audits completed in accordance with the scheduled audit plan.
- Number of integrated audits (operational and IT auditing).
- Internal audit department cost per internal audit full-time equivalent.
- Internal audit department cost components.
- Reduction in internal audit effort and/or increase in audit coverage due to use of data-mining and data-analytics technologies.
- Staff utilization (% of time charged to non-administrative audit tasks and amount of overtime).
- Cost savings generated by implementing audit recommendations.
- Average time it takes to issue an audit report.[3]

Auditor competency is another key concern as we move from the financial/compliance perspective to one of considering all aspects of an enterprise-wide risk management process. The Institute of Internal Auditors has built a competence framework that covers:

- Interpersonal skills.
- Tools and techniques.

- Internal audit standards, theory and methodology.
- Knowledge areas.

The idea is to develop the ideal auditor and since IT is a core area it is integrated throughout the framework. The ideal auditor is able to consider risks as negative threats and risks as positive opportunities that others will grasp if simply sidestepped. Auditor competency sits high on the CAE's agenda and this includes good interpersonal skills. As well as working with senior people, the internal audit is required to get along with other internal assurance teams:

> Respondents expect to work much more closely with other assurance providers by 2012. Interaction is currently only 'limited' with assurance functions related to the environment, CSR, insurance and health and safety. They do already consult and share information with management, compliance and external audit – by 2012 they expect to rely more on each other's work to avoid duplication. None of the respondents said they had a fully integrated assurance plan.[4]

Finally, we look at the way internal audit is resourced since auditors are now talking to very senior people as they work on high-risk projects and strategic parts of the business. Steve Bundred gives some sound advice on how to meet this challenge:

> 'The best-performing internal audit functions employ professional people – at least in the senior roles – and have "clout",' says Bundred. 'They work in organisations where risk management processes are embedded, and will have contributed to achieving that. They will be influencing the way in which managers across the organisation think about the internal control environment when they're managing change processes, when they're introducing new systems, or when they're re-engineering business processes,' he adds. 'The question is: how strong is the culture of the risk control environment and what contribution has internal audit made to that? Improving the quality of internal audit is not just a matter of telling internal audit functions to do better,' says Bundred. 'Internal auditors need to look higher up the organisation, influencing the top people about where internal audit should be and persuading them of the contribution that good internal audit can make to the way the organisation is run.'[5]

## Summary and Conclusions

The quality movement has been established for many years and there are various standards, guidelines and tools that can be used to incorporate quality into the internal audit shop. Moreover, there are benchmarks, measures and full-blown accreditation schemes that can be used so as to avoid reinventing the wheel. In one sense, we could argue that an independent review activity must have its own house in order before it can embark on this review activity with any real credibility. The IIA standards make it clear that there must be a system of quality assurance in place and that any noncompliance should be formally reported. There is also a need to secure 'audits' of the auditors to ensure a sense of fair play. All IIA audit shops will need to engage a formal external review at least once every five years and this somewhat simple requirement brings to bear a major process for isolating problems in internal auditing that may have sat quietly as nagging concerns for many years. External reviewers will ask: What is the system for assuring quality in use in this internal audit shop and is it adhered to and does it work in practice?

This very same question should sit at the top of the CAE's agenda. Real quality happens when the CAE, audit managers, senior auditors, team leaders and basic audit grades ask the parallel question: What is the system for assuring quality in use in this internal audit shop and have I developed myself so that I can live up to the set standards?

When internal audit has arrived at this juncture, quality will be secured and it is only a matter of developing strategies for adjusting quality systems to meet the changing needs of stakeholders. One way of getting people involved in the quality equation is to set up a CRSA workshop where we consider the risks that confront the internal audit mission and go through the usual tasks of prioritizing and managing key risks, in the context of the adopted quality management system. We can repeat here the crucial demands set by Attribute Standard 320, which states that: 'The CAE must communicate the results of external assessments to the board.' There is no room for complacency where any gaps in quality management will be placed in front of the top executives. Major gaps will question the ability of internal audit to deliver the audit objective and may undermine the whole basis of assurance, as well as consulting work.

There is really no excuse for failing to reach the exacting levels of performance and high profiles that many internal audit shops are now achieving. Professional standards abound, and the IIA with their professional practices framework have been knocking on the boardroom door for many years now. The last 10 years has seen a major shift in the roll call of professional disciplines that has placed internal auditing right up there with the accountants, lawyers, top-flight consultants, business analysts and so on. Professional standards create the targets that need to be aimed at, even where the audit shop is small. It is essential that each internal audit team tracks developments in professional standards and incorporates new aspects into their own policies and interpretations of the audit role.

## Endnotes

1. *Ethics and the Accountant in the Public Sector*, March 1999, ACCA, p. 8.
2. Kubr, Milan (ed.) (2002) *Management Consulting, A Guide to the Profession*, 4th edition, International Labour Organisation, p. 10.
3. 'Business upheaval: internal audit weighs its role amid the recession and evolving enterprise risks', in *State of the Internal Audit Profession Study*, 2009, PricewaterhouseCoopers' Fifth Annual State of the Internal Audit Profession Study, p. 23.
4. 'Towards a blueprint for the internal audit profession', Research by the Institute of Internal Auditors UK and Ireland in association with Deloitte, Deloitte & Touche, 2008, p. 11.
5. 'Audit centre stage'. *Internal Auditing & Business Risk*, IIA Magazine, May 2008, Steve Bundred tells Neil Baker, pp. 1821.

# Chapter 7

# THE AUDIT APPROACH

## Introduction

Internal auditing may be performed in many different ways and there are a variety of models that may be applied to discharging the audit role. The organization will define its audit needs and this will help to establish which types of audit services are provided. The CAE is then charged with providing this service to professional auditing standards. This chapter explores some of these different approaches and the way that they relate to the role of internal auditing. The development of internal auditing, as a profession, is based on the premise that the practice of internal audit is a defined discipline subject to professional standards. At the same time it is clear that there is a great deal of variety in the way the audit role is discharged. This results from different approaches and, in some cases, a different interpretation of the underlying principles, although the wide variety of audit-based terms does not necessarily mean that there is no clear discipline of internal auditing. It is not merely commonsense work that any untrained person may perform. What is evident is that the way the audit role is discharged will vary according to the agreed terms of reference (or audit charter). Variety creates a richness and degree of flexibility in the type of audit work that is undertaken. In many cases an audit department will contain different types of auditors who collectively discharge the audit function.

Note that all references to IIA definitions, code of ethics, IIA attribute and performance standards, practice advisories and practice guides relate to the International Professional Practices Framework (IPPF) prepared by the Institute of Internal Auditors in 2009. The sections addressed here are as follows:

7.1 The Risk-Based Systems Approach
7.2 Control Risk Self-Assessment (CRSA)
7.3 The CRSA Process
7.4 Integrating Self-Assessment and Audit
7.5 Fraud Investigations
7.6 Information Systems Auditing
7.7 Compliance
7.8 Value for Money (VFM)
7.9 The Consulting Approach
7.10 The 'Right' Structure
7.11 New Developments
     Summary and Conclusions

## 7.1  The Risk-Based Systems Approach

There are many different ways that internal auditing may be approached and some are investigatory/transactions based while others move towards a systems approach focusing on the risk management process. There is an argument that the most efficient use of audit resources occurs where one concentrates on reviewing risks to the proper functioning of systems and processes as opposed to the in-depth examination transactions that result from these individual systems. In terms of professional standards, there are aspects of an organization that clearly fall within the scope of audit work. Performance Standard 2100 means that the internal audit activity must evaluate and contribute to the improvement of governance, risk management and control processes using a systematic and disciplined approach. In terms of systems work, Performance Standard 2110 asks that the internal audit activity evaluates and contributes to the improvement of governance, risk management and control processes using a systematic and disciplined approach.

Performance Standard 2120.A1 makes it clear that the internal audit activity should evaluate risk exposures relating to the organization's governance, operations and information systems regarding:

- Reliability and integrity of financial and operational information.
- Effectiveness and efficiency of operations.
- Safeguarding of assets.
- Compliance with laws, regulations and contracts.

These systems need to be assessed by internal audit as part of the assurance role. There is a choice in the way internal auditing is carried out and although professional standards do set conceptual guidelines, they do not promote a particular methodology. The final approach will result from a combination of factors that affect the audit role and resultant work carried out. The premise upon which this *Guide* is founded considers risk-based systems auditing as a valid interpretation of the assurance role of internal audit, with all other matters falling under the generic term investigations – most of which is part of the consulting service along with direct assistance and advice in establishing business risk management. The risk-based systems approach to internal auditing has provided an extremely powerful technique for conducting audit reviews and in the past has led to a change in auditing concepts. This requires an audit policy that stresses the importance of establishing good systems so that risks such as failure, errors and abuse may be avoided in the first place. Management is charged with devising and maintaining these systems with advice from internal audit. The move is away from error spotting with more emphasis on getting the system of risk management right.

## Entropy

This may be seen as a disorder, disorganization, lack of patterning or randomness of organization of systems. A closed system tends to increase in entropy over time in that it will move towards greater disorder and randomness. Entropy provides a justification for the audit role as systems fail to keep up with moving risk landscapes and controls deteriorate over time unless they are reviewed and made to keep pace with these changing risks.

We can use the principles of systems thinking to conduct risk-based systems auditing. We are concerned with reviewing and then advising management on their systems of internal controls that discharge these four objectives. Therefore an activity should be undertaken with due regard for compliance with laws and procedures, and this feature should be built into the system. Systems in control will subscribe to these key control features, in contrast to those that are at risk. There is one problem inherent in Performance Standard 2060, which includes the following line:

> The chief audit executive must report periodically to senior management and the board on the internal audit activity's purpose, authority, responsibility, and performance relative to its plan. Reporting must also include significant risk exposures and control issues, including fraud risks, governance issues, and other matters needed or requested by senior management and the board.

Reporting should also include significant risk exposures and control issues, corporate governance issues and other matters needed or requested by the board and senior management.

## Stages of Risk-Based Systems Auditing (RBSA)

Systems thinking is used twice in RBSA. First, we break down operations as systems, components of a system, subsystems, parallel systems and parent systems. An overview may be adopted and links between operations may be identified and understood. Second, RBSA is in fact a systematic audit approach in itself, with defined stages and clear links between each step. The stages of a systems-based audit are shown in Figure 7.1.

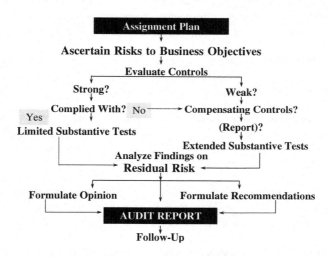

**FIGURE 7.1**    Risk-based systems auditing process.

Risk-based systems auditing cannot be carried out without following the above steps. Once the assignment plan has been determined (after a preliminary survey) we have clear terms of reference and an outline of the system in question. The next stage is to determine what risks may prevent the business goals from being achieved and ensure these risks are understood, classified and prioritized. Having discovered the key risks, we can go on to weighing up and evaluating the specific controls that form the main aspect of the risk management strategy and assess whether the controls are adequate. Adequate controls (strong) should be further considered to judge whether they are working properly through compliance tests. Some auditors argue that even when controls are in place and working, there needs to be a small amount of further testing to ensure the correct results are obtained (i.e. the system objectives are being achieved). Weak controls mean there is an unacceptable level of residual risk and this may be reported straight away. Again, some auditors wish to test the implications of these weaknesses and seek out actual error, abuse, failure and other such risk exposures to demonstrate the implications of poor controls. The findings on the state of the residual risk lead to assurances where all is well and recommendations where there are further improvements needed to mitigate aspects of the residual risk that need to be contained. The results are reported back to the client and any action required monitored during a follow-up audit that is scheduled for the future.

Returning to the stages of the risk-based systems audit, there are a number of matters to be considered at each stage:

**Define clear objectives for the stage** What we are aiming to achieve should be clearly stated at each stage so that the actual output can be measured against this.

**Plan the work and approach to be adopted** Planning is a continuous process that occurs before the audit and throughout the various above-mentioned stages. It is possible to set a separate time budget for the stage and then seek to monitor hours charged before finalizing the audit. It is also possible to carry out a review of work as the stage is completed to provide an ongoing supervision of the project by audit management.

**Obtain a good understanding of the risks to the operation** This may be achieved through analysis, discussion with client staff or through a structured workshop where the client team members consider their risks and how they impact on their business and team goals.

**Define any testing strategy** Testing is applied at ascertainment (walkthrough), compliance (after evaluation) and substantive testing (after evaluation and compliance tests). The detailed work programme may be drafted and agreed as the appropriate stage is arrived at.

**Define the techniques that will be used** Audit techniques such as interviewing, flowcharting, database interrogation, control self-assessment, negotiating and statistical sampling should be agreed again at the relevant stage of the audit. This will assist when timing the work and enable additional skill needs to be identified.

**Brief staff working on the project** With a team approach it is useful to break down each stage so that a briefing can be held to discuss problem areas, progress and other matters. Not only will this act as a feedback device but it will also promote team working where ideas are exchanged.

**Ensure that the work is formally documented** Standardized documentation ensures all key points are covered and that the work is fully recorded. The stage end is a convenient time to consider whether the documentation meets quality standards (according to the audit manual) and contains all the necessary detail. The opportunity to obtain missing material is more readily available during and not after the audit. There is an obvious link between this and the audit manager review procedure.

**Look for high levels of unmitigated risk** It is good practice to report as the audit progresses to save time and ensure that the report is fresh and dynamic. The auditor has the opportunity to assess the impact on the work done so far on the report and the testing strategy that will have to be developed at some stage. Details of excessive risk can enter the report so long as the repercussions have been tested. Since evaluation of risk occurs throughout the audit, the whole package of views on the ability of key controls to mitigate risk is developed as work progresses. This is a major part of the auditor's work.

**Agree the direction of work for the next stage** The link between stages comes naturally from the systems approach to auditing as one moves smoothly from one to another. The direction of the next stage must be considered by the auditor not only from a planning point of view but also from the wider perspective of whether work should be expanded, curtailed or adjusted. This is the point to discuss matters with the audit manager and also advise that the stage in question is complete.

There are several important tasks that the auditor needs to perform to ensure the work is carried out with due professional care. The IIA Attribute Standard 1220.A1 addresses the minimum that must be considered during an audit:

- Extent of work needed to achieve the engagement's objectives;
- Relative complexity, materiality, or significance of matters to which assurance procedures are applied;
- Adequacy and effectiveness of governance, risk management, and control processes;
- Probability of significant errors, fraud, or noncompliance; and
- Cost of assurance in relation to potential benefits.

## Business Systems Model

It is possible to view all the business as a series of systems that cover the operations, financial management, support services, processes, partnering arrangements and so on to form a complete Business Model. The business systems model is illustrated in Figure 7.2.

**FIGURE 7.2**   Risk-based systems auditing process (1).

For simplicity we have broken the organization down into three types of elements:

1. Teams – defined groups of people put together for the purpose of delivering a set objective. For example, an operational team working in production. Internal audit is also one such team.
2. Processes – a function that runs across an organization such as a complaints procedure or a performance management system.
3. Projects – a temporary resource assigned to develop a new system or product. For example, a project for designing and implementing a new information system.

For all parts of the organization there would be set objectives, risk and a risk management strategy to address these risks. Hence all such systems throughout the organization may be reviewed by internal audit, as Figure 7.3 shows.

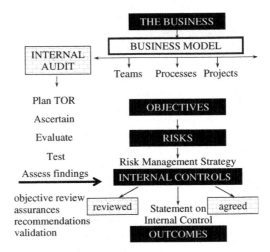

**FIGURE 7.3**  Risk-based systems auditing process (2).

The internal audit function will examine aspects of the system for managing risks that fall within the agreed terms of reference for the audit in question. Audit will ascertain the objectives and system to deliver these objectives and evaluate whether the controls in place are able to handle the significant risks that get in the way of achieving the objectives. Testing will determine whether what should be happening is actually happening in practice and provide evidence to support the audit opinion. The products from internal audit are assurances on the way risk is being managed, recommendations for improvement where appropriate and an objective validation of current practices adopted by management. Audit will also consider the feedback loop within the system and how management is able to measure the expected outcomes against the actual results so that the system may be adjusted to ensure improvement. All of this feeds into the statement on internal control and helps ensure the desired outcomes are achieved. We will look at self-assessment (CRSA) in the next section and how this technique may be used for getting better systems to manage risks. Systems auditing is meant to provide an objective review of the system in hand, but here we have to issue a word of warning on just how much the internal auditor can achieve and where the limits lie. Complete objectivity is not possible, even where the auditor is totally impartial, because the audit process can never be removed and separated from the system being audited.

## 7.2  Control Risk Self-Assessment (CRSA)

Control risk self-assessment is a tool that is used by businesses to promote risk management in teams, projects, through processes and generally throughout the organization. This tool can be used by the executive board, partners, middle management, work teams and of course internal audit. In other words, CRSA is both a management tool and audit technique depending on what the CAE wishes to apply to the audit process and the views of the corporate body. In its purest form, CSA integrates business objectives and risks and control processes. Returning to the model of business systems, we can illustrate where CRSA fits into the process of managing risks in Figure 7.4.

**FIGURE 7.4**    Risk-based systems auditing process (3).

All business systems have objectives, risks and ways of managing these risks. CRSA is a process for agreeing the set objectives, identifying the inherent risks that stop one from achieving the objectives and then working out which risks are most significant. Chapter 3 on risk management provides information on the risk management cycle and the way risks may be categorized and assessed. This section simply describes the CRSA technique where it is used in the self-assessment mode. Having isolated the key risks, the team members will go on to refine their strategy for managing the risks, which will tend to focus on internal controls as a main component of the strategy. Note that Chapter 4 deals with internal control in some detail. Allowing the work team (or project team, or representatives from a cross-organization process) to assess their risk management strategy leads to a better understanding of the specific risks and controls in question, more buy-in as people agree their approach and ensuring action plans are realistic. In addition, the CRSA approach reinforces the view that the responsibility for controls lies with those that operate them and those that manage the operations.

## The Internal Audit Role

The IIA have accepted the consulting aspect of helping to establish CRSA in organizations against the background of the internal auditors' expertise in this area. Professional Practices Pamphlet 98-2 makes it clear that: 'The IIA recommends using the synergy created by the interaction of the auditor–facilitator and CSA participants to add increased value to the organisation through the internal auditing function.'[1]

Some internal auditors feel they need to stand back from the CRSA drive and allow management to assume full responsibility for managing operational risk. Others have thrown themselves into the development and lead from the front under the 'value-add' banner. Still others kick-start CRSA in their organizations and then stand back and validate the system when it has settled down to some extent. There is no finite solution and much depends on the approach that is adopted. Whatever the final format, the internal auditor must be equipped with the right skills to perform the audit role. Note that the next section has a brief account of facilitation skills. There is further advice available from the IIA in the form of Practice Advisory 2120.1 and a pertinent extract on where internal audit fits into the overall equation, as follows:

> Determine the effectiveness of management's self-assessment processes through observations, direct tests of control and monitoring procedures, testing the accuracy of information used in monitoring activities, and other appropriate techniques.

## 7.3   The CRSA Process

There is obviously no one way of conducting CRSA workshops. In practice many organizations have interpreted the process to fit the way its people work. Some call them business risk management workshops; some describe them as teambuilding events based around clarifying team objectives. One large organization used the CRSA process to implement a major change programme that saw regional teams totally reorganized over a short period of some six months. The biggest risk they faced was not achieving the reorganization properly. Another organization could not get their people together in workshops and could only use a questionnaire-based approach with extra time added to group meetings to discuss risk areas. They went on to establish a small number of representative groups to analyze risk across organization-wide processes, and included several stakeholders to ensure all views were considered.

This results in the adopted approach being developed within the culture that is part of the way the organization works. External consultants should really work alongside the person commissioning the work and pass over skills to employees. When the person charged with setting up the CRSA comes from the finance department there will tend to be a narrow focus on the concept of risk assessment. One of the best approaches is to locate initial responsibility for setting up the process with the corporate planning officer, so that the link between risk management, planning and performance management is clearly established. If there is a formal board sponsor, close monitoring by the audit committee (or risk committee) and a nominated chief risk officer (e.g. from corporate planning), then we are well on the way to the successful implementation of risk management.

## 7.4   Integrating Self-Assessment and Audit

The internal auditor may review the CRSA process and the way it is developed and applied in an organization or the internal auditor may provide a consulting service to help facilitate the CRSA process in a hands-on manner. Since no one can be a judge in their own case, these two approaches can create a potential problem. As mentioned earlier, some audit teams start off the CRSA process and then withdraw to a position of safety and resume the review roles thereafter. Other teams split their staff into audit and consulting services and make sure that the CRSA facilitation aspect of audit is kept separate from the main risk-based systems work. Meanwhile, the IIA Performance Standard 2201 on planning considerations states quite clearly that the internal auditors must consider:

- The objectives of the activity being reviewed and the means by which the activity controls its performance;
- The significant risks to the activity, its objectives, resources, and operations and the means by which the potential impact of risk is kept to an acceptable level;
- The adequacy and effectiveness of the activity's risk management and control processes compared to a relevant control framework or model; and
- The opportunities for making significant improvements to the activity's risk management and control processes.

In other words, the internal auditor should recognize the risk management activity in the area that is being audited and take on board all the effort the client is making to manage risks and establish good controls. This is endorsed by the IIA Standard 2201.A1, which makes it clear that:

> When planning an engagement for parties outside the organization, internal auditors must establish a written understanding with them about objectives, scope, respective responsibilities, and other expectations, including restrictions on distribution of the results of the engagement and access to engagement records.

If we produce a complete model of the CRSA/audit process it may look something like Figure 7.5.

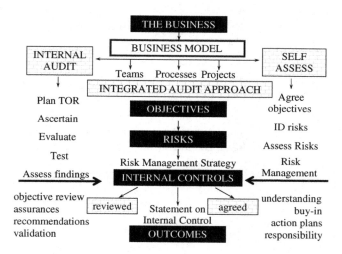

**FIGURE 7.5**   Risk-based systems auditing process (4).

A mixture of audit objectivity and testing alongside the inside knowledge and commitment from the self-assessment process may create a useful solution. This integrated approach mixes audit with the close involvement of client staff in workshop format to identify risks and help define suitable solutions. Internal audit has been added to the model: reviewed and agreed; i.e. the risk management process will have been objectively reviewed by internal audit and also agreed by the people who actually operate the system, creating many benefits. Integrated audits can provide an interesting way of refining the audit process and adding more value to the audit product.

## 7.5   Fraud Investigations

Fraud is big business and the real scale may be unknown. CIPFA has defined three categories of fraud:

(a) those which are known and recorded publicly;
(b) those which are known only within organisations and which will not be brought into the public arena; and
(c) those which are, as yet, undiscovered.[2]

It is the last category that is most worrying – frauds that have not yet come to the surface. Frauds arise when 'things go wrong' and this has implications for the system of internal control.

Because it is so sensitive, management becomes desperate to investigate and solve alleged frauds. They need as much support as possible and generally turn to internal audit for guidance. The audit function should have extensive knowledge of frauds and how they are investigated, if the service is provided by them as opposed to being the responsibility of a specialist fraud team. The ACFE's 2008 Report to the Nation provided the following worrying conclusion:

Participants in our survey estimated that U.S. organizations lose 7% of their annual revenues to fraud. Applied to the projected 2008 United States Gross Domestic Product, this 7% figure translates to approximately $994 billion in fraud losses.[3]

It is notoriously difficult to obtain reliable statistics on employee fraud. CIFAS (the UK's fraud prevention service – www.cifas.org.uk) makes clear that not all fraud cases make it to court so figures on court cases can be unreliable.

## What's at Risk?

An analysis of theft and fraud in government departments by Her Majesty's Treasury in 2001 reported that some 51 government bodies had completed the fraud return, while 51% of government bodies reported no frauds and the other 49% reported 539 cases, to a value of £1.6 million. The types of fraud reported included:

| Types of fraud | Number (%) | Value (%) |
| --- | --- | --- |
| Fraudulent encashment of payable instruments | 1 | 1 |
| Misappropriation of cash | 14 | 4 |
| Theft of assets | 33 | 25 |
| Works services projects | 2 | 3 |
| Travel and subsistence | 12 | 8 |
| Instruments of payment received on false documents | 6 | 49 |
| False claims for hours worked | 11 | 3 |
| Other | 21 | 7 |

## Defining Fraud

The IIA define fraud as:

Any illegal act characterized by deceit, concealment, or violation of trust. These acts are not dependent upon the threat of violence or physical force. Frauds are perpetrated by parties and organizations to obtain money, property, or services; to avoid payment or loss of services; or to secure personal or business advantage.

The ACFE define occupational fraud as: 'The use of one's occupation for personal enrichment through the deliberate misuse or misapplication of the employing organisation's resources or assets.'

The UK's 2006 Fraud Act was designed to address the growing threat of fraud by making provision for, and in connection with, criminal liability for fraud and obtaining services dishonestly through:

1. False representation,
2. Failing to disclose information, and/or
3. Abuse of position.

The act also creates new offences of possession and making or supplying articles for use in frauds and obtaining services dishonestly. The offence of fraudulent trading is extended to sole traders.

## The Four Components

Fraud can develop where an innocent error has gone undetected so that the ability to breach a system's security becomes evident. Once a member of staff spots a system weakness, it can be used to perpetrate fraud. This weakness may consist of unclear procedures covering access privileges to a computerized system where there is little distinction between authorized and unauthorized work. Some argue that this equation is important:

$$\text{Motive} + \text{Means} + \text{Opportunity} = \text{Fraud}$$

Fraud is an act of deceit to gain advantage or property of another with four main components:

1. **Motive** There should be a motive for the fraud. This may be that the employee is dissatisfied or is in financial difficulties. In the case of nonemployees there should be a reason why the fraud is perpetrated. Good human resource management keeps employees satisfied and lowers nonfinancial motives for engaging in frauds.
2. **Attraction** The gain or advantage secured must have an attraction for the perpetrator. This varies and may provide a gain for an associated person, e.g. a mortgage applicant.
3. **Opportunity** There must be adequate opportunity. Someone may wish to defraud an organization and know exactly what is to be gained, but with no opportunity it may never occur. Preventive control should be used to guard against the possibility of fraud by reducing opportunities.
4. **Concealment** In contrast to theft, fraud has an element of concealment. It can be by false accounting, which is a criminal offence. This makes it difficult to uncover and allows the fraud to be repeated.

## Defining Roles in an Organization

In terms of fraud detection there is a clear difference between management and internal audit's roles:

1. Management and the internal audit activity have differing roles with respect to fraud detection.
2. Management has responsibility to establish and maintain an effective control system at a reasonable cost.
3. A well-designed internal control system should not be conducive to fraud. Tests conducted by auditors, along with reasonable controls established by management, improve the likelihood that any existing fraud indicators will be detected and considered for further investigation.

Before we consider individual roles in more detail, we can refer to previous guidance from the IIA UK&Ireland, which suggests that all organizations need to identify the risk of fraud and its impact on the organization, and as such should:

- Set the tone from the top by having a policy that fraud will not be tolerated and fraudsters will be prosecuted;
- Have a fraud mitigation strategy to detect and deter would-be fraudsters;
- Have a fraud response plan setting out exactly what steps to take if a fraud is reported or detected.

The internal auditor needs to take care when carrying out the audit task and take into consideration the risk of fraud. The IIA's Attribute Standard 1220.A1 reinforces the need to exercise due professional care by considering the:

- Extent of work needed to achieve the engagement's objectives.
- Relative complexity, materiality, or significance of matters to which assurance procedures are applied.
- Adequacy and effectiveness of governance, risk management, and control processes.
- Probability of significant errors, fraud, or noncompliance.
- Cost of assurance in relation to potential benefits.

## Investigating Fraud

When employee fraud or irregularity comes to the attention of the auditor there are a number of alternative courses of action. It is essential that each course is carefully weighed up and the most appropriate action selected, based on the circumstances and the strength of evidence so far secured. These options should be kept under review:

**Call the police** This will be necessary where there is strong evidence of a fraud. The policy should be that the police are informed at the earliest opportunity. For more complicated concealed crimes, the police would expect the organization to have done some basic background work beforehand.

**Commence a management enquiry** This may involve a manager or management team being assigned to formally enquire into the circumstances of the case. This represents a responsible approach by management that acknowledges the importance of resolving frauds at once, say, by interviewing all staff working in the area in question. It can spoil an investigation where those responsible are alerted and so are able to cover their tracks. If management, through lack of experience, do not cover all eventualities then records could go missing, potential witnesses may be pressured and the investigation thwarted.

**Commence an audit investigation** The matter may be referred to internal audit for formal investigation. It may be kept confidential while a suitable strategy is formulated. An issue that is increasingly relevant is securing data held on PCs. If a suspect is alerted the files may be irretrievably wiped clean or destroyed.

**Commence a joint management/internal audit investigation** This is normally the best approach since it combines audit expertise with management's local knowledge in a suitable strategy. It also recognizes that management is responsible for investigating frauds.

**Interview the employee in question** There are times when this is the simplest option. It is possible to spend weeks investigating a matter which when presented to the culprit, he/she admits to straight away. Some fraudsters seek attention and want to be caught. It also allows simple explanations to be presented before the investigation has gone too far, e.g. a case of mistaken identity or someone using another's computer access ID and password. The problem here is that, if little work has been done on the investigation, suspects may cover their tracks before any real evidence has been secured.

**Suspend the suspect** Where the evidence is strong and there is a real risk that losses may ensue if action is not taken straight away, then the suspect may be suspended. There needs to be a clear case and the decision should be reasonable and in line with the organization's disciplinary policy. The main difficulty is that while suspension does not imply guilt, an assumption of guilt tends to be made by others. Suspension means that evidence cannot be tampered with. It also makes a stronger case for dismissal at a later disciplinary where one may be arguing that the person's presence at work can no longer be tolerated. However, it could stop audit catching the person as the fraud is being perpetrated. Another disadvantage is that it may make it difficult to quickly convene an interview with the suspect who may resign before a case has been built up.

**Instruct disciplinary proceedings** We may wish to move straight into a formal disciplinary based on the facts that are available. This is possible where we find that an employee has been convicted for fraud at court and this affects his/her position at work. It is better to carry out a full investigation beforehand and base the disciplinary on the findings.

**Check the system of internal control** This is an important step and there are times when there is little that may be done. If a cheque has been stolen and fraudulently encashed then apart from advising the police there may not be much more that can be done. On the control side we might wish to issue a strict instruction that cheques issued by the organization should not be left out on desks and should be locked away overnight.

**Issue a formal instruction to staff** This may sometimes be the most appropriate response. If it is clear that staff are overenthusiastic in, say, travel or overtime claims then it may be necessary to remind them that this is unacceptable and further distortion may constitute a disciplinary offence. We must be sure of the facts before making general comments and there are varying degrees of severity. Best practice suggests that employees should be told what constitutes a disciplinary offence and given sufficient warnings before a formal disciplinary is applied.

**Do nothing** This depends on policy. It is possible to have a policy where anonymous phone calls making allegations where the person refuses to be seen (in confidence) are not followed up. This must be justified and arises where there are resource constraints and excessive levels of unfounded allegations.

The above options should be considered with care as soon as information is received on possible fraud and irregularity. A process of assessing the circumstances and selecting the right response should be established so that a sound decision may be made. Each of these options should be reconsidered periodically as an investigation progresses. It is possible to establish a formal policy whereby internal audit is informed immediately of all frauds, actual or alleged. Some argue that there is no one way to investigate a fraud since each one varies depending on the circumstances. This does not preclude us from developing principles for the investigation of fraud. One framework is shown in Figure 7.6.

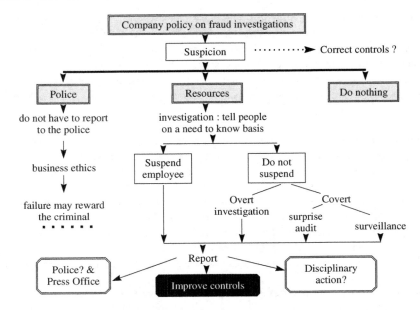

**FIGURE 7.6**   A process for investigating frauds.

## Main Considerations

During a fraud investigation consider:

1. **Planning the investigation**  The adopted strategy will have to be carefully selected, taking on board all relevant factors.
2. **Surveillance**  The use of this technique should be considered.
3. **Resources required**  The need to reassign resources will be high on the agenda. The IIA UK&Ireland's Fraud Position Statement suggests several questions for the internal auditor to consider before becoming involved in fraud investigation:
   - Does internal audit have the necessary investigative skills?
   - Does internal audit have the necessary knowledge of the law?
   - When is the right time to involve the police?
   - Should internal audit be involved in this type of work and if so to what extent?
4. **Recovering any lost funds**  At the outset of the investigation, identifying the extent of losses should be a major concern. This will affect the way that the ensuing work is carried out so that a confirmed 'schedule of losses' may be documented at the conclusion of the investigation.
5. **Legal status of the allegation**  Is it theft or simply breach of procedure? The police may be able to have an input on this matter. We have already suggested that a simple breach of procedure may turn out to be a major fraud.
6. **The level of evidence that has to be secured**  This will depend on the materiality of the fraud and the degree of difficulty in securing the available evidence.
7. **Limiting access to required documents**  It may be necessary to take immediate steps to protect files, documents and computerized records that contain evidence of the fraud. Where there is a clear suspect then this may be the best course of action.

8. **Management's role and the way that it will support the investigation** This will vary depending on organizational policies. Where management shows no interest at all then the fraud will be very difficult to penetrate. Where management is overenthusiastic then mistakes may occur and a sensible middle ground needs to be achieved.

9. **The need to refrain from unfounded accusations** Shooting from the hip is unacceptable. Even if we are sure who perpetrated the fraud, the case will rest on the evidence that supports our views and this can only be gathered through a careful process of investigation.

10. **Police involvement and advice** Having a key contact at the local police station is very useful and this may be the first place for advice when the allegations first come to light.

11. **Staff interviews** It may be necessary to meet with staff from the area in question as soon as possible. This may provide good leads to the culprit who may, unknown to the auditor, be one of the interviewees. It also has a deterrent effect as staff see that the problem is being taken seriously by management.

12. **The need for tight confidentiality** One of the biggest questions that needs to be addressed is who to see. It is as well to keep the enquiries one step removed from the area of the fraud and work with a more senior level of management. Much information can be secured from sources that are accessed centrally and it is here that the auditor's right of access becomes very useful. This also means that people outside the investigation's team need not be alerted to the fact that the investigation is taking place.

13. **Surprise audit** This technique may be used where there is a history of audit carrying out unannounced checks at organizational locations. Where this is possible much inside information may be secured as well as checks made on relevant records without alerting the suspect(s).

14. **Recovery** It may be possible to seek a restitution order to recover losses from the fraud. The judge should be advised of this during the hearing and may make a ruling if the defendant is found guilty.

The IIA make it clear in Attribute Standard 1210.A2 that the internal auditor should have sufficient knowledge to identify the indicators of fraud but is not expected to have the expertise of a person whose primary responsibility is detecting and investigating fraud. Moreover, the most effective way of managing the risk of fraud is to build this factor into risk assessment workshops that are performed by teams across the organization and so ensure prevention is part of the overall business risk management strategy.

## 7.6 Information Systems Auditing

We return to IIA Performance Standard 2120.A1, which states that the internal audit activity must evaluate risk exposures relating to the organization's governance, operations and information systems regarding:

- Reliability and integrity of financial and operational information.
- Effectiveness and efficiency of operations.
- Safeguarding of assets.
- Compliance with laws, regulations, and contracts.

Standard 2110.A2 makes it clear that:

The internal audit activity must assess whether the information technology governance of the organization sustains and supports the organization's strategies and objectives.

The information systems auditor has a particular interest in the first item – the reliability and integrity of financial and operational information. Meanwhile Practice Advisory 2130.A1-22 goes on to say that:

1. The failure to protect personal information with appropriate controls can have significant consequences for an organization. The failure could damage the reputation of individuals and/or the organization, and expose an organization to risks that include legal liability and diminished consumer and/or employee trust.

2. Privacy definitions vary widely depending upon the culture, political environment, and legislative framework of the countries in which the organization operates. Risks associated with the privacy of information encompass personal privacy (physical and psychological); privacy of space (freedom from surveillance); privacy of communication (freedom from monitoring); and privacy of information (collection, use, and disclosure of personal information by others). Personal information generally refers to information associated with a specific individual, or that has identifying characteristics that, when combined with other information, can then be associated with a specific individual. It can include any factual or subjective information – recorded or not – in any form of media. Personal information could include:

    • Name, address, identification numbers, family relationships;
    • Employee files, evaluations, comments, social status, or disciplinary actions;
    • Credit records, income, financial status, or
    • Medical status.

3. Effective control over the protection of personal information is an essential component of the governance, risk management, and control processes of an organization. The board is ultimately accountable for identifying the principal risks to the organization and implementing appropriate control processes to mitigate those risks. This includes establishing the necessary privacy framework for the organization and monitoring its implementation.

4. The internal audit activity can contribute to good governance and risk management by assessing the adequacy of management's identification of risks related to its privacy objectives and the adequacy of the controls established to mitigate those risks to an acceptable level. The internal auditor is well positioned to evaluate the privacy framework in their organization and identify the significant risks, as well as the appropriate recommendations for mitigation.

The internal audit activity identifies the types and appropriateness of information gathered by the organization that is deemed personal or private, the collection methodology used and whether the organization's use of that information is in accordance with its intended use and applicable legislation. Given the highly technical and legal nature of privacy issues, the internal audit activity needs appropriate knowledge and competence to conduct an assessment of the risks and controls of the organization's privacy framework.

## Information Systems Risk

The risk of poor information systems and unreliable security and back-up arrangements leads to possible fraud, error, noncompliance with data protection rules, customer dissatisfaction and security breaches. Poor information systems can undermine an organization and impact on the entire reputation may be at stake. The IIA UK&Ireland's Information Technology Briefing Note Three covers Internet Security (A Guide for Internal Auditors) and suggests a number of IS risk areas:

| | |
|---|---|
| Theft of proprietary information | Sabotage of data or networks |
| Eavesdropping | System penetration |
| Abuse of Internet access | Fraud |
| Denial of service | Spoofing |
| Viruses | |

Meanwhile, a Computer Crime and Security Survey highlighted the growing problems of cybercrime:

> Computer Crime continues to hit organizations hard, yet most don't report information security breaches to law enforcement, a recent U.S. survey reports. Ninety percent of the 503 U.S. organizations that responded have detected computer security breaches in the past 12 months and 80 percent acknowledged suffering financial losses, according to the seventh annual 'Computer Crime and Security Survey' conducted by the U.S. Federal Bureau of Investigation and the Computer Security Institute (CSI). The 44 percent of organizations that disclosed the amount of financial damage they suffered reported losses of $455.8 million. Last year, 85 percent of respondents detected computer crimes, and organizations lost $377.8 million, according to the 2001 survey.[4]

## The Role of the IS Auditor

The role of audit in computerized information systems is vital to the continuing welfare of the organization. The high cost of investing in information technology in terms of set-up costs and its impact on achieving objectives results in an abundance of control implications. The biggest task may be to control this aspect of the organization and if audit is kept out of these issues, their role will be relegated to minor matters only. The IS auditor may review a system (Figure 7.7), e.g. creditors, and must be able to bring into play important operational matters such as setting out terms of reference for the audit clearly:

- Start with the business objectives.
- Recognize that many controls are operational and interface with automated controls.
- Plan computer auditor's work with this in mind.

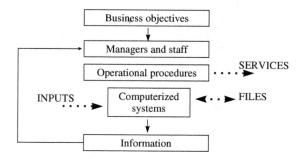

**FIGURE 7.7**   Business objectives and information systems.

The new-look internal auditor must recognize the link between the business activity and the computerized systems used to facilitate this process of setting and achieving business objectives. The IS auditor will concentrate on risks to the input, process and output aspects of the system (below operational procedures), while the operational auditor will pay more attention to the controls located in the upper section. Both audit approaches must acknowledge each other in a supportive and communicative manner. Application controls have to be tested by the auditor in line with the requirement that all audit findings should be supported by suitable evidence. Auditing around the computer means relying on management to provide all the necessary testing information and schedules and this does not promote audit independence or enhance the audit knowledge of the systems under review. The auditor may incorporate a systems control review file within the software to extract interesting information. In addition, parallel simulation may be used to set up the auditor's own model of the programmes that are being run. Interrogation software may also be used to obtain suitable audit samples for analysis while test data may be used to test the correct functioning of the documented controls. Internal audit may use application audits to establish a level of credibility within the organization and among computer specialists. Lessons for the audit approach may be learnt and this might affect plans for developing audit expertise, software packages and review techniques. The auditor should ensure audit objectives are met and there are no 'no-go areas' where the auditor is locked out of the system. IT skills will be required so that systems controls may be identified and tested without undue reliance on the computer department. Applications audits follow the same principles as other system audits and have the same audit objectives. The main difference is the nature of information systems that are reviewed and the type of controls that management needs to implement. IIA Standard 1210.A3 makes it clear that not all auditors will have specialist computing skills:

> Internal auditors must have sufficient knowledge of key information technology risks and controls and available technology-based audit techniques to perform their assigned work. However, not all internal auditors are expected to have the expertise of an internal auditor whose primary responsibility is information technology auditing.

## Information Systems Security

The internal auditor should periodically assess the organization's information security practices and recommend, as appropriate, enhancements to, or implementation of, new controls and safeguards. Threats such as computer fraud, espionage, sabotage, vandalism and natural disasters can bring down the corporate network and damage important databases. The ISO Standard 7799 addresses IT security and has the following sections:

1. Business continuity planning
2. System access control
3. System development and maintenance
4. Physical and environmental security
5. Compliance
6. Personnel security
7. Security organization
8. Computer and network management
9. Asset classification and control
10. Security policy

Much of the classification of information systems is based around risk assessment in terms of the impact on the business. Moreover, ISO 7799 recommends that audit requirements and activities involving checks on operational systems should be carefully planned and agreed to minimize the risk of disruptions to business processes, and suggests the following be observed:

- Audit requirements should be agreed with appropriate management.
- The scope of the checks should be agreed and controlled.
- The checks should be limited to read-only access to software and data.
- Other types of access should be allowed for isolated copies of system files which should be erased when audit is complete.
- Requirements for special or additional processing should be identified and agreed with service providers.

- All access should be monitored and logged to produce a reference trail.
- All procedures, requirements and responsibilities should be documented.

The ISO standard (7799) goes on to list several key controls that support the security infrastructure:

- Information security policy document.
- Allocation of security responsibilities.
- Information security education and training.
- Reporting of security incidents.
- Virus controls.
- Business continuity planning process.
- Control of proprietary copying.
- Safeguarding of company records.
- Compliance with data protection legislation.
- Compliance with security policy.

The growth in e-business makes encryption, third-party access and rules on remote or teleworking important as controls must keep pace with new developments. The Ernst & Young's 12th Annual Global Information Security Survey (GISS) came up with some interesting findings:

1. Our 2009 survey shows that companies and information security leaders are facing an environment of change; escalating levels of risk, new challenges and increasing regulatory complexity are now driving information security decisions. Companies are also struggling to leverage new technology – to get the most benefit and cost savings possible – while understanding the potential security impact to the organization.
2. Our survey also revealed that many organizations continue to be challenged by a lack of skilled information security resources and inadequate budget. These challenges have been identified in our previous surveys, but this year they have become more significant, driven by heightened economic uncertainty.
3. To address the risks and challenges of the changing environment, information security leaders are abandoning the old paradigms and taking a more information-centric view of security. It is a more flexible, risk-based approach that is focused on protecting the organization's critical information, and more suited to supporting a connected business model and today's increasingly mobile and global workforce.
4. By leveraging the information in this survey and taking action on the suggestions for improvement, organizations can achieve more effective information security and continue to outpace change.[5]

## 7.7  Compliance

The IIA Attribute Standard 1220.A1 deals with due professional care and says that internal auditors need to consider the following:

- Extent of work needed to achieve the engagement's objectives;
- Relative complexity, materiality, or significance of matters to which assurance procedures are applied;
- Adequacy and effectiveness of governance, risk management, and control processes;
- Probability of significant errors, fraud, or noncompliance; and
- Cost of assurance in relation to potential benefits.

We have indicated before that IIA Performance Standard 2120.A1 says that the internal audit activity must evaluate risk exposures relating to the organization's governance, operations and information systems regarding:

- Reliability and integrity of financial and operational information.
- Effectiveness and efficiency of operations.
- Safeguarding of assets.
- Compliance with laws, regulations, and contracts.

Compliance is an issue for the internal auditor and, during the audit, an assessment will be made of the extent to which the business is adhering to laws, regulations and control standards. The Performance Standard 2210.A3 confirms that:

> Internal auditors should review operations and programs to ascertain the extent to which results are consistent with established goals and objectives to determine whether operations and programs are being implemented or performed as intended.

While compliance and issues relating to regularity and probity are generally incidental to the main audit objective in assessing significant risk and controls, there are times when internal audit may need to launch into an investigation into specific associated problems. In many developed countries a failure to demonstrate compliance with anti-money-laundering can lead to the possible closure of the business, the seizure of assets or the revocation of operating licences. Some audit teams have compliance reviews built into their official terms of reference. For example, a review of security measures may find that remote parts of the organization may have failed to meet the corporate security standards, as illustrated below:

> Police have called for an inquiry after a new age traveller was found living on a government-licensed cannabis plantation. The teenage girl had parked her rusting bus among the 12 ft high plants and was helping herself to the crop, which should have been guarded by a farmer... police visited the plantation after a tip-off found security measures were 'non-existent' .... [6]

There are many banks, financial services companies, large retail outfits and other organizations that are either highly regulated or consist of hundreds of branded branches using the same basic operational and financial systems. The main worry from the board is that parts of the organization are out of step with requirements and the internal audit team is charged with carrying out compliance reviews as a main way of tackling this high-level risk. Automated data analysis enables such audit teams to target high-risk areas of those with possible problems of nonadherence. However, the value add proposition is that compliance reviews are the main thrust of the internal audit work.

In terms of the ongoing review of compliance with laid-down procedures in those high-risk sectors such as banking, financial services and retail, regular testing and visits to local establishments are a main feature of audit work. Management must establish operational procedures and suitable standards of financial management for all operations, particularly for remote locations and decentralized activities. They must also check on the extent to which these standards are being applied. A formal programme of probity visits may be commissioned and effected possibly on a spot-check basis. Internal audit would recommend management makes these visits as part of the systems of control over these decentralized operations. It is not necessarily the primary role of internal audit to carry out these probity checks. It may be that the audit function is required to operate a series of compliance checks as part of their role in the organization. A formal terms of reference and budget for the work will be required and this should be set out and agreed with management. Probity audits should be carried out via an agreed programme of visits that may be scheduled well in advance. The term 'programme' may also refer to a schedule that records the tasks that should be completed during the audit, which should be drafted by the audit manager.

## 7.8   Value for Money (VFM)

Part of the scope of internal audit involves evaluating the adequacy and effectiveness of arrangements for securing value for money. These arrangements consist of controls that should be established by management to ensure that their objectives will be met, and is based on promoting the managerial control system. These arrangements should involve management in a continual search for efficiencies that may result in a level of savings. It is not internal audit's responsibilities to identify these savings, and our performance measures should not include the amount of money saved through implementing audit recommendations. This point must be understood and may be restated in that we would expect our audit recommendations to place management in a position to identify areas where they may make savings. An example would be recommending that better information systems are installed. As part of our testing procedures we may be able to estimate any resultant savings, but this is not the primary role of the audit. Our duty is to get management to implement improvements in systems of control where required. It is possible to resource as part of our consultancy services VFM reviews that are designed to lead to savings for management.

There are two views of VFM: VFM in its true sense is about the way management organizes and controls its resources to maximum effect. The narrow view sees VFM as ad-hoc initiatives that result in defined savings and/or a greater level of service/output. VFM is:

- **Economy**   Resources required to perform the operation are acquired the most cost-effectively.
- **Efficiency**   Resources are employed to maximize the resulting level of output.
- **Effectiveness**   Final output represents the product that the operation was set up to produce.

This may be represented in Figure 7.8.

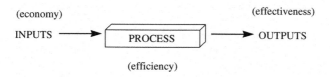

**FIGURE 7.8**   Value for money.

*Efficiency reviews* A systems-based approach to an efficiency review would consider the standards, plans, direction and type of information that management applies to controlling their operations. The investigative approach, on the other hand, concentrates on specific methods by which efficiency may be improved. This may be by applying best practice in terms of alternative operational practices or by isolating specific instances of waste and inefficiency that may be corrected. Economy (i.e. securing the cheapest inputs) is incorporated into the wider concept of efficiency because of the intimate link between these two. Efficiency covers basic matters of economy.

***Effectiveness reviews*** Effectiveness reviews are difficult to carry out and a systems-based approach would look to the application of sound managerial practices. This is the only way of guaranteeing that operational objectives may be achieved. Investigations into operational effectiveness (unlike systems reviews) determine whether objectives are being achieved. This requires an ongoing process:

1. Defining the end product.
2. Examining the current output.
3. Determining whether this output is acceptable.
4. Quantifying any shortfall.

Many of these matters involve an element of subjectivity and the auditor may be called upon to make what may be regarded as an expert opinion. There are many potential pitfalls and these should be borne in mind when embarking on the assignment. The concept of effectiveness must include a review of the customer's perceptions as recipient of the relevant services. A useful technique is to administer a client survey using a specially formulated questionnaire. This should be based on securing an idea of whether the services are having the desired effect on the final user. We wish to see suitable underlying systems in place to ensure effectiveness. Most of these are based on direction and good management practices underpinned by comprehensive communications systems. Effectiveness depends on setting clear objectives and ensuring these are resourced and properly communicated. While as auditors we cannot question the validity of the objectives or associated policy framework, we can review the extent to which they are supported by suitable managerial mechanisms. This encompasses the complex maze of underlying systems that must be in place for objectives to be translated into business activities.

## 7.9   The Consulting Approach

Internal auditors have toyed with providing a form of internal consulting service for many years. The IIA standards now make it crystal clear that internal audit may provide consultancy as well as assurance work to an organization. The IIA's Handbook on *Implementing the Professional Practices Framework* suggests six types of consulting work:

1. Formal engagements – planned and written agreement.
2. Informal engagement – routine information exchange and participation in projects, meetings, etc.
3. Emergency services – temporary help and special requests.
4. Assessment services – information to management to help them make decisions, e.g. proposed new system or contractor.
5. Facilitation services – for improvement, e.g. CSA, benchmarking, planning support.
6. Remedial services – assume direct role to prevent or remediate a problem, e.g. training in risk management, internal control, compliance issues drafting policies.[7]

It is important to make clear exactly what constitutes consulting work since IIA Attribute Standard 1000.C1 says: 'The nature of consulting services should be defined in the charter.' One difficulty is type one consulting, which consists of a formal engagement with a planned and written agreement. The IIA Handbook Series goes on to distinguish between optional consulting work and mandatory assurance services:

Assurance – adequacy of entity internal control, adequacy of process or sub-entity internal control, adequacy of ERM, adequacy of governance process, compliance with laws or regulations.

Consulting – improvement in efficiency or effectiveness, assistance in design of corrective actions, controls needed for new systems design, benchmarking.

We need to turn to the management consulting professionals to gain an insight into the type of approach that may be considered for formal consulting projects. One well-known approach to consulting assignments involves the following basic sequences:

1. **Entry**  Background work, initial contact with the client, preliminary survey (what's the problem?).
2. **Terms of reference**  Width and depth and timescales and resources and reporting lines. Make clear the requirements of Performance Standard 2120.C1, which states that: 'during consulting engagements, internal auditors must address risk consistent with the engagement's objectives and should be alert to the existence of other significant risks.' Also make clear corresponding roles and whether the work involves helping people do the analysis and solve their business problems, or whether it is more about tackling the problem and making recommendations to the client on ways forward.
3. **Contract**  In writing, why assignment is needed, TOR, what will be examined, action to be taken to interested persons, agree – respective roles, support and implementing recommendations – who does what? Monitoring arrangements for the project and reporting lines and planning and monitoring. It may also be an idea to build in any confidentiality clause and the contents of IIA Performance Standard 2130.C2 which states that: 'Internal auditors must incorporate knowledge of controls gained from consulting engagements into the process of identifying and evaluating significant risk exposures of the organization.'
4. **Analysis**  Covering:
   - **Diagnosis**  Weigh up the evidence, what's acceptable, alternative solutions, computerization, what's most cost-effective, policy constraints and then decision making.
   - **Planning for action**  Firm recommendations, based on findings, policy and social considerations, reaction of client, rate of IT development, impact on VFM, participative approach, preliminary report, verbal report.
   - **Implementation**  Management responsible for implementation, routine follow-up after six months, how much should we support management in implementation? Implementation must be planned and watch for staff reactions. Consultant may be available to help train staff (train small group who then train bigger groups), help anticipate problems, help develop action plan and checkpoints, but should not usurp management – need to set date when consultant's involvement stops. Also make sure senior management is involved in more complex projects.
5. **Release**  From the contract when all work has been completed.

The value-add proposition is that the internal auditor can add a freshness of view and comes without the in-built assumptions of the people who operate the business line.

## Managing Change

Change management is a discipline in itself alongside a growing recognition of the crucial role of clearly defined change strategies. Audit consultants are likewise primarily involved in the change process, though their concern is in seeking improvements in risk management and control. Much of the consulting role for larger strategic projects will revolve around the change management role, which is why a study of the basic principles of change management will certainly pay dividends for the internal auditor. It is clear that managers are beginning to adopt the view that poor performance can be rectified through positive and planned change. The public sector is one area that is going through a major and ongoing reform exercise in an attempt to promote efficiency, effectiveness and quality in the delivery of public services. By studying change as a topic, the auditor may be able to promote the use of change techniques by management within a specially devised strategy that allows them to manage and control the change process. In fact, there is one view that suggests that the auditor may become the change agent that underpins the fundamental process of change. Within this context audit consultancies may be a key part of management's attempts to engineer change, a point that must be fully recognized if these recommendations are to have any great impact.

## 7.10   The 'Right' Structure

Once a clear audit strategy of risk-based assurance and consulting work is in place audit management must then turn its attention to the way resources are organized. This will have a crucial effect on the delivery of audit services. Furthermore, there are many options underpinning the type of structure that should be in place, which have to be considered and decided on. Some of these options are:

- **Decentralized** Departments may arise where the audit field consists of geographically isolated segments when it may be advisable to place an audit unit in each one. This can cover a region, country or even a whole continent, where the differences in local customs are so great that a centralized audit role would be inappropriate.
- **Centralized** Where this is not the case then one *centralized* audit department may be preferable. In contrast, the current trends to devolve financial management to line managers can also affect internal audit, who may be swept up in this strategy. Unfortunately, this will tend to dilute the power base of the CAE as stronger reporting lines are established with each department.
- **Service-based** Functions may be divided into groups that provide specialized audit services such as IS, contracts, financial, consultancy, investigatory, regularity, risk-based systems and so on. The idea is to develop a level of expertise in particular audit services, in the search for enhanced professionalism. Another way is to split the assurance and consulting services. The setback is the degree of crossover that will arise where several auditors may emerge in the same work area, but with different objectives. It is also more difficult to establish a client-based view, as audit teams service the entire organization and not specified departments.
- **Client-based** Groups are each responsible for a defined range of audit fields providing audit services for their main clients. Once an audit group has been assigned to a client (say, a director) then we would expect a range of services to be provided as a contribution to developing the client/auditor relationship.
- **Mixed structures** Arise where a combination of client- and service-based approaches is applied, and the audit field is allocated to groups that also provide some specialized services. This may reflect the practicalities of working life where clients are established for each audit manager, while there are some specialist audit services (such as fraud investigations) that will run across the organization.
- **A project-based approach** Allows auditors to fall into a resource pool which forms into teams when audit projects demand. This is designed to provide a quick response-based service made up of floating expertise and mirrors the multidisciplinary team approach where resources

tackle problems as and when they arise. This can be an excellent solution but requires great skills to manage properly.

- **Consultancy-based** These models are similar to the project-based one although auditors would work separately rather than in teams. This flat structure provides no client affiliation but can give a fast response time, particularly for unplanned work. An assignment is obtained, an audit brief and budget provided and an auditor is sent out, to return with a draft report completed within budgeted hours.
- **Hierarchical structures** Involve several tiers of auditors with a range of different grades each placed within defined audit groups. We may find an audit manager, principal auditors, senior auditors, audit assistants and then trainees. This traditional approach deems control to be inherent in all staff knowing their position in the audit unit and reporting lines clearly set and applied.
- **Project teaming** Involves fixed audit groups but also selects individual auditors to form project teams for temporary assignments. Over and above this policy, auditors may be rotated between groups, say every three months, or have fixed-term secondments to specialized areas. Note that many groups that were originally set up as project teams become a permanent fixture.

There are many choices and combinations of methods that may be applied and again, as with most of the material on audit management, a suitable decision must be made. This decision should be positive, based on the available options and founded on the overriding need to achieve a quality audit service. In practice there is no one solution, although there are firm principles that should be applied along with a need to obtain a degree of in-built flexibility on the basis that change is now the norm. Furthermore, the audit structure should flow naturally from the agreed audit strategy. Once the CAE has set an agreed structure for the audit function and defined procedures and standards for the performance of audit work, then one might argue that staff should be able to deliver audit services.

## 7.11  New Developments

In the past the main characteristic of internal audit fieldwork was that the auditor was always very thorough. This means that, if the auditor did a stock check, they would count every item in their sample and track down anything that was missing or stored in the wrong place. The auditor would sit down and study detailed reports, carry out detailed analysis and would not stop until every question on the checklist was answered. The new risk management agenda means we accept some risk and we cannot give assurances on everything that happens within an organization. What is more relevant is that the auditor can give assurances on things that matter. Rather than being known as someone who can count every item of stock on the list, the auditor is becoming known as someone who is involved in governance issues that mean something to board members and strategic management. The other concern about fieldwork is that management is less interested in what happened in the past and more concerned about what is coming around the corner, and whether the risk management process picks up these concerns and deals with them.

When considering the audit approach, it may be an idea to bear in mind the shortfalls that exist in many organizations. Many managers have no real grasp of the risks that they need to manage in order to stay on top. One survey brought home this worrying fact and the key finds, as reported below:

- Only half the internal auditors in our survey felt their organisations had a good understanding of the risks they faced, could prioritise those risks, and respond to them effectively.

- Some organisations have inadequate assurance over the risks they face and this will remain a problem because there is a significant shortage of people with internal audit skills.

Internal auditors at the largest organisations are winning the argument for resources, but others must do more to make their case, especially if they want to expand their remit into areas where they believe their expertise is needed.[8]

There has been a long-running argument about the demands of auditing standards and whether smaller audit teams can meet the requirements of standards that appear to be aimed at larger units. There are some disadvantages where the audit team is fairly small, but the more intimate atmosphere does have some advantages, as described by Nicola Rimmer:

In a smaller team there is often less jockeying for position as can happen in larger teams, and so more of an opportunity for staff to get involved in audit planning and strategy, and make best practice suggestions and generally share knowledge. Also, if an individual has added value in a big way, this is more apparent, both within the team, but also amongst management, the audit committee and the board. This can provide invaluable experience for an internal auditor, although with the additional risk that they may quickly move on to bigger things. Whether working in a large or small audit team, each have their own particular challenges and advantages. However, large or small, the pressure on internal audit to deliver a quality service is increasing. One thing is clear – size really doesn't matter. What's important is how you use what you've got.[9]

One issue that has grown in importance over the years relates to the risk-based internal auditing approach that has seeped through into most internal audit units. Jeremy Opie has noted the benefits that come from using this approach:

1. Offers an independent and systematic basis for the organisation's stakeholders to judge the effectiveness of its internal control arrangements.
2. Provides the critical check that business objectives are clear and understood by all, and are congruent with the objectives of other parts of the organisation.
3. Provides an independent judgement on the effectiveness and efficiency of the risk identification and assessment process.
4. Provides an assurance of the accuracy, completeness and currency of the executive's risk picture.
5. Provides an assurance that the process for devising controls is effective and efficient, and equips the executive to manage change.
6. Provides an assurance that the executive's controls are effective and efficient, or an account of what is to be done to make them so; acknowledging, and giving due credit for, innovative management solutions to risk control. RBIA avoids merely imposing a standard control template.
7. Combats the risk of internal audit 'doing management's job for them.' Successful RBIA must work with management.
8. An RBIA programme should match the scope and objective of most annual internal control reports, offering valuable support to the reporting commitments of audit committees and executive boards.[10]

For risk-based auditing rules in most organizations, there is still a strong allegiance to building some compliance work inside many audits. Risk-based compliance reviews look at areas where the business may be breaking the rules, either through negligence, oversight or through a degree of unchecked reckless behaviour that can place the entire business at risk. Risk-based audits examine the degree to which an operation is geared up to deal with risks to its future successful delivery, but that does not mean the auditor will want to ignore actual abuse that is happening right here and now.

## The Fraud Debate

The scale and scope of fraud is captured by Arthur Piper in a special report on the rise of fraud in the UK:

> After years of uncoordinated attempts by legislators, regulators and the police to get to grips with fraudsters, the authorities seem to have suddenly woken up to the reality that tackling fraud should be a national priority: not least because fraud is big business. It costs the UK an estimated £14bn a year, which is over £230 per person in the country. In fact, fraud is on the increase because of the economic downturn. The business services firm, the Network, has recently found that the number of fraud-related reports surged from 10.9% to 21% from the first quarter of 2006 to the first quarter of 2009, in its 2009 Benchmarking Report. The report also confirmed that in-house fraud is on the rise.[11]

Internal auditors are expected to deal with fraud and when discussing current developments, the so-called expectation gap will not go away; i.e. there is often an assumption internal audit is responsible for managing the risk of fraud. Neil Baker has outlined relevant guidance from the IIA:

- Investigating the causes of fraud.
- Reviewing fraud prevention controls and detection processes put in place by management.
- Making recommendations to improve those processes.
- Advising the audit committee on what, if any, legal advice should be sought if a criminal investigation is to proceed.
- Bringing in any specialist knowledge and skills to assist in fraud investigations, or leading investigations where appropriate and requested by management.
- Liaising with the investigation team.
- Responding to whistleblowers.
- Considering fraud risk in every audit.
- Having sufficient knowledge to identify the indicators of fraud.
- Facilitating corporate learning.[12]

Some fraud investigations use surveillance to obtain evidence that cannot be gathered in any other way. In the past, this was fairly straightforward. In more recent times investigations have had to adhere to strict rules on using this approach as governments tighten up what may be seen as an infringement of human rights. The UK's Information Commissioner's Office views surveillance as the purposeful, routine, systematic and focused attention paid to personal details, for the sake of control, entitlement, management, influence or protection. Controls that track or monitor an employee's actions and communications have to be used with care so as not to be an abuse of power. Most agree that organizations need a strategic approach to fraud if they are to stay one step ahead of the international fraudsters that are fast becoming a major corporate risk. The Chartered Institute of Public Finance and Accountancy has a simple checklist on this matter:

1. Does the organisation have a counter fraud and corruption strategy that can be clearly linked to the organisation's overall strategic objectives?

2. Is there a clear remit to reduce losses to fraud and corruption to an absolute minimum covering all areas of fraud and corruption affecting the organisation?

3. Are there effective links between 'policy' work (to develop an anti-fraud and corruption and 'zero tolerance' culture, create a strong deterrent effect and prevent fraud and corruption by designing and redesigning policies and systems) and 'operational' work (to detect and investigate fraud and corruption and seek to apply sanctions and recover losses where it is found)?

4. Is the full range of integrated action being taken forward or does the organisation 'pick and choose'?

5. Does the organisation focus on outcomes (i.e. reduced losses) and not just activity (i.e. the number of investigations, prosecutions, etc.)?

6. Has the strategy been directly agreed by those with political and executive authority for the organisation?[13]

## IT Governance

IT governance is the next development on the changing approach to audit work, as IT security is starting to appear on the boardroom agenda as businesses are increasingly relying on e-business solutions. The IT auditor has an eye on IT risks and how they are being managed across the organization. In more recent years, there has emerged a new and improved chief information officer (CIO) who has much the same views, and is quite happy to listen to the auditor's views on risk management that focuses on information systems. The CIO's position is made clear in the following extract:

> Risk is an inherent part of doing business, and in a dynamic and global marketplace where change and uncertainty are the norm, risk rises exponentially. Corporate acquisitions, collaborative partnerships, global integration and accelerating technological advances all create risk, and today's most successful businesses have learned to absorb and mitigate it with relative ease. These companies are not only weathering change, they are taking advantage of it and, in some cases, even instigating it to uncover new opportunities. Such resilience is key to long-term growth and profitability. With virtually every aspect of modern business linked to information technology (IT), resilience increasingly depends on a company's ability to effectively manage the risks introduced into its IT and physical infrastructure and processes. It's no wonder that for today's top CIOs, risk management is not just a dominant theme; it has become a vocation − just as it is for their business line colleagues. Still, the scope of many CIOs' risk management efforts is often too limited to gain real value for the business. The fact is, IT executives are more likely to practice risk avoidance than risk management. And when they focus too strictly on the risks to IT and overlook the risks and benefits to the business, they limit the opportunity to drive financial and operational advantage. Good risk management in today's highly interconnected, dependency-driven business environment requires IT leaders to see and understand the business investment and financial upside of risk-taking. A holistic and more broad-based view of risk enables them to recognize the impact that IT processes and the infrastructure can have on business activities. They are better equipped to leverage IT's ability to reduce risks to the business and capitalize on opportunities for profit. A risk-aware governance framework facilitates this broader business perspective by providing decision makers across the organization with a more complete picture of risk and the potential for return. They gain the panoramic insight to make decisions that maximize revenue potential while levying an acceptable level of risk. They are better able to implement effective analysis and automation to address current risks while

protecting the emerging interests of the enterprise. In short, they can achieve a better balance of risk and return. CIOs who can communicate the business importance of risk management for IT and the related physical infrastructure can transform the way the IT leaders – and the entire enterprise – approach risk. More importantly, they can turn traditional IT risk management into a compelling, value-generating opportunity for the business.[14]

Building on the way the auditor can work with the chief information officer to raise the profile of IT as a boardroom agenda item, we can turn to a further view on this topic:

As IT represents only a part of the overall board agenda it is vital that NEDs have the right tools and information with which to challenge IT constructively and effectively ask the right questions. Coupled with the above, internal audit needs to position itself as the independent navigator of IT assurance. Given that the board will be receiving differing levels of assurance from, amongst others, compliance, IT security, third parties, project steering committees and the chief information officer (CIO), internal audit could integrate and quality assure this assurance, acting as an effective translator and trusted adviser. Chances are that existing assurance providers will be communicating risk inconsistently, providing an incomplete view of IT governance. What the board needs is effective translation of the business message embedded in technical jargon – and this is a role that an independent internal auditor is ideally placed to fulfil.[15]

Sticking to the strategic view of IT, one interesting development is work carried out by members of the INFOSEC Research Council (IRC), who are the major sponsors of information security research within the US Government. Taking a high-level strategic view of IT security issues, they have been developing a hard problem list that over the next five to ten years covers the following areas:

1. **Global-Scale Identity Management:**   Global-scale identification, authentication, access control, authorization, and management of identities and identity information.
2. **Insider Threat:**   Mitigation of insider threats in cyber space to an extent comparable to that of mitigation in physical space.
3. **Availability of Time-Critical Systems:**   Guaranteed availability of information and information services, even in resource-limited, geospatially distributed, on demand (ad hoc) environments
4. **Building Scalable Secure Systems:**   Design, construction, verification, and validation of system components and systems ranging from crucial embedded devices to systems composing millions of lines of code.
5. **Situational Understanding and Attack Attribution:**   Reliable understanding of the status of information systems, including information concerning possible attacks, who or what is responsible for the attack, the extent of the attack, and recommended responses.
6. **Information Provenance:**   Ability to track the pedigree of information in very large systems that process petabytes of information.
7. **Security with Privacy:**   Technical means for improving information security without sacrificing privacy.
8. **Enterprise-Level Security Metrics:**   Ability to effectively measure the security of large systems with hundreds to millions of users.

These eight problems were selected as the hardest and most critical challenges that must be addressed by the INFOSEC research community if trustworthy systems envisioned by the U.S. Government are to be built.[16]

One high-level approach to IT auditing is to consider the data security guidelines that are used in the organization, and this approach has been described as follows:

A widely recognised auditing standard was developed by the American Institute of Certified Public Accounts. An independent audit of an objective's 'control objectives and control activities', it normally includes checks on controls on information technology and related processes. An independent accounting or audit firm will do the audit and publish two types of report. A 'type one' report describes the organisation's controls at a specific point in time. A 'type two' report describes an organisation's controls over a minimum period of six months. Information Security Management is the only auditable international standard for information security management systems. The British Standards Institute says that being certified to ISO 27001 will help organisations manage and protect information assets. The standard is designed to ensure the selection of 'adequate and proportionate security controls'. It is based around monitoring, reviewing and improving information security management systems. The standard is applicable for all sizes of organisation and is particularly suitable where the protection of information is critical, such as in the finance, health, public and IT sectors. The standard is also used by outsourcing suppliers to assure customers that their information is being protected. ISO 27001 comprises a checklist of 133 information security controls which an organisation should consider. These controls include data backup, controlling access to a computer network, passwords, and encryption. The standard is not prescriptive; organisations must prove that their information security controls are adequate for their organisation. The certification process is usually in three stages. Stage one is a review of the existence and completeness of key documentation such as the organisation's security policy, 'statement of applicability' and 'risk treatment plan'. Stage two is an in-depth audit involving testing the existence and effectiveness of the information security controls stated in the SoA and RTP, as well as their supporting documentation. The final stage is an annual audit to confirm that a previously-certified organisation remains in compliance with the standard. The cost of certification is about £900 per day. Getting the certification can take a couple of days to a couple of months, depending on the size of the organisation.[17]

## Governance, Risk and Compliance (GRC)

One new development has been the growth in organizations seeking to integrate the concepts of governance, risk and compliance to promote consistency in the way these issues are addressed at a corporate level and across the business. The 2010 Open Compliance and Ethics Group (OCEG) Governance, Risk and Compliance Capability Model™ (also known as the Red Book) is broken into eight components:

1. **CULTURE & CONTEXT.**   Understand the current culture and the internal and external business contexts in which the organization operates, so that the GRC system can address current realities – and identify opportunities to affect the context to be more congruent with desired organizational outcomes.
2. **ORGANIZE & OVERSEE.**   Organize and oversee the GRC system so that it is integrated with, and when appropriate modifies, the existing operating model of the business and assign to management specific responsibility, decision-making authority, and accountability to achieve system goals.
3. **ASSESS & ALIGN.**   Assess risks and optimize the organizational risk profile with a portfolio of initiatives, tactics, and activities.
4. **PREVENT & PROMOTE.**   Promote and motivate desirable conduct, and prevent undesirable events and activities, using a mix of controls and incentives.

5. **DETECT & DISCERN.**    Detect actual and potential undesirable conduct, events, GRC system weaknesses, and stakeholder concerns using a broad network of information gathering and analysis techniques.
6. **RESPOND & RESOLVE.**    Respond to and recover from noncompliance and unethical conduct events, or GRC system failures, so that the organization resolves each immediate issue and prevent or resolve similar issues more effectively and efficiently in the future.
7. **MONITOR & MEASURE.**    Monitor, measure and modify the GRC system on a periodic and ongoing basis to ensure it contributes to business objectives while being effective, efficient and responsive to the changing environment.
8. **INFORM & INTEGRATE.**    Capture, document and manage GRC information so that it efficiently and accurately flows up, down and across the extended enterprise, and to external stakeholders.

The legal officer, financial controllers, risk and compliance teams, and business managers will all have a role in ensuring there is an agreed framework for promoting good governance throughout the organization. This is in contrast to a silo approach, where each team works to their own agenda focusing just on their set performance targets. GRC works best where there is a clear framework and strategy in place, with agreed roles and procedures for dealing with problems, errors, new risks and near misses. GRC is driven by the enterprise risk management process and a broad view of compliance, which looks at the impact of the organization on its wider environment and corporate policies as well as compliance with internal procedures. In the end GRC will aim to develop good control cultures where risk is properly understood and addressed by coordinating all those teams who have a role to play.

## Summary and Conclusions

The range and possibilities for internal auditors in terms of the services and approaches to their work are vast. This chapter has touched on some of these approaches and considered the specific issues and nuances of each approach. Internal audit work can be broken down into assurance-based and consulting-based. A risk-based systems approach to assurance work can be related to reviewing higher-level systems such as the corporate governance system, the risk management system and the resulting systems of internal control. Moreover, assurance work can focus on various aspects of the control spectrum such as information systems, compliance issues, value for money and systems for protecting the corporate resource from fraud and abuse. Consulting work can also relate to each of the above areas, in that it can be geared to helping an organization set up its corporate governance arrangements including risk management and control. Consulting can also be used to drill down into these arrangements and involve facilitating risk events and workshops. Top-level consulting engagements may be programmed into the audit plans to tackle corporate and managerial problems and special investigations through a formal project that may take several months to complete. Ongoing efforts to provide advice and information to line managers may also be a feature of the internal audit role, again on a consulting basis. There has never been so much choice available for the internal auditor. The response to this dilemma is to talk to stakeholders, set a strategy, publish the results, and ensure the right structure is designed and that audit staff are equipped to perform the strategy and then push ahead and monitor the success. It starts with setting the audit sights beyond what we used to do or what we have traditionally been good at. Real progress is made when the CAE is able to work 'outside the box' and develop a resource that really adds value to the direction, energies and accountabilities of the corporate body.

# Endnotes

1. 'A perspective on control self-assessment', IIA, Professional Practices Pamphlet 98-2, 1998.
2. CIPFA (1994) *The Investigation of Fraud In The Public Sector*, 2nd edition, p. 1.
3. 'Report to the Nation – The Wells Report', The White Paper, *Journal of The ACFE*, 2002.
4. McCollum, T. 'Cyber-crime still on the rise'. *Internal Auditing* – Loose, June 2002, pp. 16–17.
5. 'Outpacing change', in 12th Annual GISS, Ernst & Young's 12th Annual Global Information Security Survey.
6. *Daily Mail*, 3 September 1996.
7. Anderson, Urton and Chapman, Christy (2002) The IIA Handbook Series in *Implementing the Professional Practices Framework*, IIA, p. 21.
8. 'Towards a blueprint for the internal audit profession', Research by the Institute of Internal Auditors UK and Ireland in association with Deloitte, Deloitte & Touche, 2008, p. 7.
9. Rimmer, Nicola, 'Size isn't everything'. *Internal Auditing & Business Risk, IIA Magazine*, September 2007, p. 35.
10. Opie, Jeremy, *Internal Auditing & Business Risk, IIA Magazine*, January 2008, p. 39.
11. Piper, Arthur, 'Fraud special report'. *Internal Auditing & Business Risk, IIA Magazine*, June 2009, pp. 22–25.
12. Baker, Neil, 'Fraud special report. Self defence'. *Internal Auditing & Business Risk, IIA Magazine*, June 2009. p. 28.
13. *Managing the Risk of Fraud, The Red Book*, CIPFA Better Governance Forum, Chartered Institute of Public Finance and Accountancy, October 2006, p. 1.
14. *A CIO's Guide to IT Risk Management: Tapping the Extraordinary Potential for Business Value and Financial Growth*, IBM, September 2008, p. 3.
15. Ruddenklau, Antony and Westberg, Peter, 'Closing the gap'. *Internal Auditing & Business Risk, IIA Magazine*, September 2007, pp. 20–23.
16. *Hard Problem List*, INFOSEC Research Council (IRC), November 2005.
17. Huber, Nick, 'Finding the weakest link'. *Internal Auditing & Business Risk, IIA Magazine*, August 2009, p. 38.

# Chapter 8

# SETTING AN AUDIT STRATEGY

## Introduction

The previous chapters of *The Essential Guide* have reflected the major challenges that face internal auditors as they seek to add value to their employers. The 'value-add' proposition is a main driver for the audit services and choices need to be made in terms of what is delivered by internal audit and how this task is achieved. The IIA's Performance Standards 2000 (Managing the Internal Audit Activity) reinforces this concept by stating that: 'The CAE must effectively manage the internal audit activity to ensure it adds value to the organisation.' The most important factor in this equation is the audit strategy that is set to achieve added value. Added value is described by the IIA in the following way:

> Value is provided by improving opportunities to achieve organizational objectives, identifying operational improvement, and/or reducing risk exposure through both assurance and consulting services.

The CAE will succeed or fail on the basis of the adopted audit strategy. Note that all references to IIA definitions, code of ethics, IIA attribute and performance standards, practice advisories and practice guides relate to the International Professional Practices Framework (IPPF) prepared by the Institute of Internal Auditors in 2009. With this in mind we cover the following aspects of getting to a suitable audit strategy in this chapter:

8.1  Risk-Based Strategic Planning
8.2  Resourcing the Strategy
8.3  Managing Performance
8.4  The Auditor Appraisal Scheme
8.5  Methods of Staff Appraisal
8.6  The Audit Manual
8.7  Time Monitoring System
8.8  Audit Planning Process
8.9  The Annual Audit Plan
8.10 The Quarterly Audit Plan
8.11 New Developments
        Summary and Conclusions

## 8.1  Risk-Based Strategic Planning

Deciding clear objectives is the starting place for internal audit strategies. Directing resources towards accepted objectives sets the frame for success. There is no one way of defining audit objectives as they result from the changing influences of competing forces.

## Clear Objectives

This sounds straightforward but clarity of objectives is not always present. A basic test is to ask each auditor what they see as their main objective. It is not enough to compose a formal document entitled 'audit objectives'. There is also need for a clear but simple mission for the audit function, which should guide the entire staff. The variety of audit services is not a problem so long as an appropriate model is defined and applied.

## Scope of Audit Work

There is a need to decide what is included within the scope of audit work. It is possible to provide services outside the formal scope so long as we make a conscious decision. The scope of internal audit should be based on a professional framework. IIA standards suggest that the main role of internal audit is assurance work. Anything else is consultancy services, which should be assessed through an appropriate criteria in line with IIA Performance Standard 2010.C1, which states that:

> The chief audit executive should consider accepting proposed consulting engagements based on the engagement's potential to improve management of risks, add value, and improve the organization's operations. Accepted engagements must be included in the plan.

A discussion of scope creates an opportunity to agree on the important distinction between audit's role in contrast to management's. There are various forces that impact on the final model adopted. These range from the CAE's views, the needs of management and the type of staff employed.

1. **Communicated**   There is little point setting formal objectives for the audit function if these are not properly publicized across the organization. Communication may take the following forms:
   - Objectives embodied within an audit charter.
   - Suitable correspondence that repeats the objective.
   - The annual audit report.
   - Regular meetings with management on this topic.
   - Formal presentations to the audit committee.
   - Some mention within major audit reports.

   This is a continual process as strategy does not arise as a one-off event but changes and adjusts over time, in response to the environment.

2. **Understood by all**   Passing formal documents out to auditors and management is not enough. There is need to ensure auditors understand and work to agreed objectives. For audit staff this may involve internally organized induction training and skills workshops. We may make a formal presentation to senior management that might be used to dispel myths and misunderstanding. It is essential that members of the audit committee have a clear understanding. Dave Richards who runs the First Energy internal audit team has spent time developing a clear mission and vision based around the team's:

   1. products and services.
   2. who are our customers.
   3. what services do they use.

4. which customers are most supportive.
5. what does our feedback survey say.

The First Energy mission is that 'the IA dept is responsible for supporting improvement to corporate performance, ensuring compliance with laws and procedures and confirming accuracy of corporate records'. Their vision runs along the lines of 'We deliver objective and innovative solutions'. This is built into their audit strategies and the staff competencies needed to achieve this vision are defined. They make the crucial point that the audit department is really the sum of the behaviours of its individual members.[1]

3. **Types of services required**    The scope of internal audit sets a clear frame within which audit may operate. This will be designed to be widely applicable to most types of audit activities. The adopted scope of internal auditing can determine which services fall within the audit role. The type of services that may appear in the strategy could include:
- Reviewing the corporate risk management process.
- Visiting business units to assess their arrangements.
- Review risk management reports that are used by executive management.
- Consider whether there are any key risks not included on the corporate risk register.
- Take steps to support and encourage the risk management awareness and the overall risk management process.

Risk-based auditing is seen by most as the best way forward.

4. **Policy on fraud work**    The topic of fraud holds a special place when discussing audit objectives. Auditors understand the control cycle, which dictates that fraud is caused by poor controls. This does not detract from the need to set out our role in relation to fraud detection and investigation. The CAE must not only ensure that the audit role in frauds against the organization is documented, but also that audit is in a position to discharge this role. It is better to place a caveat by stating that the organization should provide additional resources for large projects. Management is ultimately responsible for investigating frauds but there is a growing view that fraud, where it had in the past been seen as old-fashioned audit work, should be put back on the internal auditor's list of top priorities.

5. **Geared into the organization**    Any audit objective must be linked directly into the organization's own objectives (or mission). The starting place for setting audit's role is to isolate what the organization is trying to achieve and then see how audit resources can assist this. So long as we accept that our role is located in risk management and control issues, the final audit product may take different guises in addressing control-related matters. Risk management must be set within the culture of the organization and its success criteria. Organizations range between tightly bureaucratic entities through to loosely based project teams. The growth in nontraditional audit services may be geared to the way the corporate control environment has developed. Mike Summerell has given his opinion on moving away from traditional audit approaches:

> In my experience, traditional auditing tends to focus on formal accounting control mechanisms such as signature approvals, reconciliations, and documentation manuals. The results of these audits often focus on areas considered insignificant or 'bureaucratic' by staff and management. This view reflects another deficiency of the traditional approach – its tendency to focus on symptoms instead of the real causes.... Auditors need to look for ways to enhance the services they provide. The CSA approach is not perfect, but it represents distinct advantages that more conventional approaches alone cannot offer. If the tried and trusted traditional audit techniques remain your sole approach to internal auditing, you are missing important opportunities. I firmly believe that traditional auditing simply doesn't have the potential impact of CSA. If, as a profession, we seize tradition as some virtue to maintain and champion, we may be flirting with extinction.[2]

6. **Approved**　Any audit objective must be approved by the organization. This in most cases will be the audit committee where a formally signed audit charter will be agreed along with any changes.

## Defining Audit Strategy

Strategy goes far beyond the old-fashioned annual planning updates that are described in *Brink's Modern Internal Auditing*:

> The director of internal audit today cannot develop an audit plan based solely on such factors as last year's plan and current available resources, publish the plan and proceed with audit activities. Many factors impact the type of audit activities that should be planned, and various functions and individuals within the modern organization will have some input into that planning process.[3]

The audit strategy process is a continuing cycle of events that must be properly controlled by audit management. The context is illustrated in Figure 8.1.

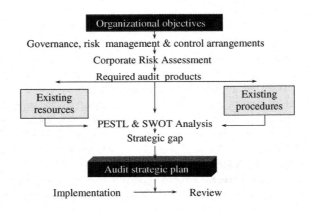

**FIGURE 8.1**　Setting audit strategy.

　This diagram highlights the link between the audit objectives, the organization's risk management process and the resultant audit strategy. This strategy helps determine what needs to be done to implement the strategy. A confidential business plan may accompany the published strategy and the CAE would seek to isolate gaps in the resources and procedures that we employ and address these gaps in the strategic plan.

## The Corporate Risk Strategy

A cornerstone of audit strategy is the corporate assessment of business risk. This establishes an organization's control needs. It involves the ongoing task of capturing the key systems that underpin an organization so that material control needs may be isolated and addressed. While audit objectives set out what we wish to achieve, control needs dictate how much work needs doing and the type of resources most appropriate. Audit plans will need to be driven by the enterprise risk management process that is in place and there should be a clear alignment between audit risk profiles and the corporat risk landscape. An audit risk survey necessitates discussion with middle management and involves:

- A definition of the audit unit.
- An assessment of the relative risks inherent in each unit.
- Research into the type of problems units attract.
- Risk ranking related to resources subsequently assigned via an audit plan.

The CAE will want to define an audit universe that will comprise all that falls within the remit of the internal audit coverage which will then be divided into audit areas. The IIA's July 2009 *GAIN Knowledge Briefing on Defining the Right Audit Universe* suggests that:

> To effectively define an audit universe, many auditors divide the organization into manageable auditable activities or units (e.g., policies, procedures, and practices; business units; IT systems; major contracts; and functions, such as accounting or operations) that can be classified in a number of ways. For instance, according to a June 2008 Flash Survey of 275 IIA members, the most frequently chosen auditable activity group was function followed by department and risk.[4]

1. **Risk assessment**   We should construct a methodology that caters for different activities being associated with different types and levels of risk. IIA Performance Standard 2010 makes it clear that: 'The chief audit executive must establish risk-based plans to determine the priorities of the internal audit activity, consistent with the organization's goals.' There is no universal formula but we need to ensure:
   - The methodology is accepted by the organization.
   - It is applied to the audit universe in a consistent fashion.
   - It is based on the corporate risk assessment and ongoing operational risk reviews.

The organization would have to be broken down into auditable units and one approach in *Brink's Modern Internal Auditing* suggests three options for identifying audit units:

   1. by function – accounting, purchasing payroll.
   2. by transaction cycle – cash receipts, production.
   3. by geography.[5]

2. **Management participation**   A further aspect of audit strategy relates to the need to involve management in the process. There is a temptation to become trapped inside the struggle to preserve audit independence, wherein contact with the outside world is avoided. Our plans and strategies are then based entirely on audit's perception of organizational needs on a 'we know best' basis. What may have been acceptable in the past can no longer be defended when all expenditure (including audit costs) must be justified to front line managers whose budgets bear the eventual recharges. Management participation is alluded to in IIA Performance Standard 2010.A1 which states that:

> The internal audit activity's plan of engagements must be based on a documented risk assessment, undertaken at least annually. The input of senior management and the board must be considered in this process.

There is the need to explain the audit process and demonstrate why resources should be directed to one area as opposed to another. Bringing management into the process means additional pressure on audit management. This derives from the need to perform one's job while at the same time communicate what is being done. A strategy not based on organizational needs and supported throughout the organization will be hard to implement. Management's participation includes:

- Explaining that audit operates to a risk-based strategy.
- Ensuring that this strategy is based primarily on addressing organizational risk and control needs.
- Publicizing the link between risk and resource allocation.
- Keeping management informed as to changes to the existing strategies.
- Securing avenues whereby relevant information may be imparted to and from management.
- Clarifying the agreed cut-off points between management and internal audit's roles.
- Retaining a degree of independence that gives audit the final say in strategy and planning.

The risk-based auditing approach to designing audit work has been explored by the IIA in their 2005 professional guidance for internal auditors in terms of three main stages:

1. **Discuss the understanding of risk maturity with the board and senior managers.**
   - Determine what has already been done to improve the risk maturity of the organization such as training, risk workshops, questionnaires about risks and interviews with risk managers.
   - Determine whether managers feel that the risk register is comprehensive. Discuss whether an understanding of risk management is embedded so that managers feel responsible not only for identifying, assessing and mitigating risks but also for monitoring the framework and the responses to risks.
2. **Obtain documents, where they are available, which detail:**
   - The objectives of the organization.
   - How risks are analyzed, for example by scoring their impact and likelihood.
   - A definition, approved by the board, which defines its risk appetite in terms of the scoring system used for inherent and residual risks.
   - The processes followed to identify risks which threaten the organization's objectives.
   - How management considers risks as part of their decision making. For example, including risks and the response to them, in project approval documents.
   - The processes followed to report risks at different levels of management.
   - The sources of information used by management and the board to assure themselves that the framework is working effectively to manage risks within the risk appetite.
   - The risk register of the organization, including the types of information described in the previous section.
   - Any existing assessment by management or the board of the risk maturity of the organization.
   - Any other documents which indicate the commitment to risk management.
3. **Conclude on the risk maturity.**
   Using the documents and information gathered assess the organization's risk maturity.[6]

## PESTL and SWOT Analysis

Audit management is like any other management process in that all relevant techniques should be applied in the course of developing a clear strategy. Two such techniques are PESTL (an assessment of political, economical, social, technical and legal factors) and SWOT (consideration of strengths, weaknesses, opportunities and threats). These assist audit management in determining the current relative position of the audit function, along with some of the forces that may influence its future progress. The factors that might be pertinent to internal audit are:

**Political**  The factors relating to government policy might affect the audit function. The government may turn towards internal audit as a safeguard against financial impropriety, particularly where large-scale scandals receive press coverage. Where government policy calls for quality control over public services or controls over executive directors for enhanced corporate governance in the private sector, audit implications have to be considered.

**Economic**  Economic factors will affect the development of the organization, and might lead to growth, retrenchment or a basic maintenance strategy that should affect the audit style. Growth calls for expansion and aggressive policies with audit advising on the risk and control aspects of takeovers and new systems. Rationalizing may require closing down parts of the organization's activities and audit recommendations involving extra resources may not be appropriate. Economic factors may affect the audit budget and the supply of new auditors. Audit will consider whether a growth, retrenchment or maintenance strategy should be pursued in internal audit.

**Social**  Social factors must be recognized since they affect the culture of the organization. These include moral aspects relating to business ethics and wider issues like environmental protection. The rate of unemployment and supply of auditors should be appreciated along with the availability of training schemes. National opinion on fraud, VFM, accountability and business practices affect the role of audit.

**Technology**  New technology has a dual role for internal audit for it will affect systems and processes used by the organization, and also expand the range of IT available for use in audit work. Audit strategy must keep up with IT developments and if possible stay a step ahead, particularly in automating audit work. It is important that audit's IT strategy flows from that adopted by the organization.

**Legal**  Audit must always keep up to date with legislation not only relating to the audit function itself but also legislation that requires compliance-based controls. Examples are health and safety, data protection, employee protection, equal opportunities, environmental issues and accounting practices.

**Strengths**  The positive factors may be developed and used to defend against threats and to seize opportunities. Strong features may relate to the quality of staff, degree of automation, special skills, a clear methodology and good client relationships.

**Weaknesses**  Areas that need attention might jeopardize the welfare of audit. It is vital these are identified and dealt with via the strategy. Common problems are:

| | |
|---|---|
| Excessive nonrecoverable hours | Low staff morale |
| Lack of audit procedures | Out-of-date audit manual |
| High staff turnover | Poor client relationships |
| Low-level audit work | Recommendations ignored |
| Poor quality of work | Assignments overrunning budget |
| No career development | Poor reputation |
| Lack of focus on risk management | |

Each of the above problems must be addressed or the audit function will fail to fulfil its full potential. It is through a carefully planned integrated audit strategy that weaknesses may be tackled.

**Opportunities** The audit function should seize opportunities. Failure may cause the downfall of the audit department in total terms or in the level of the respect that it attracts. If the organization requires new services that might be provided through the audit function, it is important that this issue is considered. If there is a gap in controls in developing new computerized information systems and audit are unable to respond to this problem, the organization will find this expertise from elsewhere. If opportunities are not seized, they may pose threats in the future. The audit strategy should ensure that required strengths are developed to maximize available opportunities. All opportunities to add value should be exploited and the IIA has provided guidance on this point in their December 2009 Recommendations:

> Once defined, CAEs should keep in mind the following four key points, as revealed throughout the interviews:
>
> 1. Adding value should be a part of every internal audit process.
> 2. Measuring an internal audit activity's added value is a quantitative and qualitative process.
> 3. When marketing an internal audit activity's added value, word-of-mouth references are best.
> 4. Opportunities for adding value are created – the process for adding value is the same regardless of an internal audit activity's staff size.[7]

**Threats** Threats can come in many guises and may affect the status of the audit function. The obvious threats come as competition, and this can arise on many fronts including external audit, management consultants and internal control teams. Developments within the organization may affect the level of independence acquired by audit and these must be countered. If the existing audit reporting line is stifling audit findings and recommendations, moves to find a direct link to the organization's power base through, say, an audit committee may be part of the strategy. If audit state their intention to perform high-level audit work they must also have an additional strategy to ensure that their staff and procedures are sufficient to meet these new demands.

## 8.2  Resourcing the Strategy

Resource management and human resource management (HRM) are major components of the strategic management process. The IIA Performance Standard 2030 makes it clear that:

> The chief audit executive must ensure that internal audit resources are appropriate, sufficient, and effectively deployed to achieve the approved plan.

We include here the main issues that impact on HRM within the context of internal auditing.

### Audit Management's Role

Audit management must ensure that HRM issues are adequately considered and dealt with. This sets the stage for defining management's role as one of managing (not performing) the audit work in larger audit shops. There are potential complications, since managers may find it hard to stop auditing and start managing. The fact that the type of work that auditors tend to handle can be very sensitive provides a convenient excuse for audit managers not to refer the work down to their staff. The position we need to reach is where audit managers appreciate the need to employ staff whom they can trust and rely on to discharge the audit role. They need to ensure the staff are properly developed and directed so that they are able to perform to accepted standards. The only way that this can be achieved is through the application of suitable HRM techniques. A further complication is that HRM matters must be set within the overall framework of the organization's own HRM policies. Audit management is restricted by the autonomy it has in the application of policies specific to internal audit. Having said this, everything that auditors do or fail to do is the direct responsibility of audit management and ultimately the CAE. IIA Standard 2000 states that:

> The chief audit executive must effectively manage the internal audit activity to ensure it adds value to the organization.

The CAE is responsible for properly managing the internal audit activity so that it meets stakeholder expectations and conforms with the IIA IPPF.

## The Human Resource Management Cycle

The audit plan must be properly resourced, which for internal audit mainly consists of getting in the human resources. This is required by IIA Practice Advisory 2030-1, which makes it clear that:

> The chief audit executive (CAE) is primarily responsible for the sufficiency and management of internal audit resources in a manner that ensures the fulfillment of internal audit's responsibilities, as detailed in the internal audit charter. This includes effective communication of resource needs and reporting of status to senior management and the board. Internal audit resources may include employees, external service providers, financial support, and technology-based audit techniques. Ensuring the adequacy of internal audit resources is ultimately a responsibility of the organization's senior management and board; the CAE should assist them in discharging this responsibility.

It is as well to define what we mean by HRM. Personnel issues are unrelated matters that concern staff, which are dealt with partly by personnel and partly by line management. These can relate to travel claims, overtime, sickness records, timesheets, timekeeping and so on. Their impact on the relationship of the employees and employer are but single-issue topics. HRM, on the other hand, is concerned with a whole system of management that is designed so that the right people are doing the right things at the right time, to ensure that organizational objectives in Figure 8.2 are achieved.

## Attributes of Auditors

Auditors will be able to deliver quality services where the following hold true:
1. The objectives are clear.
2. What is expected of them is made clear.
3. The standards of performance are made clear.
4. They have the ability to perform to the requisite standards.
5. They are motivated to do so.
6. Management removes any barriers to performance.

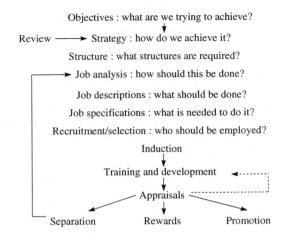

**FIGURE 8.2**    The human resource management cycle.

There is an unstated assumption that the auditor has the right attributes to perform to the requisite standards. This can only arise where audit management has defined these attributes so that recruitment and development programmes can be directed towards them. If this definition has not been carried out then it becomes guesswork. At worst, auditors may guess wrongly and behave in an inappropriate way because this is what they assume is required. Internal audit competencies are also discussed in Chapter 5.

## Realistic Resource Strategy

The realities of corporate life mean that many audit units cannot simply formulate a plan and then obtain all the resources they need. At times, it may be necessary to cut or restrict when budgets fall under pressure. A strategy of building a large audit resource needs to make sense and, at times, the CAE will want to consider ways of reducing rather than increasing the audit staff. The IIA has provided the following guidance through their *GAIN Knowledge Alert*, on maximizing the use of IA resources (February 2009):

1. Reduce the number of audits performed during the year, the frequency of audits performed, or the scope of audits performed (e.g., would not perform audits of previously reviewed areas, operational or process improvement audits, audits of special projects or extracurricular activities, and management requests)
2. Reduce internal audit staff (e.g., eliminate administrative or part-time staff and paid interns; streamline audit management staff; and eliminate positions held by auditors about to retire)
3. Reduce or eliminate IT audits or information security audits (e.g., eliminate IT auditor position and outsource function and eliminate audits of IT projects or software development projects)
4. Eliminate audits of low- to medium-risk areas based on latest risk assessment or annual audit plan and concentrate on areas of highest risk to the organization
5. Not perform consulting work or provide assistance to external auditors or consultants
6. Eliminate positions held by low- to medium-performing internal audit staff

7. Eliminate audits related to Sarbanes–Oxley compliance, controls testing, or monitoring and use Sarbanes–Oxley audit results to streamline performance of other audits where overlap is apparent
8. Cut back on travel expenses by consolidating audits on affiliate or branch operations
9. Eliminate co-sourcing or outsourcing work to save money, find a cheaper co-sourcing or outsourcing alternative, and in-source more internal audit work
10. Eliminate audits of financial areas or finance-related activities[8]

## 8.3  Managing Performance

Staff appraisal is a management control that audit would tend to recommend when undertaking an audit where staffing is included in the terms of reference for the work. Therefore one may argue that we, as auditors, should apply this technique to the management of the internal audit function. However, staff appraisal schemes can be positive motivators or complete demotivators, depending on how they are designed and implemented. The theory of staff appraisals is based on telling people what is expected of them and then telling them how far they are achieving these standards, as a way of motivating them. The other benefit is the positive steps that may be taken where performance is not on par. Appraisal schemes also underpin career development programmes, which again may be used to direct the activities of staff and ensure there is good progression so that good staff are retained and poor staff improved. It is essential that auditors are appraised in a positive fashion. This in turn depends on:

1. Keeping the accent on praise.
2. Not using the appraisal scheme to criticize but using it to develop.
3. Using performance appraisal to engender good communications and listening skills.
4. Seeking to promote a win/win environment where all sides gain.

### Appraisal Criteria

There is no way that auditors can be appraised without reference to a formal appraisal criterion. This would be based on the types of skills, abilities and attributes required to discharge the audit role. The idea is to employ, teach, develop and improve each of these factors through a formal process of appraising each auditor's ability to achieve these standards. These performance standards may cover:

• Basic auditing skills that all auditors should possess.
• Advanced auditing skills that should attach to more senior auditors.
• Managerial skills for auditors with staff responsibilities.
• Skills in related specialist areas such as computing, accounting, facilitation, law and so on.
• Other skills as required.

We are moving closer to defining a job specification that may be used to appoint audit staff. The same personal requirements may be applied to appraising the staff along with a series of personal targets. Higher levels of audit management need to acquire different types of skills, as shown in Figure 8.3.

The performance appraisal scheme must cater for the above factors if it is to have any relevance to the internal audit function. Superimposed on this are special projects that may be developed by the auditor.

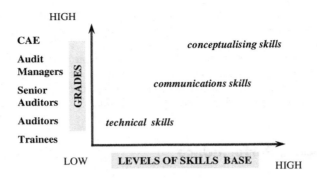

**FIGURE 8.3**  Different skills levels.

## 8.4  The Auditor Appraisal Scheme

It is one thing to design an auditor performance appraisal scheme but quite another to implement it in such a way that it produces the desired results. What looks good on paper may be different in practice. There are several matters to be considered including:

- The scheme must in fact address the auditor's performance. It should not be an alternative method of getting rid of problem staff or simply a paper exercise. The key objectives must be to assess and then seek to improve the performance of auditors at all levels in the internal audit department.
- The scheme should attempt to meet employees' needs, which should be based around a desire to obtain feedback on their achievements and approach to work. It can be sold to staff as a mechanism for providing this all-important feedback as opposed to just another management technique to increase the work rate.
- The scheme should represent a source of challenge to the auditor. The process of working to one's own personal targets engenders a form of maturity from staff but can lead to an assortment of soft targets being defined. Extremes can occur where parts of these personal targets may have already been achieved before they are applied. This positive approach can only be used in audit departments that employ highly motivated staff and use team-building approaches to work.
- The scheme must incorporate the concept of regular progress reporting. This is much better than an annual scheme whereby reports 'appear out of the blue' every 12 months. Ongoing assessment makes it easier to assimilate the scheme into everyday work that the auditor carries out.
- An auditor can compile a career plan so long as there is an awareness of the areas that have been developed and those that need further development. A shortcut to this process is via the performance appraisal scheme, which isolates one's strengths and weaknesses. To be valid the scheme must incorporate this feature rather than simply result in a finite category in the ranges of, say, 1–5. We have shown that auditors bring to their work a whole range of skills that together comprise a unique package. To simply classify a person as a category 1 (very poor) or 5 (very good), or a range between these two figures, is bad management practice. Unfortunately there are many audit sections that do just this and still have difficulty working out why their particular scheme appears to demotivate their auditors.

- We can build on this idea of motivation by suggesting that any valid scheme should be geared directly into this concept of releasing 'people power'. Performance appraisal must as the bottom line exist to improve performance. As such it must then feed into a suitable development plan that gives a sense of direction and purpose to staff as they work for an organization over the years. This simple notion is sometimes forgotten when a scheme is introduced and fast becomes a weapon of terror in the wrong manager's hands. Note that what may be acceptable in a recession, where the supply of auditors exceeds demand, may be resented in times of high economic growth.

- The scheme should acknowledge the personal goals of each auditor. In this way we should seek to establish a bridge between the organization's and the auditor's own targets. If the performance targets can become personal targets then the appraisal scheme will run automatically as it is driven by the auditor's motivation, as opposed to an obscure set of goals.

- The appraisal scheme should ideally feed into a suitable training programme. This being the case, the scheme will hopefully be used to isolate any training needs that must be met to fill gaps in the skills required to perform at the appropriate level. There is little point in identifying skills gaps without seeking to close them. Such an approach whereby training is applied to problems makes the scheme more dynamic as a positive technique rather than concentrating merely on the perceived weaknesses.

- Performance appraisal should be sophisticated enough to define an auditor's potential to work at a defined level. This requires extrapolation to move the historical achievements into projected areas. The only imponderable is the impact of training and development plans. A learning rate may also be estimated so that one uses three key factors to arrive at the auditor's potential performance (Figure 8.4).

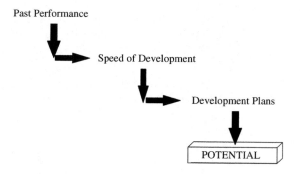

**FIGURE 8.4**  Auditor development rates.

- Using the bridge between performance appraisal and auditor development plans, we can go on to consider the future of each auditor in terms of promoting their management skills, existing job and future potential. Again the idea is to get the scheme into a positive mode that is well received by staff.

- Counselling is also an important component of an appraisal scheme. Where the scheme isolates poor performance this can lead to a great deal of stress for the auditor in question. One final implication of poor performance may be transfer/removal/dismissal. This is necessary as a final remedy that hopefully will never have to be applied so long as staff are willing to work and possess the basic skills that underpin this work. If we have to follow a line from the performance appraisal scheme to the poor performance procedures that may result in the removal of the auditor, there needs to be an interim stage based on counselling. This will seek to uncover barriers to performance that may be dealt with in addressing an inability to perform to required standards. Where these barriers can be eliminated then the final transfer decision may be delayed and the auditor given what may be seen as a second chance. Here special support programmes should be in place to address this problem. Note that counselling should not be left entirely to audit management but must include professional input from, say, the personnel department. The CAE should always remember that some employees perform badly because of their managers and this factor is often hidden from view as an interpretation of events is provided by the same manager. Again a level of sophistication built into the scheme is the keyword.

- We arrive at the final point of principle underpinning performance appraisal, which is the key ingredient: feedback. Performance appraisal provides an opportunity for the manager and audit staff to discuss performance as an issue and so develop the necessary mechanism for this feedback. Without stating the obvious, this feedback is a two-way affair. It requires both sides to listen to each other and develop a meaningful rapport.

Performance appraisal is less of a bureaucratic management technique and more of a vehicle through which performance can be addressed and developed by way of a close working relationship between the auditor and audit management.

## 8.5   Methods of Staff Appraisal

There are a variety of methods that are used to assess performance. Fortunately the internal audit arena, because of the nature of the work, provides a ready-made avenue through which auditors may be assessed. This is based around the audit review procedure, where audit work is considered by audit management before it is signed off. Ways that auditors may have their performance assessed are:

1. The audit review process. Here we can use a standardized form to allow the manager to comment on the way the auditor carried out a piece of work that can then be copied on to the person's personnel file. This brings appraisal naturally into the review process based on the hands-on work that the auditor performs rather than vague concepts.
2. A periodic review may be undertaken that deals with the auditor's performance, say, on a quarterly basis. Here one might simply take each item from the auditor's job specification along with special projects that have been assigned, and indicate the extent to which the required standards have been achieved. The manager must have reference to valid material to form the basis of this assessment and to this end one may refer to the jobs that have been charged on the auditor's timesheet.
3. It is possible to set performance targets for each auditor based around the annual/quarterly plans. This will be based on completing defined audits, keeping within budgets, performing special tasks, such as the audit manual, and achieving a percentage of chargeable to nonchargeable hours. Where these targets flow from the overall organizational/departmental targets, a form of management by achievement ensues and hierarchies may be developed so that goals cascade downwards. Examples of some specific and team and overall unit performance targets may be listed:
   - Extent to which the annual and quarterly plan has been achieved.
   - The percentage of recoverable hours charged.
   - Time taken to respond to management requests for assistance.

- Staff turnover.
- Absenteeism rate.
- Number of improvements to the audit manual.
- Time taken by auditors to get access to audit management.
- Level of managerial agreement to audit risk criteria.
- Level of involvement of auditee in the audit terms of reference.
- Number of recommendations agreed.
- Level of complaints.
- Level of staff grievances against management.
- Time taken to issue audit reports after completion of the audit.
- Level of suggestions from staff to audit management.
- Level of compliance with the audit manual.
- Regularity of group and departmental meetings.
- The percentage of staff with poor timekeeping.
- Number of aborted audits.
- Level of problems found during work reviews.
- Extent to which audit objectives have been met.
- Number of audits completed on time.
- Level of audits within the time budget.
- Number of auditors passing professional exams.
- Number of audits delegated by the audit manager.
- Level of draft reports requiring rewrites.
- Extent to which developmental plans have been achieved.
- Extent of audit automation.
- Rate of production of audit products.
- Currency of time-monitoring information.
- Currency of timesheets submitted and authorized.
- Level of satisfaction from the clients.
- Extent to which desks are kept clear.
- Extent to which files hold all relevant information.
- Time taken to find specific files.
- Extent to which follow-up audits find that recommendations from previous reports have been implemented.
- Number of audit reports issued.
- Amount of alteration as a result of management review.
- Level of recoverable hours to nonrecoverable hours charged in the period.
- Degree to which auditors keep within the budget hours for each audit.
- Extent to which the work plan has been completed.
- Level of positive comments from clients via the satisfaction questionnaire.
- Level of absences from work.

There are drawbacks in defining auditors as belonging to a certain performance group or category. It is nonetheless possible to rate each range of the performance factors by assigning a figure. It is the final overall figure that creates the problems and so this average or aggregate need not be calculated. The auditor's job specification has been quoted as one way of setting a suitable framework for the performance appraisal scheme. Most argue that performance appraisal tends to highlight existing problems rather than cause them. The concept of appraisal must be set within a mechanism to codify what should be best management practice in dealing with staff. There are many things that could go wrong with performance appraisal schemes where they are applied in an inappropriate fashion. It is important that there is a control over this process, not in terms of an appeal but in terms of referring matters for review. For this reason, it is possible to allow auditors to have specific concerns referred to the CAE to seek reconciliation or any amendments (if required). This review should revolve around the annual report and should be related only to matters connected with setting targets, reviewing performance and/or defining the resultant career development action plans.

The IIA recognizes the degree of flexibility in assessing performanance in their *GAIN Knowledge Alert, Measuring IA Performance*, September 2009:

> CAEs in different organizations use a variety of performance tools and quality assurance techniques, including satisfaction surveys and benchmarking metrics. While no single tool or technique is best, it is important that CAEs and internal audit managers choose a performance management methodology that best fits their internal audit activity's and organization's needs.[9]

The IIA go on to say that the auditor performance metrics should be organized and balances the scorecard to ensure there is a clear framework in place. CAEs around the world address various aspects of the performance management process, including the selection of performance metrics, the use of internal and external quality assessments (QAs) and tips on how to use a balanced scorecard. In selecting the right performance metrics, and prior to selecting the metrics that will be used to measure internal audit performance, CAEs should:

- Perform an inventory of the metrics being used.
- Consider existing organizational performance reporting processes, stakeholder expectations, professional requirements, and the internal audit activity's maturity level.
- Review the internal audit activity's mission and vision statements.[10]

## 8.6    The Audit Manual

The topic of audit manuals touches upon a number of subsidiary issues including standardization, procedures, controlling creativity and audit approaches and underpins professional standards for delivering the adopted audit strategy. *Brink's Modern Internal Auditing* has described the role of the audit manual:

> Audits need to be managed, and the best tool for audit management is an audit manual. An internal audit manual is an in house guide to the contents of an audit; it is a reference book which can be consulted when an audit question arises.[11]

This section brings together the main topics that should be dealt with via the audit manual as well as discussing some models that help illustrate this all-important technique.

### The Role of the Audit Manual

It is necessary to establish the role and objectives of the audit manual before considering appropriate models. Publications on internal audit procedures and performance bear on the topic and so a wide range of material has been considered. The IIA Standard 2040 covers policies and procedures:

> The chief audit executive must establish policies and procedures to guide the internal audit activity.

The interpretation goes on to say:

> The form and content of policies and procedures are dependent upon the size and structure of the internal audit activity and the complexity of its work.

The manual is a mechanism for channeling guidance for the auditor. The available material provides comments from many different sources and will give insight into the various issues that surround the design and implementation of audit manuals. Manuals fulfil the following roles:

**Defining standards and methods of work**   This is the first and foremost task of the audit manual as the vehicle for defining auditing standards. The way audit will be managed and audit resources employed are matters that have to be decided by audit management in seeking to discharge its responsibility for delivering a quality audit service.

**Communicating this to auditors**   The second role of the manual is to bring the requisite standards to the attention of audit staff. By including relevant material in the manual we can argue that this means they have to be adhered to by all staff by virtue of their position. Assorted memos, advice and documents issued to auditors have no real status if they are not delivered in a coordinated manner, and it is here that the audit manual is of great assistance.

**Establishing a base from which to measure the expected standards of performance**   So long as management has set standards and communicated these to staff (along with training if required) the auditors can then be expected to apply the standard. We then use this to determine whether audit staff are able to perform. Herein lies the third role of the manual in enabling management to consider and judge the performance of its staff. We can define three main sections of the audit manual as shown in Table 8.1.

**TABLE 8.1**   Sections of an audit manual.

| Section | Contents |
| --- | --- |
| Managerial | Concerning the management of the audit function |
| Operational | Concerning the performance of audit work |
| Administrative | All other procedural matters |

It is not possible to be more precise than this. The great diversity in style and format of audit manuals is a natural result of the diversity in audit work, approaches and quality assurance mechanisms that are applied by chief internal auditors. What we can say in addition to the managerial, operational, administrative headings is that, first, the objectives of the manual must be clearly defined and, second, the resultant document must be sufficient to achieve these objectives.

## Procedures and Working Papers

The audit manual is the device that allows audit management to consider, formulate and apply suitable audit procedures aimed at ensuring efficiency as well as compliance with standards. It is difficult to visualize any other way that this could be achieved. It must be remembered that audit procedures cannot simply be extracted from audit textbooks but have to be adapted to suit the particular audit approach. The IIA Practice Advisory 2040-1 covers policies and procedures and suggests that:

> The form and content of written policies and procedures should be appropriate to the size and structure of the internal audit activity and the complexity of work.

### Impact on Creativity

There appears to be a direct conflict between the extent of direction and standardization that a comprehensive audit manual provides and the auditor's professional autonomy. Both are essential for enhancing audit productivity. This conflict is akin to the perennial problem of reconciling managerial control and autonomy, where autonomy is defined as the freedom to succeed or fail. Auditors cannot perform if they are unclear as to what is considered successful performance while at the same time little commitment can be achieved within a bureaucratic straitjacket. Audit manuals must recognize this inherent conflict.

## 8.7  Time Monitoring System

Time management systems will tend to feature in most internal audit units and this will be an important information-based system. This should enable audit management to receive regular reports on the way their staff are working. It will be used to support performance measures that relate to a variety of performance targets that would ideally have been set for both auditors and audit teams. They should cover each of the defined information needs that derive from the management of audit time. This will involve periodic reports as well as specially requested items. The reports should revolve around the timeframe, types of work, auditors, audit groups and the entire audit unit. As such it should report on:

- Time spent on audits.
- Audits over budget.
- Nonrecoverable time charged (such as training).
- Breakdown between systems and investigations.
- Audits that should have been completed.
- And so on.

The inputs of a suitable time monitoring system are illustrated in Figure 8.5.

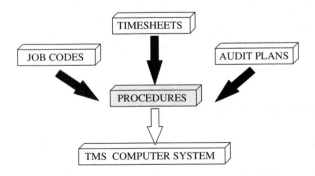

**FIGURE 8.5**  Time monitoring system inputs.

The various roles of time management information should be duly recognized and catered for. Here we would expect any such systems to cover the following functions:

1. A method of charging time to specific audit jobs.
2. A way of identifying variances from planned to actual hours though incorporating budgeted hours to each chargeable job.
3. A method of charging clients for work carried out and generating the supporting schedules and covering invoice if needs be. Accordingly, it is important to identify a client for each job that is set up on the system.
4. A method of establishing the status of each job. Suitable booknote messages may be used in any good system to compile a form of database of audit jobs, which will provide summary information. This may range from terms of reference, assigned auditor, special features, stage indicators (say, planning, field work or reporting) and so on.

The time management system will typically be a computerized package that performs the function of recording and reporting auditors' time.

## 8.8   Audit Planning Process

Planning is fundamental to successful auditing and should involve the client in defining areas for review via the assessment of relative risk. Long-term planning allocates scarce audit resources to the huge audit universe and it is impossible to audit everything. Auditors must be seen to be doing important work. The worst-case scenario is where they are unable to perform sensitive high-level investigations on management's behalf while at the same time appearing to be involved in routine low-level checking in insignificant parts of the organization. A professional audit service tends to rely more on senior auditors tackling serious high-risk issues.

### The Planning Process

Overall planning allows the audit to be part of a carefully thought-out system. This ensures that all planned work is of high priority and that audit resources are used in the best possible way. The main steps in the overall planning process are found in Figure 8.6.

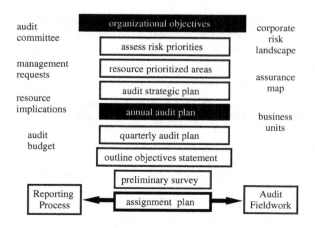

**FIGURE 8.6**   The planning process.

Some explanations follow:

- **Organizational objectives** The starting place for audit planning must be in the objectives of the organization. If these objectives are based on devolution of corporate services to business units, then the audit mission must also be so derived. Management must clarify goals and aspirations before plans can be formulated and this feedback can be achieved by active liaison and communication.
- **Assess risk priorities** The relative risks of each audit area must be identified, with reference to the corporate risk database.
- **Resource prioritized areas** Suitable resources for these areas must be provided.
- **Audit strategic plan** A plan to reconcile workload with existing resources should be developed. This should take on board the various constraints and opportunities that are influential now and in the future. The strategic plan takes us from where we are to where we wish to be over a defined timeframe, having due regard for the audit budget.
- **Annual audit plan** A formal audit plan for the year ahead is expected by most audit committees.
- **Quarterly audit plan** A quarterly plan can be derived from the annual plan. Most organizations experience constant change, making the quarter a suitable time-slot for supportive work programmes.
- **Outline objectives statement** Audit management can make a one-line statement of expectations from an audit from work done so far in the planning process.
- **Preliminary survey** Background research requires thought on key areas to be covered in an audit. This ranges from a quick look at previous files and a conversation with an operational manager to formal processes of many days of background work involving a full assessment of local business risks.
- **Assignment plan** We can now draft an assignment plan with formal terms of reference, including budgets, due dates and an audit programme.
- **The audit fieldwork** Progress should be monitored with all matters in the terms of reference considered.
- **The reporting process** Planning feeds naturally into reporting so long as we have made proper reference to our plans throughout the course of the audit.

Audit planning is driven by what is included in the audit universe and Practice Advisory 2010-1 provides some useful guidance:

> In developing the internal audit activity's audit plan, many chief audit executives (CAEs) find it useful to first develop or update the audit universe. The audit universe is a list of all the possible audits that could be performed. The CAE may obtain input on the audit universe from senior management and the board.
>
> The audit universe can include components from the organization's strategic plan. By incorporating components of the organization's strategic plan, the audit universe will consider and reflect the overall business' objectives. Strategic plans also likely reflect the organization's attitude toward risk and the degree of difficulty to achieving planned objectives. The audit universe will normally be influenced by the results of the risk management process. The organization's strategic plan considers the environment in which the organization operates. These same environmental factors would likely impact the audit universe and assessment of relative risk.

The audit universe and related audit plan are updated to reflect changes in management direction, objectives, emphasis and focus. It is advisable to assess the audit universe on at least an annual basis to reflect the most current strategies and direction of the organization. In some situations, audit plans may need to be updated more frequently (e.g. quarterly) in response to changes in the organization's business, operations, programmes, systems and controls.

## 8.9 The Annual Audit Plan

Audit will be required to publish an annual audit plan formally approved by the audit committee. This lists planned audits for the year and includes a reconciliation of audit resources to required audit cover. The annual plan may be resource-led and based on available audit staff. Alternatively, it may be strategy-led and include a bid for additional staff/expertise to fulfil the proposed workload. The annual plan is important as it represents the justification for resourcing the internal audit service. Moreover, listed audits must be material to top management's search for commercial success. Auditors will have around 214 days a year available, although it is better to form long-term plans on a week-by-week basis. The annual audit plan will set out which parts of the listed systems will be subject to audit cover over the next 12 months without assigning resources to each audit. It is probably enough simply to list against each planned audit whether it is large, medium or small. As a start these categories may be set as an estimated figure, e.g. four weeks (large), two weeks (medium) and one week (small). Some of the features of many annual audit plans are as follows:

- It should contain key audit areas from the audit universe for the next 12 months and explains why they were selected through a suitable preamble. This opening discussion should be a scaled-down version of the audit strategy with comments on the main problems facing the organization now and in the immediate future.
- It can be based around the ERM process in place and the risks that have already been identified by executive management. It should also feed into the assurance map so that internal audit sits above all other review teams to be the final independent arbiter on the state of risk management within the organization.
- Following from the above, the annual plan needs to be interfaced with the annual report. The report will talk about the state of risk management and internal control in general across the organization, whereas the plan will explain how these concerns will be dealt with by internal audit.

The plan itself should be circulated to directors for their consideration and comment before being finalized. It will explain the process of risk assessment and agreed risk criteria. The plan cannot be challenged although we would expect some degree of consultation with executive management and the basis of risk assessment may be commented on by management who may argue that it does not reflect actual risk because of new or changed information. Management cannot insist on a change to the risk assessment parameter as this can only be enforced by the audit committee, although they can certainly express reservations with the planning process. Once top management has seen the plan it will be presented to the audit committee to be formally adopted. Changes to the plan should likewise be confirmed at the audit committee. The annual plan should be well publicized both to the organization and to individual auditors.

## 8.10 The Quarterly Audit Plan

The quarterly audit plan provides an opportunity to take the planning process to greater detail where the various projects may be scheduled over a 13-week period. The quarterly period has much more meaning to both managers and auditors as a timeframe in view of the fast pace of business life. Quarterly plans are no longer short-term matters as it becomes increasingly more difficult to predict what factors may influence the organization as new developments arise. The annual plan sets a background to the quarterly plan. In today's fast-moving world, three months is often the most appropriate period within which to set priorities and assign work. Within this planning framework it is possible to:

1. Build in the planned absences of individual auditors so that a good idea of the available resources for the period in question can be obtained. The quarterly period is ideal for this, in that we will have some knowledge of staff movements and training, annual leave and sick leave.
2. Plan audit cover weekly as the basis of a work programme for each individual auditor.
3. Enter projected start and completion dates for each audit, which can be in detail (e.g. the exact date) or more realistically the week within which the planned start and finish will fall. It is possible to set this level of detail with a manageable timeframe.
4. Allocate projects to auditors. This sets the right resources to the right projects in line with relevant factors. It includes skills, experience, special interests and career development.
5. Re-prioritize projects on the annual plan. As quarterly plans are prepared, audits are reassigned on the annual plan as detailed changes are made. The link between the annual and quarterly planning mechanisms must be maintained as each is adjusted in line with changing risks.

Business risk analysis is an ongoing long-term process. It depends on extensive information on operational areas over time. It is important to make a start and write a crude model with rule-of-thumb measures and then build on it. A formal identification of the audit universe is a prerequisite to the risk assessment process.

## 8.11 New Developments

A useful approach to developing an audit strategy is to use the perspective of key stakeholders to work out how best to meet their needs. Most audit shops are working out how they can best contribute to their organizations and have a strategy for adding value as the pressure grows on all resources. One approach is to identify key stakeholders and ensure their needs are being identified and met. A review of the type of questions that an audit committee may well ask regarding the leadership, work and performance of their internal auditors has been prepared by the IIA:

- How well do I know the head of internal auditing?
- How often do I talk to him or her?
- Do I appoint the head of internal auditing? Does he or she report directly to the audit committee?
- When was the last time I reviewed the internal audit charter? Do I know what it says?
- Do I know how the internal audit activity sets its plan?
- Do I review and approve the annual plan?
- How well is the management team implementing actions agreed upon during internal audit work?
- If the chief audit executive (CAE) came to me and expressed concerns based on his or her business judgment, would I listen? How would I act?
- Does the internal audit activity comply with the IIA's Standards?
- Is internal auditing's position in the organization at a sufficiently high level and sufficiently detached from functional areas to guarantee its independence?

- Do the internal auditors avoid activities that could undermine their objectivity?
- Is the internal audit plan based on the organization's risk profile?
- How well is the internal audit activity completing its plan this year?
- Does internal auditing have a quality assurance program?
- Does it have a plan to undergo an external quality assessment every five years as required by the Standards?
- What are the results of the most recent quality assessment?
- Is internal auditing sufficiently resourced to provide objective assurance on risk and control?
- How does the CAE respond to probing by the audit committee? [12]

Improving the way the CAE interacts with the board's audit committee should be a firm part of the audit strategy and the results of one survey provide a useful insight into this topic:

Although chief audit executives (CAEs) see themselves as strong supporters of their audit committees, opportunities exist to strengthen the relationship with the committee as well as to become a stronger link between the audit committee and others in the organization who are focused on risk management efforts. CAEs educate audit committees on relevant risks and risk management strategies as well as providing updates on critical issues and information about the internal environment of the organization. To a lesser extent, CAEs are involved with audit committees on increasingly strategic activities such as defining the scope and design of enterprise risk management (ERM) projects or risk assessments. The most effective CAEs strengthen the link between the audit committee and management by effectively exercising their independence and providing proactive information and analysis on pertinent risk and governance issues. CAEs with deep knowledge, broad skills, and solid experience are in a position to serve the audit committee and management most effectively by bringing solutions to the table and acting as a translator between the committee and management on risk management issues. [13]

The conclusions from this research offer some useful advice for the CAE:

Today, CAEs interact with audit committees in a variety of ways – both formal and informal. Some CAEs are already actively engaged and feel leveraged by the audit committee. Others might have more work to do to develop the relationship. In either case, there are concrete things every CAE can do to increase the value they are able to add to the organization:

- Understand the wants and needs of the committee.
- Be the corporate governance expert the committee turns to for advice.
- Establish strong interactions with audit committee members.
- Build audit committee relationships based on skills. If the CAE has a low level of experience, he or she should ask for mentoring from audit committee members or tap into networks of other CAEs or consultants to learn from their experiences.
- Work to eliminate any inefficiency in communication between the CAE and the audit committee.
- Engage with the committee to design the internal audit department's mission, strategy, and focus.
- Position him- or herself to be a key force in bringing clarity and aligning the contributions from finance, legal, internal audit, and other management functions.

Be prepared. ERM has been identified by audit committees as well as CFOs as the biggest challenge to be faced in the coming months. [14]

One way of adding value is to ensure the needs of the audit are understood and met:

We've all seen the surveys of what an audit committee expects of an effective head of internal audit: leadership, technical skills, communication skills ... the list goes on. But nobody ever mentions one attribute – the head of internal audit needs to be a mind reader. He or she often needs to know what the audit committee wants – and to be able to deliver this – without being told what is expected! How will you know when the relationship is working? This is hard to describe, but you'll know when you get there. Some of the indicators will include: periodic emails and phone calls with the audit committee chair between committee meetings; audit committee members stopping by for a chat when they are at head office, even when there's no audit committee meeting scheduled; the audit committee chair asking to be kept informed when an issue comes up but has not been resolved, rather than asking what's being done about it; a few words of praise for internal audit at an audit committee meeting; the audit committee chair asking for your views on an issue at an audit committee meeting. What you'll find most noticeable, though, will be the fact that you've stopped being so aware of the need to make an effort.[15]

Let's take a closer look at the positive contribution that internal audit should be making:

Buchanan also expects the head of internal audit to make a positive contribution. 'You want someone who is walking into the CEO's office at least once a month and offering a bit of insight,' he says. They should be raising concerns, flagging risks that are affecting other companies, 'acting as a sounding board for the CEO as well as the CFO – someone who operates at that level.' And they must have an action based agenda, looking to get things nailed down and finished. He wants someone who is suggesting things that can be implemented, 'and not just agonising over worries that go on and on from meeting to meeting.' There should be what he calls a programme for closure: 'Who will do what for whom and by when? Then it's full stop, turn the page, next item.' Summing it all up, he needs 'a valued player to the business people, as opposed to some niggly bugger who's going to ask difficult questions without adding a lot of value.'[16]

One key question is, how does internal audit show it is adding value, in boom years and when the economy is in recession? Each and every CAE will want to address this question before it is asked by the audit committee. The value-add equation should drive the audit strategy in a way that means a successful internal audit function, even where there is an economic downturn. Help is at hand with PwC's fifth study into the state of internal auditing:

If internal audit is to demonstrate value in the face of declining resources, it must begin with a fresh look at the company's internal audit strategy and a reassessment of its own processes. We believe doing so will not only help gain credibility with organizational peers suffering the same cutbacks, it will also help internal audit preserve its capacity to address strategic, operational, and business risks, as well as today's emerging challenges. As we anticipated in our forward-looking report Internal Audit 2012,1 internal audit leaders have begun to recognize the need to redefine the function's value proposition and seek to increase its value by learning to operate more efficiently, intelligently, and quickly. Concerns over declining budgets are a reminder that greater efficiencies within internal audit won't come a moment too soon.[17]

We turn now to the important issue of contributing to IT governance in adding value to the business. For a view of ways that internal audit can better contribute we can turn to the IT profession itself:

There are numerous benefits of having information technology personnel work closely with internal auditors. For some technology personnel, the entire audit function may have a mysterious and misunderstood role, particularly when working in certain industries. Too often, auditing is viewed as a necessary evil, and therefore, will involve confrontational relationships. In high-performing organizations, there is a mutual respect and trust between the technology teams and the internal and external audit teams. In these situations, technology teams view the auditors as additional consultative resources to ensure appropriate controls are in place and effective. Just as the manufacturing world realized the need for quality control processes, technology departments are finally recognizing that processes and controls to ensure the quality of information technology services must be implemented. When IT processes are well documented and operating reliably, IT audits confirm the positive efforts of IT. Where they are not, IT audits report the gaps and numerous opportunities for improvement. The level of documentation for IT processes should reflect the risks associated with the IT processes. IT audits will provide an independent assessment of the appropriateness of the IT efforts to be efficient, effective, and responsive to the needs of the organization.[18]

Protecting and increasing shareholder value is the key to a successful organization and this may be achieved by using the following the advice:

A correctly aligned approach to risk management focuses on those risks with the greatest opportunity to reduce shareholder value. Given that definition, two factors may be to blame when management is unable to effectively identify and respond to risks that can damage shareholder value: the absence of a correctly aligned approach to risk management coupled with the lack of a sufficient engine to power the company's risk management strategy. A transformed internal audit function has the potential to become that engine – a potent force of old-fashioned due diligence that could help manage the increasingly sophisticated risk factors today's businesses face.[19]

Most argue that real value comes from transforming a service to fit new contexts. In terms of the internal audit function a 10-step plan is recommended by PwC for just this task:

1. Identify stakeholder expectations of internal audit; ask what management, the board, and the audit committee value.
2. Gather data to assess current state.
3. Link the company's strategic objectives and shareholder value drivers to internal audit's scope.
4. Consider how previously unaudited areas might be audited, then align auditable risks to the audit plan.
5. Eliminate routine, low-value audits.
6. Based on the updated audit plan, consider transformational ideas to reduce cost.
7. Identify inefficient processes.
8. Develop implementation plans for transformational concepts as well as anticipated process efficiencies.
9. Review updated internal audit plan, along with cost-reduction ideas, with key stakeholders to gain support.
10. Implement (add measurement, feedback, and adjustment processes for continuous improvement). [20]

Having got good resources in place the next stage is to re-visit the audit plan and how it can be developed in a way that is both dynamic and flexible:

During rapid transitions from one economic state to another, traditional audit cycles and frequencies may not serve organisations well. This indicates that assurance needs can (and need to) alter at a similar speed and may require key business risks to be audited more frequently. For example, how often does internal audit look at risk management arrangements – annual reviews may no longer be enough. Additionally, audit plans that run for three to five years may no longer be fit for purpose, where a greater responsiveness demanded by the business ought to result in plans covering shorter time periods, involving smaller audits with a quicker turnaround time. External factors will impact upon an organisation's function and health. Many indicators such as the retail prices index and exchange rates are 'lag' indicators showing conditions that have happened. Whilst they are useful, they are probably too late in helping an organisation in being proactive and agile to changes. To identify change, the focus needs to be on lead indicators that show which way the wind is blowing. This is what gives an organisation the ability to be ahead of the game and respond to threats in a downturn and to take advantage of opportunities before its competitors during an upturn. This would also require internal auditors to adapt their internal management arrangements to reflect the principles of agility and responsiveness for the use of resources. For example, identifying key staff with specialist skills that will be required when an organisation's future assurance needs change becomes a key consideration. Many organisations make use of tools such as PeSt (political, economic, social and technological) analysis to gauge environmental conditions and inform the business planning.[21]

One major strategic issue relates to the way audit plans its work over the year. The dynamic approach to this task suggested by some CAEs is that audit need no longer develop an annual plan as such but simply build an indicative quarterly plan that flexes as the fast-moving risk profiles change and alter with each major new event. An interesting perspective is given by one well-known audit writer:

> If your average commitment, over the course of the year, for management special requests exceeds 10%, you have a planning failure. When management continuously overrides your audit plan with excessive special requests, they are telling you that your plan is wrong, that you are directing your audit resources to the wrong areas, or at the wrong time, and that they are better at allocating your resources than you are. They may be right. The solution is to engage senior management more extensively in your planning discussions, to listen closely to their concerns and to ensure they understand the strategy behind your audit plan and the implications of changing your plans to accommodate special requests. Your audit universe should map very closely to your company's organisation chart, lines of business or process structure. You should be auditing the business that management has created and is responsible for. A logical step in the planning process is to gather any risk assessments prepared by management. If they have prepared risk assessments, your assurance strategy must include an evaluation of that assessment to determine its reliability. The solution is to include the reliability of management risk assessments as one of your audit planning criteria. Management with a track record of reliable, comprehensive risk assessments should receive much less audit coverage. Management who do not perform risk assessments should be featured prominently in your audit plan and in your executive and board reporting.[22]

We have spent some time discussing value-add and we can turn now to Paul Boyle, who has explained the concept of audit value in the following way:

> 'If governance, risk management and internal control provide the framework for business success, it is one in which high-quality internal auditing plays an important part,' says Boyle. 'Clearly, when it comes to the management of risk, the internal audit function can make a huge contribution to the board's and audit committee's understanding,' he says. 'An internal audit function can get to the facts, they can make comparisons objectively between different parts of the company, they can identify corrective actions, and they can follow up to make sure those corrective actions are being taken. It's absolutely central.' The FRC – as mentioned – makes a conscious effort to put

entrepreneurialism ahead of risk, and internal audit functions should do likewise, Boyle believes. 'A potential danger for internal audit, and one to watch out for, is that, almost by instinct, their focus would be on the management of risk and not necessarily on entrepreneurial success,' he says.[23]

## Summary and Conclusions

Most internal audit shops have moved on from the risk assessment checklists and entered into a dialogue with the board about how the audit resource can be used to best effect, i.e. utilizing the corporate assessment of risks along with auditors' special expertise in risk management, control models and specific control mechanisms (and requests for consulting projects), and the way objective assessments can be used to promote accountability and help managers deliver.

Internal audit will want to maximize its impact on the organization through a clear strategy. It could act as a nonexecutive assurance function that challenges current risk management practice as well as providing advice on areas ripe for improvement. There is a view that the adopted audit strategy would depend on the stage of maturity of the organization's risk management process. Therefore a mix of support, advice, guidance, challenge and direct assistance would be used in different ways to different parts of the organization.

Audit plans will then flow naturally from the organization's strategic direction while the underlying process should be flexible and, as strategies alter, planned reviews should be reassessed. The corporate risk landscape and the assurance map used by the board should set the context for the audit planning process. The flow of planning components should be kept in mind as we consider each aspect of audit planning. In the past internal audit would plan its work more or less in isolation from the boardroom agenda and then report the results of individual audits as the audit assurance platform. Now the internal audit plan will be driven by the state of the ERM process in place and the type of assurances that are needed by the board as they seek to manage risk to the organization.

It is one thing to set an audit strategy and quite another to ensure the audit resource is sufficiently astute to deliver the goods. The IIA standards are challenging in that they represent an ideal that can be daunting for an audit team that is staffed by low-level juniors or more senior people who have become stuck in their ways. We close this chapter with a good example of a staffing strategy, based on what the Financial Services Authority looks for in their audit resource, which includes the all-important intellectual capacity:

Hilary's strategy for staffing her team is to have around half of them coming from within the FSA, with the rest recruited externally for their professional audit skills. She has made a number of recruits – there are 16 staff in the department – but still has vacancies for senior roles to fill. A system of guest auditing – a Hilary innovation – allows staff from other parts of the FSA to spend time working in internal audit. The 'guests' get an interesting development opportunity, while the internal auditors benefit from their expertise and get to spread the word about what the function does and procurement. So that is in itself a big challenge, a big intellectual challenge. 'That means the number one requirement for an FSA auditor is "intellectual capacity",' says Hilary. Number two is gravitas and oral communication skills. 'They are key in this because as soon as we walk into a room and speak to people we have to have credibility, all auditors do.' Written communication skills are vital, too. 'The FSA puts a high premium on the written word and that applies as much internally as externally. Good writing skills, so that clear persuasive reports can be produced quickly, are very important.' However important, these skills are just what Hilary regards as 'base camp – what you need to get in the door.' What else does she look for? 'It is critical that we have people who have good influencing skills, who understand the backdrop to what they're doing, and understand how things have come about in the FSA. They need to be able to position things and add the necessary context. Auditees are always asking for more context.'[24]

# Endnotes

1. Roth, James (2002) *Adding Value, Seven Roads to Success*, Orlando: IIA Inc.
2. Summerell, Mike, 'In my opinion'. *Internal Auditor*, February 2000, p. 96.
3. Moeller, Robert and Witt, Herbert (1999) *Brink's Modern Internal Auditing*, 5th edition, New York: John Wiley & Sons, Inc., para. 8.16
4. *GAIN Knowledge Briefing, Defining the Right Audit Universe*, The Institute of Internal Auditors, July 2009.
5. Moeller, Robert and Witt, Herbert (1999) *Brink's Modern Internal Auditing*, 5th edition, New York: John Wiley & Sons, Inc., p. 494.
6. *An Approach to Implementing Risk Based Internal Auditing, Professional Guidance for Internal Auditors*, IIA UK&Ireland, 2005.
7. *Adding Value to the Organization, Question and Answer Recommendations*, The Institute of Internal Auditors' Global Audit Information Network (GAIN), December 2009.
8. *GAIN Knowledge Alert, Maximizing the Use of IA Resources*, The Institute of Internal Auditors and The IIA Research Foundation's Global Audit Information Network (GAIN), February 2009.
9. *GAIN Knowledge Alert, Measuring IA Performance*, The Institute of Internal Auditors, September 2009.
10. *GAIN Knowledge Alert, Measuring IA Performance*, The Institute of Internal Auditors, September 2009.
11. Moeller, Robert and Witt, Herbert (1999) *Brink's Modern Internal Auditing*, 5th edition, New York: John Wiley & Sons, Inc., p. 497.
12. Audit Committee Briefing, *Internal Audit Standards: Why They Matter*, Institute of Internal Auditors, August 2006.
13. Chief Audit Executives and Audit Committees: *Building a Strong Relationship*, This report highlights the results of a survey, designed and conducted by Crowe Horwath LLP to better understand the relationship between chief audit executives and audit committees, Executive Summary, Crowe Horwath LLP, 2008, pp. 4–10.
14. Chief Audit Executives and Audit Committees: *Building a Strong Relationship*, This report highlights the results of a survey, designed and conducted by Crowe Horwath LLP to better understand the relationship between chief audit executives and audit committees, Conclusions and Recommendations, Crowe Horwath LLP, 2008, pp. 4–10.
15. Barma, Hanif, *Internal Auditing & Business Risk*, IIA Magazine, August 2007, pp. 36–37.
16. *Internal Auditing & Business Risk*, IIA Magazine, July 2007, John Buchanan tells Neil Baker what he looks for in a head of internal audit, p. 17
17. 'Business upheaval: internal audit weighs its role amid the recession and evolving enterprise risks', *State of the Internal Audit Profession Study*, PricewaterhouseCoopers' fifth annual State of the Internal Audit Profession Study, 2009, p. 7.
18. Prescriptive Guide Series on *Operational Excellence: Linking Your Business, Compliance, Operations and Security*, Tripwire Inc., 2010, p. 25.
19. 'An opportunity for transformation. How internal audit helps contribute to shareholder value, Pricewaterhouse-Coopers, October 2008, p. 9.
20. 'An opportunity for transformation. How internal audit helps contribute to shareholder value, Pricewaterhouse-Coopers, October 2008, p. 27.
21. Shackleford, Steven and Hollands, Richard, 'Internal auditing'. *Internal Auditing & Business Risk*, IIA Magazine, May 2009, p. 35.
22. Corbin, Dave, *Internal Auditing & Business Risk*, IIA Magazine, October 2009, pp. 25–26.
23. *Internal Auditing & Business Risk*, IIA Magazine, July 2008, 'Why internal audit matters', Paul Boyle tells Neil Baker, p. 28.
24. *Internal Auditing & Business Risk*, IIA Magazine, October 2008, 'Fair but firm', Rosemary Hilary talks to Neil Baker about the changes she's been making to the internal audit function at the FSA, and her report on the demise of Northern Rock, pp. 12–17.

# Chapter 9

# AUDIT FIELDWORK

## Introduction

We have established that there are many different interpretations of the internal audit role and many approaches to performing both assurance and consulting work. One basic approach that has been discussed is risk-based systems auditing. This involves establishing the system objectives, finding out what risks should be addressed and then developing appropriate solutions to mitigate unacceptable levels of risk. The audit can be done by the client (with help from internal audit), by the auditor but with a great deal of participation with the client, or entirely by the internal auditor (as an outsider). These perspectives form a spectrum from objective review through to facilitated self-assessment. Whatever the adopted format, the auditor should perform fieldwork to arrive at an opinion and advice on managing outstanding risks. Apart from the self-assessment approach, which is more consultancy than anything else, the internal auditor may go through variations on several set stages in performing the audit. Note that all references to IIA definitions, code of ethics, IIA attribute and performance standards, practice advisories and practice guides relate to the International Professional Practices Framework (IPPF) prepared by the Institute of Internal Auditors in 2009. The various stages for performing a basic audit are covered in this chapter and include:

9.1 Planning the Audit
9.2 Interviewing Skills
9.3 Ascertaining the System
9.4 Evaluation
9.5 Testing Strategies
9.6 Evidence and Working Papers
9.7 Statistical Sampling
9.8 Audit Testing and Statistical Sampling
9.9 Structuring the Audit Report
9.10 Audit Committee Reporting
9.11 New Developments
     Summary and Conclusions

## 9.1   Planning the Audit

The annual audit plan lists those high-risk areas that are targeted for audit cover during the next 12 months. The quarterly audit plan provides more detail by setting out those audits that will be performed by specified auditors in the following three months. Before the full audit is started and resources committed, an assignment plan will direct and control these resources. Before we are in a position to formulate assignment plans, we need background information on the targeted operation. Preliminary work will be required, the extent of which will vary according to the size of the audit. This section sets out the principles behind the preliminary survey and assignment planning, although the approach and level of detail will vary depending on the policies of each individual audit department. The IIA Performance Standard 2200 deals with engagement planning and requires that:

> Internal auditors must develop and document a plan for each engagement, including the engagement's objectives, scope, timing, and resource allocations.

## The Preliminary Survey

The preliminary survey seeks to accumulate relevant information regarding the operation under review so that a defined direction of the ensuing audit (if it goes ahead) may be agreed. The internal audit files will be the first port of call and any previous audit cover will be considered. All assignment audit files should contain a document entitled 'outstanding matters', which will set out concerns that were not addressed via the audit at hand. The files tell only part of the story, as will the resultant audit report, and it is best to talk to the auditor who last performed work in the relevant area. It is advisable to carry out background research into the area subject to the survey. This might include national research, committee papers, recent changes and planned computerized systems. Much of this information should really have been obtained via the corporate risk assessment. It is always advisable to get some basic facts before meeting with management so as to create a good impression. We can now meet with the key manager and tour the operational area. An overview of the real risks facing the manager in question can be obtained. A feel for the audit can be gathered from impressions gained from touring the work area, where the initial impression can be used to help direct the auditor towards particular problems. A note of matters to be covered in such an opening meeting should be drafted to form the basis of the discussions, covering items such as:

- Key business objectives.
- Key risks, risk assessment undertaken and current measures to manage risk including key controls.
- Audit client, key managers and teams.
- Key managerial processes: what frameworks impact the business area covering strategy, operational, structure, human resource management, key information systems, direction, supervision and procedures.

Note that Performance Standard 2120.A1 reinforces the scope of internal auditing by requiring that:

> The internal audit activity should evaluate risk exposures relating to the organisation's governance, operations and information systems regarding the:

- Reliability and integrity of financial and operational information.
- Effectiveness and efficiency of operations.
- Safeguarding of assets.
- Compliance with laws, regulations, and contracts.

1. **What to Review?**    Recent work carried out by other review agencies should be obtained and considered, although watch out for bias where the work was commissioned for a particular reason. Reports contain natural bias set by the terms of reference. For example, a staffing review commissioned by an employee union is more likely to recommend pay rises. The preliminary survey involves assessing local business risk factors that affect audit objectives. No audit can cover all the relevant areas within a specific operation and the assignment plan states what will be done and what is not covered. It is the process of assessing local risk that allows the auditor to key into the target elements of the operational area. This is done at preliminary survey before the audit objectives and scope of the review can be finalized and agreed. This is important because management often feel that an audit will reveal all that is wrong with a system. A clear definition of what was not included in the audit will help to avoid this. Note that the IIA define engagement objectives as: 'broad statements developed by internal auditors that define intended engagement accomplishments'. The impact on audit work might be an issue either by redirecting resources or adjusting the scope of another audit that would be affected by the planned work. A major benefit of the preliminary survey is an understanding of the nature of the audit. This highlights the type of audit skills required, including special skills relating to automation and/or technically complicated matters such as contract law. Audit standards require audit management to ensure they can perform audits to professional standards. It is the responsibility of managers to use their resources properly and if it is clear that an audit is too difficult for the available resources then the project should be aborted. It is a useful policy to get senior auditors or audit managers to perform the preliminary survey and then assign the full audit to more junior staff. The survey is perhaps the most difficult part of the audit process since once the terms of reference have been set and a programme of work agreed the remainder can be fairly straightforward. It means that the audit manager has a full knowledge of the audit and can supervise and review the work as it progresses. The preliminary survey should result in a programme of work that has been identified as a result of the background work. This may be in the form of a detailed audit program or simply a list of key tasks depending on the type of audit, the approach to work and the policies of the audit unit.

2. **The audit programme**    As well as isolating the system for review and determining the direction of the audit, the assignment plan may result in an audit programme for use during the audit. Performance Standard 2240 mentions work programmes and says that: 'Internal auditors must develop work programs that achieve the engagement objectives. These work programs should be recorded.' There are also separate standards for assurance and consulting work that suggest:

> **2240.A1** – Work programs must include the procedures for identifying, analyzing, evaluating, and documenting information during the engagement. The work program must be approved prior to its implementation, and any adjustments approved promptly.
> **2240.C1** – Work programs for consulting engagements may vary in form and content depending upon the nature of the engagement.

The term 'audit program' (or 'work program') should be carefully considered since an audit programme tends to be associated with a series of predefined testing routines. This does not promote the systems-based approach since the direction of the testing procedures depends on the outcome of the risk and control evaluation. The IIA define the engagement work programme as:

> A document that lists the procedures to be followed during an engagement, designed to achieve the engagement plan.

The audit programme may be seen more as an audit guide and may include:

1. Defining the various tasks that need to be performed. Here a list of key tasks should be compiled for the lead auditor that sets the direction of the audit process that will now be carried out. This is not only a useful planning tool that can be used to monitor progress on the audit but also provides firm guidance for the auditor on work that must be completed.
2. Defining the extent of work in a particular part of the operation. For smaller audits with a probity approach it is possible to list the various testing routines. Defining testing programmes makes the audit controllable. It is based around the required tests and in basic audits this may give the number of items that should be selected and how they are tested. Audit management can exercise firm control. This would not be appropriate for a systems-based approach since it is controls that are tested after they have been assessed and testing is not carried out for its own sake.
3. **The preliminary survey report** It is advisable to present a formal preliminary survey report (PSR) once the work has been completed. Another consideration is that access to information and explanations is important to establish at an early stage and help is given here by various elements of Performance Standard 2220:

> **2220.A1** – The scope of the engagement must include consideration of relevant systems, records, personnel, and physical properties, including those under the control of third parties.
> **2220.A2** – If significant consulting opportunities arise during an assurance engagement, a specific written understanding as to the objectives, scope, respective responsibilities, and other expectations should be reached and the results of the consulting engagement communicated in accordance with consulting standards.
> **2220.C1** – In performing consulting engagements, internal auditors must ensure that the scope of the engagement is sufficient to address the agreed-upon objectives. If internal auditors develop reservations about the scope during the engagement, these reservations must be discussed with the client to determine whether to continue with the engagement.

The PSR goes to the audit manager, along with a brief description of the system to be used to prepare the assignment plan. The PSR of one or two pages will cover the following:

1. An outline of the system under review including business/systems objectives and boundaries.
2. The work undertaken in the preliminary survey in outlining the risk management process in place.
3. An initial opinion on the risk areas based on the key control objectives covering compliance, information systems, safeguarding assets and value for money.
4. Recommendations for the proposed assignment in terms of the nature and extent of audit cover now required.
5. An appendix with outline systems notes and a draft audit guide/programme for the full audit.

## Assignment Planning

Each audit must be carefully planned as this is the only way to control it. Assignment planning takes all available information and allows the objectives, scope, direction and approach to be defined. The preliminary survey will have been conducted before plans can be formulated and will provide much information for formulating the assignment plan. The preliminary survey report will set out the proposed objectives of the full audit stage. Factors to be addressed in the assignment plan are:

1. The terms of reference for the audit by audit management and disclosed to the client management. They guide audit work and feature in the resultant report with an audit opinion on each component. The precise terms of the audit should be given much consideration in line with Performance Standard 2220, which says: 'The established scope must be sufficient to satisfy the objectives of the engagement'.

2. The scope of work including areas for coverage and parts of the system not to be dealt with at this time. This may be referred to in a memorandum to client management publicizing the pending audit.

3. Target dates for start and completion and key stages. For larger audits, break the task down into defined stages. Section the audit into manageable parts that may be reported on separately. This enables the auditor to maintain a focus on the objective at hand and report before going on to deal with the next part. For example, a corporate system, which has been devolved down to departments like personnel, budgeting or expenditure processing, may be broken down into sections relating to each department. A separate report will be drafted for each department along with a composite report covering the corporate arrangements. Auditors can be drafted in to deal with each department if a suitable programme of work has been prepared and explained since the work programme requires extensive testing and interrogation of the corporate database. Once compiled, it can be completed by a variety of resources including temporary audit staff. Practice Advisory 2230-1 acknowledges that auditors may have development needs and suggests that:

> Internal auditors consider the following when determining the appropriateness and sufficiency of resources:
>
> - The number and experience level of the internal audit staff.
> - Knowledge, skills, and other competencies of the internal audit staff when selecting internal auditors for the engagement.
> - Availability of external resources where additional knowledge and competencies are required.
> - Training needs of internal auditors as each engagement assignment serves as a basis for meeting the internal audit activity's developmental needs.

Some assistance may be provided by audit management to address any particular problems experienced by the field auditor. This may include any follow-up action taken on an audit report issued previously that impacts on the audit. The auditor will also be concerned that compliance issues have been addressed by management and Performance Standard 2210.A2 covers this point by commenting that: 'The internal auditor must consider the probability of significant errors, irregularities, noncompliance, and other exposures when developing the engagement objectives.'

4. A full definition of the system under review including the points where it starts and finishes and interfaces with other related systems. This avoids unnecessary confusion over the duration of the audit, with a clear focus on exactly what the system is. It allows the auditor to think through the associated systems and their impact on the audit.

5. Identification of risk areas and critical points of the audit that may require special attention and/or resources. This may refer to the timing of the audit, say, in relation to restructuring, a new computer system, a recruitment campaign or a new staff performance scheme. On

this point, Performance Standard 2210.A1 says: 'Internal auditors must conduct a preliminary assessment of the risks relevant to the activity under review. Engagement objectives must reflect the results of this assessment.' On the other hand, consulting engagements are defined by the client and Performance Standard 2210.C1 states: 'Consulting engagement objectives must address governance, risk management, and control processes to the extent agreed upon with the client.'

6. Definition of the reporting and review arrangements including a list of the officers who will receive draft reports. Where the audit is geographically remote, the review arrangements must be determined so that this process does not hold up the progress of the audit report.

7. Establish a confirmed audit programme (or guide) for each part of the audit and the testing regimes (for compliance reviews). The audit techniques that should be applied may also be defined along with a list of standardized documents (having reference to the audit manual) in use in the audit unit. On this point, Practice Advisory 2240-1 argues that:

> Internal auditors develop and obtain documented approval of work programs before commencing the internal audit engagement. The work program includes methodologies to be used, such as technology-based audit and sampling techniques. The process of collecting, analyzing, interpreting, and documenting information is to be supervised to provide reasonable assurance that engagement objectives are met and that the internal auditor's objectivity is maintained.

8. The assignment plan will outline any travel and hotel arrangements along with subsistence allowances. This should recognize the need to save time and ensure efficient use of resources.

9. Identify the auditors assigned to the project and their roles. Performance Standard 2230 covers resource allocations and states that: 'Internal auditors must determine appropriate and sufficient resources to achieve engagement objectives based on an evaluation of the nature and complexity of each engagement, time constraints, and available resources.' The assignment planning task must identify which auditors are assigned. The audit manager or lead auditor should perform the preliminary survey so that a good insight into the audit is obtained by those directing the work. Once done, the audit proper should be assigned. A trend is for a move away from teamwork with a single auditor being given an audit to streamline resources. It fits with the development profile of auditors who, apart from trainees, should be given responsibility for whole projects. Meanwhile, the IIA Performance Standard 2201 provides a list of matters to be considered when planning the audit, such as:

- The objectives of the activity being reviewed and the means by which the activity controls its performance;
- The significant risks to the activity, its objectives, resources, and operations and the means by which the potential impact of risk is kept to an acceptable level;
- The adequacy and effectiveness of the activity's risk management and control processes compared to a relevant control framework or model; and
- The opportunities for making significant improvements to the activity's risk management and control processes.

Consulting engagements are more straightforward and are covered by Performance Standard 2201.C1, which requires that internal auditors must establish an understanding with consulting engagement clients about objectives, scope, respective responsibilities and other client expectations. For significant engagements, this understanding must be documented.

## Assigning Time Budgets to Audits

We must define an audit budget in terms of time allowed. Time is the key factor on any audit. Setting a time budget acts as a principal control over the assignment and is the single most important concern of audit management. A viable audit is achieved within budget to professional audit standards and as a full discharge of its objectives. Budgeted hours must be realistic and achievable. There are two different views. One seeks to perform the audit terms of reference to the full no matter how long this takes, even if budgeted hours are extended. This normally involves extensive testing and an inability to defer parts of the audit to a later stage. The other view is that audit management sets a defined number of hours according to the level of risk attached. When this budget expires the auditor must transfer to another work area, so recognizing the risks of not dealing with the next planned audit. Extensions are not encouraged as the auditor has to perform as much work as possible during the budget hours and then move on to the next job. The adopted policy must be explained and detailed in the audit manual since work done on one audit detracts from work that might be done elsewhere.

1. **The assignment planning process**  The audit manager should provide all guidance in the assignment plan before the full audit commences. Objectives in the assignment plan should be achieved and the audit manager review should ensure this. Performance Standard 2110 makes clear the audit link to corporate governance and states that: 'The engagement's objectives should address the risk, controls and governance processes associated with the activities under review.' The assignment plan should also incorporate review points over audit hours charged and quality of work to judge the value of work performed. Not all requests for formal consulting projects can be accepted by the internal auditor and Performance Standard 2220.C1 makes it clear that some projects will have to be declined by saying that:

> In performing consulting engagements, internal auditors must ensure that the scope of the engagement is sufficient to address the agreed-upon objectives. If internal auditors develop reservations about the scope during the engagement, these reservations must be discussed with the client to determine whether to continue with the engagement.

2. **Planning documentation**  There are many versions of documents that assist audit planning to provide standards and checklists for the work and areas that should be covered in the plan, showing each task and indicating:

| | |
|---|---|
| The audit objective | Who does what |
| For how long | Any particular guidance |
| The review arrangements | |

This control will not work unless there is an inbuilt monitoring system of continual supervision and review of progress. The audit manager should provide all necessary direction via the assignment planning process. The details above are the minimum information that should be contained in audit plans before the full audit is approved by audit management.

## 9.2 Interviewing Skills

Gathering information is a fundamental part of audit work as the auditor spends a great deal of time fact-finding. The starting place for establishing facts is simply to ask, and herein lies the importance of interviewing. Some of the synonyms for interviewing are:

> audience, conference, consultation, dialogue, meeting, talk, examine, interrogate, question

We take a wider view of the concept and mean it simply to refer to 'talking with' in a structured manner. Dale Flesher has written that:

> The audit interview is a means of gathering facts, opinions, and ideas, and therefore is an important source of audit evidence. It is a means of interpreting hard copy information ... an auditor's skills in using the techniques of audit interviewing frequently determines whether he or she is perceived to be a professional.[1]

The technique of interviewing should be mastered by the auditor and there is much material available on this topic that will contribute to this task. We see interviewing as a process, a task, a set structure, an audit standard and an exercise in understanding human behaviour. These components will be covered in the material below. Interviewing is based around effective communications and it is a good idea to remember the basic communications model to appreciate where things could go wrong and how communicating may be improved using Figure 9.1.

**FIGURE 9.1**   The communications cycle.

The sender has to decide how to transmit the message, which is then sent and decoded (rightly or wrongly) by the receiver. All this is against the background noise that consists of anything that gets in the way of clear messages being delivered and received. The positives are located in the feedback loop where understanding of the message is fed back to the giver to ensure it has been properly received and understood. Communicating is harder than it sounds and a quote from Madelyn Burley-Allen is apt: 'Speech is a joint game between the talker and the listener against the forces of confusion. Unless both make the effort inter-personal communication is impossible.'[2]

### Structuring Interviews

Interviews are structured meetings where information is provided and obtained. The interviewee must understand what information is required and the interviewer must likewise understand the information that is being provided. It is generally advisable to structure the interview since this tends to assist the task of exchanging information. The process should involve the following key steps:

**Background preparation on the subject area**  Whatever the interview it is always useful to do some background work related to the particular topic at hand. As a standard one would expect the auditor at least to consider material that has been provided to the internal audit unit. This involves reviewing files, talking to auditors who have some relevant knowledge and obtaining any previous written communications with the party in question. It is extremely embarrassing to meet with an individual who refers to correspondence that was sent to internal audit in the past, which the auditor is unaware of. The audit information systems should be capable of isolating all records of past contact with managers and with sections of the organization. A suitable central database should be maintained by the audit administration officer who collects and indexes this information. The degree of preparation will be related to the importance of the interview. This may range from a basic internal search of the filing system (as indicated above) through to an extensive review of published material associated with the matters that will form the basis of the planned meeting. Most managers are greatly impressed by auditors who display some knowledge of the matters uppermost on management's mind.

**Set convenient dates and times**  On the basis that an interview that is hurried with the constant pressure of other competing demands lowers the benefits that come from such a forum, it should be arranged properly. By this we mean that there should be sufficient notice given along with due regard for problems experienced by the client in finding the right time and place for the meeting. We obviously have to balance the need to complete our work promptly with the requirements of the client. Some leeway on our part is required if this balance is to be achieved.

**Prepare note of areas to cover**  This should entail a brief note of the areas that need to be covered as an *aide-mémoire* and as a way of thinking through the information-gathering process beforehand. It is possible to provide this checklist to the interviewee beforehand so that any preparations may be made that will expedite the process. As a rule never list a series of detailed questions as this approach will come across as being far too mechanical in terms of reading the questions and repeating them in front of the interviewee. It also stops the auditor from using professional judgement to manage the interview process by changing the order and questions to fit the responses that are being provided by the interviewee.

**Define objectives of the interview**  The next important stage is to state the precise objectives of the meeting. There are times when the auditor forgets the power of the audit's right of access, which forces managers to provide relevant information and explanation as part of their managerial duties. This results in most requests from audit to attend an interview being readily accepted by managers who are aware of their special responsibilities in respect of auditor's requirements, which makes it easier to convene meetings quickly. There is nonetheless the danger that managers are present simply because of their desire to discharge their duty and not with any belief that they may benefit from such a discussion. The act of explaining the basis of the meeting should be designed to remove this psychological barrier and allow a free flow of information in both directions. If this is not done then the level of efficiency may decline as the interviewee responds rigidly, as would someone who is forced to furnish information.

We provide an outline illustration of how we might structure a typical audit interview in Figure 9.2.

Introductions

Objectives

Questions and answers
(main part of the interview)

Winding up
(check communication)

Closure

(next steps and thanks)

**FIGURE 9.2**   Interview structure.

Explanations follow:

- **Introductions**   This involves introducing all parties present at the interview and explaining their role and position within the information-gathering process.
- **Objectives**   What is hoped to be achieved from the interview is then fully communicated and further clarification provided if needs be.
- **Questions and answers**   The main body of the interview should then proceed in a way that flows naturally and promotes the achievement of the original objectives of the meeting.
- **Wind up**   The next stage is to recheck the information that has been given and any matters (such as the exchange of specific documents) that have already been agreed.
- **Closure**   An indication of next steps, further meetings and specific arrangements such as planned meetings with key staff should be given. Formal thanks (and possibly handshakes) should also be a feature of the last stage of the interview process.

## Behavioural Aspects of Interviewing

What might appear a straightforward interview may go badly wrong and leave the auditor and client confused. There are many reasons why people act in an unpredictable way, which generally stems from a lack of appreciation by the auditor of the behavioural aspects of audit work. The actions of one aggressive auditor who may have left many years ago may still be foremost in many managers' minds whenever the auditors call. There are many behavioural aspects that the auditor should bear in mind when conducting interviews, and interviewees may possibly be asking themselves the following questions:

- What do they want from me?
- Are they human?
- Are they assessing me?
- Can I trust them?
- Should I tell them everything?
- What are they writing down?
- What about my problems?
- How can they help me?
- How will their work affect me?
- Who will be blamed if they find any errors?
- Are they going to propose drastic changes?

The auditor poses a threat in terms of the potential for making changes to the working lives of everyone they meet. People generally dislike change, particularly where they cannot be sure how it will affect them. Where these changes are based on levels of unmitigated risk the auditor finds in the manager's area of responsibility, any suggested changes may be associated with negative connotations. These feelings can affect the way the interview progresses and the auditor needs to be sure that the audit objectives and how they should build into management's needs are carefully conveyed to the interviewee. The first few minutes of the interview may consist of a clear attempt by the auditor to explain the audit role and approach before a constructive dialogue may be entered into. It is also important to indicate the next steps that will be followed after the interview is concluded. The auditor's actions must be consistent with his or her words and if he/she is seen as a spy for senior management, little or no cooperation will be received. Any mismatch between what the auditor says they do and management's own understanding can lead to fundamental conceptual problems. This has to be fought against at all times by the auditor to dispel myths and build proper working relationships. Even where the auditor is involved in investigations into irregularity, there is still a view that the auditor is primarily examining the circumstances at issue and not the people concerned. Where a name can be fitted to a problem, then this should be a natural consequence of the proceedings and not a witch-hunt. One of the hardest challenges in the audit role is seeking to reconcile the assurance and consulting roles. We would hope that the image of the jackbooted 'find the transgressor' auditor does not cross over into our main role in assurance auditing and make constructive communications with management and staff impossible. Much resistance from a client can be pre-empted by discussions on this point in a frank and open manner, so long as our actions coincide with our words.

## Types of Questions

Some interviews go on for hours while others last a few moments; these two extremes do not necessarily coincide with the auditor obtaining full or limited information. The success of an interview is not only measured by length of time. Long discussions may be constructive but can result in inefficient use of time. The efficiency of interviews increases by the selective use of different types of questions. Interviewees are guided by skilful use of questioning so that material issues are expanded on while specifics are dealt with more quickly. Types of question include:

- **Open questions** Such as, 'Tell me about your job.' There are times during an interview when we wish to give the interviewee a free hand in discussing a particular issue. It can open up a flood of material that can become uncontrollable if it is not structured at all, and in this way it should be used only where appropriate. It is best to set a scene by describing a set of circumstances and then ask the interviewee to comment on this. The answers can be structured to an extent by asking closed questions as the discussion progresses, although this may involve an amount of interruption. The technique tends to stimulate a positive atmosphere on the basis that most people like to talk about their work area. If the answers become too long, or go in different directions, we may gently interrupt the proceedings by deferring specific matters for later coverage. The topics that we deal with using open questions must be related to matters of which the interviewee has direct knowledge, so that a value-based opinion is not provided that delves not on facts but into pure conjecture. We can therefore ask questions like, 'Tell me about your latest strategic goals', but not value questions such as, 'Give me your views on whether the organization treats people fairly'.
- **Closed questions** Such as, 'Do you work in the accounts department?' This requires a basic yes/no answer that can be recorded straight away. This is a useful way of getting

precise responses to important factual questions that does not rely on judgemental material or long-drawn-out discussions. Name, post designation, start date and specific factual matters can be dealt with in this forum. Having said this, the extensive use of closed questions will elicit very limited information and can turn into an interrogation. It will also create a potentially confrontational mode as the interviewee is subject to a barrage of closed questions that result in the provision of substantial amounts of basic facts. It is best to use closed questions sparingly, perhaps at the start of the interview and whenever we need basic detail, or need to check what has been said earlier. In general they should be avoided if we wish to develop a closer relationship and understand the real issues facing management.

- **Probing questions**    Such as, 'Tell me more about xyz.' These types of questions are used where the client starts a discussion but does not go into sufficient detail. Points raised by the interviewee can be highlighted and further details requested, as a way of directing the discussions. This requires an amount of recapping, which makes the interview process longer and slightly less smooth. However, it means that we get a complete picture of items important to the audit objectives. The problem arises where the auditor probes certain areas that the client is not comfortable with. Some people purposely avoid issues that they feel can leave them open to criticism. In this environment the auditor may find a reluctance to address these particular topics even where there is some probing. Rephrasing the question is another way of returning to a defined topic, as will reviewing what has been said. Ultimately it is difficult to get someone to talk about a topic that they wish to avoid without injecting some conflict into the occasion. It is here where interview skills should come to the fore through a mixture of gentle persuasion and firm perseverance. There is a need to achieve a fine balance between the auditor's right to information and explanations while recognizing that we cannot really force people to talk openly.

- **Confirmatory questions**    Such as, 'Your job description refers to an xyz, is this correct?' Compliance auditing recognizes the realities of business life and the fact that not everything is always as it should be. Furthermore, there are times when we need to double-check an assumption or official position as a way of getting to the truth. It is within this context that we will seek to confirm our understanding of events, systems, processes, circumstances and whatever else we have to research in the course of our work. The ability to recheck matters in a factual manner without causing offence is useful where we need to obtain reliable information. Again we need to avoid the interrogation stance, which is why the use of this approach should really be restricted.

- **Clarification**    Along the lines, 'I thought you said that you worked for Mr X?', when the interviewee has just contradicted himself. We are fast moving into the territory of manipulation, where the auditor tries to squeeze otherwise classified information from a third party. Where there is an obvious inconsistency between the detail that is being provided it is best to place this problem directly in front of the interviewee and seek an explanation. There may be a straightforward reason for this and the opportunity to explain should always be provided. Where there is not then we will still need to obtain clarification as our record of the meeting will not be acceptable if gaps and conflicts remained unresolved. Again the most efficient method of solving these 'mysteries' is simply to ask.

In general one should not use the following types of questions:

- **Leading questions**    Such as, 'Surely you check these invoices before approving them?' This category of question encourages a predefined response that has been invited or hinted at, while the interviewee tends to feel obliged to provide the acceptable answer. The problem is that it does not fit with the search for the truth, which is the main aim of the interview. In this way we can more or less ban the use of leading questions as a generally acceptable practice.

- **Loaded questions**    Such as, 'You appear to be more qualified than your boss.' This incorporates a degree of emotion by being directed at a 'soft spot'. Some may feel that it will get the other party on the side of the auditor by implying a position that sides with them in favour of another outside party. Playing politics has no place in audit policy, not in terms of its usefulness but more in terms of the danger that comes with not saying what you mean or meaning what you say. Audit policy should rule loaded questions generally out of bounds.
- **Trick questions**    Along the lines, 'You say that you have worked here for three and a half years; what date did you start?' The auditor may appear to be clever by playing a game of 'one-up-manship'. This involves keeping one step ahead in terms of general knowledge and usually hiding certain pieces of information so as to rely on this extra insight for use at a later stage. There are many implications of taking a stance along these lines that have no place in the audit role. As with the other approaches there is little point in retaining the use of trick questions as part of audit standards on interviewing.

One principle that should be applied is that constant feedback should be obtained throughout the interview and matters double-checked as far as possible. For more formal occasions, the interviewee should be asked to comment on the documented interview record at the close of the meeting. Above all listen, listen and listen. It is hard to set a standard on this but we must demand that our auditors have mastered the fundamental skill of being able to concentrate not on what they are saying (or plan to say) but more importantly on what is being said to them. The significance is such that, if audit management is not able to train its staff in this skill, then these staff should be released and new people recruited.

Interviewing is widely used to secure audit information. Interviews intrude into the interviewee's world and may be resisted or encouraged depending on the relationship established. Experienced auditors set up interviews and secure information in an efficient and effective manner. The interview is a two-way process and the auditor must convey audit objectives clearly and convincingly. There are many barriers to good interviews and these should be recognized and carefully managed with the aid of a comprehensive audit manual and training workshops.

## 9.3    Ascertaining the System

Systems-based auditing relies on evaluating the whole system of risk management and internal control, which ensures operational objectives will be achieved. This task can only be performed where the systems that are being considered are properly understood, which in turn relies on the auditor's ability to document the system efficiently. There are several alternative methods, each with its own advantages. Some of the more popular ones are mentioned here.

### Alternative Methods

The main options that the auditor has for documenting the system are:

1. Narrative notes.
2. Block diagrams.
3. Flowcharts.
4. Internal control questionnaire (ICQ).

## Securing the Required Information

Before the auditor can 'capture' the system, information must be secured through fact-finding. The auditor should interview the line manager and operatives to elicit a picture of operations. Line managers will have an overview of what goes on in their areas of responsibility and this is the starting place for the full audit. It is only when the operatives are seen that a truer picture is obtained that highlights noncompliance and/or poor controls. The auditor decides how far to follow the system if it links into other systems. This is clear from the defined scope of the audit in the assignment plan. New information that extends the systems boundaries is brought back to the audit manager for further consideration. When the system is being written up, gaps in acquired information may require further investigation. Armed with predefined checklists the auditor should direct interviews to cover all important areas. Capturing the flow of documentation and information should be key concerns. The auditor should try to document the system and consider whether it equates to the 'official system'. Different versions of the same system may result from misunderstanding by operational staff and this should be seen as a finding in its own right. Walkthrough testing means that the auditor will point to examples as the system is explained by the client to help illustrate underlying processes. The information-gathering process may bring out weaknesses that might be discovered by the auditor or expressed by the interviewee. This aids the auditor in evaluation, and it is not necessary to keep ascertainment and evaluation separate. It is dangerous for the auditor to jump to conclusions and start recommending action at the ascertainment stage no matter how impressive this might appear during initial interviews.

## Narrative

Systems are set out by straightforward narrative, where the main parts of the system are noted in point format. The processes are described from start to finish to convey the required information on which to base an evaluation. For the bulk of these systems notes may be taken direct from the interview with the operations manager. For simple systems that do not involve much document flows, this may be sufficient. For more complicated systems it may be necessary to go on to draft a block diagram and/or a detailed flowchart. Narrative provides a useful shortcut to systems documentation and as long as it conveys the right information clearly, it is a valid technique. It should be possible to cross-reference relevant documents to the narrative and then attach them to the notes for future use. Structured narrative notes divide the operation into sections or people alongside brief notes on each activity to form a diagrammatic representation of events. This might appear as in Table 9.1. This captures the system simply on a single document without needing detailed symbols and keys.

**TABLE 9.1**   Structured systems narrative notes.

| System Stage | Dept A | Dept B | Dept C |
|---|---|---|---|
| 1 | notes xxx | notes xxx | notes xxx |
| 2 | notes xxx | notes xxx | notes xxx |
| 3 | notes xxx | notes xxx | notes xxx |
| 4 | notes xxx | notes xxx | notes xxx |
| etc. | | | |

## Block Diagrams

Block diagrams fall in between detailed flowcharts and narrative. They consist of a series of boxes each representing an operation or control. It provides a simple diagrammatic representation as in Figure 9.3.

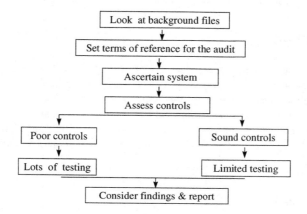

**FIGURE 9.3** A block diagram.

One may show the flow of information and the organizational arrangements. The main advantage is that this technique is quick and simple, and sample diagrams can be incorporated within the audit report to aid understanding by outlining the system. For high-level work that does not require a detailed analysis of documentation this can be an efficient way of recording the system. This contrasts with flowcharting, where there is an obsession with the detailed movement of documents.

## Balancing the Level of Details Required

There must be balance in the use of ascertainment techniques so that efficiency is maintained and there is perspective involved in applying flowcharting. For the best ascertainment options consider:

- **Narrative**   A simple descriptive overview gleaned directly from the interviews. It should be used wherever possible unless the level of documentation becomes too detailed to deal with in note form.
- **Block diagrams**   Illustrate the main stages of a system and the relationships between components. With the growing use of graphical presentation software, there is scope for attractive diagrams that can be imported into the audit report for ease of reading. Main systems stages have to be summarized for block diagrams to be of any use, although the advantage is simplicity in design and ease of use.
- **Detailed flowchart**   These should be used sparingly and only where absolutely necessary. Because of time constraints and the move away from basic operational detail, they have limited use. Where a sensitive system, such as pre-signed cheque ordering, use and dispatch, must be carefully accounted for, monitored and controlled at all stages, detailed flowcharts will probably be required.

Standards on the above including appropriate conventions should be comprehensively dealt with in the audit manual. It is pointless to seek to flowchart in detail for all organizational systems as this would be a momentous task. They would need constant change with little or no benefit to the audit service. The choice of ascertainment technique depends on the type of audit and approach adopted. There is a wide variety of available methodologies and this adds to, rather than dilutes, the auditor's skills base. The audit manual is the right vehicle for setting such standards.

## 9.4  Evaluation

Evaluation may be seen as the most important stage in any audit review since this provides an opportunity for auditors to apply professional creativity to the fullest. The audit opinion and recommendations should flow from the systems weaknesses identified during the systems evaluation. Audit testing routines are carried out to confirm the original evaluation in terms of the application of controls and the effects of control weaknesses. If the evaluation is flawed then all the remaining audit work will suffer. Audit recommendations will provide substandard solutions to risk exposures.

### Defining the System

The preliminary survey establishes which system is being audited. The statement on scope of audit work in the assignment plan will document what is being reviewed and it is this system that will be subject to evaluation. We then have to turn to the model of the system that is being evaluated. Successful evaluation requires that the right techniques are applied in the right way, based on a good understanding of the system. The auditor's understanding of the system should include:

1. **Understanding the needs of the parties who rely on the system**   This not only includes front line staff and middle managers but all those involved in systems that interface. These may sometimes conflict where one user (say, line managers) requires readily available financial information while another (say, the accountant) demands high accuracy rather than speed.
2. **Understanding the adopted success criteria**   This concerns what the system is about in terms of the competing factors of quality, timeliness, quantity and value of the system's product against the need to ensure that risks to these attributes are managed.
3. **Understanding the risk landscape**   This is an understanding that impacts the objectives and success criteria including the adopted risk appetite.
4. **Understanding systems constraints**   This considers the relationship between the cost of risks and benefits of control in containing these risks.

### Evaluation Techniques

The system being reviewed is the system being applied in practice in line with management's operational objectives. The evaluation applied should be based on those controls required to ensure systems objectives are achieved with no great loss or inefficiency. Evaluation techniques include:

1. **Flowcharts**   These help identify systems blockages, duplication of effort and segregation of duties along with controls that depend on documentation flows and the way work is organized.

2. **Transactions testing**   By testing transactions one might pick up system malfunctions that cause error conditions identified by the tests. Where we are able to manipulate large amounts of data, the ability to carry out a limited range of tests quickly arises. This cannot be seen as a systematic evaluation since it does not rely on a full understanding of the operation under review, but leaves matters to chance as samples are selected and examined.

3. **Directed representations**   One cannot deny the usefulness of information provided by persons who have knowledge of the system. If management states that there are defined system weaknesses at the outset of an audit, one would be ill-advised to ignore this source of information. Complaints from users, operatives, middle management and third parties can provide a shortcut to the evaluation process. One would look for bias in these comments as they could not be taken without some degree of substantiating evidence.

4. **Internal control questionnaires (ICQ)**   Dealt with below.

5. **Risk-based internal control evaluation system (RBICES)**   Dealt with below.

## Internal Control Questionnaires (ICQ)

Internal control questionnaires (ICQ) are widely used to assist the control evaluation process and there are many standard packages. They consist of a series of questions applied to a particular operation and designed so that a 'no' answer indicates a potential control weakness. One might ask:

> Is the task of receipting income separated from the recording of this income?

The idea is that a 'no' answer may mean that official duties are insufficiently segregated. The potential weaknesses are then further explored and compensatory controls looked for before testing routines are applied. Parts of the ICQ that relate to a stores system appears in Table 9.2.

**TABLE 9.2**   Control-related ICQ.

| Question | Yes | No | Test no. |
|---|---|---|---|
| Ordering System | | | |
| Control objective: to ensure that stores are authorized, delivered, correct, safeguarded and available | | | |
| Q.1 Is person certifying the order independent of the storekeeper? | | | |
| Q.2 Are orders placed only with approved suppliers? | | | |
| Q.3 Does the order make reference to a purchasing contract? | | | |
| Q.4 Are stock level reports issued regularly for re-ordering purposes? | | | |
| etc. | | | |

Do not give them to the manager to complete but use them for fact-finding discussion. The ICQ should be completed by using all available sources of information from interviews, observation, initial testing, documents, manuals, representations and past audit files. It is compiled as the audit progresses, taking on board a wide range of information, although it is seen by many as a rather old-fashioned approach to performing audit work. In fact, there is an ongoing debate about the use of checklists in internal audit work and there is a large swell of opinion that suggests this approach does not support the modern audit role.

## Risk-Based Internal Control Evaluation System (RBICES)

The internal control evaluation system/schedule (RBICES) is partly a conceptual model linked directly into the systems-based approach and partly a mechanism for setting out the evaluation process in matrix format. Unlike ICQs, it involves setting out the components of good evaluation in a schedule (or matrix) format so that a systematic series of steps can be undertaken before testing, conclusions and recommendations are made. The main headings may appear at the top of the schedule as:

- Business objectives.
- Risks to the achievement of objectives.
- Available control mechanisms.
- Existing control mechanisms.
- Initial evaluation.
- Testing strategy required.
- Test results.
- Conclusions.
- Recommendations.

The entire audit process is established in a formal systematic fashion, although this technique tends to be used by more experienced auditors with a full understanding of the system. Note that this format appears very similar to the risk registers that are prepared through the CRSA process. An example of this audit evaluation approach applied to an audit of a local authority small business grant approval system is given in Table 9.3.

There are several advantages to this approach:

1. It treats controls as part of the process of mitigating risks to achieving objectives and therefore it starts with what management is trying to achieve (i.e. the systems objectives). The entire audit process is seen to flow from this start point.
2. The auditor does not possess a pat answer to controls as suggested by the ICQ approach. It is a question of working out what control objectives are relevant (having regard to the systems objectives) and then seeking to determine what control mechanisms should be in place. This technique is more difficult to master as it requires a commitment to systems auditing. Instead of being armed with a list of questions, the auditor is armed with a database of control mechanisms that fit various risk scenarios.
3. The RBICES requires the auditor to analyze the system and break it down into logical components as it flows from input and processes through to the final output in chronological order.

**TABLE 9.3** Business advice service risk/control evaluation.
(business aims – to encourage business regeneration through local grants)

| Process stage and control objective | Inherent risks | Desirable controls | Existing controls | Initial assessment | Testing strategy ref and results | Audit recommendations |
|---|---|---|---|---|---|---|
| Grants available<br>I. A Awareness of grant | Little appreciation of grant availability | Wide publicity | Word of mouth only | Inadequate | I.A.I Survey of local businesses<br>Result – awareness poor | I. Need to launch scheme properly |
| Eligibility established<br>I. B Objective eligibility criteria | Many ineligible businesses applying | Information package | New leaflet and website in use | Very detailed material | I.B.I Check that applying businesses receive info<br>Result - OK | n/a Audit assurances provided |
| Businesses approved<br>I. C Meet criteria | Wrong businesses approved | Formal assessment | Subjective selection | Open to abuse | I.C.I Check whether wrong approvals made<br>Result – poor | 2. Prepare formal assessment criteria |
| Grants paid<br>I. D Pay the correct person | Cheques going astray | ID and collection | Posted out | Can go astray | I.D.I Check that ID system adhered to<br>I.D.2 Cheques received by businesses<br>Result – no fraud | n/a Audit assurances provided |
| Businesses grow<br>I. E Effects of grants known | Grants have no impact on local community | Database follow-up | Not done | VFM not assured | I.E.I Examine failure rates of aided businesses<br>Result – poor | 3. Monitoring and new tracking system required |

4. The RBICES deals with control risk and exposures as an extension of the evaluation procedure. This requires a considered understanding of the activities under review. A good appreciation of risk enables the auditor to direct control mechanisms at the right parts of the system.
5. The RBICES flows naturally into the testing routines as, after compliance has been reviewed, the poorer parts of the system are then subject to substantive testing.
6. The RBICES forms a record of control weakness to be placed in front of management and discussed before the draft audit report is prepared. We are able to provide a full audit process encapsulated within the RBICES schedules. This contains details of objectives, how existing controls compare with desirable ones, the test results obtained, and final opinion and recommended improvements derived from resolving weak controls that were confirmed by tests applied.
7. The RBICES means a move away from the old audit programme approach where a list of basic tasks is given to the auditor to work through. This method leads to creative, thinking auditors who can operate more at strategic levels.
8. An even better format may be the integrated audit approach (see Chapter 8) where the business advice would embark on a risk workshop to get to the key risks that would then be used to drive the resulting audit. They would then resume to work through ways forward (rather than audit recommendations) before the audit report and agreed management action plan was prepared and issued in draft.

During control evaluation the auditor's judgement is perhaps the single most important factor and this will be based on experience and training. The whole process of reviewing the system will arise throughout the audit and the formal evaluation techniques may be used to confirm the auditor's initial opinion. Control findings will impact on the way risk is being managed in the area under review and these initially will have to be tested. First, they must be checked to see if controls are being applied as intended. Second, the effects of weaknesses on the level of risk exposure must be established and quantified by gathering sufficient evidence.

## 9.5 Testing Strategies

Testing is the act of securing suitable evidence to support an audit. It confirms the auditor's initial opinion on the state of internal controls. It is a step in control evaluation, although many auditors test for the sole purpose of highlighting errors or nonadherence with laid-down procedure. It depends on the audit objective. The IIA Practice Advisory 2240-1 requires audit procedures to be in place to ensure the required evidence can be gathered:

> Internal auditors develop and obtain documented approval of work programs before commencing the internal audit engagement. The work program includes methodologies to be used, such as technology-based audit and sampling techniques.

> The process of collecting, analyzing, interpreting, and documenting information is to be supervised to provide reasonable assurance that engagement objectives are met and that the internal auditor's objectivity is maintained.

### The Testing Process

The auditor should gather sufficient evidence to support audit findings. This means the information should be factual, adequate and convincing so that a prudent, informed person would reach the same conclusions as the auditor. Competent information is reliable and is best attainable through the use of appropriate engagement techniques. Relevant information supports engagement observations and recommendations and is consistent with the objectives for the engagement. Useful information helps the organization meet its goals. The testing process may be noted as follows:

**Define the test objective** There must be a clear reason for performing the test. In systems auditing this relates to the adequacy or effectiveness of controls. For example, if we are concerned that there is no proper system for ensuring orders are properly authorized, then we may examine a sample of orders to see if they comply with the purchasing code of practice. The test objective is to judge the extent of problems.

**Define the testing strategy** How test objectives are achieved is determined by the testing strategy. This lists the tests required and groups them to aid their efficient execution. If we need to examine application forms for a sample of newly recruited employees as part of an audit of personnel procedures, we need to decide how this will best be achieved, the use of statistical sampling and how data will be extracted.

**Formulate an audit programme** The testing strategy can be defined in more detail and form an audit programme of work. This programme becomes a schedule containing space for the samples to be listed and the tests performed and documented. It provides a ready-made guide to the completion of the testing strategies. The programme may appear in matrix format with space on the left for a list of payments made to subcontractors that are selected at random. The rest of the schedule will be broken down into columns for each part of the tests. This could cover checks over order, contract number, payments, certificates, invoices, select list of suppliers, budget provision and tax exemption. This checks whether procedures over the employment and payment of subcontractors work.

**Perform the test** The detailed work of performing the tests is the main part of the testing process. The key point is that there is a tendency for the test objective to be lost in the vast amount of work that may be required during the test performance stage.

**Schedule the evidence** The results of testing should be summarized and fed into the report (via the RBICES) and be cross-referenced in the working papers. Test results give an overview of results and provide detailed schedules that may be sent to management for action. They may be referred to in the audit report as examples of actual problems. Where we have examined hundreds of payroll payments and found several categories of errors (say, the wrong pay rates applied) we may mention the amount of over/underpayments in each department in the report. The working papers should assist by allowing summaries to be compiled without extra effort. Interesting examples may be highlighted and the design of schedules should enable these items to be readily extracted.

**Interpret the results** The meaning of what is found feeds into the testing strategy. If we examine a series of performance reports for indications of misleading information being provided, we must have set criteria against which to measure findings. We must consider whether what was found is accurate and have access to a suitable model to make this judgement. If we check authorizations for new accounts on a computer system, the checks will only make sense if we have a list of authorizing officers.

***Determine the impact on audit objectives***  The link back to the original objectives should be firmly in place so that we take the mass of data and decide what it means for the audit. Auditors should give an opinion on areas covered. This will be based on the state of controls and whether this led to unacceptable levels of risk being identified through testing. This part of the testing puts the detailed work into perspective by providing an outcome. This cannot be to list errors found by internal audit, since this would be for management to do. The goal is to support an audit view of risk management and controls resulting in a recommendation. We would want to see that the operation in question is properly aligned to corporate values. In both audit and consulting work, this is an important consideration, as laid out in IIA Performance Standards 2110:

> The internal audit activity must assess and make appropriate recommendations for improving the governance process in its accomplishment of the following objectives:
>
> • Promoting appropriate ethics and values within the organization;
> • Ensuring effective organizational performance management and accountability;
> • Communicating risk and control information to appropriate areas of the organization; and
> • Coordinating the activities of and communicating information among the board, external and internal auditors, and management.

***Determine the next step***  Taking into account all that has been found, the direction of the audit should be agreed, particularly if there is a need to change plans. One outcome may be to extend the testing routines into greater detail or other areas, or ask management to look into particular problems. We may find matters that were totally unexpected and there must be an opportunity to review the audit and current position before going headlong into the next stage of the project.

## The Four Types of Tests

***Walkthrough***  This involves taking a small sample of items that are traced through the system to ensure that the auditor understands the system. It occurs during the ascertainment stage of the audit and may lead to further tests later. The client may be asked to refer to named documents representative of the transaction cycle that will be cross-referenced to the interview record to assist this process of 'capturing' the system.

***Compliance***  This determines whether key controls are adhered to. It uncovers noncompliance or unclear procedures. If key controls are not being applied, and this is not compensated for by the system, they become reclassified as weak controls. Note that internal auditors should review operations and programmes to ascertain the extent to which results are consistent with established goals and objectives and to determine whether operations are being performed as intended.

***Substantive***  These determine whether control objectives are being achieved. Weak controls imply objectives will not be achieved and substantive tests are designed to confirm this initial audit view on the impact of residual risk. Substantive tests may isolate risks that materialize in the form of error, poor information, direct loss or poor value for money.

***Dual purpose***  This is not a test but a recognition of the practicalities of testing controls, where one may wish to combine compliance and substantive testing. An example is to examine an invoice that is certified for payment (compliance test) and is valid (substantive test). It would be impractical to select this invoice twice for two different tests to be separately applied.

The important tests are deemed to be compliance or substantive, as these are the two main techniques used to support audit work. The relationship between the four tests is shown in Figure 9.4.

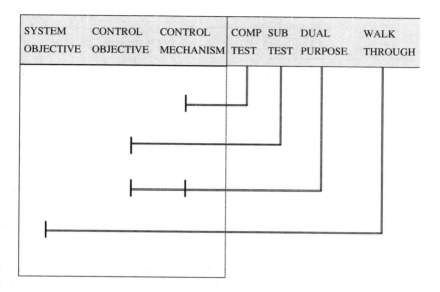

**FIGURE 9.4**   The various test patterns.

We can summarize our discussion:

- Walkthrough tests seek to determine how the system's objectives are achieved.
- Compliance tests seek to determine whether control mechanisms are being applied.
- Substantive tests seek to determine whether control objectives are being achieved.
- Dual-purpose tests check for both compliance and actual error, abuse or inefficiency.

## Comparing Compliance and Substantive Tests

There are key differences between the two main types of test. We re-state the systems-based approach to auditing and how these tests fit into the audit process in Figure 9.5.

We look first for compliance with key controls and then review results. Substantive tests are then directed towards all known weak areas including those where key controls are not being observed or revealed through compliance testing.

## Testing Techniques

There are many ways that one can gather the necessary evidence to support the testing objective. The number and types of techniques are limited only by the imagination of the auditor.

**Re-performance**   Rechecking a calculation or procedure can give evidence as to its reliability. This enables the auditor to comment directly on the accuracy by which transactions are processed,

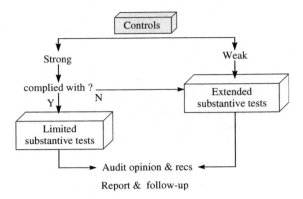

**FIGURE 9.5**   Compliance and substantive tests.

although it does depend on the auditor being able to perform the necessary task. As an example we might wish to recalculate the amount of money paid to staff who are made compulsorily redundant to ensure that controls, such as supervisory review over payments, are working properly.

***Observation***   This is a useful method of information gathering since it is obtained first-hand by the auditor. There are drawbacks in that what is presented to the auditor may be stage-managed, although this may be a somewhat cynical view. For example, during one audit staff were observed exchanging passwords when they were already keyed into a terminal under their own password and wanted to use another terminal, which was a clear breach of procedure. Structured observation may be used to check controls that have a physical presence such as security and, for example, this may be used to check how cashiers carry out their end-of-day cash balancing operations.

***Corroboration***   Having facts from one area confirmed by reference to another party is a good way of verifying the accuracy of these facts. The more independent the third party the more reliable the results. This technique should be used with care as it should not be an obvious act of rechecking what has been said elsewhere and is best used to follow the natural flow of a system. For example, a payment can be written off by an officer who has placed a stop on the cheque by writing a memo to a financial controller. Meanwhile, the financial controller should be asked to confirm this, as he/she is visited as part of the audit.

***Analytical review***   Analytical review is a technique that tends to be applied by external auditors and there is an APB statement on this. This involves looking at two or more sets of comparable information, say two years' balance sheets, and extracting new data that can be used to direct audit attention towards areas of particular interest. The auditor would be looking for:

- Changes in key ratios.
- Absolute changes in key figures.
- General trends.
- Movement in the level of purchases and creditors.
- Movement in the cash and bank account balances.
- Movement in sales and debtors.

This directs the auditors' attention towards areas for investigation, although because of the emphasis in comparing financial data the technique is mainly used by external auditors.

**Inspection**  Inspection is a formal way of observing physical attributes against a set criterion. It implies the use of an amount of expertise to discharge this exercise that the auditor may or may not possess. One might imagine the auditor wishing to inspect building work done by subcontractors that has been certified and paid for by the organization. Again the auditor will not necessarily be able to carry out this inspection but may commission a consultant to make the required checks and provide a status report. In this case controls over the work certification process can be reviewed through this process of examining previous building jobs. Inspection can also be used to check the existence of assets that have been acquired by the organization.

**Reconciliation**  The process of balancing one set of figures back to another is based mainly on the principle of double-entry bookkeeping that ensures the accounts balance at all times. The reconciliation may be something that is done by management as part of its normal work and this may be reviewed by the auditor using re-performance where necessary. It is also possible for the auditor to perform a new reconciliation to provide evidence of the adequacy of controls. For example, the auditor may seek to balance payroll to personnel systems to establish how well these two systems interface. Any discrepancies may indicate a breakdown of communications between the two functions that could lead to real or potential loss to the organization.

**Expert opinion**  This is less a technique and more a source of assistance linked to another technique. There are many times when the auditor has a problem in terms of securing relevant evidence pertinent to the audit at hand but being unable to perform the underlying work. For example, a stores audit may disclose losses on fuel that management argues is due to the natural process of evaporation. The extent of these losses, having reference to this factor, may be reviewed for consistency by an expert who would examine the facilities and provide an opinion on the validity of the stated argument. The auditor in turn may then be able to comment on the state of controls over safeguarding fuel from unauthorized removal, where there are clear losses that cannot be fully explained through evaporation.

**Interviews**  More often than not the best way to find something out is simply to ask and much useful information can be obtained through the interview forum. This facility is extremely convenient, although the reliability of representations can vary, depending on the circumstances. Where persons provide information this must be verified as far as possible by asking for the document, report, policy, memorandum, minutes and so on that should support what is being said. There are some pointers that are simple to examine, where, for example, we wish to discover whether managers are using the organization's financial regulations. If they are asked whether they possess a copy and cannot find one, then we can argue that they do not make reference to this document in their everyday work. If some of them have never heard of the regulation then we may comment adversely on the adequacy with which this procedure has been implemented in the organization.

**Review of published reports/research**  Another source of supportive evidence is to be found in reports that impact on the area under review. These can range from internal reports, say on staffing levels, externally commissioned reviews of, for example, the potential for new IT, or national reports that contain relevant base data on, say, productivity levels. They may provide information that may be referred to in the audit report covering, for instance, the average cost per employee of payroll services. Alternatively, the existence of a report may simply be used as evidence that management had access to specific advice, that may or may not have been acted on. Any matters raised by the external auditors may also be of use when seeking material to support the internal audit opinion. Obviously reports must be used with care, since the auditor cannot verify the contents of most reports unless prepared from official sources (e.g. government statistics).

**Independent confirmation**  An obvious source of evidence is to get someone to independently agree defined facts. Where opinion is involved this becomes more difficult as subjective matters can be interpreted in different ways. Direct facts relating to dates, times, figures, agreements and so on can be readily double-checked. The usual example of this technique is debtors' circularization, where moneys due to the organization are confirmed by writing direct to the debtor in question. This is a useful device for the external auditor during asset verification. Independent verification may involve checking a representation made by the independent third party. A stocktaker's certificate, for example, may be checked for authenticity by contacting the firm that has issued the document. The rule that the best evidence comes from people who have no vested interest in providing incorrect information is applied. However, this is not a way of viewing all others as somehow untrustworthy, but simply part of the drive to seek the best evidence wherever possible.

**Receiving the service as a client**  Most operations that produce goods or services recognize the key concept of client care, which means there must be a net value from what is being delivered. If we were going to audit a company with a chain of restaurants, for example, the first thing to do would be to purchase a meal from the outlet. Taking this further, it is possible to visit or phone and experience the service as a client to obtain a feel for the way controls over this service are operating. If, for example, a line manager has said that all clients receive a complaints form so that feedback is obtained where the service user has experienced a problem, we can find out if this is the case. This technique may be used in conjunction with observation so that an overall impression can be gleaned. We would not be able to refer directly to evidence from this source but it may be used to concentrate attention in the direction of service delivery, if this suggests a breakdown in controls. The approach is not always possible to use but, where it can be, it gives an important 'feel' for the operation.

**Mathematical models**  The auditor may construct a model that may be used to gauge particular features of an operation. This is generally not easy as there is a set-up cost involved and the question of credibility when it is used to support an audit report. However, where we have a large audit and it is possible to apply conceptual models, this is a consideration. The example that students will see in most textbooks relates to setting reorder levels in a stores environment. Here the auditor may use a suitable model to test whether controls over stock reordering result in acceptable reorder quantities and frequencies. Other factors such as slow-moving stock and stock-outs will also come into play to support or not support the findings from such a mathematical model.

**Questionnaires**  Formal surveys can be used to assist the audit process. This is a useful device in an audit of an operation that has equivalents either within the organization or in other comparable ones. Because an organization does things differently from other bodies does not mean that this is wrong or right. Telephone surveys can be used to save time so long as full records are made and important matters separately verified in writing. We can elicit data on staffing levels, decentralized operations, use of new IT and other matters from asking questions from other services. We can compute averages and trends to be used to assess the existing position. These devices are best used for more comprehensive reviews that examine controls over value for money.

**Comparison**   Vouching comes under this heading in that we can seek to check one item against another one that has an associated factor. There is little that can be said about comparison over and above the basic checking of two or more facts (usually documents). One point to note is that the auditor should maintain accurate records of these comparisons as they may be challenged at a later date. Furthermore, where there is a discrepancy we would have to discover which item is wrong before such matters can be reported. We should also bring the actual error to the attention of management if it is material in terms of the need to make corrections.

**User satisfaction surveys**   Obtaining direct feedback from persons who use the service/product delivered by the operation under review can provide an insight into the success or otherwise of the operation. These mainly test controls over the marketing function attached to the operation. In addition, they can provide a commentary on the quality assurance (QA) procedures that have been installed (these QA procedures would be deemed a key control). Such surveys can reveal much more than hours of conversations with management, as they should give a completely unbiased view of the service being audited.

We have already suggested that there is an open-ended list of testing techniques, although whatever techniques are applied it is important to record all results carefully. Clearly, testing is not just limited to basic financial systems but can be applied in any environment. For some of the more sensitive ones, such as the client satisfaction survey, the auditor should make it clear to management that the exercise is being undertaken. Copies of the pro forma documentation that is being used for the purpose should also be provided. Whatever the approach we must beware of appearing to be spies, performing some type of undercover work, as this will probably impair the audit image.

## Can Controls be Compensated for?

There are times where controls fall out of date or become inappropriate as the system adapts to its environment. Front line controls fall out of place and back-up controls appear as staff seek to ensure the operations work. We find staff deal with problems by establishing another level of control to fill in for any perceived gaps. A system for car mileage claims may state that managers should certify claims before they are paid as a key control. Where this task is not taken seriously, we may find payroll staff querying the claims where they are obviously inconsistent. This check by payroll acts as a compensatory control that may not appear in the official procedure in line with the principle that people generally want good controls. Systems of internal control operate together and where one part is weak (i.e. not adhered to) another part may well take over. Auditors may need to look for these compensating controls. They will need to decide whether to recommend that management adopts them as official procedures, on the basis that they reflect the shifts in control balance that occur over time. Most compensating controls depend on a good control culture, which means an organic view of procedures is adopted to a better effect. We cannot always take extra procedures as being the most efficient method, as they may not be based on an overview of the entire operation and interfaces. The auditor must test compliance with official controls and apply the same tests to compensatory ones.

## 9.6   Evidence and Working Papers

Audit testing results in much material that should support the reported audit opinion and associated recommendations. The test results along with other material gathered throughout the audit process will constitute audit evidence and this will be held in suitable audit working papers. Standards of working papers and documentary evidence are a topic that all auditors come across in the course of their work and generally there is a view that good standards are a prerequisite to good control. Practice Advisory 2330-1 covers documenting information, based on Standard 2330:

> Internal auditors prepare working papers. Working papers document the information obtained, the analyses made, and the support for the conclusions and engagement results. Internal audit management reviews the prepared working papers.
>
> Engagement working papers generally:
>
> - Aid in the planning, performance, and review of engagements.
> - Provide the principal support for engagement results.
> - Document whether engagement objectives were achieved.
> - Support the accuracy and completeness of the work performed.
> - Provide a basis for the internal audit activity's quality assurance and improvement program.
> - Facilitate third-party reviews.
>
> The organization, design, and content of engagement working papers depend on the engagement's nature and objectives and the organization's needs. Engagement working papers document all aspects of the engagement process from planning to communicating results. The internal audit activity determines the media used to document and store working papers. The chief audit executive establishes working paper policies for the various types of engagements performed. Standardized engagement working papers, such as questionnaires and audit programs, may improve the engagement's efficiency and facilitate the delegation of engagement work. Engagement working papers may be categorized as permanent or carry-forward engagement files that contain information of continuing importance.

Note that the external auditor may be sued where their work may have been performed negligently and their working papers may be used in any defence to this charge. Here we look at some of the requirements for internal auditors' working papers and filing systems.

### Evidence Attributes

The evidence the auditor uses for the audit opinion should be:

**Sufficient** This is in line with materiality, level of risk and the level of auditors' knowledge of the operation. Sufficient means enough, which depends on circumstances. It should be enough to satisfy the auditor's judgement or persuade management to make any changes advocated by audit. It could mean enough to ensure there is a wide spread of material or an acceptable sample. Evidence is adequate when it meets the desired purpose. The audit opinion may range from 'it is clear that . . . ', 'it would appear that . . . ', 'there are indications that . . . ' to 'there is the possibility that . . . '. In the current environment of cost constraint, the amount of evidence secured should be the minimum to form an opinion in that it takes more resources to obtain relevant proof that conclusions are sound.

**Relevant** This ensures that evidence is directed to the control objectives. Relevance brings into play the legal concept of admissibility, which requires material to relate specifically to the issues at hand. It is wrong to refer to matters that do not impact on the arguments that appear in the audit report, as a way of blurring the issues at hand. The auditor must use professional judgement in deciding what is important. Test results that refer to low-level detail cannot be used to comment on material considerations that have a far-reaching effect on management's ability to achieve. Relevance means that the evidence is associated with the key concerns and that it is material to them.

**Reliable** The information should be accurate, without bias and if possible produced by a third party or obtained directly by the auditor. The term 'reliable' stimulates images of the evidence being 'dependable, honest, sound, and true'. This may in turn be applied to the audit report that is based on this evidence, as, in one sense and in contrast, unreliable evidence creates an opposite impact by lowering the credibility of the auditor's work. The rules on obtaining audit evidence require it to be done in a way that minimizes bias. The reliability factor must be applied by the auditor to satisfy him/herself and must also satisfy the perceptions of the report reader. Independence and accuracy are the main components of the reliability index that need to be fully addressed by the auditor in the search for good evidence.

**Practical** One would weigh up the evidence required, the cost and time taken to obtain it and sensitivity. Some matters cannot be discovered through audit since it would take too much research. There are many examples of this that range from getting a definitive verdict on the state of the MIS database, through to obtaining a view on whether staff are well motivated. Not all matters may be studied and documented by the auditor since the general equation suggests that the greater the value of evidence the more resources will be applied to securing it. There is a constraint that means there is a strict limit on the time that can be applied. The IIA Performance Standard 2300 makes it clear that: 'Internal auditors must identify, analyze, evaluate, and document sufficient information to achieve the engagement's objectives.'

## Standardization

One way to formalize the process is to define standardized working papers aimed at getting to the audit opinion with supporting evidence. The IIA's Practice Advisory 2330-1 (Recording Information) suggests that: 'The CAE should establish working paper policies for the various types of engagements performed. Standardized engagement working papers such as questionnaire and audit programs may improve the efficiency of an engagement and facilitate the delegation of engagement work.' These standardized documents will form the current file while the background material will either be held as a bundle of general papers or, if relevant, will enter into the permanent filing system. This approach forms the basis for an automated filing system where standardized forms are maintained on disk. Standardized documentation enables auditors to follow a systematic audit methodology and can contribute to overall audit efficiency. This point is explored later in the section on the audit manual. These are certain types of documents that might be standardized including, for example:

| | |
|---|---|
| Preliminary survey report | Assignment plans |
| Flowcharts | Interview records |
| Internal control evaluation forms | Compliance and substantive test strategies |
| Record of risks and control weakness | Risk assessments |
| Constraint analysis | Objectives statement |

## Access to Working Papers

The IIA have issued guidance on controlling engagement records and granting access to these records, extracts of which follow:

- **2330 – Documenting Information:** Internal auditors must document relevant information to support the conclusions and engagement results.
- **2330.A1** – The chief audit executive must control access to engagement records. The chief audit executive must obtain the approval of senior management and/or legal counsel prior to releasing such records to external parties, as appropriate.
- **2330.A2** – The chief audit executive must develop retention requirements for engagement records, regardless of the medium in which each record is stored. These retention requirements must be consistent with the organization's guidelines and any pertinent regulatory or other requirements.
- **2330.C1** – The chief audit executive must develop policies governing the custody and retention of consulting engagement records, as well as their release to internal and external parties. These policies must be consistent with the organization's guidelines and any pertinent regulatory or other requirements.

## 9.7  Statistical Sampling

All auditors need knowledge of statistical sampling and it is advisable to adopt a clear policy regarding its use. We summarize popular ways statistical sampling may be applied, although a specialist textbook will provide a fuller understanding. Statistical sampling has a clear role and auditors make a decision during systems audits, as shown in Figure 9.6.

An auditor has to decide whether statistical sampling will be used based on knowledge and an appreciation of the technique and its application.

### The Normal Distribution

The bell-shaped curve represents the normal distribution. The shape of the curve is determined by the mean and the standard deviation (SD) of the underlying values whereby the greater the range of values the flatter the curve. This feature is used in statistical sampling to allow the area under the curve to equate to 1. If the mean is seen as 0 then we can calculate that each SD from the mean will cover a defined portion of the normal distribution curve. This appears in Figure 9.7.

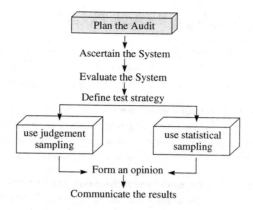

**FIGURE 9.6** Role of sampling.

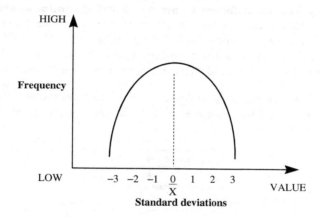

**FIGURE 9.7** The normal distribution.

The area under the curve is:

$$+ \text{ or } - 1 \text{ SD} = 68.3\%$$

$$+ \text{ or } - 2 \text{ SD} = 95.4\%$$

$$+ \text{ or } - 3 \text{ SD} = 99.7\%$$

The relationships between the values and the SDs have been translated into statistical tables. These may be used to form conclusions about the population that are derived from an examination of a sample of the population. This is based on the theory that the mean of a distribution of sample means is equal to the mean of the population from which the sample is drawn. It is important to know the SD of the sample that is used and a formula may be used to calculate this figure. This is not reproduced here but it should be noted that the smaller the range of values the smaller the SD, while the greater the range (i.e. variation from the mean) the larger the SD.

## Applying Statistical Sampling to the Audit Process

It is important that statistical sampling is considered in terms of its actual role in the audit process. It is used when performing the testing routines required to confirm or otherwise the initial evaluation of internal controls. To this end the samples and ensuing tests may be used for:

**Quantifying the effects of control weaknesses** Substantive testing reveals the implications of a lack of control. This is where statistical sampling may be used to allow a generalist comment based on the results of a predetermined number of transactions. We have already agreed that one can only give an overall opinion on the entire database where the sample has been statistically prepared.

**Getting management to act on audit recommendations** Ensuring that internal audit recommendations are supported by indicating the extent of risk in failing to take remedial action encourages management to adopt them. Therefore, where we find excessive levels of non-compliance with a key control, this must be quantified and set against the corresponding recommendation.

**Highlighting implications of failure to act on identified control weaknesses** We use statistical sampling to predict the extent of uncontrolled error. This need not be in terms of one-off examples that give no indication of the scale and extent of the problems, as in some audit reports. Scientific sampling can result in matrix boxes in the report where the type of errors found can be given global values based on extrapolation, to increase the impact of the findings.

Statistical sampling is a means to an end. It assists in achieving defined test objectives, without examining the entire population. The role of statistical sampling within the testing routine is described in Figure 9.8.

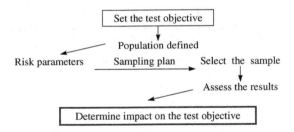

**FIGURE 9.8**   Testing using statistical sampling.

## Sampling Techniques

There are two main aspects to statistical sampling. One is how the number of items to be examined is defined. The other relates to the methods used to extract the required information. The latter is called the sampling method or selection technique. Methods used to define numbers tested are called sampling plans. This section deals with sampling methods and these may be set out as:

**Random sampling** This technique is used to select samples such that each item in the population has an equal chance of being chosen. Random number tables may be used to choose the required items and these may be generated by an appropriately programmed computer.

**Stratified sampling** If we recall that the normal distribution places values in the shape of a bell, then a skewed distribution will not appear symmetrical. This may mean that the auditor can divide the population into several segments that may consist of, say, a small number of high-value invoices for revenue contracts and a large number of small-value ones for one-off supplies. The auditor may wish to pay more attention to high-value items and in so doing can split the population into two and apply statistical sampling plans with different confidence levels to each one. The auditor may have decided that payments to overseas agents are not adequately controlled and there is a significant risk that many such payments may fall foul of anticorruption legislation and may wish to examine a sample of these payments. The population of payments to 1755 overseas agents may be divided into the strata. The auditor may wish to examine all 60 payments over £80 000 and then extract a sample of 100 further payments using three value-based strata:

| Stratum | £ Range | Total amount | Initial sample |
|---|---|---|---|
| 1 | 0–9 999.99 | 2 800 000 | 28 |
| 2 | 10 000–29 999.99 | 3 500 000 | 35 |
| 3 | 30 000–79 999.99 | 3 700 000 | 37 |
|  | 80 000 and over | 20 800 000 |  |
|  |  | 30 800 000 | 100 |

The initial sample of 100 items distributed per value:

$2.8 + 3.5 + 3.7 = 10$, which gives $2.8/10 \times 100 = 28$ $3.5/10 \times 100 = 35$ $3.7/10 \times 100 = 37$

and then all 60 that are over £80 000.

**Cluster sampling** This is a convenient way of selecting items for testing where, once the number of transactions has been defined, they are then taken from one filing area. This may be a single drawer of a filing cabinet and is based on simple working practicalities.

**Interval sampling** Here the population should be homogeneous, with no cyclical bias or missing items. If we divide the population size by the sample size, the sampling interval is obtained and every nth item is chosen for testing. One might imagine a computer being asked to select, say, every 20th item from a particular file.

**Automated sampling** This may be seen as a selection technique where the auditor uses sampling software to set parameters, determine the number for testing, access the relevant file and then download the selected items into a separate spreadsheet for later analytical testing by the auditor.

## Setting Risk Parameters

Statistical sampling is based on probability theory and therefore one must set upper and lower limits within which the results may be placed. It is similar to saying that on average a die will fall on the number six on 1/6 occasions. With statistical sampling one has to set the criteria within which the results should be evaluated, and this falls under three basic parameters:

**Error rate** This is the level of error that one may expect from the population being tested. Error may be seen as, for example, the number of invoices that are incorrect. This is normally set at 5%

and most statistical sampling tables are based on this figure. If the actual error rate is different then a revision to the quoted risk boundaries has to be made. The rate is determined by the auditor and is based on pilot studies, discussions with management and the results of previous audits.

**Confidence**  Confidence is the degree to which the results derived from the sample will follow the trend in the actual population. A 95% confidence means that 95 out of every 100 items examined will reflect the population. The position on confidence levels is given in Table 9.4.

**TABLE 9.4**    Confidence levels.

| Level | Perception |
| --- | --- |
| Below 90% | Is too low to be of any real value |
| 90% | Is where the auditor knows a lot about the population but wishes to convince management |
| 95% | Is the level that is generally used and is high enough to satisfy the auditor and management |
| 99% | Is too high and will result in most of the population being selected |

**Precision**  This shows the margin within which the results can be quoted and defines the degree of accuracy that is required. It may be in terms of the quoted error being expressed as a figure taken from testing the sample plus or minus the degree of precision, say, 2%. The real result relative to the population will be somewhere within the lower and upper levels. If one needs to be accurate to 2% one may find an error in the sample of, say, £100, which may be quoted for the population as between £98 and £102. The level chosen will depend on the objective of the test and how the results are used.

**Extrapolation**  This occurs when results taken from a sample are grossed up and applied to the whole population. The average result from the sample is multiplied by the value of the population to give the estimated total error. Risk parameters are set by the auditor and depend on the test objective. It is common practice to use 5% error rate tables, with 95% confidence at plus or minus 2% precision. Using these standards, most statistically extrapolated results will be accepted by management.

## 9.8   Audit Testing and Statistical Sampling

The two main types of audit testing are compliance and substantive testing, although one may perform some walkthrough tests during the ascertainment stage. Note the following:

- **Compliance tests**   Here one is testing the existence or otherwise of a particular control. The test is of a yes/no nature where an attribute (i.e. control adherence) is either present or does not exist. An example may be a test to determine the number of purchase invoices that have not been authorized by a designated officer before being paid.
- **Substantive tests**   These tests are carried out to establish the extent to which the implications of a control weakness may be quantified. We may be concerned to discover the total value of purchase invoices incorrectly posted to the wrong year due to poor cut-off procedures.

These two testing conventions require different statistical sampling plans geared into the objectives of the tests. Compliance testing is concerned with specific attributes so that a frequency may be quoted. Substantive testing looks for variables and enables the auditor to quote a range of values from the test results. The sampling plans mentioned below may be placed in Table 9.5.

**TABLE 9.5**   The sampling plans.

| Compliance testing | Substantive testing |
| --- | --- |
| Attribute sampling | Variable sampling |
| Stop–go sampling | Difference estimates |
| Discovery sampling | Monetary unit sampling |

Statistical sampling is not a mandatory technique although it should not be ignored by the auditor as it can be used to comment on a system through the use of a relatively small sample. The audit department should define a clear policy on the use of this technique and where and how it should be applied, and this should appear in the audit manual. The use of automated statistical sampling via a suitable software package encourages auditors to use statistical sampling. If judgement sampling is, in the main, being applied this should be stated as clear policy having reviewed the applicability of statistical sampling.

## 9.9   Reporting Results of the Audit

Some auditors argue that the audit report is the fundamental end product of any audit and IIA Performance Standard 2400 states that: 'Internal auditors must communicate the engagement results.' In reality the impact of the audit should be the actual changes that are created as a result of the investment of audit resources and here the report forms just part of this process. Whatever the view, the fact is that audit reporting is one of those fundamental techniques that must be mastered by the auditor. Sawyer has made clear that:

> Reports are the auditor's opportunity to get management's undivided attention. That is how auditors should regard reporting – as an opportunity, not dreary drudgery – a perfect occasion to show management how.[3]

There are many components and principles that underlie audit reporting, the most important of which is the quality of audit work that has been carried out prior to the reporting stage. Reporting is important and a useful phrase to express this importance comes from the IIA Handbook Series:

> An auditor's greatest idea or discovery is only as effective as his or her ability to express the concept to others and elicit the desired response.[4]

### Interim Audit Reports

Before the full audit report is produced one would expect interim reports, particularly on larger projects. These have three main uses:

1. It forces the auditor to build the report as work is progressed. As such the findings are fresh in the auditor's mind as they appear and are captured in written format. This allows a

greater link between the audit report and underlying work that is being carried out by the auditor. Furthermore, it should be possible to complete a draft audit report quite soon after the fieldwork is finished and not have to wait unduly long periods for the report to be made available.

2. It keeps the audit manager up to date and allows interim reviews of work performed. If the audit has to be aborted or suspended for any reason, then it is possible to report the results to date very quickly. This will act as a position statement that may be picked up again when the audit is being resumed. The worst case scenario occurs where the auditor introduces the audit to managers and heightens their expectations, carries out detailed audit work and after several weeks appears to disappear completely. Just when the managers have forgotten the audit, a draft report appears on their desk that contains many surprises. The correct model is where the auditor briefs management at the end of each week on findings to date and general progress on the audit. This is where the interim report comes to the auditor's aid as a useful communication device.

3. In this way it may be given to the client and so act as a continuous report clearance device as well as bringing the client into the audit process itself. Furthermore, it is possible to produce the final draft shortly after conclusion of the fieldwork. This approach will also allow audit to comply with the IIA reporting standards, which suggest that nothing in the report should come as a surprise to management. In fact, the IIA's IPPF Performance Standards endorse this view and says that:

> **2410 – Criteria for Communicating:** Communications must include the engagement's objectives and scope as well as applicable conclusions, recommendations, and action plans.
>
> **2410.A1** – Final communication of engagement results must, where appropriate, contain internal auditors' overall opinion and/or conclusions.
>
> **2410.A2** – Internal auditors are encouraged to acknowledge satisfactory performance in engagement communications.
>
> **2410.A3** – When releasing engagement results to parties outside the organization, the communication must include limitations on distribution and use of the results.
>
> **2410.C1** – Communication of the progress and results of consulting engagements will vary in form and content depending upon the nature of the engagement and the needs of the client.

## Audit Assignment Reports

This is what most auditors think of when considering the topic of audit reports and is dealt with in some detail below:

1. **Executive summaries**   A two or three page summary can be attached to the front of the report or issued as a separate document. It provides a concise account of objectives, main conclusions and the steps that management should be taking. This recognizes that managers are busy and wish to take a shortcut in getting to grips with any material issues that may result from an audit. A groundbreaking article that helped focus audit effort to top executives was produced in 1997 by Francis X. Bossle and Alfred R. Michenzi in the 'One page audit report':

> Previously, our misguided audit goal was to create an all-inclusive final document that would make sense to all users, from the operating level all the way up to the CEO. We constructed

long narratives that gave everyone a detailed analysis of the audit findings. As a result, completing and distributing the final report usually required several months. Unfortunately, the report was often dated and of limited usefulness by the time it was eventually issued.... Our solution to this dilemma was to develop a series of one page audit reports.

1. **One Page Audit Report** – supplies executive management with a nuts and bolts summary of the audit findings and recommendations and covers – subject, responsible officer, scope, risk exposure, overall audit comment, significant audit recs, management response, planned follow up.
2. **Corrective Action Report** – addresses each audit finding and concerns and covers – title, observation, risk, recommendation, implementation date, management response, department responsible.
3. **Special Project Report** – addresses limited scope activities of internal audit, covering – subject, nature of request, procedures informed, key audit concerns, contribution of internal audit, follow up action.

Operating management reviews and comments on all three reports, but only the One Page Audit Report and the Special Project Report go to executive management... Our one page reporting process has become a win-win situation for everyone involved. Overall customer satisfaction with the efforts and work of our department has improved.[5]

2. **Follow-up reports** All audit work should be followed up and it is possible to establish a standardized reporting format to check on outstanding audit recommendations. These audits tend to be simple to perform but sensitive in nature. They involve forming a view on whether management has done all it promised to. Practice Advisory 2500.A1-1 deals with the follow-up process:

**2500.A1** – The chief audit executive must establish a follow-up process to monitor and ensure that management actions have been effectively implemented or that senior management has accepted the risk of not taking action.

1. Internal auditors determine whether management has taken action or implemented the recommendation. The internal auditor determines whether the desired results were achieved or if senior management or the board has assumed the risk of not taking action or implementing the recommendation.
2. Follow-up is a process by which internal auditors evaluate the adequacy, effectiveness, and timeliness of actions taken by management on reported observations and recommendations, including those made by external auditors and others. This process also includes determining whether senior management and/or the board have assumed the risk of not taking corrective action on reported observations.
3. The internal audit activity's charter should define the responsibility for follow-up. The chief audit executive (CAE) determines the nature, timing, and extent of follow-up, considering the following factors:

- Significance of the reported observation or recommendation.
- Degree of effort and cost needed to correct the reported condition.
- Impact that may result should the corrective action fail.
- Complexity of the corrective action.
- Time period involved.

1. The CAE is responsible for scheduling follow-up activities as part of developing engagement work schedules. Scheduling of follow-up is based on the risk and exposure involved, as well as the degree of difficulty and the significance of timing in implementing corrective action.
2. Where the CAE judges that management's oral or written response indicates that action taken is sufficient when weighed against the relative importance of the observation or recommendation, internal auditors may follow up as part of the next engagement.
3. Internal auditors ascertain whether actions taken on observations and recommendations remedy the underlying conditions. Follow-up activities should be appropriately documented.

It may be necessary to criticize management where it has failed to implement agreed recommendations while at the same time maintaining a degree of diplomacy. It is necessary to weigh up all excuses for a lack of action before deciding whether management has acted reasonably. The follow-up process is crucial and IIA Performance Standard 2500 states that the chief audit executive must establish and maintain a system to monitor the disposition of results communicated to management. Assurance and consulting work is covered:

**2500.A1** – The chief audit executive must establish a follow-up process to monitor and ensure that management actions have been effectively implemented or that senior management has accepted the risk of not taking action.

**2500.C1** – The internal audit activity must monitor the disposition of results of consulting engagements to the extent agreed upon with the client.

Follow-up procedures revolve around the view of residual risk. Where the internal auditor has failed to convince client management that the risk needs addressing then any associated audit recommendations may not be agreed. Where the internal auditor is convinced that this level of residual risk is outside the remit of the corporate risk appetite then the matter should be reported upwards, even up to the board. Performance Standard 2600 deals with this tricky issue and says:

When the chief audit executive believes that senior management has accepted a level of residual risk that may be unacceptable to the organization, the chief audit executive must discuss the matter with senior management. If the decision regarding residual risk is not resolved, the chief audit executive must report the matter to the board for resolution.

### Performance standard 2410 covers communicating audit work:

Communications must include the engagement's objectives and scope as well as applicable conclusions, recommendations, and action plans.

There are other standards that provide more detailed requirements depending on the type of audit in question:

**2410.A1** – Final communication of engagement results must, where appropriate, contain internal auditors' overall opinion and/or conclusions.

**2410.A2** – Internal auditors are encouraged to acknowledge satisfactory performance in engagement communications.

**2410.A3** – When releasing engagement results to parties outside the organization, the communication must include limitations on distribution and use of the results.

**2410.C1** – Communication of the progress and results of consulting engagements will vary in form and content depending upon the nature of the engagement and the needs of the client.

**Final published assignment report** A final report should be prepared along with a clear definition of reporting lines and people who should be given copies. There are many audit units guilty of producing 'draft' reports that remain in circulation without a final version, much to the confusion of all involved with this document. Where there are problems with the accuracy of the final report these should be corrected. The IIA Performance Standard 2421 sets a direction here: 'If a final communication contains a significant error or omission, the chief audit executive must communicate corrected information to all parties who received the original communication.'

It may also be an idea to consider any developments that have occurred since the completion of the audit fieldwork and refer to them in the final report if appropriate. Meanwhile, two IIA standards address the publication of audit reports to external parties:

**2201.A1** – When planning an engagement for parties outside the organization, internal auditors must establish a written understanding with them about objectives, scope, respective responsibilities, and other expectations, including restrictions on distribution of the results of the engagement and access to engagement records.

**2201.C1** – Internal auditors must establish an understanding with consulting engagement clients about objectives, scope, respective responsibilities, and other client expectations. For significant engagements, this understanding must be documented.

**Follow-up** The process is still not complete until we have set up a follow-up routine in line with best audit practice. These standards can be mentioned within the report or the accompanying letter.

**Quarterly reports** The audit report should feed into the quarterly reporting cycle that seeks to summarize what has been found and reported on in the relevant three-month period. Reference to the quarterly plan makes this a dynamic process that is linked to a defined reference point.

**Annual report** The above is equally true for the annual reporting cycle that again should be set within the context of the plan for the year in question.

**Management action** We arrive at the true audit product in terms of management action based on the audit report. All else is simply to set a foundation within which this action may be stimulated by the auditor. The objective of the reporting process is to get management to act on audit's advice. A report that suggests no action is required is just as significant as one that asks for many changes. Assurances (of good control) allow management to channel resources into riskier areas. The reality of corporate life is that there are many reports and other types of communications that bombard managers.

The CAE is responsible for communicating the final results to individuals who can ensure that the results are given due consideration. This will depend on the type of organization, the type of audit work performed and the circumstances of the audit. Ordinarily the report will go to the line manager for the area under review and the next tier up.

The audit terms of reference and clear qualifications set out within the report will clarify the extent of audit coverage. There is a variety of views and approaches adopted by audit report writers and each has justification. The audit role may be derived from these three objectives. The underlying goal may be to act as a catalyst for all material improvements to controls necessary to ensure that systems objectives are achieved. The four main functions of the audit report are:

- To *assure* management that business risks are well controlled.
- To *alert* them to areas where this is not the case and there are defined risk exposures.
- To *advise* them on steps necessary to improve risk management strategies.
- To support *action* plans prepared by client management.

The internal audit report should reflect the new agenda of corporate governance, risk management and control. Jeffrey Ridley has provided advice on this matter:

> This year watch your language. Create your own dictionary of words and phrases, based on today's internal auditing agenda of 'assurance', 'consultancy' and 'training'. One linked to the IIA Inc.'s Glossary and the new image of internal auditing. One that all will understand. Use this to link all internal auditing processes, from charter, recruitment and training to planning, risk assessment, audit programmes and reporting. Use it to influence all those to whom you report and with whom you co-ordinate, including your audit committee, external auditing and other auditors. Use it to create the vision for your services and to market internal auditing professionalism for 2001 and beyond.[6]

## Underlying Components of Action

The audit report is the result of a comprehensive process and is a means to an end. There are several clear parts of the audit process that directly impact on the audit report: this working paper is called a risk-based internal control evaluation schedule (RBICES) and contains details of each major control weakness that appears as an audit finding in the published report. The aim is to lead the auditor into creative thinking so that problems may be solved. A logical foundation will have been built, which these ideas can be founded on. The RBICES will form the main reference document for the wrap-up meeting, where material issues will be discussed with the auditee. This working document will also feed directly into the draft audit report in that it will set out what was done, what was found, what it means and what now needs to be done. The stage at which the ICES appears in the report drafting process may be illustrated in Figure 9.9.

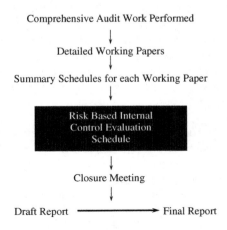

**FIGURE 9.9**    Risk-based internal control evaluation schedule.

The RBICES that we described in Chapter 8 should form a high-level summary of the working papers (properly cross-referenced), which lends itself to being fed directly into the audit report itself. Moreover relevant material, which will enter into the report's standards, findings, conclusions and recommendations, will be found in the RBICES that promotes a structured approach to drafting the formal audit report. The auditor should point management in the right direction and stimulate effective management action. It is possible to adjust the tone of audit recommendations and choose from:

- We recommend...
- We strongly recommend...
- It is advisable for management to...
- It is essential that management...
- Management needs to urgently address...
- Management should consider...

Auditors may make many recommendations and these should be structured for maximum impact, with the most important first. There should be a few enabling steps that management should take and these should be detailed in the opening part of the recommendations. They should be designed to place management in a position to effect the various recommendations. This would also appear in any executive summary and should not consist of more than two or three items in the discussion mode. The remaining recommendations should follow in order of priority (see the section below on change management). One useful approach is to document a series of recommendations for each main section of the report and then repeat them as the final part of the executive summary (cross-referenced to the main report). Recommendations should be presented to create maximum impact. There are many busy executives who are primarily interested in what is being recommended, and why.

## The Clearance Process

The draft audit report, once reviewed, has to be cleared and management given the opportunity to comment on the contents. The findings should not come as a surprise to management and it is advisable to bring them to the manager's attention as they arise. Regular progress reports (probably oral) and a brief meeting at the end of each week will assist this process. A wrap-up meeting with the line manager should be held at the end of the audit, where the main findings are discussed. The reviewed draft should be sent to the line manager (only) and an informal meeting held to discuss this as soon as possible after completion of the work. Factual matters should be dealt with and the auditor may well revise the draft as a result. The auditor's conclusions will only change where the factual corrections materially affect audit findings. Once this has occurred a further draft should be formally sent to those affected by the work, including the next tier of management. Formal written comments will be taken on board and a final report published. This is a useful technique for involving the actual operational manager as the report will be more reliable and we would have hopefully secured this officer's full support before it goes to a wider audience. Note that where management accepts without question all audit recommendations, this may mean they are not particularly interested in the results and wish to get rid of the auditor. Effective action normally starts with close discussions with management on each audit recommendation. Again see the section below on change management for a different perspective on this issue. Management is entitled to choose not to follow audit recommendations and in this instance it is the auditor's responsibility to ensure they understand the implications and are prepared to assume the associated risk. Management will then assume full responsibility for this documented decision and this issue may be brought to the attention of the audit committee.

## Formulating the Action Plan

It is a good idea to form an agreed action plan with management based on the audit. This allows management to take over the audit recommendations and so be fully involved in implementing them. An action plan may be devised during the drafting procedure and once agreed may be included in the published report. Where management is allowed to form its own action plan, this becomes a very efficient way of getting audit recommendations implemented, although we would expect a degree of negotiation by both sides. Accordingly the auditor should work out which recommendations should be pursued and which may be partly given up for a greater good. The best solution is to include the action plan within the executive summary as part of the agreed solution and we would look for items such as work required, by whom, deadlines and reporting lines as a way of ensuring that the recommendations will come about. Once complete the action plan should belong to management as it seeks to embark on the necessary workload.

## 9.10   Structuring the Audit Report

The flow of information contained in an audit report should follow a logical path that takes the reader through the audit process itself. There are many ways that this information may be presented, although the principle of providing a logical flow of problems, causes, effects and required action should stand. A defined structure for audit reports should be implemented by the CAE and this should be followed when drafting audit reports. This will vary from department to department depending on the nature of the work that is carried out and the type of officers who will be receiving the audit report. One example is shown in Table 9.6.

**TABLE 9.6**   Report sections.

| Section | Coverage |
| --- | --- |
| One | This will contain the executive summary to the report. |
| Two | This will outline the objective, scope, approach and work done. |
| Three | This will contain a background to the area under review. |
| Appendices | Restrict these to the minimum. |

The CAE should adopt a suitable policy on responses from the client, which may be:

- **Incorporated into the report**   Here adjustment is made throughout the report to reflect the comments received from management. A note to this effect may also appear in the report, which is a technically correct approach, but can lead to delays in achieving a final draft for publication. There will also be some comments that the auditor does not agree with, and again the way that these are presented will have to be thought about.
- **Built into a management action plan**   The important part of the report is the action plan and it is possible to build management's views into this section without making numerous adjustments to the main body of the report.

- **Included as an appendix** A convenient method for dealing with responses is simply to include them as an appendix to the report. The problem here is that they may be taken out of context if a form of audit responses to the comments is not also included. We may imagine, however, that a continuous exchange of memoranda based on responses to responses could become an embarrassment to all sides and this should be avoided.

Some audit departments send the draft for consultation without the executive summary and formulate recommendations after the client has been able to comment on the findings. The participative approach comes into its own where the auditor forms joint recommendations with the client after discussing the findings. This agreed action plan is then reported in the executive summary. Note that where there has been close cooperation throughout the audit, problems with formal responses will probably not arise. One IIA standard insists that each paragraph in the report is attached to a unique paragraph number from one onwards, for ease of reference. Practice Advisory 2410-1 (extracts only) gives some sound advice on audit reporting and possible communications criteria:

> Although the format and content of the final engagement communications varies by organization or type of engagement, they are to contain, at a minimum, the purpose, scope, and results of the engagement.

> Final engagement communications may include background information and summaries. Background information may identify the organizational units and activities reviewed and provide explanatory information. It may also include the status of observations, conclusions, and recommendations from prior reports and an indication of whether the report covers a scheduled engagement or is responding to a request. Summaries are balanced representations of the communication's content.

> Engagement observations and recommendations emerge by a process of comparing criteria (the correct state) with condition (the current state). Whether or not there is a difference, the internal auditor has a foundation on which to build the report. When conditions meet the criteria, communication of satisfactory performance may be appropriate. Observations and recommendations are based on the following attributes:

> **Criteria:** The standards, measures, or expectations used in making an evaluation and/or verification (the correct state)

> **Condition:** The factual evidence that the internal auditor found in the course of the examination (the current state). Cause: The reason for the difference between expected and actual conditions.

> **Effect:** The risk or exposure the organization and/or others encounter because the condition is not consistent with the criteria (the impact of the difference). In determining the degree of risk or exposure, internal auditors consider the effect their engagement observations and recommendations may have on the organization's operations and financial statements. Observations and recommendations can include engagement client accomplishments, related issues, and supportive information.

IIA standard 2420 on the quality of communications states:

> Communications must be accurate, objective, clear, concise, constructive, complete, and timely.

The interpretation explains this concept:

> Accurate communications are free from errors and distortions and are faithful to the underlying facts. Objective communications are fair, impartial, and unbiased and are the result of a

fair-minded and balanced assessment of all relevant facts and circumstances. Clear communications are easily understood and logical, avoiding unnecessary technical language and providing all significant and relevant information. Concise communications are to the point and avoid unnecessary elaboration, superfluous detail, redundancy, and wordiness. Constructive communications are helpful to the engagement client and the organization and lead to improvements where needed. Complete communications lack nothing that is essential to the target audience and include all significant and relevant information and observations to support recommendations and conclusions. Timely communications are opportune and expedient, depending on the significance of the issue, allowing management to take appropriate corrective action.

Audit reporting procedures play a crucial role in the success of audits. The reporting mode should be geared to the culture of the organization and the needs of management. We have set out the minimum information that the auditor needs to consider when acquiring expertise on communicating the results of audit work as required under audit standards. We should also refer to the internal audit department's own reporting standard, which will reflect the audit role agreed with the organization.

## Presentations as Part of the Audit Clearance Procedures

One approach to audit presentations is to use them in the report drafting procedure to involve management and get an interactive response from them:

1. Complete field work with ongoing discussion with management on findings as they arise.
2. Draft a report that sets out work done, findings and recommendations.
3. Hold a presentation where the report is discussed, concentrating on the outline recommendations as the most important part. Give out the draft report at this meeting and 'sell the ideas'.
4. Ask management to consider the detailed report and meet again for its response. An action plan should then be formulated.
5. Review the report to take on board any matters that management has brought to your attention.
6. Send the report out for wider consultation with all who feature.
7. Prepare final report for formal publication.

There is no point in convening a presentation where the relationship between internal audit and the client is impoverished or has broken down. The presentation then becomes point scoring with little constructive work possible. There is nothing to be gained from a presentation where the underlying audit has not been professionally done. Where findings are flawed, recommendations unworkable and/or the auditor has not been objective, the work cannot be defended in a presentation.

## 9.11  Audit Committee Reporting

Activity reports are produced periodically by the CAE to formally report the activities of the internal audit department. These would typically go to the audit committee and may be based around an annual report and four separate quarterly reports.

## Quarterly Reporting Cycle

The quarterly reports will tend to include:

**Planning and control matters for the audit department** This will explain whether there are issues and developments that affect the scope and effectiveness of the audit function now and in the near future. This may be seen as a form of self-audit and if an internal or external review of audit has been completed then this will also feature in the quarterly report.

**An outline of audit's performance for the quarter** This provides results of performance indicators that measure quality and quantity of audit work, normally using a balanced scorecard.

**Statistics on types of work performed and departments charged** This will indicate the work that has been performed over each main department/section. These figures can be compared to planned profiles as a way of gauging the success and viability of the audit function. We would also expect statistical analysis to be carried out over periods as well as between components (e.g. types of work).

**Brief summary of reports issued** A brief account of the conclusions from final cleared reports may be provided for information. It may be possible to enclose the executive summaries of these reports as appendices to the quarterly audit report. The audit committee may take action where there are matters that remain unresolved arising from audits that have been carried out. However, it should be noted that audit credibility may be damaged where we have 'cried wolf' too often.

**Details of staff turnover** Information concerning starters, leavers, training programmes and exam success, transfers and any skills gaps should be included since it may have a direct impact on the audit plans. Where additional resources are required to cover audit plans then this should be discussed before a formal bid is submitted via the agreed mechanism.

**Overall productivity per output within time budgets** This will be based on achieving the quarterly plan, the monthly plan and the requirements of the assignment plan. Thus actuals will be set against the plan and conclusions drawn about any variances that are so highlighted. Managerial concerns such as budget overruns, excessive unrecoverable time and incomplete audits will have to be fully explained in the quarterly report, which will act as a high-level control over the audit function.

Many are now seeking to assess internal audit's performance in terms of outcomes rather than outputs. For example, some people feel that an organization should measure the state of its control environment (through surveys and assessment) and assess the extent to which it is improving. If audit is contributing to a better understanding of internal control, compliance and the management of risks generally throughout the organization then targets may be set and considered in respect of these matters. Richard Chambers, the president and CEO of the IIA, shares his personal reflections and insights on the internal audit profession in regular posts. His remarks in a post entitled ' Effective Communications: An Enduring Challenge for Internal Auditors' (posted on 11 August 2010) gave some important tips for improving the way we communicate. Richard has often warned about some of the observations from audit committee members, management officials and others:

- Internal audit reports are too voluminous or not well written.
- Too many reports or too much content is provided to the audit committee.
- Internal audit results are 'not synthesized' in a way that would permit users to 'connect the dots'.
- Internal auditors are 'introverts by nature' and reluctant to communicate informally.
- The CAE and senior internal audit staff are not very effective at delivering presentations.
- The CAE is reluctant to offer/issue opinions.

He goes on to offer some useful ideas to counter these criticisms and enhance internal auditors' communications style and content, including the following ideas:

- Flexible and customized reporting formats – including electronic reports or summary reports with hyperlinks to more in-depth discussion of key findings.
- Synthesized reports to audit committees with ratings or indicators of reports to which audit committee members should pay particular attention.
- Capstone or summary reports that 'connect the dots' in terms of the overall effectiveness of internal controls or risk management.
- Regular informal meetings with executive management and business unit leaders to build relationships and continuously identify emerging risks.
- Striving to develop succinct and visually impactful presentations for management and audit committee presentations.
- Annual opinions on the effectiveness of internal controls. However, care should be taken to ensure that users of such reports clearly understand pertinent limitations.

## 9.12  New Developments

One emerging topic is the growing importance of corporate assurance maps. Closely related to positioning the audit function to add value to the business is high-impact auditing, which derives from a strategic focus on the corporate risk management process. It is a good idea to get straight to the point on performing fieldwork. Gone are the days of working through a detailed checklist of tests that are applied to the audit as a standard routine. There are still many audit checklists in existence but their use is being questioned as we move to a risk-based approach. Audit fieldwork can be boiled down to five basic elements:

1. Being clear about the operational objectives in the area being audited and how these objectives create and preserve value for the business.
2. Understanding the business model in place and the way risk is dealt with through the adopted business strategy and effective leadership in delivering the strategy through performance review and meaningful incentives.
3. Working out how the risk management process ensures that these controls work to retain risk within an acceptable risk appetite that the process owner is then accountable for.
4. Considering how the manager obtains an oversight of the way the operation is governed, compliance is ensured and how assurances along with significant risks are reported upwards.

5. Reviewing the business management reports for consistency, reliability and whether the reports themselves enable management to make good decisions on high-risk issues and account for their responsibilities.

The auditor may want to take a view on each of these elements although it is the final point, 5, that is most interesting. The auditor should encourage business managers to be a firm part of the assurance-giving process along with the other assurance teams that work in the organization. However, what do we do when the business has not got a handle on risk management in that it is risk immature?

> Let us consider risk immaturity. All organisations are risk immature to some degree. Managers across many sectors fail to set clear objectives, identify risks that flow from those objectives and adequately mitigate those risks. Looking at recent corporate failures, including an entire business sector, can we really argue that risk maturity is prevalent, or even dominant? As the private sector suffers from an economic recession, it is clear that many management teams have failed to take risk management seriously, or have struggled to apply it effectively. The public sector, as it shortly enters its recession, is likely to be similar.... These circumstances mean that internal audit must have a new paradigm and professional culture that recognises risk immaturity. Internal audit needs to adjust to the reality of a risk immature world. This is not to say that risk immaturity is acceptable or desirable, more to recognise that it is more prevalent than currently publicly acknowledged or accepted.... I think, therefore, it is time for the profession to recognise the risk immaturity of many organisations and their management teams. Now is the opportunity, with such a widespread recognition of risk management failure in so many organisations, for internal auditors to lead in the identification of nominal or poor risk management. Internal audit should be brave enough to report where risks are not being assessed and managed properly rather than being complicit in the box-ticking risk management exercise undertaken in some organisations. Internal auditors should be recognised as the risk management professionals that they are.[7]

The auditor needs to work out how well the business is doing in managing risk and providing an account of this task. During the audit, it is possible to consider the way assurances are being provided on controls and whether there is an integrated approach to this task. Health and safety, legal compliance, IT security and other teams may each have had an input to opining on controls in various business units. Some of the risks that are considered during the audit may have been reviewed by other assurance teams and it may be possible to view their results as part of the audit fieldwork process. This approach is organic and is far removed from the old approach of working through a checklist of audit tests to complete the fieldwork. Some auditors argue that they use checklists to make sure they have covered all key areas or have completed all important tasks. Others develop their own checklist as they progress through the audit fieldwork rather than use an off-the-shelf version. Still others refuse to use any form of checklist at all. At the end of the audit fieldwork, the audit may be able to report on whether:

1. Operational objectives are clear and they create and preserve value for the business.
2. The business model and the adopted business strategy are delivering these objectives through effective leadership and meaningful performance incentives.
3. Controls work to retain risk within an acceptable risk appetite.
4. The manager is able to govern the operation and provide assurances that significant risks are addressed and, where appropriate, reported upwards.
5. Management reports are consistent, reliable and lead to risk-smart decision making.

This is far removed from audit reports that simply reproduce detailed lists of minor errors in specific processes that need to be put right by management. The auditor is really looking for the assurance map that reflects the oversight responsibilities across the organization. This map is either present or needs to be developed to show:

- The types of assurances required by the board.
- Who gives these assurances and in what format.
- How these assurances are verified to ensure they are entirely reliable and kept up to date.
- How executives can be assured that reckless behaviour is not happening in the organization.

This last point is significant. How can a board know if people they employ are exceeding the risk appetite, i.e. they are being reckless with corporate resources? Senior Supervisors Group, of banking representatives from Canada, France, Germany, Japan, Switzerland, the UK and the US, have commented that:

> A key weakness in governance stemmed from what several senior managers admitted was a disparity between the risks that their firms took and those that their boards of directors perceived the firms to be taking. In addition, supervisors saw insufficient evidence of active board involvement in setting the risk appetite for firms in a way that recognizes the implications of that risk taking. Specifically, only rarely did supervisors see firms share with their boards and senior management a) robust measures of risk exposures (and related limits), b) the level of capital that the firm would need to maintain after sustaining a loss of the magnitude of the risk measure, and c) the actions that management could take to restore capital after sustaining such a loss. Supervisors believe that active board involvement in determining the risk tolerance of the firm is critical to ensuring that discipline is sustained in the face of future market pressures for excessive risk taking.[8]

With the increasing reliance on assurances it is clear that they must be reliable and give value to the business. Essentially, assurances give confidence to the recipient that all is well, or that current action is in hand, or that something new needs to be done. It is implicit in the assurance that the provider of these assurances is professional, independent and has carried out sufficient examinations to be able to hold an opinion, and that there is documentation that supports the assurances and the process from which they were developed. The big question, then, is can the summation of individual audits enable the CAE to provide assurances that comment on the entire organization? Or should the CAE start to prepare corporate-wide reviews of the assurance infrastructure and implant audit work within these maps to give a holistic picture of the quality of risk management within the organization? One way of getting to grips with the assurance map is to take the various committees and forums that report to the main board and argue that these bodies represent the assurance infrastructure in that each committee is there to give assurances on a major aspect of the corporate issues that are uppermost in the minds of the board. Internal audit may be moving to a position where they will be reviewing the extent to which these committees work in giving assurances on areas that they are charged to take care of. Although internal audit can never set the level of acceptable risk, it can comment on the extent to which managed risk is aligned to what is viewed as acceptable by the board. It may be the case that the internal auditor will need to select a position from one of four points:

1. Being part of the corporate assurance map by giving assurances in defined parts of the business.
2. Coordinating the assurance map by ensuring all assurance teams work together and fit into the enterprise-wide risk management process.

3. Reviewing the assurance-giving process to ensure it makes the best use of available resources and gives the board the service it requires.
4. Leading the assurance process that seeks to review and help improve the enterprise risk management process.

## Summary and Conclusions

This chapter has provided an introduction to audit fieldwork, from planning through to performing and reporting the engagement. Note that IIA Practice Advisory 2210.A1 suggests that internal auditors consider management's assessment of risks relevant to the activity under review. The internal auditor also considers:

- The reliability of management's assessment of risk.
- Management's process for monitoring, reporting, and resolving risk and control issues.
- Management's reporting of events that exceeded the limits of the organization's risk appetite and management's response to those reports.
- Risks in related activities relevant to the activity under review.

The need to build the state of risk management into the audit approach calls for some flexibility in the way audits are undertaken. We have mentioned interviewing and the wider task of ascertaining the system, evaluation, testing techniques and communicating the results. In one sense, we have tried to write about something that is impossible to capture in one idea, i.e. the combination of risk-based systems audits, reviews, investigations, consulting projects and short exercises that typify the internal auditors' work. Moreover, there really is no such thing as audit fieldwork. There are only different types, and approaches to audit work suit different contexts and challenges. One possible approach is to frame the audit work around a model that we have called risk-assessed control evaluation (RaCE), as shown in Figure 9.10.

The model is an interpretation of an audit approach that does not start with the need to 'catch people out'. It is based on adapting the approach to the context in question and moving between the extremes of *audit review, facilitating* the client's assessment to simply *validating* the current self-assessment process. Using the alpha references A to L, the RaCE is explained in outline:

**A:** First identify exactly what business area is in the annual audit plan. This may be a section, team, project, process, change programme, local office, establishment, contract, business unit or whatever is deemed to be a distinct auditable area.

**B:** The next step is to find out where the business area (BA) stands on the corporate risks database in terms of relative risk in the organization. This should have been done to form the basis of the annual audit plan.

**C:** It may then be possible to assess the control environment in the BA. COSO and CoCo each have assessment questions and guidance that can be used to judge whether the BA is on a sound footing in terms of having an environment that reflects the corporate position in a trustworthy and reliable manner.

**D:** The next stage is to assess the extent to which risk and control assessment is understood and practised in the BA. Where there is a developed risk assessment procedure and good appreciation

RISK and CONTROL EVALUATION

A. Business Area
B. Corporate Risk Database
C. Control environment
D. Business risk awareness
E. Business objectives

AUDIT APPROACH
AUDIT REVIEW ←→ VALIDATION
FACILITATION

| F<br>RISKS | G<br>RISK RATING | H<br>CONTROL STANDARDS | I<br>KEY CONTROLS | J<br>RaCE & TESTING | K<br>RISK OWNER | L<br>INTEGRATED ACTION PLANS |
|---|---|---|---|---|---|---|
| | | | | | | |
| | | | | | | |
| | | | | | | |
| | | | | | | |
| | | | | | | |
| | | | | | | |
| | | | | | | |

Comments..........................................................

**FIGURE 9.10** Risk and control evaluation.

by managers, supervisors and staff generally, then we can start to judge where the BA stands in terms of having a robust risk management process in place and reliable risk registers.

**E:** This is simply isolating the agreed business objective of the BA in question.

Armed with the knowledge secured from the assessments A to E above, the audit approach may be determined. This may entail performing a standard audit (Audit review) where the control environment and level of risk appreciation is such that it is not possible to rely on a facilitated self-assessment review. Where the BA has a good control environment but is not equipped to carry out the risk assessment, then a facilitated (Facilitation) approach may be provided by the audit team to help the client get up to par. Where both the control environment promotes integrity, compliance and competence and self-assessment is being applied, then audit may simply validate (Validation) the self-assessment already used by the BA and concentrate on key controls that have been deemed important in managing the more material risks.

**F:** Risks to the achievement of business objectives are defined and updated to reflect current changes. For well-performing BAs the risk assessment will be based more on the future strategy, since the current position is already successfully managed.

**G:** Risk rating is simply the degree of materiality and likelihood that forms the basis for most risk assessment models.

**H:** Control standards are mechanisms that may be applied to managing the business risks that have been isolated in G.

The tasks F to H may be performed by the auditor (for the Audit approach), a convened workshop of client staff facilitated by the auditor (Facilitated approach) or through an examination of the current risk assessment already carried out by the client management (Validation audit approach).

**I:** This involves identifying the key controls in use.

**J:** The evaluation stage comes next, where the key controls are considered in terms of whether they are sufficient to manage the risks, as compared to the control standards developed in H. Testing is carried out using the audit approach, while audit effort will focus on judging whether the client is able to assess compliance under the current arrangements. Where the RaCE is found to be sound on a self-assessed basis, then the auditor may focus on validation and may perform some limited independent testing to check that controls are working properly.

**K:** Each risk assessment should be assigned to a risk (or process) owner so that it is clear where responsibility and accountability lie.

**L:** This part of the RaCE simply states that action required to manage risks is integrated within the current performance management arrangements. The way this is done is entirely up to the manager so long as the risks in question are dealt with in an efficient and effective manner in line with the corporate risk policy and defined risk appetite.

Where the auditor captures the above information in the RaCE, this process can drive the audit so that ascertainment is about identifying the system and risk (e.g. the flowchart and interview record), evaluation features in column J cross-referenced to the auditors' records and testing schedules are referenced to the lines in column J. Audit recommendations are based around findings from the evaluation and test results and feature in the final column L. The audit report is then a representation of the RaCE and describes the system, the risks, how they are managed and anything more that needs to be done to help ensure business objectives can be achieved. Where the RaCE has been performed by the client staff and facilitated by the auditor, it becomes a joint effort between audit and client with some formal testing performed by the auditor. Where the RaCE has already been recently performed by the client, the auditor validates the work, updates the RaCE, performs selective testing and then is able to provide assurances on the adequacy of risk management and the underlying systems of internal control. The RaCE process depends on all parts of the organization embracing the risk management concept and using internal audit to assist this task with a mixture of assurance and consulting input, depending on which approach best suits the business area in question. In this way the auditor:

- Recognizes that some business areas can be relied on to self-assess their systems and audit only needs to validate (and check) the arrangements in place.
- Helps those business areas that need to develop their risk assessment practices and so assesses their progress at the same time.
- Reviews areas where there are obvious problems and makes recommendations to improve the control environment and get risk management practices put in place. Audit will be concerned that the integrity and competence of people within the business area is properly developed.

In this way, audit field work may then be performed in a way that is both flexible and dynamic and makes sense to the client manager, board and the audit committee. The Appendix contains a brief case study using the RaCE approach.

## Endnotes

1. Flesher, Dale (1996) *Internal Auditing: A One-Semester Course*, Florida: The Institute of Internal Auditors, p. 149.
2. Burley-Allen, Madelyn (1995) *Listening – The Forgotten Skill*, New York: John Wiley & Sons, Inc.
3. Sawyer, Lawrence B. and Dittenhofer, Mortimer A., Assisted by Scheiner, James H. (1996) *Sawyer's Internal Auditing*, 4th edition, Florida: The Institute of Internal Auditors.
4. Anderson, Urton and Chapman, Christy (2002) *Implementing the Professional Practices Framework*, IIA Handbook Series, Florida: The Institute of Internal Auditors, p. 167.
5. Bossle, Francis X. and Michenzi, Alfred R. 'One page audit report'. *Internal Auditor*, April 1997, pp. 37–41.
6. Ridley. Jeffrey, 'Mind your language'. *Internal Auditing and Business Risk*, January 2001, p. 13.
7. John Buchanan tells Neil Baker what he looks for in a head of internal audit, August 2009, pp. 27–31.
8. *Risk Management Lessons from the Global Banking Crisis of 2008*, Senior Supervisors Group, 21 October 2009, p. 4, published by the Financial Stability Board.

# Chapter 10

# MEETING THE CHALLENGE

## Introduction

Our final chapter provides a brief account of some of the challenges for the profession based on comments from writers from the internal audit community and beyond. Note that all references to IIA definitions, code of ethics, IIA attribute and performance standards, practice advisories and practice guides relate to the International Professional Practices Framework (IPPF) prepared by the Institute of Internal Auditors in 2009. The areas that are touched on include:

10.1 The New Dimensions of Internal Auditing
10.2 The Audit Reputation
10.3 Globalization
10.4 Providing Audit Assurances
10.5 Meeting the Challenge
        Summary and Conclusions

## 10.1 The New Dimensions of Internal Auditing

We accept that internal audit must deliver added value to the organization and this is defined by the IIA as:

> Value is provided by improving opportunities to achieve organizational objectives, identifying operational improvement, and/or reducing risk exposure through both assurance and consulting services.

Against this measure is the changing context of internal auditing which is summed up in the IIA's work on the context for internal auditing competency frameworks, in Chapter 5 of the IIA Handbook Series on *Implementing the Professional Practices Framework*:

| Past Focus | Additional Focus |
|---|---|
| hard controls | soft controls |
| control evaluation | self-assessment |
| control | risk |
| risk | context |
| risk threats | risk opportunities |
| past | future |
| review | preview |
| detective | preventive |
| operational audit | strategy audit |

| | |
|---|---|
| auditor | consultant |
| imposition | invitation |
| persuasion | negotiation |
| independence | value |
| audit knowledge | business knowledge |
| catalyst | change facilitator |
| transaction | processes |
| control activities | management controls |
| control | risk |
| consciousness | consciousness[1] |

This sets the new dimensions of internal auditing as the concepts on the right-hand side become a benchmark for each chief audit executive (CAE) to consider.

## 10.2   The Audit Reputation

There is a view that the organization of the future will revolve around its reputation and that the so-called chief risk officer could become the chief reputation officer. In turn, the internal audit shop will have to consider its own reputation and what it means to the organization. William E. Chadwick has considered the importance of the audit image:

> Internal auditors should be proud of the contributions they make to the internal controls of an organization. Unfortunately, they rarely receive the recognition they deserve, because their accomplishments often are overshadowed by the bad news they must impart. Therefore, it is important for internal auditors to educate their clients on the value of internal auditing and build relationships that can withstand a negative audit. Using humor is a great way to begin that process. Internal auditing doesn't have to be doom and gloom. Auditors need to let the world in on this well-kept secret and, at the same time, improve their image and enhance communication with their clients.[2]

The internal auditor helps drive and is driven by the corporate governance agenda. In the past auditors would define their role and responsibilities by considering what they would most enjoy doing and what fitted their skills base. Nowadays, the internal auditor can only really view their role by reference to societal expectations and the challenge is being able to judge how business and public services will develop. Richard Chambers, the president and CEO of the IIA, shares his personal reflections and insights on the internal audit profession in regular posts. His remarks in a post entitled 'Beyond bean counting' (posted on 26 July 2010) gives some important tips for moving away from the bean counting image some have of internal auditors to develop business acumen and much more professional credibility:

- Become a 'sponge' for information about the business. Read and learn everything you can about your organization and the industry in which it operates. While a typical 10K report for a publicly traded company can present a lot of dry reading, it also presents a 'treasure chest' of information about the business and strategic risks facing your company.
- Seek out variety in your internal audit assignments. While it is great to become an expert in a specific area of business operations, you will be even more valuable if your expertise spans multiple areas of business operations.

- Be passionate about every internal audit assignment. At the Postal Service, those auditors who truly impressed management were the ones who quickly became conversant enough to discuss business risks and controls with 20-year veterans of the business.
- Seek rotational assignments in business operations. As much as we would like to think we can learn everything we need to know about the business by wearing an internal audit hat, there is simply no substitute for hands-on experience.
- Identify your own gaps in understanding the business, and seek out training or other professional development opportunities. As the newly appointed IG at the Tennessee Valley Authority in 2001, I enrolled in a basic utilities course so that I could better understand the fundamentals of electric power generation, transmission, and distribution. Certainly no one directed me to do it. However, I felt it was critical for me to understand the essence of the company for which I was the newly appointed chief audit executive.
- Be patient. Gaining comprehensive knowledge of the business and enhancing your overall business acumen takes time.

PricewaterhouseCoopers considered new developments in their 2010 report, *State of the Internal Audit Profession*, which noted that:

Among the activities most performed for boards and audit committees were assessing key enterprise risks, measuring risk-mitigation effectiveness, assessing ethics and codes of conduct, and reviewing and assessing IT governance.

However, PwC go on to warn that:

... there remain a number of areas where many internal audit departments can increase their contribution to and support of corporate governance. These include work in the executive and board compensation area, training and orientation of the board and audit committee, and benchmarking and facilitating board and committee self-assessments. What is clear, though, is an expectation for better clarity and context for risk assessment to bring a strategic focus to the effort. While management has become accustomed to answering the age-old question – what keeps you up at night – our research shows that there is a better approach as highlighted in the accompanying case study. Another particular area of need is to better identify emerging risk, not necessarily the 'one in a million black swan' type risk, but those that would be evident if one were focused on looking for them in the right way.

Moving further into the role of internal auditing, in the IIA's Question and Answer Session in July 2010 entitled *The Expanding Role of the CAE*, three key points emerged from these interview sessions regarding the role and reputation of internal auditing:

1. CAE roles are continuing to expand into business areas outside the internal audit activity. Business functions that CAEs are continuing to provide oversight for are part of the organization's governance, risk, or compliance (GRC) structure. CAEs are also being called upon to provide oversight for non-GRC processes or activities requiring business skills similar to those demanded of internal auditors.
2. CAE oversight responsibilities outside the internal audit activity mostly focus on assurance and the facilitation of information to senior management and the board. As a result, the internal audit activity's independence and objectivity is not impaired.
3. Prior to accepting oversight responsibility for an area outside the internal audit activity, the CAE should take into consideration the needs of the organization, the skill sets of

internal auditors, and the new area of responsibility to mitigate issues of independence and objectivity. CAEs should not be responsible for making strategic business decisions or providing assurance for processes, controls, or activities pertaining to business functions for which they have oversight. In organizations where the CAE is responsible for a function that needs internal audit assurance, the internal audit charter must clearly state this role and how assurance will be provided to maintain the internal audit activity's independence and objectivity.

## 10.3   Globalization

One real development in internal auditing coincides in the way business (and public services) are becoming increasingly internationalized. Physical location is no longer an issue as consumer activity is moving away from the local high street as it launches into hyperspace through the Internet. The global IIA was established in 1941 and represents over 170 000 members across 165 countries and territories. The IIA has built on this platform and is developing the profession into a truly global internal auditing organization whose broad business objectives include:

- establishing global standards for the practice of internal auditing.
- promoting the professional certification of internal auditors worldwide.
- fostering the development of the profession around the globe.
- representing and promoting internal auditing across national borders.
- facilitating the timely sharing of information among Member associations.
- searching for globally applicable products and services.[3]

Looking at Europe, there is further activity to bring like-minded professionals together. Neil Cowan, past president of IIA UK&Ireland and past vice president of the European Confederation of Institutes of Internal Auditing (ECIIA) and director general of the ECIIA 1999–2002, has described the European Scene for *The Essential Guide to Internal Auditing*:

The profile of professional internal auditing received a significant boost when, at the beginning of the millennium, the European Union (EU) established a separate Directorate General for Internal Audit (DGIA). At the same time, an independent Audit Progress Committee was set up. Together, these innovations reflected a new determination in the EU to drive forward a more effective approach to matters of audit, risk and control. These moves also encouraged further development of internal auditing in member States where the profession was already well established and gave further impetus in countries where less developed approaches were evident.

All of this was a recognition at European level of the contribution that professional internal auditing can make to good governance, not just within the European Commission (EC) itself, but also in countries throughout the wider European geographic area. Given the depth of involvement of the EU in all areas of economic activity, this was also a signal that the benefits of internal auditing were available to all types of organisations in every economic sector.

Staffing of DGIA sought to reflect the right professional qualifications required to undertake a value adding internal audit service. A prime requirement also was the acceptance of global internal auditing standards in order to establish an effective benchmark. By this example, the EC sought to provide a lead for EU member States in establishing their own approach to the provision of assurance on the application of good governance principles, risk management and internal control.

Many EU member States actively encourage internal auditing in the knowledge that this service to management provides a valuable contribution to public confidence in the way in which organisations in both the public and private sectors are governed. However, countries may differ in the role which is expected of internal auditing and the means by which the service is provided. Some countries seek a confirmation from internal audit that controls are effective in the financial area only whilst others see internal audit as a full partner with an organisation's Board and management in providing assurance over effective governance processes which embrace risk assessment and operational control.

In some EU member States the professional body for internal auditors – the Institute of Internal Auditors (IIA) – has been long established, is a crucible for driving the profession forward and promotes the adherence to the IIA Standards for the Professional Practice of Internal Auditing. These countries are involved in the debates about the way in which firms and other organisations operate and are a full party to developing laws and regulations in appropriate areas of activity. In other countries which have not reached this level of professional development, the IIA assists in raising standards and promoting professional practice.

Professionalism of the internal auditor is the key factor in providing risk and control assurance to Directors and Management Boards. Skill, knowledge, ability and experience – and, thus, credibility – are reflected in the qualifications that an internal auditor can bring to an organisation. Whether directly audit related, or generally in business, the qualified internal auditor is part of the comfort factor which Boards seek in gaining assurance over effective management processes. Other factors should come from an effective Audit Committee.

A well constituted Audit Committee of the Board, made up of independent non-executive Directors, should challenge the Board in its approach to good governance. The Audit Committee role should be to provide an oversight of risk management and internal control activities and advise the Board where problems may occur. The Committee should seek meaningful input from both internal and external audit and should be instrumental in providing the Board with on-going control information in addition to having significant influence over the Board's annual control statement.

The internal audit function, together with an effective Audit Committee, provide two significant pieces of the corporate governance jig-saw puzzle. Separately they can make a strong contribution to effective corporate governance; working closely together they become formidable.

## 10.4   Providing Audit Assurances

The task of providing reliable assurances has never been more crucial to the internal auditing profession. There are several key issues that underpin the need to ensure internal auditors are able to step up to the plate and not only discharge their professional duties but also fill a gap in the governance framework, where the captains of industry need to be sure that all is well below decks. The CAE will need to consider the following five questions.

### What Is the Sate of the Audit Shop and Is It Fit for Purpose?

IIA Standard 2120 says that 'the internal audit activity must evaluate the effectiveness and contribute to the improvement of risk management processes', while Practice Advisory 2120-2 acknowledges the expectations of internal audit to deliver the goods and deal with the high level of risk facing high-profile internal audit units. The interesting question arises as to how internal audit is able to take the necessary steps to ensure that it is managing its own risks. Practice Advisory 2120-2 argues that risks facing internal audit fall into three broad categories: audit failure, false assurance, and reputation risks. Some of the steps the CAE can consider are summarized below:

- Quality assurance and improvement programme.
- Periodic review of the audit universe.
- Periodic review of the audit plan.
- Effective audit planning.
- Effective audit design focused on understanding the system of internal controls.
- Effective management review and escalation procedures.
- Proper resource allocation.

The above forms a high-level system of internal control over the internal audit unit and as a beacon for good control, the CAE should ask for assurances from the audit managers that each of these controls is in place and working. As part of the 'physician heal thyself' syndrome, the CAE will want to prepare a risk register that caters for key risks to the audit service and ensures a continual review of the accepted controls and other arrangements to promote a successful audit function. The IIA's Knowledge Report considered the attributes of highly effective quality assurance and improvement programmes in January 2010 and found that highly effective programmes had the following three traits:

1. They have dedicated staff who are passionate about quality assurance and improvement. This person or group of individuals is responsible for performing the internal self-assessment, gathering all information in preparation for the external QA, and performing ongoing monitoring of the internal audit activity.
2. They leverage the use of technology and invest in the right technology tools based on the internal audit activity's quality assurance and improvement needs. Tools are used to document all internal audit work papers as well as secure information in a central location.
3. They have the support of senior management and the audit committee. Getting the support of these two entities is especially important when performing an external QA and in ensuring internal auditors are onboard with quality assurance activities.

## How Does the Audit Service Fit into the Corporate Assurance Map?

If the primary role of internal audit is to provide independent assurances on the risk management, control and governance process, then these assurances need to fit into the assurance map. Practice Advisory 2050-2 comes to the rescue by explaining how Standard 2050 is met in terms of coordinating the activities of other internal and external providers of assurance and consulting services to ensure proper coverage and minimize duplication of efforts. Practice Advisory 2050-2 acknowledges that the board will want to gain assurance from the various sources that processes are operating properly by suggesting that there are three main classes of assurance providers, differentiated by the stakeholders they serve, their level of independence from the activities over which they provide assurance and the robustness of that assurance:

1. Those who report to management and/or are part of management (management assurance), including individuals who perform control self-assessments, quality auditors, environmental auditors, and other management-designated assurance personnel.

2. Those who report to the board, including internal audit.
3. Those who report to external stakeholders (external audit assurance), which is a role traditionally fulfilled by the independent/statutory auditor.

These assurance providers include:

- Line management and employees.
- Senior management.
- Internal and external auditors.
- Compliance.
- Quality assurance.
- Risk management.
- Environmental auditors.
- Workplace health and safety auditors.
- Government performance auditors.
- Financial reporting review teams.
- Subcommittees of the board.
- External assurance providers, including surveys, specialist reviews (such as health and safety inspectors).

The advisory makes it clear that the internal audit activity will normally provide assurance over the entire organization, including risk management processes showing how key risks are classified and the effectiveness of the risk assessment and risk reporting systems.

The question of where internal audit fit into the assurance landscape brings many issues to the fore. The growth in risk committees and the converged *Governance, Risk and Compliance* strategies that some organizations are now embarking on, raises the question of the CAE leading the risk management team or even the entire GRC functions as well as internal audit. There are no hard and fast rules, although there is a strong argument for suggesting that internal audit sit above and review everything that goes on in the organization, including any integrated GRC teams. In this sense, audit do not run risk management and compliance teams but independently review the way risk management and compliance are run by management. Another view is that internal audit should define a role that fits with the state of risk management appreciation within the organization, which for simplicity is divided into three states:

- **Risk immature**   Internal audit should champion risk management practices.
- **Risk irresponsible**   Internal audit should challenge risk management practices.
- **Risk mature**   Internal audit should appraise risk management practices.

## How Does the Internal Audit Plan Ensure the Best Use of Audit Resources?

Most agree that the CAE will use the risk management process to drive internal audit plans. Practice Advisory 2010-2 covers the way this may happen. The advisory recognizes that internal auditors may not be qualified to review every risk category and the ERM process in the organization (e.g. internal audits of workplace health and safety, environmental auditing or complex financial instruments). Factors the internal auditor considers when developing the internal audit plan should include:

- Inherent risks – Are they identified and assessed?
- Residual risks – Are they identified and assessed?

- Mitigating controls, contingency plans, and monitoring activities – Are they linked to the individual events and/or risks?
- Risk registers – Are they systematic, completed and accurate?
- Documentation – Are the risks and activities documented?

## Does Audit Work Build into High-Level Assurances?

Most auditors are used to planning an audit, working through the fieldwork and preparing a report with a formal opinion. What is less straightforward is how to align this audit work into macro views that can be applied to large parts of the organizations, major business processes and isolate key risks to the organization. The IIA's Practice Guide on formulating and expressing internal audit opinions was issued in April 2009 and this highlighted some of issues that internal audit may need to give opinions on, covering, for example:

- The overall system of internal control over financial reporting.
- Organizations' controls and procedures for compliance with laws and regulations.
- Effectiveness of controls such as budgeting and performance management in multiple sub-sidiaries.
- System of internal control at a subsidiary or reporting unit.
- Compliance with laws and regulations in single or a few business units.

IIA guidance suggests that stakeholders also need to understand the nature of the opinion, what it covers, the criteria used to express the opinion and the time period in question. It goes on to show how macro opinions need to be expressed with care to make sure the user understands the purpose, the basis of the opinion, the risk appetite used by the organization, and the work done to support the opinion, including reliance on others. These types of opinions may result from the aggregation of different audits each carried out at different times, although micro opinions are easier as they are based around an individual audit. In essence the framework against which the audit opinion is set is very important as this gives the context for the work and results. Negative opinions result where nothing has come to the auditor's attention that causes concern. Where the internal auditor places any reliance on the work of a third party assurance provider it will need to be assessed for competence, independence and objectivity before it can be relied on by the internal auditor. The practice guide gives examples of the way in which some audit units use a tiered grading of controls as:

- Effective
- Some improvement needed
- Major improvement needed
- Unsatisfactory

Opinions can be given on the areas that have been audited but there is still a need to consider the way audit work contributes to the overall assurance map. We can return to Practice Advisory 2050-2 for guidance on the way in which an assurance mapping exercise can be used to map assurance coverage against the key risks in an organization. This process allows an organization to identify and address any gaps in the risk management process and gives stakeholders comfort that risks are being managed and reported on, and that regulatory and legal obligations are being met. Organizations will benefit from a streamlined approach, which ensures the information is available to management about the risks they face and how the risks are being addressed.

Each significant unit within an organization could have its own assurance map. Alternatively, the internal audit activity may play a coordinating role in developing and completing the organization's assurance landscape. In organizations requiring an overall opinion from the CAE, the CAE needs to understand the nature, scope and extent of the integrated assurance map to consider the work of other assurance providers (and rely on it as appropriate) before presenting an overall opinion on the organization's governance, risk management, and control processes.

## How Can Internal Audit Move Forwards?

There is so much to choose from when considering developments in the future positioning of internal audit. We can start with the work carried out by PricewaterhouseCoopers on the future of internal auditing:

> As organizations consider new techniques to manage risks and controls, our study suggests they will look to both internal audit and other functional areas to assess risk as well as to perform the more traditional assessments of controls. Spurred by Sarbanes–Oxley and other reform measures, organizations have taken steps to strengthen controls and expand their controls-related monitoring activities. As a consequence, the value ascribed to traditional controls-focused assurance activities will likely diminish and potentially erode some of the newfound stature that many internal audit functions have attained in recent years. As other risk management functions assume new responsibilities in areas such as controls (and, in the process, enhance their value in the eyes of management), internal audit, with its strong association with controls assurance, could be perceived as being limited in its ability to deliver comparable value. Internal audit thus finds itself at a crossroads, with two possible paths to the future. One is to continue doing what it does today and nothing more, a path that brings with it the inherent risk of future obsolescence. Alternatively, internal audit may choose the path we believe is more likely to lead it to meet the evolving needs of modern organizations, and the rising expectations of senior management and audit committees. This path involves moving beyond the fundamentals of risk and controls to create a new internal audit value proposition. The new (and inherently more strategic) value proposition would include the provision of risk management assurance along with the traditional responsibility of assurance over controls. Adding risk management capabilities would inevitably help internal audit align itself more closely with an organization's maturing risk management functions. But doing so would require something not always associated with today's internal audit function: a risk-centric mindset.[4]

One major concern is how the internal auditor should act if the risk appetite applied in the organization is unacceptable or excessive. What does the auditor do when confronted by reckless behaviour? The chief risk officer may also have a view in this situation. There is a big difference between smart risk taking and reckless risk taking. New challenges for internal audit revolve around the theme of daring to go into danger zones, as well as safe areas. One such danger zone is pay and incentives and even bonuses. Huge risks emerge where bonus systems incentivize the wrong set of behaviours and it is here that internal audit can step into areas of corporate controversy. Governance danger zones, such as where inappropriate bonus schemes hit the risk agenda when they start to appear in the press and impact corporate reputations. We can turn now to solid supporters of the internal audit role in the form of Professor Mervyn King, chairman of South Africa's 'King Committee' on corporate governance, who opened the 2008 IIA conference:

> . . . with a rousing call for internal audit to take its rightful place in 'the boardroom, not the backroom'. In an address titled 'Governance, strategy, sustainability and internal audit', King

argued that the role and status of internal audit was changing because boards were demanding greater assurance on strategic issues. 'Two years ago I said the profession would be changed completely within five years and so far I have been proved right,' he told delegates. 'Internal audit can no longer be divorced from strategy,' he continued. 'Internal audit has to be involved with management in developing strategy, otherwise how can you know whether controls are adequate, that the quality of corporate information is such that the non-execs and the board can have confidence in relying on it? Strategy is the board's responsibility,' he stressed, 'but who is in a better place to understand the risks and opportunities in developing that strategy than internal audit? I believe no one. Internal audit was becoming a risk-centred and "intellectual" discipline,' said King, adding: 'The days of internal audit being compliance centred are dead forever.'[5]

The IIA UK&Ireland's annual conference sounded their continued support for risk-based auditing:

> Outgoing Institute president Simon D'Arcy told delegates that the profession had come a long way in recent years, but needed to change yet further if it is to meet boardroom expectations. 'We must consolidate our progress by future-proofing, honing our communications skills and constantly thinking about what we are doing, in order to give the quality of assurance required by senior management,' he said. D'Arcy outlined what he called 'intelligent internal auditing'. This did not mean esoteric or 'boffinlike' auditing, he said. 'It means thinking about what you are doing.' Internal auditors should adopt a risk-based approach and make sure they provide 'assurance around things that really matter,' otherwise their value to their organisation is open to question. This is particularly true in the current economic climate, where financial firms are collapsing under the burden of unforeseen or badly assessed risks, he said.[6]

It is one thing to ask for a seat at the top table and quite another to ensure you get invited back. IIA Standard 1111 takes internal auditing way beyond the old days of checking accounting records and physical inventories by stating that the CAE must communicate and interact directly with the board. This interaction will include committees, such as the audit committee and risk committee, set up by the board, and in terms of reinforcing this most important relationship Practice Advisory 1111-1 provides some much needed guidance:

> Direct communication occurs when the chief audit executive (CAE) regularly attends and participates in board meetings that relate to the board's oversight responsibilities for auditing, financial reporting, organizational governance, and control. The CAE's attendance and participation at these meetings provide an opportunity to be apprised of strategic business and operational developments, and to raise high-level risk, systems, procedures, or control issues at an early stage. Meeting attendance also provides an opportunity to exchange information concerning the internal audit activity's plans and activities and to keep each other informed on any other matters of mutual interest. Such communication and interaction also occurs when the CAE meets privately with the board, at least annually.

A key interaction is where the CAE challenges the board on whether key risks are being adequately addressed. The sticking point is whether management and internal audit agree with the way this is happening and when there is a gap, Standard 2600 swings into action:

> When the chief audit executive believes that senior management has accepted a level of residual risk that may be unacceptable to the organization, the chief audit executive must discuss the matter with senior management. If the decision regarding residual risk is not resolved, the chief audit executive must report the matter to the board for resolution.

The acceptance of risk and the resolution gaps between the opinion of internal audit and the views held by senior management will be the question that all chief audit executives will face now and in the future. In one sense this will define the audit role as, when all is well, the auditor can be a trusted advisor but, when there is a problem, this role turns to one of critical friend. The adopted approach comes back to the question of risk appetite and how it can be used to drive the risk governance agenda and is one challenge that will not go away. Deloittes has a view on how we can use a series of key questions to assess the risk appetite within an organization:

- What size risks or opportunities do we expect management to bring to our attention?
- How does management determine the organization's risk appetite? Which risk categories are considered, and how do they relate to management's performance goals and compensation metrics?
- In developing the risk appetite, how did management incorporate the perspectives of shareholders, regulators, and analysts – and experiences of peer companies?
- How are risk tolerances set? How does that process account for risk appetite? How do risk tolerances relate to the risk appetite and to risk categories?
- What scenario-planning or other models are used in setting the risk appetite and tolerances?
- How do these tools account for changing circumstances and for the human factor? [7]

Ernst and Young go on to describe their research into areas where there is room to improve risk management in most organizations:

- Improving the risk assessment approach to better anticipate, identify and understand risks.
- Aligning risk management focus with business objectives to drive greater value and focus on the risks most likely to affect the business.
- Enhancing coordination of risk and control groups to achieve greater efficiencies and eliminate redundancies, duplication and gaps among risk activities. Organizations that improve their risk management activities will not only provide better protection for their businesses, but also improve their business performance, improve their decision making and, ultimately, increase their competitive advantage.[8]

The coordination of risk and control groups is where internal audit needs to step up to the plate. The question is, are we just another risk and control group? Or can we rise above the rest and ensure our job is to review the way risk is managed including the way these risk and controls groups help drive and improve the agenda? We cannot leave the examination of challenges facing the internal audit profession without referring to the proposition set by Professor Andrew Chambers that these challenges call for a new breed of 'Super Auditor':

The enhancement of the internal audit role I am suggesting will need the development of a cadre of 'super auditors' with requisite skill sets and accreditation mechanisms. Outsourced assistance to the internal audit function is likely to become even more important. CAEs will need a status and a quality equivalent to that of an executive director, and they will be held more to account for any failures to provide timely warnings to the board. In medium to large internal audit functions there will need to be a mezzanine level of internal auditors, immediately below the CAE, also able to interface on equal terms with members of the board. We will need to reconsider the continued applicability of the term 'chief audit executive', which implies an affiliation to the management team. I notice I am not alone in thinking along these lines. Indeed, if internal audit is not to fill the board's assurance vacuum, other professionals probably will. BBC's *Today* programme on October 30, 2008 reported that Paul Moore, head of regulatory risk at HBOS from 2002 until he was made redundant in 2004, considers that 'people like him need

326 THE ESSENTIAL GUIDE TO INTERNAL AUDITING

to report direct not to executive management but to non-executives whose job it is to rein in management.' In the age of the sound bite, the idea of the 'super auditor' resonates strongly. Of course, I am keen to engage in consideration of whether and how the board's assurance vacuum needs to be filled, and the other changes to internal audit, in addition to the fostering of super auditors, that will be needed if the internal audit profession is to rise to this latest challenge.[9]

One important development during 2009 was a slight change of wording applied in internal auditing standards from 'should' to 'must'. There is no hiding place and each audit shop across the world will need to ensure it is able to stand up to the rigours of the IIA's International Professional Practices Framework as it asks that the standards are applied by setting out clearly what it means when the requirement is a 'must':

The Standards use the word 'must' to specify an unconditional requirement.

Meanwhile, the president of the IIA UK&Ireland, Sarah Blackburn, has presented a serious challenge to all internal auditors across the world:

People sometimes concentrate on the outputs of internal audit: the reports, the recommendations, the advice given. But the value to stakeholders is the outcome – ultimately they feel more confident because of what internal audit is telling them. If the audit committee and the board are confident that the regulator will be satisfied and that management's assurances and the risk management process are sound, they are more likely to undertake new opportunities to grow the business and achieve more stretching goals.[10]

We warned in Chapter 1 of *The Essential Guide* that it is important not to throw the baby out with the bathwater. Professor Andrew Chambers has warned about the dangers of getting swept away on the tide of consulting styles and not retaining a semblance of our original role, by suggesting that:

I am a bit of a traditionalist. Rather than looking for some jazzy, sexy new horizon to strive for (as has been internal auditors' wont since the start) my view is that the pendulum may swing back. Someone has to provide the good old fashioned assurance through control assessment (including detailed testing) comprehensively covering all the affairs of the enterprise over time. When will managements and internal auditors learn! Boards are already convinced, I think – they know the importance of assurance.

## 10.5  Meeting the Challenge

All countries to a greater or lesser extent are coming to recognize the great value from an internal audit service. It is hard to think of any other corporate service that is enshrined in laws and regulations and which carries the burden of the societal expectations that we have mentioned. Keeping to the international theme, we can quote an example from the complementary Listing Requirements of the Malaysian Stock Exchange, which describes the value from internal auditing:

- Reviewing objectives and activities – review with management the operational activities and ensure the principal objectives are aligned to overall company's objectives.
- Evaluating risk – identify all auditable activities and relevant risk factors, and to assess their significance.

- Confirming information – research and gather information that is competent, factual and complete.
- Analysing operations – analyse and examine that operations are effective.
- Providing assurance on compliance – provide assurance on compliance to statutory requirements, laws, company policies and guidelines.
- Recommending internal controls – recommend appropriate controls to overcome deficiencies and to enhance company operations.
- Assuring safeguards – evaluate procedures in place to safeguard company assets.
- Consulting and facilitating – assist management in establishing a proper risk management framework, assessing risks and monitoring the effectiveness of the risk management programme and ensuring the adequacy of the internal control system.[11]

The new-look internal auditor will have a view on whether effective risk management has been implemented and will help this task wherever possible. Good auditors will be able to relate to business imperatives and understand the way risk taking is an important part of finding new income streams and increased value creation. It means a slight mindset shift with the internal auditor speaking management's language and not just hiding behind the staid accounting jargon of 'risk mitigation and internal control routines'.

Much progress is made where internal audit feed into the way the business seeks to achieve its objectives that goes beyond a control and compliance mentality. This point is now uppermost in the minds of many CAEs and the IIA's November 2009 knowledge report on becoming a more effective CAE argues that the number one response was to ensure internal audit efforts help senior managers meet their business objectives. It was felt that CAEs needed to establish effective, regular two-way communication and partner with the organization's other risk, control and governance functions and other management committees, as well as ensuring they are able to communicate with committee members on sensitive matters that are ignored or cannot be discussed with senior management. We cannot do much better in meeting the challenge than dip into the IIA's *Tone at the Top*, Issue 46 (February 2010), which discussed exactly what it means for an organization to have a healthy dependency on internal auditing:

> It might be obvious that the board of directors should rely on management for pertinent information about the organization that it serves. However, through its audit committee, the full board has access to the internal auditors' assessment of risks throughout the enterprise, and to their opinions on how well the internal controls that are in place are working. Because objectivity and independence help define their role in the organization, the internal auditors are in a position to provide to the audit committee and the board valuable insights on both strategic and operational risks. Based on their extensive training and experience in risk assessment, proficient and professional internal auditors can bring immeasurable value and support to the board by ensuring it has a realistic picture of the state of the organization's risks. And this can achieve a great deal of progress toward helping shift the entity's environment away from a culture of risk.[12]

## Summary and Conclusions

There is much that internal audit is expected to contribute and much that can be done to make this contribution. Back in August 2002, LeRoy E. Bookal, chairman of IIA Inc., wrote that:

> With our unique viewpoint as independent but inside observers, internal auditors play a vital role within governance processes by keeping the board, senior management, and external auditors

aware of risk and control issues and by assessing the effectiveness of risk management .... Audit committees and boards are facing skyrocketing liability costs and ever-increasing workloads. It's no wonder that liability costs are rising – boards have to meet more governance challenges each year, but their resources for information about their increasingly complex organizations are limited. In the post-Enron era, it is surprising that boards of directors for any publicly held companies would choose to do without internal auditing. It is also surprising that investors, liability insurers, and other stakeholders have not questioned the decision to do without internal auditing more often .... There is no simple checklist showing everything internal auditors can do to add value, because, at times, techniques for adding value are as unique and personalized as the organizations for which we work.[13]

We have featured the words of Larry Sawyer in *The Essential Guide* and there is no reason not to include something in the final chapter. Many years ago Sawyer wrote out Ten Little Maxims for the internal auditor:

1. Leave every place a little better than you found it.
2. You can't stomp your foot when you are on your knees.
3. Know the objectives.
4. Nothing ever happens until somebody sells something.
5. Every deficiency is rooted in the violation of some principle of good management.
6. Never believe what the first person tells you.
7. The best question is, 'Mr or Ms Manager, how do you satisfy yourself that . . . ?'
8. Politics and culture will usually win over rules and regulations.
9. When you point your finger, make sure your finger nail is clean.
10. Murphy was an optimist.[14]

When an auditor is considering an operational risk during an assignment, but cannot quite see the big picture in relating this task to the top boardroom corporate governance agenda, regard can be had to a famous poem by George Herbert:

For want of a nail the shoe is lost;
　　For want of a shoe the horse is lost;
　　　　For want of a horse the rider is lost;
　　　　　　For want of a rider the battle is lost;
　　　　　　　　For want of the battle the kingdom is lost.

My view of the changing world of the internal auditor is quite simple, and it is summed up in the following dimensions that move through stages 1–10; from old to new-look contexts:

1. We're here to check on you.
　2. We're here to check your controls.
　　3. We're here to check your risks.
　　　4. We're here to check your risk management system.
　　　　5. We're here to help you establish risk management.
　　　6. We're here to help you protect your business.
　　　　7. We're here to help you prove you can be trusted to take care of the business.
　　　8. We're here to support the way you grow the business in a sustainable way.
　9. We're here to help you deal with the the risks that impair your corporate reputation.
10. We're here becase we are internal audit – the impartial professionals you can trust.

We close this book with a powerful quote from the IIA from their publication, *All in a Day's Work*:

Sitting on the right side of management, modern-day internal auditors are consulted on all aspects of the organization and must be prepared for just about anything. They are coaches, internal and external stakeholder advocates, risk managers, controls experts, efficiency specialists, and problem-solving partners. They are the organization's safety net. It's certainly not easy, but for these skilled and competent professionals, it's all in a day's work.

## Endnotes

1. Chapman, Christy and Anderson, Urton, (2002) *Implementing the Professional Practices Framework*, IIA Handbook Series, Institute of Internal Auditors, p. 91.
2. Chadwick, William E. 'Oh no the auditor is here'. *Internal Auditor*, April 2002, pp. 52–55.
3. *Global IIA, The Case For Globalization*, 1 October 2001 (www.theiia.org).
4. Advisory Services Internal Audit, *Connected Thinking, Internal Audit 2012*, A study examining the future of internal auditing and the potential decline of a controls-centric approach, PricewaterhouseCoopers LLP, 2007, p. 5.
5. Annual Conference Special, *Internal Auditing Magazine*, November 2008, Institute of Internal Auditors UK&Ireland, Neil Baker and Arthur Piper report, pp. 38–47.
6. Annual Conference Special, *Internal Auditing Magazine*, November 2008, Institute of Internal Auditors UK&Ireland, Neil Baker and Arthur Piper report, pp. 38–47.
7. *Risk Intelligent Governance, A Practical Guide for Boards*, Risk Intelligence Series, Issue 16, 2009, Deloitte Development LLC, Member of Deloitte Touche Tohmatsu, p. 9.
8. 'The future of risk: protecting and enabling performance', Ernst and Young, 2009, p. 3.
9. Chambers, Andrew, *Internal Auditing & Business Risk*, IIA Magazine, December 2008, p. 21.
10. Blackburn, Sarah, President of the IIA UK&Ireland, *Internal Auditing*, December/January 2009, p. 15.
11. *Complement KLSE Listing Requirements–Malaysia*, Guidance on Internal Audit Function, Task Force set up by the Securities Commission of Malaysia, IIA Malaysia acted as Secretariat to the Task Force, July 2002.
12. *Tone at the Top*, Issue 46, February 2010, Institute of Internal Auditors.
13. Bookal, Leroy E., Chairman of IIA Inc. 'Internal auditors–integral to good corporate governance'. *Internal Auditing*, August 2002, pp. 44–49.
14. Sawyer, Lawrence B., 'An internal audit philosophy'. *Internal Auditor*, August 1995, p. 46.

## Appendix A

# AUDITING THE RISK MANAGEMENT PROCESS: A CASE STUDY

Our aim in this presentation is to illustrate the way the corporate risk management process may be audited through a simple case study using the risk-assessed control evaluation (RaCE) approach discussed in Chapter 9. The presentation covers an audit of the corporate risk management arrangements that exist in a large organization with a head office and hundreds of local offices.

The audit was taken from the annual audit plan that was agreed by the audit committee. It was seen as a high-profile audit in that it would examine the overall arrangements for providing a robust risk management process that covers the entire organization.

The auditor prepared a draft terms of reference, objectives and approach to the planned audit. The terms of reference were reviewed with management prior to the commencement of the audit to provide a comprehensive understanding of the areas to be covered and the approach to be adopted. The objectives, scope of the corporate risk management audit, along with selected extracts of key audit documentation, are set out below. Note that detailed audit planning documents, interview records and testing schedules that would normally be prepared for this type of audit are not included in this case study.

## Systems related business objectives

It is a requirement of the corporate risk management strategy that potential opportunities and threats to the achievement by the service of its objectives are effectively managed. The purpose of the risk management policy is to establish corporate standards and clear procedures in the management of business risk to ensure the following:

- Integration of risk management into the culture of the organization.
- Raising awareness of the need for risk management by all those concerned with the delivery of services, including partners, suppliers and contractors.
- Enabling business managers to anticipate and respond to changing social, environmental and legislative conditions.
- Introduction of a robust framework and procedures for identification, evaluation, prioritization, control and monitoring of risk and the reporting and recording of events, based on good practice.
- Minimization of the cost of insurable risk.

The overall audit objective is to review and evaluate the adequacy of the control framework in place to ensure the effective assessment and management of risk. We will review the adequacy and effectiveness of controls to ensure that:

1. There is a clearly defined risk management policy and implementation strategy that is properly approved, appropriately issued and regularly reviewed to meet the challenges from new legislation and recognized best practice.

2. Effective structures and procedures are in place to support the delivery of the strategy and to ensure that the policy is understood and complied with.
3. Risk management is being suitably integrated within strategic business planning and performance management.
4. Risks are properly identified, evaluated and appropriately managed in a way that facilitates good decision-making by defined risk owners.

## Scope of the audit

The scope of the audit covered the overall risk management arrangement. Most of the work involved reviewing the measures put in place by the Enterprise Risk Management Team and the impact on head office and all business units involved in management at strategic, programme, project and operational levels. We also considered the measures used to evaluate progress in embedding risk management into the culture of the organization. The audit determined whether the entire risk management process is able to underpin adequate and effective internal control and provide the necessary level of assurance on the effectiveness of systems of internal control. To this end it was necessary to perform the various tasks, including the following:

- Meet with the head of the ERM Team and other members of the team.
- Meet with personnel from safety and health, business continuity and information management, human resources and others where appropriate.
- Visit selected personnel in a sample of business units and ensure that any findings from a relatively small sample of units are placed in context to provide a fair assessment of progress in implementing enterprise risk management.
- Meet with appropriate managers.
- Review a sample of risk registers from different parts of the business.
- Consider the extent to which significant decisions are made with regard to inherent risks.
- Review the degree of integration of risk management into strategic business planning.

## Audit approach

We adopted the risk-assessed control evaluation approach, which involves the following:

- Discussing and agreeing with management the terms of reference.
- Ascertaining and recording the risk management system.
- Evaluating and testing the adequacy and effectiveness of the arrangements in place.
- Forming an opinion based on the audit assurance criteria, on the extent to which the system related business objectives have been met, as well as considering improvements that can be made to the way risk is being managed.
- Issuing an emerging findings note for any areas of significant importance that may arise during the fieldwork.
- Discussing findings and recommendations with line management and the Enterprise Risk Management Team.
- Issuing a formal report to the head of ERM to obtain a written response indicating the level of acceptance of audit recommendations.
- Issuing the agreed final report to the chief executive, head of ERM, the director of operations and the director of resources.

- Copies of all final reports will also be sent to the audit committee.
- Reviewing progress towards the implementation of recommendations 6 months after the issue of the final report.

A further meeting was held between the head of ERM and the lead auditor to discuss the control objectives, which were agreed as:

## Control Objective One

There is a clearly defined risk management policy and implementation strategy that is properly approved, appropriately issued and regularly reviewed to meet new challenges from legislation and recognized best practice.

## Control Objective Two

Effective structures and procedures are in place to support the delivery of the strategy and to ensure that the policy is understood and complied with.

## Control Objective Three

Risk management is being suitably integrated within strategic business planning and performance management.

## Control Objective Four

Risk is properly identified, evaluated and appropriately managed in a way that facilitates good decision-making by defined risk owners.

## Abbreviations

| | |
|---|---|
| BU | Business Unit (e.g. ZZZ BU is Business Unit ZZZ) |
| CEO | Chief Executive Officer |
| CIO | Chief Information Officer |
| CRSA | Control Risk Self-Assessment |
| ERMT | Enterprise Risk Management Team |
| H&S | Health and Safety |
| HoS | Head of Strategy |
| QA | Quality Assurance |
| RM | Risk Management |
| RR | Risk Register |
| SIC | Statement on Internal Control |
| SMT | Senior Management Team |
| REF | Reference (Normally refers to an interview record) |

The next stage involved obtaining the required evidence to support the initial evaluation regarding the state of controls in line with the four control objectives.

# Control Objective One – Evidence Obtained

**Control Objective:**

**1. There is a clearly defined risk management policy and implementation strategy that is properly approved, appropriately issued and regularly reviewed to meet new challenges from legislation and recognized best practice.**

| RISKS | EVALUATION | SUPPORTING EVIDENCE |
|---|---|---|
| 1.1 Policy does not address important aspects of RM | Policy not cross referenced to other risk elements and no real stakeholder engagement | (REF) There is scope to improve ERM in all parts of the business<br>(REF) The ERM team has a key role in ERMT and may be used in a more dynamic way to facilitate the spread of good RM practices. The concept of an ERM may be used to derive a holistic RM process based around a suitable website that uses upside as well as downside risk and appropriate tools made available to suit the context and issue at hand. |
| 1.2 Implementation does not address culture of organization | Risk maturity model flawed No surveys carried out | (ZZZ BU) ZZZ is in an unusual position with a recently-appointed Manager new to the RM process. Manager sees it as important to drive what is a stagnant RM process. Many gaps in current arrangements due to frequent staff changes meant the RR was out of date but this is being addressed by the new manager. ERM process does not take on board the many frequent staff changes that occur at BUs as a norm. New RR author had no training before taking on the role. Lack of feedback on their RRs and no overall monitoring causes a gap in ensuring that the RRs make sense and are current. |
| 1.3 New challenges are not being addressed | ERMT positioned to be involved in new developments but business risk management not applied as a change project | (REF) There is a formal ERMT in place with clear roles reporting the task of embedding ERM into the business alongside the current operational RM approach. This a challenging task and audit will work in a partnership mode with the ERMT in promoting effective ERM. |
| 1.4 Best practice is not applied to risk policy | Good arrangements in place | (REF) The Chief Information Officer (CIO) is working with ERMT on integrating risk processes and is supportive of the ERM process. They recognize the problems with lack of Main Board buy in and the knock on effect to reduce the perception of ERM at the Information Board. There is a need to express the value add from ERM and sell these messages in a joined up manner<br>(REF) The Head of Strategy (HoS) has been included in the range of ERMT contacts and is currently working alongside them to develop a holistic approach to RM with website summaries and links to specific risk elements. There are issues around getting managers to own their RRs and using the ERMT as a centre of excellence with a good user-friendly website. The HoS is particularly interested in the reputational risk where professional standards are impaired. |

# Control Objective Two – Evidence Obtained

**Control Objective:**
2. Effective structures and procedures are in place in MPA/MPS to support the delivery of the strategy and to ensure that the policy is understood and complied with.

| RISKS | EVALUATION | SUPPORTING EVIDENCE |
|---|---|---|
| 2.1 Main Board does not have full oversight of RM process | Lack of expertise at audit committee and assessment model is flawed | *(REF) Two issues arise from this meeting:*<br>BU: RR may not be fully aligned to the Corporate RR. Main board should have its own fully inclusive RR and this issue should be explored with the CEO.<br>(REF) Strategic issues should drive RM and there may be support for better use of CRSA and ERM in bringing together the RM components and engaging people around real issues<br>(REF) The risk maturity model is misleading and does not give a real picture of where they stand. The Audit Committee seems not to challenge this model even where aspects are scored Amber. ERM needs to reach inside the business and CRSA may be one way of making this happen. Much hinges on the Corporate Risk Review Group and their role in getting the Main Board to engage properly with ERM. The audit view is that, as long as ownership is not set with the Main Board then there will always be problems. |
| 2.2 Main Board does not fully engage with RM at a senior level | Expected controls not in place due to resistance from MB | (REF) ERM is the responsibility of the CEO and there is a need to make much more progress perhaps using the new Corporate Governance Guidance as a stepping stone to making ERM implemented in a way that is more practical and useful to the business.<br>(Main Board Minutes) No mention of ERM in Board discussions. Only mention was a view that RM was an undefined process |
| 2.3 Policy is not really understood across senior management | Risk not set as a new competence and only aimed at risk authors and not wider organization | (REF) FFF BU have an enthusiastic approach to ERM and have recently been visited by the ERMT. SMT did their risk assessments from a blank sheet of paper and appear to have bought in to the overall concept.<br>(REF) There is a view that a lack of resources within ERMT impairs progress. There is no apparent Training for Trainers approach in use.<br>(JS) The training product appears highly professional, but is constrained by the lack of clear role definition and strategy to embed RM within the business and not just train junior people to prepare risk registers for their senior management. This strategy would complement the training of a cadre of senior risk advocates that is currently being rolled out. Training is designed to instil relevant competence amongst all levels of employees and is therefore a crucial aspect of efforts to embed ERM into the business. |
| 2.4 Policy is not being complied with in the organization | ERMT should do more coaching due to lack of resources.<br>Head Office not monitoring results and no self assessment in place | *(REF) QA is a mix of visits and one to one coaching. There is no scoring and final report does not contain an agreed action plan. Audit could recommend that the QA process may be sharpened up. There are concerns over the resources to cover the business unit (BU) and there is no clear plan to cover the many BUs. It may be possible to clarify the position and assign the QA role to Head Office and use ERMT as Risk advocates and facilitators as a separate role.*<br>(REF) Business Support is an unit with around 100 staff and they have not had any contact from the ERMT. This meant they had not prepared risk registers in line with the ERM Policy although the manager expressed an interest in meeting with ERMT and having a formal risk management process in place. The ERMT appears to have left out this support unit from their portfolio. This demonstrates the difficulty in sweeping up all units within the ERM process and it may mean a better and more dynamic ERMT website<br>(REF) Head Office receive copies of the BU RRs that they summarize into themes but they do not monitor red risks. Head Office does not appear to have its own RR apart from aspects such as the performance unit. They also do not appear to use accelerated risks from BUs as a high level steering document. There is some uncertainty about the respective quality roles of Head Office and ERMT. If Head Office were to assume a QA role, this would free the ERMT to have more of a consulting role. |

# Control Objective Three – Evidence Obtained

**Control Objective:**
**3. Risk management is being suitably integrated within strategic business planning and performance management.**

| RISKS | EVALUATION | SUPPORTING EVIDENCE |
|---|---|---|
| 3.1 There is insufficient integration of RM into the business | RM seen as annual exercise as part of planning. Many BUs do not link with plans. Performance management system does not feature ERM and action plans | (REF) GGG BU has used ERM but much has fallen behind because of a lack of timely feedback and real engagement from senior management and the BU and head office. Top ten risks scored then 94 risks added on with no scores or action plans provided. People seemed to have added them in to protect themselves from criticism if not achieved. Many of the risks may be causes rather than risks. Year end cycle for RM is unhelpful as RR should be live document. In terms of risk appetite – people work in silos and no meetings held to discuss. The risk author compiled the RR and e-mailed it out for ideas for the RR and asked for responses – but not assessed as a working group so no brain storming and no asking the troops. There are gaps in the RR where items have not been scored or reviewed. This year is a learning curve and it will need to be firmed up as it has now lost momentum. |
| 3.2 Strategic planning activities do not apply risk assessment properly | Most plans including the Strategic plan make no mention of risk assessment. | Review of Strategic plan 20xx/yy |
| 3.3 Performance management framework does not incorporate action points from the RM process | Risk owners not always defined and BU action plans left blank. No real escalation of high level risks and ownership in risk standard not helpful. | Review of RRs and meetings at ZZZ BU, GGG BU, HHH BU and PPP BU |
| 3.4 ERM is not being embedded into the culture at operational levels | Implementation patchy with RRs being prepared but of variable quality and poor buy in from senior managers. | (REF) The lack of early contact with ERMT may have led to problems with getting ERM in place at the BUs. (REF) The focus on risk authors means a move away from true SMT ownership with some RRs not being very strategic. HHH BU appear to have bought into the ERM process and have been recently visited by the ERMT on the QA reviews. However the RR is prepared by a data analyst (who sits on SMT as a Union Rep) and then sent to SMT for agreement. |

# Control Objective Four– Evidence Obtained

**Control Objective:**
4. Risk is properly identified, evaluated and appropriately managed in a way that facilitates good decision-making by defined risk owners.

| RISKS | EVALUATION | SUPPORTING EVIDENCE |
|---|---|---|
| 4.1 Risks are not being designed and prioritized in a meaningful way | Risk standard and training does not deal in depth with appetite, escalation and senior management ownership | (REF) While there is a competent trainer in place there may need to be more work on obtaining feedback and assessing the quality of training. An advocacy role may be built into the programme along with a move towards facilitated workshops and better website interaction as well as post course contact. Refresher training may incorporate a 'training for trainers' aspect although this would extend the programme. May need to do more on risk tolerance and upside risk and links to SIC.<br><br>(Audit Test QA process) The QA process has resulted in visits to half of the BUs and the results demonstrate that there are many issues regarding the poor quality of risk registers and the lack of engagement from SMT. Because of a lack of resources, the ERMT will find it difficult to visit the remaining BU and cover the many support teams that together form the workforce. Moreover, the ERMT have re-set the quality strategy by focussing on more of a coaching/consulting role in terms of helping the BU risk authors in their efforts to make ERM a success in their various Business units. Head Office receive copies of the BU risk registers and in the past assumed a quality assurance role and this is being reviewed in light of the involvement of the ERMT. |
| 4.2 Decision making is not informed by effective RM activities | Committee papers do not contain risk assessments and training aimed at risk authors not decision makers. | General knowledge that committee papers have no section on Risk assessments and mitigations |
| 4.3 RM does not lead to more effective internal controls | No real attempt to link ERM with SIC or certification process. Top ten risks misses chances of full SIC involvement | Analysis of BU RRs and evaluations at ZZZ, HHH, HHH and PPP business units<br>Review of risk standard and RR training material |
| 4.4 Risk ownership is not properly defined | Definition poor and training and website material not aimed at senior people | (REF) There is a well understood need to get the Main Board fully engaged with ERM and the strategy is based around the Risk Strategy Group. The CRSA approach means getting ERM as an accepted complement to the more usual reactive operational risk assessments that are applied across the organization. The challenge is to get ERM into the business and not just a compliance based add on. Much hinges on accelerating risk to the Main Board. |

One important aspect of the audit is to check the way that business units interpret the enterprise risk management procedures in the way that they handle risk at a local level. An audit evaluation schedule was prepared to check the position at a sample of business units.

# Audit Evaluation – Local Business Units

| RISK | EXPECTED CONTROLS<br>*Suitable local mechanisms to ensure that:* | ANALYSIS REQUIRED |
|---|---|---|
| **1. ERM Policy is not properly understood** | 1.1 Copy of Policy readily available to all staff<br>1.2 Staff awareness training or refreshers<br>1.3 Policy referred to when appropriate<br>1.4 Policy seen as an important development | Local copy of policy<br>Any local RM guidance<br>Staff training days and feedback<br>Memos on ERM |
| **2. ERM standard is not being complied with.** | 2.1 Staff aware of procedures and how they relate to their work<br>2.2 Appropriate training, presentations and seminars<br>2.3 Refresher and induction training.<br>2.4 Procedure seen as important in prioritizing work<br>2.5 Procedure seen to contain all that is needed to enable the RM process.<br>2.6 Active steps taken to monitor the procedure.<br>2.7 Management team refer to procedure when appropriate.<br>2.8 Management team work in compliance with the procedure. | Copy of standard.<br>Local Guidance ERM procedures.<br>Training days and feedback.<br>Targets for ERM implementation.<br>Memos on ERM and non compliance.<br>Local guidance on compliance.<br>Reports on success of process. |
| **3. Business Unit Senior Management has no real engagement with ERM or the benefits that should accrue for adopting this approach.** | 3.1 Management team have contact with the ERM team when appropriate.<br>3.2 Management team in turn promote and publicize ERM within their command.<br>3.3 Management team have a belief that the ERM process helps them perform and improve controls.<br>3.4 Benefits are built into targets for management team and other managers and staff. | Actual contact with ERM team.<br>Memos to and from ERM team.<br>Promotional material on ERM team.<br>Meetings agenda and minutes.<br>Documented achievement of target benefits.<br>Internal control documentation. |
| **4. RRs do not reflect current priorities that ensure appropriate decisions are made to achieve set objectives.** | 4.1 Risk Registers (RRs) are prepared in a way that is consistent with the ERM Standard<br>4.2 RRs are linked to the key objectives<br>4.3 RRs are used to drive decision making<br>4.4 RRs are up to date and reflective of current priorities.<br>4.5 RRs are a regular feature of management team meetings<br>4.6 All personnel contribute to the compilation of RRs<br>4.7 RRs are set with a clear risk appetite. | Actual RR<br>Updated material<br>Links with management team minutes<br>Sources of RR materials<br>Guidance on scoring and appetites<br>Risk assessments mentioned in decision documents |
| **5. The stated benefits from the ERM process are not being achieved.** | 5.1 Management team have a good understanding of the benefits that accrue from ERM.<br>5.2 The ERM process is fully aligned to reviews of and improvement to internal controls.<br>5.3 These benefits have or will be achieved through suitable measures adopted by the unit. | Any suitable supporting documentation |

The auditor assessed the way training in risk management was provided by the ERM team as this was important to ensure business managers were able to implement the ERM policy and use the tools properly.

# Evaluation of ERM Training (1)

### OBJECTIVES OF THE TEST
To assess the training material provided by ERM Team in terms of the extent to which it underpins the implementation of a robust risk management process.

### AUDIT FINDINGS
The training product appears highly professional, but is constrained by the lack of clear role definition and strategy to embed RM within the organization and not just train junior people to prepare risk registers for their senior management. This strategy would complement the training of a cadre of senior risk advocates that is currently being rolled out. Training is designed to instil relevant competence amongst all levels of staff and is therefore a crucial aspect of efforts to embed ERM into the organization.

Several observations and recommendations resulted from this review.

# Evaluation of ERM Training (2)

**Possible audit recommendations:**

1. The ERM Team should prepare a session file that sets out what was covered during each slide and session sub-objectives for each part of the programme along with details of the exercises and examples that may be used as and when required.

2. The Risk Register basic and refresher courses should include the following additional aims:
   a. Explore processes for escalating high risk issues.
   b. Look at risk management responsibilities.
   c. Selling the ERM concept.

Short sessions should allude to the importance of these three items to ensure the highest impact from the investment in training time and resource even is this means the programme is extended by an additional half hour.

3. Document the course objectives on the course assessment form.

4. The course assessment form should be re-designed to ensure feedback on whether:
   a. The course achieved its objectives
   b. The course achieved the delegates' personal objectives.

5. The scores achieved for items 1 (course objectives achieved) and 2 (personal objectives achieved) should be compiled for each course and a course report should be prepared by the trainer stating the scores, comments on the course and whether any changes are required – in response to comments from the course assessment forms. Each course file should be reviewed by the trainer's line manager and the success of such training should form part of the annual performance appraisal scheme.

6. It may be possible to set a target for course feedback scores for example over 80% of delegates should score the training as having achieved its objectives 'excellent' or 'good'.

7. The rest of the form should remain as it is apart from the last box 'Any other comments' where it should say – 'please continue overleaf if required'.

The auditor assessed the way the ERM team checked that their procedures were being applied at local offices through a quality assurance process – to ensure business managers were implementing the ERM policy and used the tools properly.

# Evaluation of ERM QA Process (1)

## OBJECTIVES OF THE TEST

To assess the Quality Assurance regime applied to providers of risk registers in terms of the extent to which it underpins the implementation of a robust risk management process.

## AUDIT FINDINGS

The QA process has resulted in visits to half of the Business Units and the results demonstrate that there are many issues regarding the poor quality of risk registers and the lack of engagement from the Management Team. Because of a lack of resources, the ERMT will find it difficult to visit the remaining Business Units and cover the many support teams that together form the organization. Moreover, the ERM Team have re-set the quality strategy by focussing on more of a coaching/consulting role in terms of helping the Business Unit risk authors in their efforts to make ERM a success in their various Business Units. Head office receive copies of the Business Unit risk registers and in the past assumed a quality assurance role and this is being reviewed in light of the involvement of the ERM Team.

Several observations and recommendations resulted from this review. The auditor has done a lot of background work and has obtained a good understanding of what is going wrong with the current arrangements and where improvements are needed to make risk management work properly.

# Evaluation of ERM QA Process (2)

**Possible audit recommendations:**

1. The ERM Team should focus on a consulting role by being available to Business Units to help support and help them in their efforts to embed ERM and prepare meaningful risk registers.

2. The appropriate Head office team should be assigned the task of quality assuring Business Unit risk registers in conjunction with the overall monitoring and oversight role. The Business Unit self assessment process (see below) may be used as an initial input to the QA process.

3. The ERM Team should assume a consulting and QA role for the various Business Units' self assessment process (see below).

4. The Business Units should apply a form of quality Self-Assessment using a simple form attached to the risk standard and available on the IntraNet (with suitable guidance) that covers key questions to be addressed by the Business Unit for example:

• Is the RR prepared by the Management Team in a way that reflects the key risks impacting on objectives?

• Do the Management Team assign ownership to all risks and ensure these are managed within the risk tolerance set by the Business Unit Manager?

• Are the risks prioritized so that high impact, high likelihood matters receive the most attention and are suitably mitigated through decision based action plans?

• Is the risk register a key feature on the Management Team agenda so that it is refreshed on a regular basis to reflect the current priorities facing the Unit?

• Are old risks archived so that they do not obscure current risks?

• Does the Management Team review the risk register to ensure the scores reflect the current position with existing and planned controls?

• Does the risk register focus on strategic issues so that there is a focus on the top ten risks impacting the main objectives?

• Does the risk register reflect best practice as documented in the risk standard?

• Are portfolio heads encouraged to develop their own risk registers based around their key objectives, while ensuring that key issues are discussed when developing the more strategic Management Team register?

• Does the Business Unit Manager assume responsibility for ensuring ERM is embedded in the operational unit and is being applied to best effect?

• Does the Business Unit Manager use the ERM process to ensure that internal controls focus on high risk areas in a way that means there is no exposure to unacceptable levels of risk across all categories of the Business Units so that a certificate of internal control may be prepared and signed?

The auditor prepared the risk-assessed control evaluation covering Control Objectives One to Four.

# Risk Assessed Control Evaluation (1)

**Control Objective:**
1. There is a clearly defined risk management policy and implementation strategy that is properly approved, appropriately issued and regularly reviewed to meet new challenges from legislation and recognized best practice.

| RISKS | EXPECTED CONTROLS | ACTUAL CONTROLS | EVALUATION | INITIAL RECOMMENDATIONS |
|---|---|---|---|---|
| 1.1 Policy does not address important aspects of RM | Wide policy coverage<br>Links with other policies<br>Stakeholder engagement | Policy and risk standard in existence | Policy not cross referenced to other risk elements and no real stakeholder engagement | Implement ERM across all risk groups<br>Allow stakeholders to build solutions<br>Drive process from Operational/business perspective |
| 1.2 Implementation does not address culture of organization | Policy review stages<br>Culture change measures<br>Targets set<br>Surveys and analysis | Regular updates of procedure<br>Risk maturity model<br>Tracks progress | Good use of updating<br>Risk maturity model flawed<br>No surveys carried out | Obtain a better risk maturity model<br>Involve all staff in the implementation |
| 1.3 New challenges are not being addressed | Horizon scanning<br>Scope reviews<br>Change programme impacts | Corp Governance codes assessed<br>ERM Team's own RR | ERM Team positioned to be involved in new developments but ERM not applied as a change project | Develop a clear vision and use culture change techniques |
| 1.4 Best practice is not applied to risk policy | Best practice forums used<br>Continual improvements | Contact with other organizations and central bodies. ERM Team in place | Good arrangements in place | Support ERM Team and track developments in risk practices. |

# Risk Assessed Control Evaluation (2)

**Control Objective:**
2. Effective structures and procedures are in place in all Business Units to support the delivery of the strategy and to ensure that the policy is understood and complied with.

| RISKS | EXPECTED CONTROLS | ACTUAL CONTROLS | EVALUATION | INITIAL RECOMMENDATIONS |
|---|---|---|---|---|
| 2.1 Board does not have full oversight of RM process | Clear oversight role defined<br>Board review strategy<br>Careful analysis | Reports to Audit Committee | Lack of expertise at Board and Audit Committee level and assessment model is flawed. | Board training and better risk maturity model as well as QA reports on progress tracking |
| 2.2 Top management does not fully engage with RM at a senior level | CEO responsible for buy in<br>RM used by CEO Team | N/a | Expected controls not in place due to resistance from Main Board | Change ownership of risk policy to align to Main Board. |
| 2.3 Policy is not really understood across business | Staff awareness programme<br>Measurement of effect<br>Competence set for RM | Training in place for basic RRs, Refresher training, projects and programmes and proposed Senior Risk Champions | Risk not set as a new competence and only aimed at risk authors and not wider organization | Set ERM in staff competence and use training for trainers approach as well as better website and interaction |
| 2.4 Policy is not being adopted by the main board | Programme easy to apply<br>Central support effort<br>Monitoring programme<br>Incentives/benefits defined | Copy of RRs to Head Office and ERM Team's QA programme. | ERMT should do more coaching due to a lack of resources.<br>Head Office not monitoring results and no self assessment in place. | Give Head Office QA role for Business Units<br>Introduce self assessment model<br>Give ERM Team a QA role for all parts of the business. |

# Risk Assessed Control Evaluation (3)

**Control Objective:**
**3. Risk management is being suitably integrated within strategic business planning and performance management.**

| RISKS | EXPECTED CONTROLS | ACTUAL CONTROLS | EVALUATION | INITIAL RECOMMENDATIONS |
|---|---|---|---|---|
| 3.1 There is insufficient integration of ERM into the the business lines | ERM activities coordinated Gaps/duplication addressed Common language defined Road maps in use | Risk terminology defined in risk standard. Attempts to link risk to planning Action plans in risk template | RM seen as annual exercise as part of planning. Many Business units do not link with plans. Performance appraisal system does not feature ERM and action plans. | Ensure RRs are living documents at all levels of management and not a mechanistic year end process. |
| 3.2 Strategic planning activities do not apply risk assessment properly | Planners role in project plans risk assessed Planning improvements note | Links to planning encouraged by ERM Team | Most business plans make no mention of risk assessments. | Build Risk assessment into planning and RM into implementing strategy through set objectives. |
| 3.3 Performance management framework does not incorporate action points from the RM process | Action points owned by staff Performance targets for RM RM top priorities KPIs | Risk owners should be defined via the ERM Template and action plans | Risk owners not always defined and Business units action plans left blank. No real escalation of high level risks and ownership in  risk standard not helpful. | Develop better roles and responsibilities and assess use of RM at work for all levels of management. Implement escalated reporting through colour coded models |
| 3.4 ERM is not being embedded into the culture at operational levels | Roll out of ERM to all Business lines and support services | Training for risk authors and requirement that Management Teams prepare RRs each year | Implementation patchy with RRs being prepared but of variable quality and poor buy in from senior managers. | Implement a dynamic and flexible CRSA programme along with a new definition of risk ownership at senior management level |

# Risk Assessed Control Evaluation (4)

**Control Objective:**
**4. Risk is properly identified, evaluated and appropriately managed in a way that facilitates good decision-making by defined risk owners.**

| RISKS | EXPECTED CONTROLS | ACTUAL CONTROLS | EVALUATION | INITIAL RECOMMENDATIONS |
|---|---|---|---|---|
| 4.1 Risks are not being designed and prioritized in a meaningful way | Effective risk standard in place<br>Training for consistency<br>Risk appetite defined<br>Results monitored | Risk policy in place and process for Business Units to prepare RRs each year | Risk standard and training does not deal in depth with appetite, escalation and senior management ownership | Add escalated reporting to risk standard and notes on risk appetite and upside risk.<br>Implement CRSA across the organization. |
| 4.2 Decision making is not informed by effective RM activities | Effective training for RM<br>Decision model for risk<br>Documented RA<br>Committee papers RA<br>Business cases RA | Investment board risk assessment. | Audit Committee papers do not contain risk assessments and training aimed at authors not decision makers. | Ensure all audit committee papers define risks and mitigations.<br>Widen training through interactive website. |
| 4.3 RM does not lead to more effective internal controls | RM linked to better controls<br>Assurances based on RA<br>Clear role in improving controls<br>Upside risk addressed | Brief mention of control<br>ERM Team involved in Statement on Internal Control (SIC) | No real attempt to link ERM with SIC or certification process.<br>Top ten risks misses chances of full SIC involvement | Re-set the ERM process to make links with SIC – all levels of management need to prepare RRs and internal control assessments |
| 4.4 Risk ownership is not properly defined | Formal role definition<br>Accountability rules<br>RR actions clear | Risk standard definitions | Definition poor and training and IntraNet website material not aimed at senior people. | As above |

The auditor is now in a position to write the audit report.

The detailed fieldwork has been done and a summary schedule sets out the exact position covering all aspects of the audit. Let's go through a suggested executive summary. The introduction will provide some background to the audit and explain why it was undertaken – normally as part of the annual audit plan.

# Audit Report - Introduction

## 1 INTRODUCTION

This audit was carried out as part of the 20xx/yy internal audit plan and is the first systems review of the corporate risk management process.

1.2 The Main Board is responsible for the management of risk in the organization. There is a Enterprise Risk Management Team (ERMT) headed by the Head of Risk Management who reports, through a Director of Strategy, to the main board. The ERMT has operated since 200x with a remit to oversee the development of the Risk Management Framework and User Guide and to quality assure risk registers.

1.3 The regulator's code requires effective risk management in terms of taking informed and transparent decisions, which are subject to effective scrutiny. The Director of Strategy has overall responsibility for ensuring that the risk register is reviewed and kept up to date while the Audit Committee monitors the risk management strategy.

1.4 Risk Management is seen as an important aspect of managing complex organizations in both the private and public sectors. The concept of ensuring risks to achieving objectives are effectively managed in a way that ensures there is a reasonable chance of achieving them is straightforward, but it can be difficult to actually install these ideals within an organization. Risk management is a fundamental component of a successful organization and any organization will experience adverse publicity whenever one of the following factors apply:

- A significant risk has not been identified.
- The consequences of a significant risk have not been fully appreciated.
- Poor controls have led to the realization of a significant risk.
- Sound controls that guard against a significant risk have been by-passed.

The audit objectives will indicate what we hoped to achieve from carrying out the audit work.

# Audit Report - Objectives

## 2. OBJECTIVES

2.1 The objectives of the audit were to evaluate the adequacy and effectiveness of the control framework established by management to ensure the effective assessment and management of risk. In particular, we set out to provide assurance that controls exist and are operating effectively to ensure that:

• There is a clearly defined risk management policy and implementation strategy that is properly approved, appropriately issued and regularly reviewed to meet new challenges from legislation and recognized best practice.

• Effective structures and procedures are in place to support the delivery of the strategy and to ensure that the policy is understood and complied with.

• Risk management is being integrated within strategic business planning and performance management.

• Risks are properly identified, evaluated and appropriately managed in a way that facilitates good decision making by a defined risk owner.

The scope gives the coverage and states what was included in the audit and, by definition, what was left out.

# Audit Report - Scope

## 3 SCOPE

3.1 We reviewed the role of Main Board and the measures put in place by the Enterprise Risk Management Team. Assessing the impact on Directorates, Business Groups and Business Units involving managers and staff at strategic, programme, project and operational levels. Business unit (BU) risk registers were analyzed and several BUs were visited during the course of the audit. We also considered the measures used to evaluate progress in embedding risk management into the culture of the business. It was not possible to analyze all the BU risk registers. As well as carrying out interviews with various managers and staff, internal audit assessed the application of ERM at operational unit level by:

• Analyzing the collective knowledge gleaned by internal audit from audit visits to various BUs during 20xx.

• Analyzing copies of BU risk registers provided to Head Office and the ERMT.

• Visiting four BUs and one central unit.

• Reviewing the results of a sample of quality assurance visits made by the ERMT.

The audit opinion is quite important. It gives the audit view and this feeds into the overall assurance on whether internal controls are working within the organization.

# Audit Report - Opinion

## 3. AUDIT OPINION

Our overall opinion is that the control framework for assessment and management of risk is in need of significant improvement to ensure that risk management is fully embedded within all business lines. We identified a number of areas where the existing arrangements could be improved.

3.1 The risk management policy is out-of-date and does not adequately reflect the way risk management should be applied within the organization.

3.2 We found that the current focus on Business Risk does not encourage a more integrated approach to managing risk across the organization.

3.3 The current implementation strategy has not been fully effective in supporting the implementation of the risk management policy.

3.4 The structures and procedures in place are not fully effective and need to be repositioned to ensure that risk management is fully supported within the organization.

3.5 There is little evidence to demonstrate that risk assessment is integrated into the business planning and performance process.

3.6 The current arrangements have not led to risk management being embedded into business culture in a way that promotes good decision-making by defined risk owners. In terms of promoting a risk astute culture across all parts of the organization, there are calls for a major shift in strategy to secure the buy-in to ensure risk management is part of everyday life throughout the organization.

The recommendations point to ways forward and these should be discussed with line management before they get into the draft report. When the current arrangements are very poor, under the RaCE approach, the auditor may apply a consulting role and provide further guidance on improving the system.

# Audit Report - Recommendations

## 5. KEY RECOMMENDATIONS

5.1 The Head of Risk Management has recently re-focused the approach to the Enterprise Risk implementation strategy. This is to ensure that a high-ranking Risk Review Group helps engineer greater involvement from the Main Board as well as taking steps to move the business through a staged risk maturity programme. All members of the Enterprise Risk Management Team are fully engaged in this important change programme.

5.2 We have made recommendations throughout the report aimed at introducing effective controls or improving those already in place. To mitigate those risks that, in our opinion, need to be improved before system objectives for corporate risk assessment and management can be achieved, we make the following key recommendations:

5.3 Main Board review the approach to business risk management to incorporate an Enterprise Risk Management Process (based on the enterprise wide risk management approach)[1] as a way of integrating all risk activities across the organization.

5.4 Main Board approve a clearly defined strategy for the implementation of the new approach along the lines of a Risk Management Framework that is integrated within planning, performance and day-to-day business.

5.5 The ERMT focus on providing a consultancy and Q&A role available to Business Groups, BUs to help support them in embedding Risk Management and facilitating the preparation of meaningful risk registers.

5.6 Risk management training incorporates an advocacy dimension, with a move away from the concept of risk authors, to promote local risk assessments as the adopted way forward.

5.7 Risk registers are re-designed to constitute varying degrees of sophistication, from Rapid Risk Reports, to basic registers through to more detailed SMT versions – and these registers should be aligned to the ongoing process for reviewing internal controls.

5.8 Audit Committee papers incorporate a section on associated risk assessments to inform the relevant user/decision makers.

5.9 The Risk Management Policy and supporting guidance are revised to reflect any agreed changes in risk management strategy and approach.

5.10 A user friendly version of CRSA is implemented throughout the organization.

Without going into too much detailed design, the auditor may point to structural and concept issues that may be adopted to ensure a better way of managing risk in the organization. Various models can also be included in the detail of the audit report to help management get to grips with sorting out the current weaknesses.

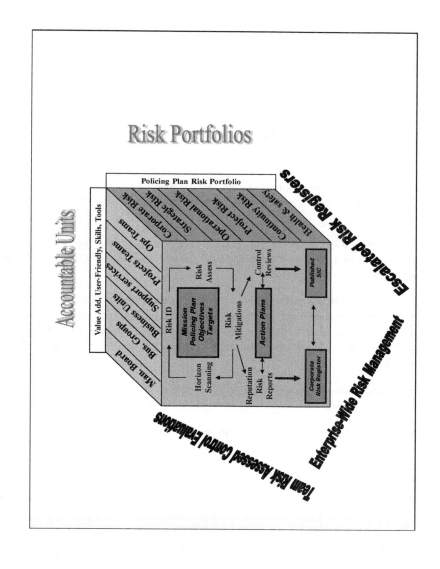

The first model shows how ERM may be applied across the entire organization. The audit report will contain some explanatory narratives:

## Clear roles and accountabilities across the organization

Applying risk management throughout the organization for the main board, business groups, business units, support services, programme and project teams.

Re-packaging the enterprise risk management process to promote value added in helping teams deliver their goals in a user friendly format that does not entail excessive degrees of paperwork or extensive training.

Delivering the necessary skills and tools to all staff that fall within the risk management framework and not just the current 'risk authors'.

## Integrating risk management

It is essential that risk assessments are related to plans and priorities.

Applying the application of risk management throughout the business to cover all categories of risk assessments, including corporate, strategic, operational, project, continuity and health and safety risk.

Giving responsibility to senior managers for coordinating all risk activities and ensuring that they are integrated in a consistent and meaningful manner, driven by strategic priorities rather than the narrow business risk approach.

Creating a one-stop website facility to enable users to log on to the risk category that they are addressing and view consistent material that they can become familiar with. On-line training tutorials may be used to support the new risk competencies along with training notes and multichoice tests. A refereed interactive discussion forum may also be used to help share experiences.

Performing on-line risk assessments, with user-friendly tools and aids that help the user develop a series of simple and more complex risk registers to suit the local context.

## Application of a generic risk management cycle

Defining and agreeing a straightforward and generic risk cycle for use in all types of risk assessments and risk management exercises.

Basing the enterprise risk management cycle around the mission, plan, objectives and targets.

Linking risk registers to the process of preparing formal statements on internal control across the organization. Denoting how existing controls that mitigate against key risks are reviewed and how planned controls are tracked through to their full implementation. All local SMT risk registers denote any 'Red Risks' used to populate a board's reputational risk register that is accelerated upwards through the management command until it arrives as a top-level report for the main board as an aspect of its own corporate risk register.

Applying horizon scanning across the organization to ensure there are effective mechanisms to capture important new and potential risks.

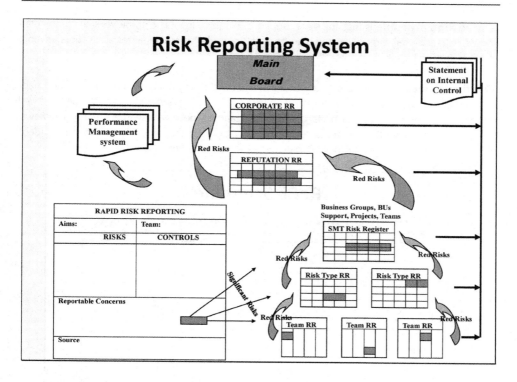

## A suitable reporting structure

This is designed to take on board the enterprise risk management process, which acknowledges the need to simplify reports and escalate significant risk through the business, in quick time. The model illustrates one possible approach whereby high-profile tactical teams, working parties, special interest groups and officers, given nonstandard tasks, can complete a simple rapid risk report to help them focus their collective energies. Any unusual or high-level risks that they are not able to control can be reported upwards to go on another more senior risk register. Meanwhile the permanent teams will complete a slightly more detailed register (called 'Team RR' in the diagram) that will also accelerate difficult 'Red Risks' upwards. In line with the current practice, risk assessments will be carried out as normal for activities such as health and safety, dynamic risk assessments, business continuity, tactical operations, projects and so on (called 'Risk Type RR'). Red Risks will go upwards into the more complex senior management team (SMT) registers. This integrated approach to risk management means SMT Red Risks that pose a particular concern may populate the board's reputation risk register. This reputation register will then inform the main board's corporate register. It is essential that the performance management systems incorporate outcomes from various risk assessments to ensure the resulting action points are sufficiently aligned to personal and team performance targets. The various different types of risk registers could be completed on-line with links between the hierarchy to capture high scoring, or designated 'Red Risks', for input to the next level of registers.

**The first important principle** is that less senior personnel complete very simple rapid risk registers and it is only at SMT and beyond that the registers need contain the detailed information used in the current template.

**The second principle** is that any significant concerns from front line employees and junior staff should be quickly relayed upwards and addressed before the risk materializes and causes adverse publicity for the business.

**The final principle** is that this arrangement will allow the organization to compile a statement on internal control based on the risk-based reviews of controls that naturally occur when carrying out risk assessments across all parts of the organization. These management control reviews, as well as management's own self-assessments, may be used to complement the independent reviews by internal audit and other internal and external review teams.

# RaCE Schedule

| KEY RISKS & RATING | KEY CONTROLS | INITIAL EVALUATION | TEST PLAN | OPINION & RECOMMENDATIONS |
|---|---|---|---|---|
| | | | | |

Some audits can become quite complex, particularly those that consider a corporate-wide system that reaches into most parts of the business. A great deal of information, views and robust evidence can be secured by the auditor who works through such a difficult and high-profile system. The risk-assessed control evaluation (RaCE) system is a good way of dealing with these types of audits by detailing:

- Key risks & ratings column. Key risks that have been rated high in terms of impact and likelihood before controls are applied.
- Key controls column. These risks drive the evaluation in terms of controls that are in place to mitigate the risks.
- Initial evaluation column. The auditor's initial evaluation of these control measures.
- Test plan column. Which tests should be applied to assess the reliability of these controls and the impact of noncompliance and general weaknesses through poor controls.

- The testing column represents the test strategy. Test schedules will be prepared and performed and the results summarized and entered back on to the internal control evaluation schedule. After this, the main RaCE schedule will contain the audit opinion and recommendations that will then feed into the management action plan.

We have had a look at an audit case study based on one version of the risk-assessed control evaluation approach to assurance audits, with some consulting aspects tacked on to the end. Each audit team will have their own way of carrying out and documenting their audit work and we have gone through only one of the many different approaches that may be used.

# INDEX

CPSIA information can be obtained
at www.ICGtesting.com
Printed in the USA
LVOW03s1956150616

492793LV00019B/108/P

9 780470 746936